SYD ENEVER
THE MG MAN

SYD ENEVER
THE MG MAN

BY DAVID KNOWLES

Herridge & Sons

MICHAEL SEDGWICK
MEMORIAL TRUST

Syd Enever – The MG Man is published with the financial assistance of the Michael Sedgwick Memorial Trust. The M.S.M.T. was founded in memory of the motoring historian and author Michael C. Sedgwick (1926–1983), to encourage the publication of new motoring research, and the recording of Road Transport History. Support by the Trust does not imply any involvement in the editorial process, which remains the responsibility of the editor and publisher. The Trust is a Registered Charity, No 290841, and a full list of the Trustees and an overview of the functions of the M.S.M.T. can be found on: www.michaelsedgwicktrust.co.uk

Published 2025 by
Herridge & Sons Ltd
Lower Forda, Shebbear
Beaworthy, Devon
EX21 5SY
United Kingdom

© Copyright David Knowles 2025
No part of this work may be reproduced in any form or by any means without the prior permission of the publisher.

ISBN 978-1-914929-14-4
Printed in China

Contents

Foreword by Roger Enever 6

Introduction 7

Acknowledgements 8

Prelude: Syd Enever in the Words of Others 9

Chapter One: The Lad from Winchester 19

Chapter Two: The Shop Boy at Morris Garages 26

Chapter Three: Fledgling Engineer 31

Chapter Four: Magic Midgets and Magnettes 49

Chapter Five: War Years at Abingdon 103

Chapter Six: Export or Die 110

Chapter Seven: Final Furlongs 153

Chapter Eight: Into the Sunset 219

Appendix 227

Index 234

Foreword By Roger Enever

My father was a strong family man – he had been looked after by his mothers and sisters when he was small, after his father left when he was a small boy. The beloved aunties that I remember were Auntie Ethel, Auntie Flo and Auntie Lena; in his youth young Syd had been the only boy in the family, and so his closeness to his own family echoed that.

Some of my earliest memories of spending time with my father were our frequent trips into the Abingdon MG factory, often on a Sunday when the place was otherwise quiet. Whilst my father would be 'in the zone' – probably talking to Alec Hounslow while they had a record-breaker engine on the test bed, I would wander off around the factory, and I remember in particular walking among the rows of drawing boards, with the many blueprints and drawings laid over them. Meanwhile, those two – Alec and my father – never rested: they were always thinking of the next challenge...

Dad was always bringing blueprints home, and laying them out on the dining room table, and he would carefully pore over them – he'd always be considering what needed doing, including alterations he wanted to see. He was in the habit of producing long lists of things in the evening that needed to be actioned the next day.

Often the families at the heart of the MG design and development world would meet up at various pubs in the Oxford area – places like The Perch, The Trout and others – typically the Enevers and the Hounslows would all come together. Sometimes, dad would take me over to Jacko's house in Kennington – I remember it had the railway line at the end of his back garden.

People revered my father – so many of them eulogised about him, his knowledge and his abilities. If I went to a race meeting with him, while I was still at school, his contemporaries would be saying how marvellous he was. But despite all this, he didn't like to talk about himself – he much preferred to focus on the job, the challenge at hand. So, unlike some others, he didn't court celebrity, and he certainly wasn't a self-promoter, which is why it is so marvellous that at last, his story is coming out into the world.

We are lucky, as a family, that my father squirreled away a wealth of material – photo albums, notebooks and drawings amongst a plethora of other aspects of a life spent at Morris Garages and MG. We're immensely proud of my father and all that he achieved, and it has been a pleasure to help David Knowles in his mammoth task of bringing the story to light. I hope that, once you have read this book, you will have some greater understanding of what a remarkable contribution to the motoring world – and to MG in particular – that my father made.

Syd Enever was a handsome man; this image originates in a studio photo from the early 1950s. (Enever Archive)

Roger Enever
Oxford, January 2025

Introduction

Although MG has accumulated a hundred years of history, this book is intended to be more than just another marque treatise: it aims to put into context the story of a man whose brilliance and dedication helped make the MG marque all the more remarkable. If, in telling Syd Enever's story, it is possible to advance the general understanding and appreciation of the MG mystique, then that is all to the good: but it is really intended to convey the story of a reluctant hero who just happened to spend 51 years of his life, first with Morris Garages and then with MG, and had some exciting and remarkable adventures along the way – not least in the rarefied atmosphere of automotive racing and record breaking with smaller vehicles.

Great people can come in many forms; some are alive to and enjoy their reputation, basking in the light of the adulation it generally brings. Others avoid the public limelight and all it both illuminates and implies; for many of these individuals, their preference is to knuckle down, get on with the task at hand, and let others who are keen to do all the talking court the attention. For some onlookers, looking past the more voluble, the publicity-shy may appear as intriguing individuals, but all too often, their story goes untold: they have spent their lives toiling away at whatever it is that makes them great, but after it is all over, history may forget them because of their political shyness. Syd Enever was definitely one of the latter brigade; more of a doer than a talker, and like many creative engineers he was often simply focused on the next challenge as soon as the present task was completed. But he is not someone who should be forgotten.

For me, that quiet fame was a key driver in wanting to write a biography of a man who has long been one of my own automotive heroes; it is fair to say that he was a hero to many others too – some of them his colleagues and many just simple enthusiasts like me who have cause to thank him for his selfless devotion to the development of some of the best affordable sports cars that the world has ever known.

Syd Enever was certainly not the only man worthy of the title 'Mister MG', as this book will show, but he nevertheless became known by most of his peers as such. There is, however, already an excellent biography of another worthy candidate for that title; 'Mister MG' is a heartfelt tribute to a much-loved father by Peter Thornley, and is an important book for any true student of MG history. For that reason, this book is called '*Syd Enever – MG Man*' – because to many of the people he met, he was precisely that – for most of the marque's history during his tenure, 'Enever' and 'MG' were indivisible.

Roger Enever in the cockpit of his father's creation, the 'Roaring Raindrop', at Silverstone in 1958. 'Uncle' Alec Hounslow looks on. (Enever Archive)

Acknowledgements

It is often difficult when setting out to acknowledge the help received on a mammoth multi-year project like this to avoid leaving out names of people whose input, however small or large, proved invaluable. Added to that is the sad fact that when dealing with events from up to more than a century ago, many of the lead players are no longer with us. Obviously, I should begin by thanking Roger and his family for allowing me access to their memories of Syd, in particular his copious and illuminating photo albums whose photos populate the chapters which follow. I should also acknowledge the people who worked with Syd, including those with wonderful memories of those heady days gone by, such as Mike Allison, Jim Cox and Pete Neal. I am also indebted to that internationally renowned, knowledgeable and infectiously enthusiastic South African MG enthusiast Norman Ewing, who had laid tentative plans for his own book about Syd Enever some thirty years ago, and generously shared papers from his own archives to ensure that I could deliver a better biography as a consequence. I am also indebted to fellow author Jon Pressnell, who generously shared some of the instances where people he had interviewed also opened up about Syd. In some cases, where the individuals concerned have long since departed, I have been fortunate to have spoken to the relatives whose proud memories of their loved ones has been similarly illuminating; the list is again a long one but includes the families of Reg 'Jacko' Jackson, Alec Hounslow, Terry Mitchell, Jim O'Neill, Denis Williams, Bill Renwick and many more besides. My hope is that in sharing their stories, this book will be a fitting testimony to a man who was at the heart of the remarkable MG story. As for Syd Enever, we shall surely not see his like again.

Prelude: Syd Enever – in the Words Of Others

Relatively little has been written specifically about Syd Enever, although, as will be seen later, we are extremely fortunate that he committed to paper his own memories of his early life and career. I am forever indebted to his son Roger for kindly sharing these papers – photos included – which it is hoped will help bring this elusive figure to life and especially illuminate the seldom told story of his early years, including the original path that brought him to make MG his working livelihood and passion. Syd was often reluctant to talk about himself, usually steering any conversation back to the cars and the engineering challenges.

We are fortunate that several of his contemporaries spoke warmly of him to others and several committed memories of him to paper; accordingly, before launching into the main part of the story, some of these memories are included below, with grateful acknowledgment to those fellow travellers in the world of MG, whilst also acknowledging that some of them are, like Syd, sadly no longer with us.

Syd Enever was highly thought of by all of his colleagues – whether they served over, under or alongside him. **John Thornley**, who got to know Syd from 1931 onwards, just as his automotive creativity was in the ascendant, said that he would put his friend and colleague on a par with the much more famous Alec Issigonis – high praise indeed, for whatever people may have thought of the latter, either as colleagues or by reputation, surely all of them would have agreed that the man best known for the Morris Minor and Mini was something of a genius, albeit someone who knew that fact and revelled in the reverence it brought.

When interviewed by his old friend (and fellow MG Car Club founder) Harold Hastings for *Motor* magazine in December 1969, Thornley related how Cecil Kimber had built a great team and that he felt privileged to '...*carry on more or less where Kim left off. None of those he picked could be said to be overburdened with formal education, but they succeeded by the application of innate common sense and an ability, stimulated by love of motor sport and the challenge of the times, to learn as they went along*'.

Thornley said that Syd was probably the most outstanding example of this select group, many of whom are covered later in this book. '*While George Propert and Cecil Cousins were translating the early rudimentary sketches into the early MGs, Syd was learning in an atmosphere where everyone was expected*

Syd Enever was already part of the British motor industry establishment through much of the post-war period; here he is seen in a distinguished line-up which includes Donald Healey, John Thornley, Sergio Pininfarina and Alec Issigonis, posing with the famous Dewar Trophy, which BMC was awarded, for the Mini, in 1959. Perhaps Syd was too much of a diplomat to have pointed out that two years earlier, the trophy had been awarded to his good friends at The Dunlop Rubber Company Limited for their work on 'disc brakes and research and development of tyres for the MG car, which secured various international speed records'? (Enever Archive)

to turn his hand to anything, and did. There was something of everything to be had at MG during his early years with them, and before long he had begun to take a leading part in design discussions'.

Thornley credited Syd with the ability to seek out knowledge in unusual places: 'I remember, at a time when the air was full of argument about the harsh ride of the early cars, finding Syd with a large book which he had drawn from the local library. It proved to have been published before the turn of the century and its subject was the suspension of railway locomotives. He had found in this the basic principles for which he sought, unclouded by "all the highfalutin' clap-trap modern designers write". And who else in the world can claim to have designed two sports cars, each of which has sold 100,000 examples, with one still going strong?'

The author is aware of at least two occasions where this statement of evident delight by John Thornley in his friend's capacity for lateral thought has been re-quoted by others; one occasion within a gloomy treatise on the malaise of British industry, and in particular its historic reluctance to recruit graduates but to rely instead on the practical person, whose skills were born from experience. Frankly whilst there is much to concede concerning the lack of suitably qualified graduates in UK industry in the sixties and seventies, all the same it seems grossly unfair to label Syd – whose genius was evident throughout his career – as some kind of watchword for the incompetence of industrial management.

As Thornley added: 'it is not correct to describe [Syd] as an untrained engineer, because he trained himself; he had an insatiable curiosity about why things happened, a curiosity which went far beyond purely engineering and automotive matters, so that he had knowledge of a wide variety of subjects which would hold one spellbound – if only one could get him talking. By nature he is a quiet man – except when something stings him – and it is because of this taciturnity that he was not more widely recognised in his heyday.'

John Thornley's son Peter – whose biography of his father, *Mister MG*, deserves a place on all MG enthusiast's bookshelves, added: 'a master of his element, Syd was very specific on how far the competitions department could go in tuning a vehicle for a particular event, so that the compromise between performance and reliability was always maintained to advantage. Similarly, he would react very strongly if he had found production had deviated from the strict process he had laid down for the construction of the vehicle, and would go down on the shop floor in a tirade to ensure that things were "dun right". A man of remarkable ability, who was also in the right place at the right time.

John Thornley's Last Tribute to Syd

John Thornley and Syd were always close allies and friends, and shortly before Thornley died, he wrote a final touching tribute. Peter Thornley does not recall it; written in March 1994, it might be the last such piece John wrote, as he died that July. In fond tribute to both men, it is reproduced here, acknowledging duplication with other Thornley quotes.

ALBERT SYDNEY ENEVER
An Appreciation
by
John Thornley

Sydney Enever came over to Abingdon from Oxford with the nucleus of the MG Car Company in 1929, came up the hard way to be made Chief Designer in 1953 in which position he continued until his retirement in 1971. Very early on it became clear that he was a 'one off', with a questing mind and a penchant for direct action. His great pal, Reggie Jackson, often told the tale of Syd, noticing an apprentice tapping away at a piece of bent metal, went up to him saying "Don't stroke it, mate" and took it out of his hands. He squinted at it – from two angles – laid it on the bench and fetched it one almighty swipe with a hammer. The piece flew across the shop and 'everything jumped off the bench' but, when they found the piece, it was dead straight Apocryphal maybe, but fair comment on Syd in his younger days. Don't infer from that that I think he grew more staid as time went on – not a bit of it. He always was a terror with 'the girls', though he didn't flaunt it. It was only those of us who knew him well who knew what he was up to. But getting back to this 'one off' business. I found him once with a fat tome under his arm which he had just drawn from a library in Oxford. Published in the 1890's it had to do with the suspension systems of railway locomotives. We were, at the time, in some difficulty with the road-holding of the prototype MGB. Syd's philosophy was that, if you could persuade 100 tons and more of railway locomotive to stay on track at 100 mph or so, you must know something about what went on between road and vehicle. The learned papers which were read, from time to time, before the Institute of Automobile Engineers were all very well but, in Syd's view, often enough by-passed fundamentals. So it was his habit to go back to

PRELUDE: SYD ENEVER – IN THE WORDS OF OTHERS

basics and take it from there. From the end of WWII there was always something going on that Sydney had his thumb in but it will serve to compress the story if we confine ourselves to the most important items, the MGA, EX181 and the MGB. Racing had been brought to an official end in 1935 but somehow we contrived to achieve some success in Sports Car racing from the moment we got the TC into post-war production. How we got away with it I have never been quite sure. Either we had a very tolerant Top Brass who had probably given me up as a hopeless case or I had a very skilful and co-operative Chief Accountant who was able to 'lose' the cost! Anyway, we supported a team of Jacobs, Lund and Phillips in TCs and subsequently TDs in, for instance, the Production Car Races at Silverstone and the Ulster TT. The cars were generally to Sydney's specification. From these three George Phillips emerged as an ambitious loner who had special bodies built for his car and then entered it for Le Mans. He did well enough that we took him very seriously. This gave Sydney the opportunity to follow his cherished ideas and design what was to be the prototype of the MGA. This remarkable car caused the BMC Board to return MG design authority to Abingdon with Sydney as Chief Engineer. In 1955 we entered a team of three for Le Mans and went on to produce over 100,000 of them. EX181 was something else again. Syd had brought Goldie Gardner's car to the point where it exceeded 200mph in 1939 in Germany . From then on he had his sights set on 250 and, after extensive work in the wind-tunnel, produced what must have come very close to the ultimate shape. The car, fitted with an MGA Twin-Cam engine, supercharged, was driven in excess of 250mph by Phil Hill in 1959, on the Utah salt. The MGB was a very great exercise in original thinking in that it was Syd's first assay into monocoque construction and possibly the first series-produced monocoque open car anywhere. It is interesting and enlightening to take an MGB Roadster, with the hood down, open both doors wide and then look at the car full side on from a point about a foot off the ground. You will see two large chunks of motor-car joined together by very little, and into that 'very little' Sydney had designed sufficient torsional and beam strength to secure impeccable road manners. For reasons that we won't go into here, Syd's car stayed in production for 17 years and sold over half-a-million. Genius is not too high a label to put on him. He deserves his place in the automotive history books. He was, moreover, an inspiration to work with.

JWT

March 1994

Captain Goldie Gardner came to know Syd during the record breaking endeavours described in later chapters; in his book *Magic MPH*, Gardner recalled how he first came to appreciate Syd (who had already worked on his record car; Gardner would probably have known Syd on sight at least as a riding mechanic too). Syd joined 'Jacko' on the team that accompanied Gardner and his sleek green record car to Frankfurt in November 1938: '*This was the first occasion on which Kim had included Syd Enever in my party. From then onwards, I have been lucky enough to have not only the support of these two great technicians, Syd Enever and*

Goldie Gardner in his famous MG Record Breaker, in which his exploits – aided by Syd and his colleagues – extended from 1938 to 1952. (Jackson family archive)

A characteristic portrait of George Eyston – a 'Boys Own' hero like Goldie Gardner, although for many years Eyston also participated in the more rarefied stratosphere of land speed record breaking irrespective of engine capacity. Eyston would have known Syd prewar but their mutual respect and friendship came more to the fore in the mid-1950s. (Author Archive)

Jacko, in some cases during the preparation of the car and on the site during the actual attempt at record, but also that of Les Kesterton of the SU Carburettor company – truly a very great team.'

In a similar manner, Gardner's fellow record breaker **George Eyston** also had cause to be grateful for Syd's skills; the two corresponded extensively when it came to the 1950s record breaking efforts, by which time Syd's expertise in that arena was probably the equal of anybody in such a rarefied field.

Jim O'Neill first got to know Syd after arriving at Cowley and working under Gerald Palmer, his MG work including the TD Midget and Z Magnette, although in the main his contact then tended to be with John Thornley, as Abingdon and Cowley were a little more 'distant' than their physical proximity might have suggested. It was when Jim got to work on what became the MGA – described later in this book – that he and Syd got to know each other better and Jim was one of the first people that Syd 'poached' from Cowley when he set up the new drawing office at Abingdon in June 1954.

O'Neill told the author of his arrival at Abingdon that summer: *'our first task was to beg, borrow or steal as much equipment as possible. Two 18-foot layout tables were made up by the works carpenters, improvised wooden sweeps also made up in the carpenters' shop. Drawing boards were 'borrowed' from Morris Motors'.* This began the basis of Syd's new enhanced fiefdom. With the MGA under way, as we shall see,

attention soon turned to its replacement (engineers, in common with many creative people, swiftly turn their interest to the new thing at the expense of the old): *'During a visit to the Geneva Motor Show, Syd Enever handed to me a scrap of paper with a very crude sketch of the future MGB. He wanted the Headlamps set into scallops in the wings and in the flattish area between the headlamps an elongated traditional MG Radiator. The body sides would have a similar rounded section to the Jaguar E Type'.*

Don Hayter, the man most frequently associated with the body design of the MGB, recalled his former mentor with enormous respect and affection, writing about Syd for the MG Car Club magazine *Safety Fast* in 1993: *'The vast width of engineering knowledge which he acquired was largely self-taught and his ability to identify and solve problems and to design and engineer improvements in engine output and performance were unique. Syd had the ability to transmit his ideas and enthusiasm to all he worked with and his attention to even the tiniest detail was legendary. He always said that information on any aspect of engineering or materials was available somewhere in a book so that it could be taken and adapted to design use'.*

Speaking to the author in recent years, Hayter remembered an example of Syd's interest and concern to ensure that MG continued to embrace its famous 'Safety Fast' philosophy. *'A safety related problem came when Syd called me into his office and showed me a damaged steering wheel. The wheel was available on the market copying the Italian cars. It had an alloy centre but with a hard rim in polished wood riveted on. The cherry wood riveted damaged wheel which came to Syd had bent considerably when the driver was thrown forward in an accident. The wood rim had broken from the rivets and produced a nasty spear shape which drove into the driver's chest causing a bad injury. We issued a sales and service note to make sure no more steering wheels of this type were to be used. All our future steering wheels were in steel or alloy with a one piece moulded plastic rim. These performed well in later crash testing with calibrated dummies both here and in the USA'.*

Hayter recalled one of his visits to the Enever family home in Oxford: *'he introduced me to his wife Ivy and his daughter, Jane. Ivy showed me a collection of pottery she valued, including Moorcroft. Jane was home telling me of her historic prints from the Paris flea market where she was dealing. Elder daughter Susan was, I believe, nursing and was trying to get a cheap ticket to Australia'.* Roger Enever was also around: *'Syd had brought Roger into Development to look at a Midget for him to race. Alec Hounslow and Jimmy Cox had been told to fit a larger B-series engine to be tried by Roger and Tom Haig for club* use, which he did'.

Hayter also recalled Syd's interest in a new six-cylinder powertrain: *'it was a light-alloy 3-litre C series engine for competitions and development for which Engines Branch were making test units. Jimmy Cox and Cliff Humphries were to fit these in the lightened MGC GTs'*. As we shall see much later in this book, Syd had many thoughts regarding the kind of engine needed for motorsports supremacy, but was often baulked by senior management hovering well above the immediate concerns of MG – difficult enough in the days of Nuffield and BMC; tougher than ever when British Leyland came about.

Lastly, as far as Don Hayter's recollections are concerned, he told the author: *'Syd left behind relics of his interest in car colours as paint swatches from Glasso and ICI all over the place'* adding that in connection with this: *'the MGB side chrome moulding was there to give a split line for the then-popular two-tone colour schemes.'*

Roy Brocklehurst owed the start of his career to Syd and the respect was affectionate, strong and mutual. Brocklehurst spoke of the design dynamics at Abingdon in an interview with Wilson McComb in late 1986: *'I guess the feeling for where we should go [on the MGB in particular] was more inspired by John Thornley than by any other person. Syd might invite comments from us in a very democratic way, but I think he reckoned that John knew what he wanted, and he wasn't about to argue with him. Syd shouldn't be under-estimated though. He never had any formal engineering training, but he was so intuitive in his approach – except that he had this thing about the proportions and fixing of components; he wouldn't tolerate anything less than a 5/16-inch bolt. "A man of massive brackets and powerful bolts", I always called him...'*

In the same interview, Brocklehurst also recalled Syd's sometimes eccentric driving techniques: *'Syd liked big steering wheels, and he always referred to the handbrake as the side brake'* adding that Syd's driving style was strange, and that he was not especially interested in the ergonomics of the control layout (something shared with Issigonis). When Syd retired, Roy took over as Chief Engineer – a role his mentor had long promised him – although his talents were soon called elsewhere.

A fellow member of the so-called 'Insomnia Crew' (see Chapter Four) was **Henry Wright Stone** (November 7th 1910 – March 1990), one of the MG mechanics who initially worked alongside Syd in the racing heydays of the 1930s, and saw him rise due to his brilliance at solving issues. Writing in his own autobiography, published in 1983, Stone recalled that

'Syd was known to a few of his very early work mates as "Squeaker" because his voice would sometimes squeak when he got excited. Syd was a fantastic bloke with a photographic memory and unlimited engineering know-how. He could read an engineering paper and anytime later hold a talk explaining the technical details. If asked, Syd would always take the trouble to explain why he wanted something done in a special way. Like all clever men, Syd appeared absent-minded at time. I knew him and worked for him for many years, but there were times when it would seem he didn't know my name. He would look at me vacantly, hesitate, and say "Stoney – ah, ah – oh, yes, Henry... well, I want you to do so and so..." The next morning he would bowl in and say "where is it? Oh yes, that is very nice, but I had a rethink last night. What we should really do is this..."

'He wrote notes on cigarette packets, wrapping paper, and, in fact, anything he could get his hands on when the ideas came to him. He even drew sketches on tablecloths when he got carried away. His drawings were something – they were never to scale, but all of the detail was there. Syd had an uncanny knack of getting to the root of a problem. What Syd didn't know about power units you could write on a postage stamp with letters a foot high. He never should have retired from MG, but should have been retained as a consultant. His heart was with MG. I remember he was close to tears on his last day when he wished us all good-bye.

'Many MG enthusiasts used to corner Syd to expound their theories about MG tuning. Syd always listened patiently, then quickly said "that's no good; we tried that back in '37". The enthusiast would have an instant long

Syd was always happy to be part of the celebrations; here he is seen at right at the Churchills nightclub in London's Bond Street, with Ivy sitting third from left. Others at the table include Mr & Mrs Thornley (Joanne far left) and Les and Pan (aka 'Pam') Lambourne in the centre. (Enever family)

face, but would cheer up when Syd would offer. "you could well pursue such and such a course with greater reliability."

'I remember being called into John Thornley's office in 1956. Syd was there and he said quietly to me "How would you like to visit the salt flats, Henry?" I enthusiastically agreed, and Syd involved me immediately in the project. The very next day we went up to Austin's where Dr. Stuart was in charge of the engine being developed for the Healey car. One of Syd's first questions concerned the planned fuel. Well, they hadn't tried it on straight methanol, and really weren't finding out anything useful. So, he and I took over. I was given a squirt can of methanol and Syd took the throttle. We quickly determined that the jets were all wrong, so Syd drilled them out on the spot. It took him an amazingly short time to solve many problems for them, and we exited leaving them in silent wonderment. On the way home, Syd observed "lot to learn" to no-one in particular".

'One of my first memories of Syd was an Abingdon fair in the early 1930s. He and Frankie Tayler were enjoying themselves. They went on the ghost train and got off the car in the bowels of the machine. They spent some time playing peek-a-boo with the operators, which seemed to amuse the onlookers quite a bit.'

'I knew him for a long while back and worked under his guidance most of the time I was at MG. He was admired and respected by everyone at MG. At first, he appeared aloof, but he was a deep thinker and it was always worth the wait for his pearls of wisdom.'

Henry Stone also spoke of Syd's enviable understanding of fundamental engine tuning issues: *'Syd decided to write the TC Tuning Manual; he issued the instructions, and I did the tuning. There was a Heenan & Froude DPX2 Tuning and Test Bed installed in the corner of the shop and the TC engine was run on that… Syd did all the brain work and wrote the manual. What Syd Enever didn't know about engine tuning wasn't worth knowing; he was an expert in the field. I have personally heard Syd discussing technicalities with other well-known engine designers who always respected his opinion.'*

Jim Cox often found himself working closely with Syd on some engine problem – engines being very much Syd's forte as we shall see: *'Syd was a brilliant engineer with an excellent memory – he always knew exactly what you were supposed to be doing – whether or not you were actually doing it. I remember that we had three special camshafts for some purpose and five years later he came to see me and said he thought we'd got one left to which I replied that I didn't think we had. Syd said to go and check and of course when I did he was absolutely right'.* Cox spent much time working closely with Jack Crook, both under Syd, and more of his tales are told later in the main text.

Through the course of this book, there are many examples of instances where Syd Enever's ever inventive mind was always coming up with bright ideas – and some would be ones which Jim Cox would be asked to investigate, for example, with the B-Series engine. In the process of developing the EX182 Le Mans car in 1955, Jim Cox recalled Syd's ever inventive mind thinking outside the box again: *'Syd wanted to use a cross-flow head – four or five were made – and he wanted to use two sets of carbs; one pair each side of the head. The idea was that there would be a normal pair on the conventional side and two smaller ones – I think they were one inch SUs we tried – on the opposite side. The theory was that the smaller carbs would give improved low-end power, but this didn't work, and so we finished up with a 5/8-inch balance pipe around the back of the engine.'* Those ideas came from no text book but instead from a man who was experienced at drawing seemingly impossible outputs from engines.

Mike Allison worked at the MG factory from 1964 for the best part of a decade and so got to know many of the people such as Syd, Jacko (his boss for much of this period) and others who had such great stories to tell – if only he could entice them to share. Writing about Syd in his brilliant book on MG motorsport history, 'The Works MGs' (Haynes, 2000) co-written with Peter Browning) Allison recalled: *'Reg [Jackson] and Syd were friends from the earliest days, and it was natural that Syd should follow along the road opened up by the older man, although they were barely eighteen months apart in age. Syd was involved with the racing when he earned his sobriquet ['Squeak'] because he was apparently inclined to chirp into conversations with "but…". [the origin of Syd's nickname again – see Henry Stone, earlier] The name stuck, and even the drivers knew him as that. In due course he was commandeered into H. N. Charles's drawing office where he learned about design. His thinking out of problems from first principles was developed by Charles and stood him in good stead for his best work on the MGA and MG models. …always a hands-on man, Syd was not one to suffer fools gladly, and was often thought to be autocratic and uncommunicative, but in fact he was a good man to work for, with a sharp mind who could always see a fault if it existed in a proposal.'*

Although Allison never really managed to encourage Syd to 'open up' to him about his past, he did elicit some insights from 'Jacko', who claimed to have first met Syd when the latter was working at Cowley as a fitter (this interlude does not feature in Syd's own notes; Jacko told Allison that *"Syd is blessed with a poor recall of his early days".*) Jacko continued: *"when we started with racing, Syd was dead keen to be involved, and I suppose he came over to MG when the C-types were being prepared for the*

Double-Twelve, so we were at Abingdon then... after a time he became a permanent fixture, and was eventually taken under HN Charles's wing when we were developing the R-type chassis. The way Syd works to this day was HN's... everything worked from first principles, but he does tend to get fixated with some ideas! Syd was brilliant at solving problems on the hoof, at race meetings and the like, and we were a team when working on Goldie's and George's record breaking...although not so much with George's pre-war stuff.'

Peter Neal, more recently the MG Car Club's Archivist, worked at the MG factory at Abingdon from soon after the drawing office was re-established in 1954, and understandably has many memories of his one-time boss. 'He would scribble ideas down overnight and bring them in to be worked up...' and as junior draughtsman in the small team that task often fell to Neal. The trouble was that although detailed and impressive, the sketches were not necessarily proportionally correct. An airbrush was purchased and Neal practiced so that he could produce presentation-worthy artwork – but when he asked his immediate boss Jim O'Neill if he should alter the perspective, Jim told him not to change it. 'I mean that sounds like me making excuses for my poor work, but that was exactly how it was; I had learned quite a bit about perspective because I wanted to be a technical illustrator when I set out.'

Echoing the words of Mike Allison, Neal says that Syd was not what one might term a 'people person' but he knew how to get the best out of people who could help him; but at the same time, 'Syd was very much a family man and was very proud of his family; he would do things like drop them off at school in the morning, that sort of thing. I remember his daughter Susan and him bringing her to "Our Lady's Abingdon" before he came to work. He was always very supportive of his children as well; naturally he thought a great deal of Roger because of his racing, and he did an awful lot to support him in this'. This might have given rise to charges of nepotism, but as Neal explains: 'what some of us hadn't initially realised was that Roger was a very talented driver and Syd knew that, and so did the best he could provide for him, whether that was an MG or a suitably warmed up Mini.' As getting the job done, and done right, was such a focus, sometimes normal home time considerations for himself and other often did not seem to register; 'for Jim O'Neill and Terry Mitchell, it was often as though he thought that they'd stay here till he was ready to finish for the day'. Geoff Healey echoed this, telling Jon Pressnell: 'he had no regard for time, and at eight, nine or ten o'clock at night he'd be talking away, before deciding to go home.'

Terry Mitchell told the author of his first experience of working with Syd, when from February 1954, the latter recruited him to work on the design of the EX179 record breaker. This was before the creation of MG's new drawing office that summer (to which Mitchell was an early recruit) and whilst Mitchell's main place of work was still the main MG drawing office at Cowley, he would come over to Abingdon to work on the new record breaker drawings. 'Syd had said he wanted EX179 to be "same as EX135 but different". About one inch thicker at the scuttle' Mitchell said, adding 'I'd be there at ten or eleven at night working on it, and Syd and Jacko [Jackson] would be standing either side of my drawing board, telling me about their exploits before the war with Gardner and Eyston... originally, Syd really borrowed me at Cowley; he would come over on Thursdays and he'd chat to us through the windows, and I remember that he told me he had managed to get a XPAG engine through valve crash, which I'd never heard of being done before.'

Mitchell also confirmed the stories from others of Syd's propensity for sketching ideas on discarded cigarette packets turned inside out, and sometimes leaving them tucked on the drawing board. As with Peter Neal's recollections above, Terry Mitchell said that Syd's sketches were seldom to scale or precise proportion, but that he got used to how Syd's mind worked in practice; he also got to appreciate some of his boss's eccentricities: 'Syd used to sit next to the wheel, but we all wanted to drive straight-armed like Farina. He couldn't really see all that well in the dark; he'd slow up by the kerb if there were lights coming towards him. He was cleverest of all on engines more than anything else'.

Interviewed by Mike Taylor for *Thoroughbred & Classic Cars* in 1992, Mitchell said 'Syd was a great one for leaving sketches on opened-out cigarette packets on your drawing board; it was difficult at first because often many of the dimensions would be missing but after a while I began to know how his mind worked. He also had a habit of using unusual phrases, such as 'massive brackets and powerful belts'. That said, he had a very, very good memory.'

On the subject of engines, which as we shall see were Syd's key interest, Mitchell told Mike Taylor of how this benefited the 'Roaring Raindrop', described in Chapter Six: 'Without doubt, Syd's main forte was engine design; it was Syd who produced the specification for the engines to go into EX 181, including camshaft profiles, con-rod types and so on. Eddie Maher, however, thought he knew better, putting the engines together the way he thought they should be built'. When tested they proved to be well down on power; Maher telephoned Enever to say there was something wrong. 'Syd immediately went up to Coventry and spent the night rebuilding the engines to his specification. Under test, one unit produced 293bhp, the other 303. Syd could really make an engine talk but he'd had no college education ...I think, like so many of us, *his flair for engineering and engine development was born in him'.*

In recent years, Terry's daughter Theresa told the author of her own reflections on her father's boss: *'Syd Enever came to our house many times – I just remember him as a gentleman, always smart-suited and tidy – he was a good looking man. Dad had the utmost respect for him and loved working for him – I think he taught dad a great deal. I know they had fun in the drawing office too – Dad would rather be there than at home with us girls! I sensed that dad felt free to be creative under Syd'.*

David Ash was employed by J. S. Inskip, MG's premier New York dealership, raced a MGAs at Sebring in 1956 and 1957, took part in the record-breaking in period and became a firm friend of Syd Enever, chiefly through record-breaking on the Salt Flats in the fifties. Shortly after Syd retired, Ash produced a tribute for his *Sports Car* magazine; *'[Syd] admits to getting a tremendous satisfaction when he sees 'his' cars winning motor races. His son, motor racing driver Roger Enever has pulled off many successes in cars designed by him. Motor cars are his work, his hobby and his whole life. He is happiest when surrounded by drawing boards solving mechanical problems. The most difficult thing of all is to get him to talk about Syd Enever. How will he spend his retirement? "I'm certainly not retiring to take up gardening," he says, and then switches rapidly to explaining how the 1973 safety regulation proposals could be met – accompanied as ever by sketches on a scrap of paper'.*

Expanding on the theme about his hero in 1975, Ash said *'Sydney Enever is that rare kind of genius who had a special gift for quantum. Cars such as the MGA and B and an assortment of land speed record cars came off his drawing boards with a rightness and perfection, not just of line and style, but balance and practicality that were uncanny. Like most men of this unusual stripe, Enever has always been frank and utterly unpretentious. In his years at MG there was never any posturing and while many others deferred to him constantly, Syd Enever saw himself always as a very mortal, even ordinary human – although automotive history will record that he was a good deal more important and gifted than that'.*

Another firm friend of Syd's was ex-pat **Gordon Whitby**, who worked for many years in the US side of the BMC business and corresponded extensively with Syd over much of that period and also participated in some of the record-breaking sessions. He wrote: *'Syd, a self-educated engineer, had the ability to design and build with limited funds, solid and safe sports cars and engines that were exciting to drive. He also excelled more than anyone in building beautiful, streamlined cars, which would run for hours on end, establishing new speed and endurance records, using small cubic inch engines. Amazingly, this was accomplished with limited funds from BMC which was "par for the course". I have often wondered what Syd could have accomplished had he been Chief Engineer/ Designer with General Motors or the Ford Motor Car Co.'*

Writing a further tribute in 1988 to his friend in the short-lived US publication *MG Magazine*, Ash noted that Syd was no prima donna, despite his talents: *'[he was] always frank, almost blunt, even; utterly unpretentious. In his years at MG, there was never any posturing. While many others deferred to him constantly, Syd Enever seemed always to see himself as a very mortal even ordinary human – although history will record that he was vastly more important and gifted than that.'*

Geoffrey Healey often spoke highly of Syd, noting his professionalism, camaraderie and focus on the job without any rancour about the potential rivalry between MG and Austin-Healey. Writing in his book '*The Story of the Big Healeys*' (Gentry Books, 1977) about the time when the Austin-Healey six-cylinder cars were transferred to Abingdon, Healey wrote: *'Syd Enever had a small team with a very large workload. Roy Brocklehurst, Jim O'Neill, Terry Mitchell, Don Hayter, Cecil Cousins, Reg Jackson and Alec Hounslow were to work on the project with no less enthusiasm than that which they gave to the MG models, at the same time dealing with competition requests and problems'.* All of those names feature later in this book. Geoff Healey went on: *'The high quality of the cars produced at Abingdon is a testimony to the devotion and skill of the team. It is no accident that those firms who have been actively concerned with racing produce a better result.'*

He also credits the role that Syd played in helping raise the Big Healey's capabilities in rallying, talking about the development of an Austin-Healey 100/6 'UOC 741' in 1957: *'Syd Enever redesigned the rear spring to reduce stress under load and produced the legendary 14-leaf rear spring that was to contribute so much to the success of the six-cylinders.'* In his book *More Healeys*, Geoff Healey notes how MG always made his family welcome at Abingdon, and how Syd's way of studying a car was distinctive: *'Warwick and Abingdon are only 60 miles apart, and linked by a very pleasant route over the Cotswolds, and we would drive to get Syd's expert opinion on some engineering detail. Syd had a characteristic pose when considering a problem, crouching down on his haunches. Naturally, anyone else involved in the discussion would be forced to do likewise, to the amusement of curious onlookers.'*

Geoff clearly had many fond memories of working with Syd, but he was also alive to the higher politics within BMC. *'Some of the BMC hierarchy had a* barely hidden dislike for John Thornley and MG. They were jealous of the favourable publicity MG and John Thornley received, whilst they felt that they were getting slanged in the press... Alec Issigonis actively discouraged any closer co-operation between Syd and myself including telling me not to talk to Syd about the facelift for the Sprite. I think he thought that rivalry and competition would spur people to greater efforts. This was not an isolated incident but was repeated in many areas'. Finally, writing in his third book for Gentry Books (*Healey – The Specials*, published in 1980) Geoff Healey commented succinctly that '*Syd Enever was one of those experienced and highly competent engineers, so sadly missing in today's automobile industry*.'

Jon Pressnell interviewed Geoff too: '*Syd was involved with the Jensen Interceptor drophead, with Eric Carter, formerly of Morris Bodies Branch – "ringing up mates, here there and everywhere, and turning out a first-rate job."* The Interceptor story – including Eric Carter – pops up in Chapter Eight. '*Syd was a very practical engineer, aware that he had to make things strong enough for the people at Abingdon not to break them when assembling the cars. He wanted things to be right first time – and if anything failed, he'd probably make it three times as strong as necessary, and it would never fail again. He was very easy to get on with. Syd wasn't at all political, and he made no attempt to score points for MG*.'

Nuffield and later BMC Engineering lead Charles Griffin told author Jon Pressnell that Syd was, in his words, '*Nobody's mug... He shattered everyone. He used to prepare the engines for the land-speed-record cars. He'd say 'You never know, it might work' – his ultimate philosophy was that it might be alright. He wouldn't risk it on the bench...*'

Another former member of the MG team, who became involved – largely after Syd left – on vehicle impact testing – was **Dave Seymour**, who spoke to Pressnell about his former boss with enormous respect: '*he was a very competent and clever engineer. The great thing about Syd was that if you couldn't do it, he'd take off his coat and show you how to do it. Syd was very down to earth, and it was said that Syd used to have a pad by the side of his bed. If he woke up in the middle of the night and suddenly thought of something, it was written down, for the next morning.*

"*He used to leave all these notes around if he was going out for the day, of what he wanted everyone to do*'.

Motoring author **Doug Nye** interviewed both Syd and his friend **Eric Carter** (of Morris Motors Bodies) for articles that appeared in 1979 in *Automobile Quarterly* and the short-lived publication *Collector's Car Magazine*; these were rare examples where Syd opened up slightly, in this case on the story of the creation of the MGA. The author asked Nye of his impression of Syd; he said '*I spent a day at his modest home in the Oxford suburbs; he was a taciturn, modest guy – it was hard work to get much out of him at first. I got the impression that there was a tinge of bitterness about BMC; he was one of the less frequently praised engineers within the Organisation – and there'd be mutterings along the lines of "what's he done?" and "he's always been messing about with specials" – and there was no doubt some jealousy of his fame. He wasn't self-promoting, unlike Issigonis, and yet if you look at many of the magazines from the period when he was at his height, he got a lot of coverage – far more than most Midlands engineers ever did!*'

In connection with the MGA in particular, Carter said to Nye of his friend: '*Syd Enever was responsible for this model and for so many others. He lived for his work, and worked all hours. He had to sell the MGA to top management, he had to take any kicks and he deserves any credit. MG, BMC, BLM all owe him a lot...*'

Another motoring writer who tackled Syd was **Edward Eves**, for many years Midland Motoring Correspondent for *Autocar*; in the summer of 1975, Eves (who had worked in Humber's photographic department before the War) went to see Syd at his home by the Oxford Bypass and like others before him tried valiantly to encourage his interviewee to open up about himself as well as his work. '*I talked to Syd at his home in Oxford where he still thinks and dreams motor cars. Asked which of his achievements he considered the best, his unhesitating reply was the Gardner car, because it raised*

Syd's August 1960 certificate of Fellowship of the Motor Industry – a recognition by his peers of his status. (Enever Archive)

the records by something, like 40mph when previously constructors had been scratching for the odd one or two miles per hour'. Eves also asked about the origins of the MGA (described in Chapter Six): *'Syd told me how he started the MGA design on his dining room table basing the chassis on that of the TD but sweeping the chassis side members outwards round the cockpit area to allow the occupants to sit between them, nearer to the road, thereby making the car lower. When the design was completed and the prototype built it proved so free of faults that it was put into production after only fifty miles of road testing'.*

Michael H. Dale was a former BMC Salesman who moved to the USA and rose the ranks to become, by the time of his retirement in 1999, President of Jaguar Cars Inc. As a British ex-pat he got to see BMC – in particular Austin Healey and MG – through the golden post-war expansion. *'I only met Syd a few times but he impressed me as a most down to earth gent. The discussions were around what should replace the MGB. He was searching for a mass produced car from which he could take the basics, as he had done with previous sports cars, and the only offering was the Mini which had a detrimental effect on styling; front wheel drive doesn't lend itself easily to long hood short deck approach'* Dale sold Enever's MGAs in the Personal Exports showroom on at 41-46 Piccadilly and the American bases before he switched to the USA. *'As the twin cam didn't make it there were lots of disc brakes and wheels left over. MG, inventive as usual, offered them on the standard car and I did a land office business selling them. A great sports car for its time'*.

Alec Poole wrote of his experience as a 'Morris Commercial' Apprentice, spending part of his time with Syd in 1964; Alec and Roger Enever got on like a house on fire, both being sons of people 'in the business' with high expectations on their shoulders, and doubtless a need to prove themselves on merit to avoid the inevitable sneers about nepotism. Poole said that he heard that in the 1950s, MI5 had supposedly said that they found that Syd's name was included on a 'persons of interest' list retained by the Nazis if they had invaded; it's a nice story – although the author checked a copy of *'Sonderfahndungsliste G.B.'* – the so-called *'Hitler's Black Book'* and there are no Enevers in there; perhaps he was on another list? Undoubtedly the Germans would have been intrigued as to how Syd managed to extract so much power and speed from such tiny engines.

Alan Edis, who eventually proved to be the final Plant Director overseeing the Abingdon factory, had a number of meetings with Syd, and told the author: *'Syd Enever was a very nice man indeed; he just quietly got on and did the best he could; he was a very important man for MG in the way things evolved'*.

Finally, for the purposes of this prelude to the main story, is this quote from the pages of a 1951 issue of the Nuffield Organisation's in-house staff magazine *Teamwork* within an article about the Gardner record car: *'it is not surprising that Sydney Enever has not found time for any of the usual hobbies. Motor cars are his work, hobby and whole life. Like most men of outstanding engineering ability, he is quiet, has some difficulty in expressing himself. The most difficult thing of all is to get him to talk about Syd Enever'*. The author hopes that this book will go some small way to redressing that problem.

Chapter One: The Lad From Winchester

Albert Sydney Enever was born in Colden Common, a small village near Winchester, Hampshire, on March 25th 1906, the youngest of six – and as the only boy, you can be certain that in the mostly female household, he was royally spoilt by his four surviving sisters (one had died aged sixteen months in June 1899, and so Syd obviously never knew her). The patriarch of this household was Francis Albert Sydney Enever, who according to his son had been an ironmonger's assistant, but had been apprenticed to the making of stained-glass windows, and according to his son was also remembered as an accomplished pianist.

Mother was Maud Matilda Enever (née Harper) whose family were dairy farmers based at Littlemore and Long Wittenham, the former a rural south-eastern district of Oxford, and the latter a village and civil parish in Berkshire (nowadays Oxfordshire) which was a few miles east of the town of Abingdon-on-Thames – a place which will later feature prominently in this story. The Harpers also owned a butcher's shop, bakery, baker's shop and dairy on the Cowley Road in Oxford at its junction with Bullingdon Road. Francis and Maud were married at Cowley Parish Church on May 23rd 1895.

Looking smart in his woollen jacket, waistcoat and knickerbockers, this is the young Syd Enever as a school student. (Enever Family)

> **Francis Albert Sydney Taylor Enever**
>
> Syd Enever's parents were married in 1895; they were at the time Francis Albert Sydney Enever (the obvious source of their son's name when he was born nine years later) and Maud Matilda Harper. This was not the whole story, however; Francis had been born Francis Albert Sydney Taylor in Reading, Berkshire in 1873 but later adopted the surname of his own natural father (Frederick Francis Enever) making Syd Enever's father's full name 'Francis Albert Sydney Taylor Enever'; by curious coincidence his initials could be said to spell the word 'Fast-Enever'; nonsense perhaps, but an amusing harbinger of the future?
>
> Family records of Francis Enever's departure are unclear beyond the fact that he left his family in 1909 and seemingly never saw his family ever again, leaving Maud alone in charge of their considerable family, including young Syd. In June 1918, he is recorded as living in Brighton, Sussex – having married Beatrice Hestel Bourdon on June 1st at Brighton Registry Office, describing himself falsely as a widower; he was working at the time as a Commercial Traveller. Research by the late

Enever/ Enever family historian Barry Ennever showed that Francis had two daughters, Lorna and Eugenie, the former born in August 1905 and thus a year older than Syd; it seems therefore that Francis was already sowing the seeds for his eventual break with his Oxford family in 1909.

Further research shows that Syd's errant father left for North America in 1920, in order to seek his fortune, being recorded at Gloucester, Massachusetts, USA, and although he appears to have returned to Brighton, he is recorded travelling from Southampton on the Berengaria, bound for New York. The last known record of him is as a tobacco salesman in New York in April 1930, living (as one of 16 families; 40 people in total) in a lodging house at 2474 Eight Avenue, New York City. One is tempted to wonder if this man – now in his fifties – ever heard how well his son, Syd, was doing, by this stage?

Syd's parents had separated by 1909 when he was just three years old; '*my mother was living on ten shillings a week, which she had been left by her father, and she supplemented this by going out to work*' he wrote. With a young family, the oldest child still only fifteen, one can imagine the challenges this posed for a single woman in her mid-thirties in Edwardian England. All the children were sent to school – even three-year old Syd, who recalled that his headmaster in Colden Common was Mr. Busby, who lived just across the road from the school. As for the Enever family: '*We lived in a two-storied cottage, one of a row of eight, with a Christian Bible Chapel – where I was baptized – built on one end, and the 'Rising Sun' public house on the other – and the rent was two shillings and ninepence a week.*' Despite Mrs Enever's modest income, she somehow managed to arrange for her daughters to learn to play the piano.

Two years after Francis Enever had departed – never to be seen again by his family, as far as is known – the family moved to Oxford, which was understandable as it was near to Maud's family; their first home in the area was at Howard Street, by the Cowley Road, but they soon moved to Cranham Street where they ran a grocery and general store which Syd ruefully recalled as being '*not being very profitable*'. While there, Syd attended St Barnabas School. In 1913, the family moved to Paradise Square; '*we had a four-storied house which was in a district where most of the theatrical people from the Oxford Theatre came to lodge, and my mother ran this as a boarding house for these people*.' At this juncture, Syd was sent to South Oxford School, where the headmaster was named Benson, Living a few doors away was Arthur Leslie Cook, who was to become Syd's life-long friend until dying in 1966.

South Oxford School

South Oxford School had opened in Thames Street, Oxford in 1910, so was still quite new when Syd first entered its classrooms; a sign of the different times was that girls' classes were accommodated on the top floor, students entering through dedicated Girls' Entrances at either side of the front of the building. Boys were taught in the ground floor classrooms; the infants were in a separate building with an entrance from Luther Street, whilst the main school was accessed through a passage at St. Aldates. The school converted to a secondary modern with a mixed junior school in 1948, and finally closed its doors in 1981.

An 1837 engraving of St. Ebbe's Church, the heart of the local community and a depiction from 75 years before the arrival of the Reverend John Stansfeld, in turn an early influence on the young Syd Enever. Whilst the church remains, much of the original suburb and community it once served was swept away by the progress of modern development. (Author Archive)

By the following year, just as Europe erupted into what became known as the 'Great War', eight year old Syd and his friends could often be found in typical youthful pursuits: '*like most boys, we built a number of variations of wooden go-carts, consisting of boards or boxes and axles taken from a pram; these could only be pulled along or run downhill*'. The author recalls making something very similar in the late 1960s when around the same age. Enever's were rather more adventurous, however, with even thoughts of mimicking contemporary air aces; he recalled wistfully that *'one was built with wood and canvas wings on it, but on going down a steep hill, it never took off.'*

As the First World war continued, the sight of military presences in and around Oxford became a common occurrence; soldiers sometimes billeted at the Enever household at Paradise Square. The association also became even closer to home when Syd's sister Florence, then twenty years old, married a Captain Cyril Howitt in 1915. Syd also remembers rationing (which began in the summer of 1918) as food supplies became scarcer; he would sometimes collect the family's margarine ration from a central distribution point at Gloucester Green, nowadays Oxford's main bus station.

Around this time, too, Syd encountered someone who would prove influential to the young boy; *'the Rector of the Parish of St. Ebbes was the Reverend Stansfeld, who lived in the Rectory opposite our house – and he was also the parish doctor.'* Syd recalled, adding that Stansfeld was *'one of the best and kindest men I have known, in the way that he looked after his parishioners.'* Rev'd Stansfeld, whose story is covered in a panel later, appears to have been thoughtful and kind to his parishioners, putting their needs first, and clearly was very fondly remembered by Syd Stansfeld promoted a scouts and guides group and a boys club; *'in the Rectory Grounds we helped him build a large wooden building of a number of rooms, including a club-room, doctor's surgery, reception and other rooms.'*

A typical street in St. Ebbes in the early 1900s; it was a vibrant community, if not a wealthy one. The inexorable winds of progress in the 1950s blew much of the old housing and shops away. (Author Archive)

The Reverend John Stansfeld – known frequently to his parishioners as 'The Doctor' (he combined medical and religious care amongst his many talent) seen here in a 1915 photo; he was the Rector of St. Ebbe's from 1912 to 1926, and was described by Syd as being one of the kindest men he ever knew. (Portrait from 'The Doctor. The story of John Stansfeld of Oxford and Bermondsey' (B Baron, 1952))

Paradise Square And St. Ebbe's

Just to the south of Oxford Castle, in an area now dominated by post-war and later development, there used to be a distinct area of the city which thrummed with life, and was home to quite a wide cross-section of the local population – some moderately well-off, but many more somewhat lower down the scale of affluence, on the borderline of middle and working class. Built largely on the site of former Greyfriars Paradise Gardens (paradise in this context meaning 'walled garden'), and bordered along its western flank by the Castle Mill Stream, with Oxford Castle to the east, by the Edwardian period, the area of the parish of St. Ebbes had been developed with many small, terraced houses, some originally with dubious sanitation although later Victorian interventions had mitigated this problem.

St. Ebbes was described in the 1952 biography of John Stansfeld (*'The Doctor'*, by Barclay Baron) as being home to around 750 'slum houses'; the parish

Syd and Ivy's wedding day; also in the photo left to right are seen Sarah Davis Cyril Howitt (Florence's husband) Maud Enever, Will Muddock (Uncle). (Enever Family)

A studio portrait of a young Ivy, complete with fashionable Marcel Wave in her hair. (Enever Family)

was regarded as a blight on the area dominated to the south by Matthew Arnold's 'city of dreaming spires' of academia: *'there is nothing to attract a sightseer save the great mass of the Castle keep, towering above a neglected reach of the Rover. A jumble of old lanes, little yards and workshops lead down to the unlovely gasworks near the railway station.'* Despite this, Baron described the level of life as vibrant; it was *'... hard-up but hard-working, cheerful and neighbourly – the authentic pattern of a community, long-established.'* The popular Victorian and later view of St. Ebbe's as a seemingly recalcitrant poor part of Oxford had become deeply entrenched in the wake of cholera outbreaks in 1832, 1846 and 1854, associated in part with the open drains – although these were partially tackled in the wake of a report following the second outbreak.

It was to this busy, low-income but vibrant suburb that Maud Enever, her husband having left, moved with her young school-age son and some of his older sisters moved just two years before the start of the First World War. Proximity to the theatres and colleges meant that lodging houses were commonplace in St. Ebbes, and Mrs Enever took on such an establishment which provided her with a reasonable source of income.

The 1921 Census records Syd (as Sydney Albert Enever) living at 6 Paradise Square, Oxford along with his mother, Maud Matilda Enever, sister Leonora Grace Enever and a pair of lodgers in their mid-fifties, one of them a retired Publisher's Agent for 'Kelly's Directory' (a kind of 'Yellow Pages' of its time) called Walter Scott and the other, Ernest Lawrence, described as a General Manager for 'North & Co. Ltd', then a well-known local Mineral Water business known for its 'codd bottles', which used a glass marble as an internal stopper for carbonated drinks. Maud is described as an *'Apartments Lodging Housekeeper'* whilst Syd is a *'Garage Hand'* at Morris Garages in Queen Street, Oxford. Syd was still living there ten years later, on the basis of contemporary correspondence.

By the late 1930s, the authorities in Oxford were focused on what would later perhaps be termed slum clearance, although such language would doubtless have offended many who lived in St. Ebbes at that time, because there was a sense of community spirit and a well-supported church and associated rectory in the heart of the parish. The Second World War intervened and meant that plans were suspended, but they never went away; a 1948 document 'Oxford Replanned' (by Thomas Sharp, for the Architectural Press) set the blueprint to sweep away the old St. Ebbes, and from the 1960s some 700 households were moved out and the old gasworks dismantled to allow the area to be cleared and re-developed, including the Westgate Centre and flats where St Ebbe's School once sat.

Whilst the Rectory survives, as does the basic street layout of Paradise Square, very little of what exists around it would have been familiar to Maud, Syd and Leonora; their old community, both good and bad, has been erased.

Reverend John Stansfeld

To Syd, with no father at home from the age of six, and that home overwhelmingly female, it was perhaps understandable if he latched on to a trusted father substitute. At Oxford, that role seems to have been fulfilled in part by the Reverend **John Stedwell Stansfeld** (December 16th 1855 – December 17th 1939) who was a doctor, Anglican priest and philanthropist. Although he had arrived in Oxford by the time that Syd got to know him, Stansfeld had already founded the Oxford Medical mission in Bermondsey, London, and the Stansfeld Oxford & Bermondsey Club Football Club in 1897.

At the time, there were a number of church-sponsored groups centred on Oxford that reached out to the poorer parts of society, notably in the East End of London, aiming at a practical, philanthropic and Christian ministry amongst the poorest members of society, at a time when public welfare was at best minimal, and the impacts of poverty in some places breathtakingly awful. Stansfeld left school in 1869 and briefly tried engineering, but finding he was not best suited to that profession, tried a few jobs in the City of London before successfully sitting a Civil Service entrance examination in 1876, after which he joined the offices of Customs & Excise, initially in London but before long moving to Oxford.

He then became caught up in the life of the University, meeting like-minded friends with similar religious leanings, and embarked on Classics studies at Exeter College; later he decided he wanted to go into the church and so studied further at Wycliffe Hall. All these studies were in evenings and at weekends while he worked at Customs & Excise.

Gaining a BA in 1889 and an MA in 1892, he then decided to study medicine as well, and even found himself working part time as a doctor at Charing Cross Hospital. By the turn of the century, he was a fully-qualified doctor – at which point he was encouraged by friends to join a medical mission to Bermondsey. Being both a medical doctor and a minister of the cloth, Stansfeld was not atypical of his time; with such a spread of talents he would have truly been the centre of gravity of his local community, and furthermore his force of character meant that he was respected by the majority of his parish – who knew him simply as 'The Doctor'.

In the Edwardian years, Stansfeld founded a boys' club in Bermondsey, and extended its reach further when he acquired some land at Horndon in Essex to create a holiday camp – in the days just before the Boy Scout movement came into being. In 1912, Dr Stansfeld accepted an offer to minister in a 'poor parish' of Oxford – and so he arrived in St. Ebbes – around the time that the Enever family moved to Paradise Square. As explained in the

Young Syd, around 1926, cutting a dashing look. (Enever Family)

> main text, Syd greatly admired 'The Doctor' and had cause to be especially grateful when a boyish experiment went badly wrong.
>
> Stansfeld's wife Janet died on October 29th 1918 and in 1925 he set off to Africa as a medical missionary as he approached his seventieth birthday, spending five years in Kenya before returning home to live in Spelsbury, 16 miles northwest of Oxford. There he lived the bucolic life of the country parson, dying three months after the Second World War had been declared.

One gable of the main room was designed to feature a triangular pattern of red and white glass on a fretwork of wooden framing; Syd recalled he took on the task of cutting and fitting the glass in this structure (perhaps this was something he remembered seeing his father do): '*I had never tackled cutting such large sheets of glass before, but managed without any drastic breakages.*' Others also had a go – including Syd's friend Arthur Cook. As a reward for helping build his surgery and rooms, the Reverend-cum-doctor Stansfeld sent the troupe on a camping holiday at Shotover Hill, where Stansfeld had bought some land (see panel). Whilst there, Syd and his pals were roped in to help demolish an old brick cottage that was lying derelict; their adopted technique – pulling down the chimney stack after attaching a rope to it – was frowned on, even if it did achieve the desired demolition in a cloud of dust; '*with a crash the whole roof and walls crumbled down*' Syd recalled.

Meanwhile Syd's early school years saw him show aptitude in the vital basics of reading, writing and arithmetic, and he showed an interest and ability in drawing – clearly one of the skills which would eventually serve him in good stead – and (like his later colleague Cecil Cousins – see later) he also enjoyed the practical joys of carpentry. Sports-wise he was less interested in football than in swimming and running. '*During this time, my pal and I constructed a number of bicycles from parts we bought very cheaply from the local scrap dealers.*' This early type of 'up-cycling' facilitated a certain amount of freedom: '*we were able to go out into the country, which we enjoyed doing – we visited the local open-air swimming baths fairly often – no matter how cold!*'

Syd and Arthur's enthusiasm and carpentry skills led them to make bows and arrows, stilts and the pièce de résistance, a small boat like a coracle – although the latter was not so successful; '*it was short and wide, and terribly hard to steer, and consequently it tended to go round and round in circles, although we did manage to use it for swimming and fishing adventures.*'

Syd's next hobby could nearly have been his last, when he and Arthur discovered the joys of explosives: '*in those days you could purchase loose black gunpowder from the local gunshop, by the ounce. This you could use in various ways to make small bombs and the like, but I constructed a cannon from a pieces of drain pipe about two feet long, and fixed to a base*'. One day in the garden, Syd had loaded his cannon; '*by some means or other it went off when my face was over the barrel – and the blast of flame hit me full in the face, burning off all of my hair except for the back part, and scorching my face completely all over*'. Syd notes that somehow he had managed to close his eyes in time, but he certainly was in a bad way: '*the pain was terrible; my mother rushed me over to Doctor Stansfeld, who fortunately was nearby*'. The good reverend was clearly a multi-talented asset to the local community.

Syd came back with his head completely bandaged, with just small slits for his eyes: '*for days I laid on my bed, and for weeks I remained bandaged, as the whole of the skin of my face became rigid and gradually came away.*' Eventually the time came to review the damage: '*at last the bandages came away, and I looked in the mirror – it was ghastly to behold – the charred hair and the patchy new and old pieces of parchment-like skin. But it was marvellous how eventually none of this showed and I returned to normal, with new eyelashes and darker and more prolific eyebrows*'.

Syd and Ivy dressed up as 'Bonnie & Clyde' (Enever Family)

CHAPTER ONE: THE LAD FROM WINCHESTER

Syd's Family

Syd married Ivy Mildred Davis (born April 13th 1910) at St Ebbes Church on September 8th 1932 and they went on to have four children; Susan (November 6th 1938), Jane (March 4th 1942), Roger (June 8th 1944) and Michael (December 7th 1945 – June 2003). From the evidence of letters to Syd from the Earl of March in June 1931, thus when he was still a bachelor, we can deduce that at that time he was living at 6 Paradise Square, Oxford. By the time of the 1939 England and Wales Register, the couple were living with Ivy's 53-year old mother Sarah at 2 Albert Place, Oxford.

Roger Enever remembers visiting St Ebbes to see family: '*my mother's mother – Sarah Davis – née Muddock –– lived just round the corner; there was a pub nearby, and they used to send us out to get some beer or milk stout – and there was a parrot at this pub; they were all little old back-to-back houses – it was very humble...*'

Jane married Claude Moufflet, a French student who had studied at Ruskin College, and they moved to Paris where they in turn had two children – Nicholas (born May 2nd 1963) and Tamsin (Born October 8th 1964). Roger married Londoner Marguerite Ruth Tobin in 1971 although they later divorced. Ivy died, a few months before her husband, in on September 9th 1992.

Syd and Ivy Enever and family at the then relatively new Jam Mound - Boars Hill, Oxford; the mound comprised an artificial hill, built in 1931, and had been designed by Sir Arthur Evans to provide a view of Oxford as described by Matthew Arnold in his poem, Thyrsis, "that sweet city with her dreaming spires". (Enever Family)

Building on his carpentry interests, Syd enrolled in evening classes in carving at the Oxford Technical School; '*I was able to carve some pieces for our local church – I could do this quite well, but it was such a long job.*' Syd eventually gave up this pastime in favour of more time out and about with his friends. Meanwhile at school, Syd ended up in the top form, where he was second in his class; he remembers that the boy above him, named Grimsby, went on to work at an accountant in Cornmarket and ultimately had a career as financial controller for an international company.

Proud grandfather with his daughter Jane's children, Nicholas and Tamsin. (Enever Family)

Chapter Two: The Shop Boy at Morris Garages

The headmaster at South Oxford School evidently had good connections in the local Oxford business community, and knowing Syd's mechanical interest and aptitude, suggested he secure a job as a 'shop boy' at the Morris Garages salesroom in Queen Street in the heart of the city. *'This I did, at the initial wage of twelve shillings and sixpence in early 1920'* he recalled.

The young William Morris, a keen cyclist, photographed on an old 'boneshaker' around 1895. He would later go on to found the Morris Garages, where a young Syd Enever began his career. (Author Archive)

William Morris – Lord Nuffield

Much has been written about William Morris – later Sir William and ultimately Lord Nuffield – without whom, obviously, the stories told in this book would never have happened. Born in the village of Hallow near Worcester in 1877, Morris and his family soon returned to their original stamping ground of Oxford, as Morris's father became a bailiff at Headington when Morris senior's father-in-law became blind. As a young man, Morris was an enthusiastic early adopter of the new-fangled bicycle, already in the nowadays familiar form of parallelogram frame, equal-sized wheels with pneumatic tyres and chain drive to the rear from chain wheel and pedals. In due course, Morris began to buy in components and assembled them into complete bicycles which he sold locally in Oxford with increasing success; he was also a highly accomplished cycle racer in his youth.

Despite an early business set back which clouded his views on being, in his mind, subservient to outside investment, Morris eventually established the Morris Garages with premises dotted around the centre of Oxford, notably a garage in the large yard behind the Clarendon Hotel in Cornmarket (see separate panel about the business).

Although his fascinating life and career need not trouble us here in detail, Morris nevertheless facilitated the atmosphere in which Syd Enever and his many colleagues could thrive. He would become one the greatest philanthropists that the United Kingdom ever knew, donating what today would equate with well over a billion Pounds Sterling; many endowments bearing the 'Nuffield' name are still thriving today, even if, rather sadly, many of the people who still benefit in some manner may have little if any knowledge of the man who made it all possible.

The Morris Garages Premises

William Morris started his working life in a modest but entrepreneurial manner, building and repairing bicycles, largely from components he bought in from third-party suppliers (indeed that practice largely set the tone for the remainder of his career); a financial hiccup which saw him having to queue in the rain in order to buy back his own tools somewhat coloured his attitude to business partnerships, but he nevertheless surrounded himself with a small coterie of trusted acolytes (some of whom, it has to be said, lost little time in back-biting in order to curry favour). By the time that he was ready to expand into the new-fangled motorcycle and automobile business, it was clearly no longer sufficient to operate from a high-street shop with its traditional front-door bell; a yard was needed and a workshop where repairs could be undertaken unhindered by weather or neighbourly concerns.

Between 1910 and 1911, Merton College (Morris's landlords) built a new building along Longwall Street, to become Morris Garages, and it was here in 1912 that Morris designed and built his first car, the prototype 'Bullnose Morris'. He bought new showrooms at 36 and 37 Queen Street in 1913, and in 1914 a further large garage in the hotel yard of the Clarendon Hotel in Cornmarket. Syd Enever's first time at Morris Garages was spent in the show room in 36-37 Queen Street, seven years after William Morris had acquired it, and later he moved to the larger site where more of the practical mechanical work was undertaken.

The Clarendon Yard included an entrance from the street which soon benefited from the requisite 'Morris Garage' sign above it; the hotel itself – at 52 Cornmarket, Oxford – survived until 1954 when, in the manner of the time, developers did what Hitler never did and demolished the building, in favour of a new Woolworths store (later in turn knocked down in favour of yet another development). The yard was to the rear of the hotel, and one can imagine that occasionally the noise from the various workshops and open space caused disturbance to guests and staff of the hotel, but for many years there appears to have been a symbiotic relationship between the two cheek-by-jowl businesses.

Syd wrote that hire cars were always available; in 1921 for example he recalled the three makes on offer were Hudson, Essex and a Daimler – the latter chauffeur driven by 'Jock' Cockburn and Harry Newbold. *'Most of the owners of cars with whom we dealt with in those days were the business people of Oxford and surrounding districts, including many farmers and titled people.'*

There were changes at the Clarendon Yard in 1924, according to Syd's notes: *'the yard was completely reconstructed, the whole being turned into one large covered-in garage, and a car repair shop only. Petrol pumps were installed, and the repair shop itself was a larger and more pleasant place to work.'* Before long there was new management at the site too: *'the rebuilt garage was now run by a Mr. Critchall, who was brought in on an efficiency basis; he only lasted a couple of years, and then "Copper" Crease was made Manager, with George Bullock becoming Foreman of the Repair Shop.'*

In later years, 'Morris Garages' opened in 1932 as a separate retail franchise opened in grand premises at St. Aldates (nowadays Oxford Crown Court). Although there are plaques on some of these former homes to the business, little else remains – although of course there is still to some extent a legacy in the Oxford suburbs in the form of the BMW MINI factory.

The Morris Garages was a major business in Oxford offering to hire out, sell and service motor cars. This frontage in Longwall has been preserved by New College. (Author Archive)

William Morris, seated in a 10hp Bullnose Morris Oxford Standard Model with his passenger, Mr Varney, after they had completed a reliability trial from London to Edinburgh and back in May 1913. The picture was taken outside Stewart & Ardern's original premises, 18 Woodstock Road, London (Author Archive)

Edwin Armstead And Carl Breeden

Manager of the Morris Garages from January 1919 was Edwin Clipsham Armstead (1865 – May 13th 1922), an old associate of William Morris, who Syd recalled as *'a brusque large gentleman with a big moustache, but of a kindly demeanour.'* Before linking up with William Morris, Cambridge-born Armstead had run his own cycle business (shops at 9-10 Broad Street, and 18 Little Clarendon Street). Armstead resigned as General Manager in 1921 but it seems that Morris kept him on in some capacity. Thus a new arrival, as General Manager of the Morris Garages in early 1921, was Charles (Carl) Louis Breeden (February 10th 1891 – November 2nd 1951).

Breeden, had, until a major falling-out early in 1921 with his brother-in-law, Oliver Lucas, held the exalted post of Sales Director at Joseph Lucas Limited, but before that schism Breeden had extended a generous credit line to Morris during the troubled economic times of late 1919, a period when most of the British car industry suffered a dramatic collapse in sales. Morris seldom forgot those who had helped him, and Breeden would prove to be a classic example.

However, Breeden was not destined to stay long yoked to Morris Garages; in 1922 he left and bought into the *'Wilmot Manufacturing Company'* of Birmingham, which went on by 1927 to become the famous Wilmot-Breeden concern, which supplied thousands of parts for British car makers for many decades to come; Wilmot-Breeden long benefited from the relationship Breeden had forged with Morris. The author is grateful to Peter Seymour, an expert in Morris and Nuffield history, who came across a fascinating letter from Cecil Kimber to his friend Frank Woollard, dated February 16th 1922, when he studied Woollard's papers. In the letter, Kimber said:

'Since I last wrote you Breeden has come – and gone! Something rather more attractive engaged his attention in Birmingham from which City he seemed very loath to part. I immediately tackled WRM with the result that I am now General Manager at 500 per, with a decent percentage in profits – if any! Old Armstead says goodbye to us at the end of the month, thank goodness, and Findlater becomes my right hand man. Some work ahead'.

The sad fact was that the 57-year old Armstead had indeed resigned, and subsequently took his own life on May 13th 1922 – leaving no note. Peter Seymour sought details of the inquest which included the comment, about Armstead, that *'... he worried a lot about giving up his* [self-owned] *business. He thought he had made a great mistake. He gave up his business in Broad Street during the war, and just recently he had been somewhat depressed.'* As Peter Seymour notes, it was hardly the first or last instance where someone would regret giving up being their own boss in favour of working for someone else – as we have seen, William Morris himself having been a good example.

Syd's own notes confirm Armstead's departure, without the sad detail, but adds another name to the mix: *'a Mr Anderson had temporarily taken over, and subsequently a Mr. Cecil Kimber was appointed by William R. Morris; he had begun as Sales Manager, driving around on a small two-stroke Triumph motorcycle; after a short while he became General Manager.'* Syd remembered Kimber as *'... a man with great drive and initiative, a personal enthusiasm for cars, and a desire to enter the sports car market with a car of his own conception.'*

As well as the obvious Morris cars, the garage also handled a variety of other makes: *'there were the American Hudson and Essex cars, also Humbers, Talbots, Wolseleys, Singers, Standards and others, as well as motorcycles such as Douglas, Enfield, Indian, Sunbeam and Triumph'.* Meanwhile Syd was provided with a carrier cycle; *'it was fixed with a "Morris Garages" display plate, and I used it to travel between Queen Street, Longwall Garage and the Clarendon Garage, and out to Morris Motors at Cowley with messages, parcels and so forth.'* When not out on his errands, Syd generally found himself in the sales room, where he would be cleaning cars and motorcycles and moving them around. *'I also kept Mr. Newport's stock of large brass headlamps highly polished'* he recalled.

Syd recalled others too; as well as the afore-mentioned Edwin Armstead: *'there was a Miss Stepney, secretary; Mr Tobin, hire car driver and salesman; Vic Young, salesman; Mr Newport, counter-sales; Freddie Gardner, hire driver; and Miss Cooper, telephone operator'.* In addition, *'Mr Bradbury gave driving instructions using an open two-seat Morris Cowley'.* Mr. Tobin, meanwhile, moved on from being hire driver to become Sales Manager and a few years later the General Manager. According to Syd, *'the usual practice when taking on school leavers, in the Sales Rooms, was to move them on fairly quickly to their garages where they could be trained as mechanics.'* Syd was eventually replaced at the Sales Room by 'new boy' Frank Smith: *'he subsequently became an electrician at the Clarendon Garage and finally a car repair foreman.'*

During 1921, the year after joining (and after that year's Census in June – see later), Syd was moved to the Morris Garages Clarendon Hotel Yard in Cornmarket Street, Oxford, at the time a large open yard adjacent to the Clarendon Hotel itself: *'it had a row of lock-up garages all down one side which included a motorcycle repair shop. Across the lower end was a large, covered garage. "Bill" Bailey, as foreman, ran the motorcycle repair shop, and one of his mechanics was a tall fellow named Cecil Cousins who later was detailed by Cecil Kimber to take charge of the production construction of the Morris Garages sports cars, and eventually finished up at the MG Car Company at Abingdon, as Deputy to the Managing Director.'*

The Clarendon Yard mainly comprised facilities for garaging, washing and polishing cars, with a tyres repair section supervised by a Mr Cullimore, the Yard Foreman. Petrol was dispensed to customers via two-gallon cans of various brands; Syd recalled these included Pratts, Shell, BP (British Petroleum), National Benzole and Red Line.

The car repair shop was in a separate building, situated behind the hotel; this was where Syd was working by 1921: *'I was detailed to work here, under the Foreman Mr Crease, more generally referred to as "Copper" Crease'.* Syd noted that "Copper" (real name William) had already worked with William Morris for nearly two decades: *'he was one of the original boys who had started at the "Oxford Automobile and Cycle Agency" at New Road, Oxford, being taken on there in 1903'.* Syd clearly remembered Mr Crease with some affection: *'he was a most considerate man, helping me as much as possible, and he was eventually instrumental in bringing me to the attention of Mr. Cecil Kimber, leading to my transfer to the MG Car Company Limited at Abingdon.'*

Writing fifty years after these events, Syd also looked back fondly at some of the other people with whom he worked at a time when he was still just fifteen years old: *'the mechanics I can best remember at that time included Horace Draper, Dave Resuggan, Archie Sheldon and George Bullock – later to become Foreman; there were about six in all.'* Syd's own work was varied: *'I had to record all the mechanics' time sheets and keep all the job cards in order, with time and materials recorded so that the customer bills could be prepared.'*

In addition to the paperwork, Syd would be asked to keep the workshop clean, fetch any spare parts from the Longwall Garage, Morris Motors at Cowley or the train station; *'I often had to do cleaning jobs for the mechanics and if I had any time free, to help with the*

The Morris Garages.

Proprietor - W. R. MORRIS

Queen Street, Longwall Street and Clarendon Yard, Oxford

MR. W. R. MORRIS wishes to inform his many customers and friends that MR. E. C. ARMSTEAD, who is well known to so many of the citizens of Oxford and district, has been appointed " General Manager of the Morris Garages " in the place of Mr. F. G. Barton, who owing to ill-health was compelled to relinquish the position. Mr. Armstead is a well-known business man with considerable energy, and I feel confident that of all those clients who have entrusted me with their patronage in the past will continue to do so, they will find in him a man who will be only too anxious to do all he can to carry out anything in the way of business entrusted to him with courtesy and expedition and in addition will, in the course of a few months be in a position to execute orders for the 1919 Morris Cowley Cars.

Sole Agent for " Morris Oxford " and " Morris Cowley " Cars
Orders taken now for Triumph, Royal Enfield, B.S.A., Douglas, Matchless And Levis Motor Cycles

Edwin Armstead was a Cycle Dealer before the First World War; he joined The Morris Garages at the start of 1919 and was still in charge when Syd first arrived. (Peter Seymour) dismantling of an engine, axle or car.. this is what I was interested in and enjoyed doing, no matter how dirty I got in the process – and I always worked as quickly as possible, giving myself a sense of achievement.' Because the Morris Garages business was a general agency that dealt with a wide range of cars, the experience that Syd gained was wide-ranging and obviously encouraged independent thinking and a broad knowledge of the many different systems and equipment; *'car makes typically included Ford, Hupmobile, Singer, Standard, Belsize, Humber, Wolseley, Daimler, Bugatti, Studebaker, Hispano-Suiza, Delaunay-Belleville and many others – and including the original Morris cars with their White & Poppe engines of 1913'.*

'With this sort of variation, I soon picked up the practical side of car mechanics including all the hand-fitting of those days, especially the scraping and close fitting of the crankshaft and connecting-rod bearings. At that time, most cars had magneto ignition systems and many of the old cars that I worked on had leather-faced clutches. Starting by handle was usual, the exception being the beautiful Delaunay-Belleville, which had compressed-air starting.'

The sheer variety of motorcars and their nascent technology in those early days of the twentieth century was both a blessing and a curse; the evolution of equipment, fittings and techniques associated with them was in a constant state of flux, and any mechanic needed to keep abreast of the latest developments or risk becoming out of touch. *'Having great interest in anything mechanical, I became perhaps far more proficient in terms of the intricacy of these cars than the mechanics were. One day Dave Resuggan was trying to dismantle the differential of an old Fiat car, and could not work out how to do it; I visualised that it must be that one pin crossed through the other; I suggested this to Dave, which only made him wild, and he went off to get a bar. Meanwhile, I had slipped the pin out and got it all apart; this only enraged him even more and he told me to 'eff off.'*

In those days, Model T Fords were commonplace, and illustrating the variety of car systems he got to work with, Syd remembered working on these popular rugged but eccentric cars when they came into Morris Garages for repair: *'they had flywheel dynamos, vibrating ignition coils and two-speed epicyclic gearboxes'*. Many cars required some degree of parts improvisation, in a day long before the later widespread parts availability; quite a few of the original parts themselves had been handmade and when you add in the fact that some of the cars were out of production, the need to use workshop skills to make new parts – often from scratch – can be appreciated.

'In the workshop there were several machines, such as a lathe, grinder and pillar-drill' Syd wrote; *'one day after time, I was alone in the workshop and I was using the pillar drill. I had a rather long lock of hair over my eyes, and leaning over the machine this became wound around the spindle, pulling my head up abruptly with a feeling as though I had been scalped. I suppose the belt slipped as I put my foot on the stop peal and found myself fixed to the machine. Winding the spindle back by hand, I managed to get loose, leaving me with a dreadful headache – but this later cleared up with no ill effects'.* Syd ruefully added that this was a clear lesson for him of the perils of long, loose hair when working by a machine with rotating parts.

Chapter Three: Fledgling Engineer

Natural curiosity and the experience of working with a wide range of cars and their parts meant that Syd became very interested in the workings of engines; his was very much a practical education at this stage and arguably none the worse for that. '*On one visit to the Longwall Garage I examined, with great enthusiasm, an Opel sports car of about 1912 vintage, and on which my colleagues were dismantling the engine; this one had hemispherical cylinder heads and twin camshafts.*'

Meanwhile at home, the teenager and his friends dabbled with their first motorcycles: '*mine was an old De Dion with a single-speed belt drive, while my friends also managed to get hold of some similar machines; we used to drive out on these into the country, pushing them up the steep hills, repairing them en-route, and somehow getting them home again.*' Over time, these older machines were exchanged for ones that were slightly less archaic; '*I remember a small "Diamond", a vee-twin "Ivy", a two-and-three-quarter horsepower flat twin Douglas and later on a six-horsepower flat-twin Douglas – the latter a lovely smooth machine and fitted with a side car.*'

By the age of sixteen, Syd was keen to learn to drive a car, and in this endeavour he was aided by his Foreman, "Copper" Crease: '*he taught me the fundamentals of driving in a few short lessons, and I was then allowed to use the shop car, which was an old two-seater Morris Cowley, used for carrying around any material and equipment as necessary. Early on in the use of this car, I had one of the few mishaps I ever had in a car. It was on the way to Cowley, when they light was fading, and I did not brake soon enough to prevent running into a young fellow on a delivery bicycle, loaded up with groceries.*' No real harm was done to the boy, but the wheels of his bicycle were bent and the groceries went everywhere. '*I got into hot water with Mr. Crease over this, but all was soon forgotten!*'

According to Syd, the old two-seater was subsequently fitted with a small van body by a local coachbuilder and good use was made of it for a number of years; '*it was painted in brown and cream, which became the company colours for the MG Car Company*'.

A 1912 Model D1 Douglas motorcycle, of a kind similar to the one that Syd owned... (Thijs Lempens 'Yesterdays' (NL))

... and here is a 1919 4HP Douglas with sidecar.

Kimber undoubtedly owed much of his continued success to the benevolent patronage of Sir William Morris – later Lord Nuffield. Here we see the two of them in January 1930, on the day that the Abingdon factory was formally opened with a celebratory luncheon. (Author Archive)

The Oxford Undergraduate Customers of Morris Garages

Some of the Oxford undergraduates had cars that were exciting to the young Syd; he remembered *'there were two fierce-looking chain-driven Mercedes one driven by "Bubbly" Johnson and the other by Horsfall, who was stroke for the varsity eight. Another was a beautiful one-and-a-half litre Cordon Blue Bugatti owned by a graduate who it was said had purchased it from Raymond Mays. This car was entered in a hill-climb, but he had an unfortunate accident where he drove into the crowd – an event which stopped that hill-climb from continuing. It was also said that he was one of the undergraduates who climbed the Martyr's Memorial in Oxford and placed a chamber pot on its pinnacle.'*

The relationship between William Morris and the large cohort of Oxford undergraduates was forged long before he ventured into motorised transport; speaking in March 1953 on the popular BBC TV programme 'Any Questions', the novelist Sir Compton Mackenzie (1883- 1972, perhaps best-known as author of 'Whisky Galore'), recalled how, as an Oxford undergraduate (he studied at Magdalen College) he had ventured into Morris's first shop: *'Fifty years ago I went into a small cycle shop in the High Street, Oxford, to have a puncture repaired. I was told by a Napoleonic little man with a smart, brushed-up moustache, that although he was very busy, my cycle would be attended to if I cared to leave it.'*

Mackenzie further recalled that two days after his puncture had been mended, he noticed that W.R. Morris had opened up the Morris Garage, and in doing so had taken over what, according to Mackenzie, was half of the then Oxford Market; asking Morris why he had expanded to this extent, the reply was *'that won't be big enough to hold half the cars in ten years' time!'* Mackenzie told his fellow panellists that *'even then I knew I was in the presence of a man who would do great things.'* The Chairman of the panel, BBC's Freddie Grisewood (1888- 1972) had also been an undergraduate at Magdalen and similarly recalled the shop, and how he used to take his bicycle to Morris for repairs *'after we had been playing cycle polo.'*

Work to create Kimber's sporting cars began at Longwall Garage, where according to Syd, Kimber *'... took five or six Morris Cowley chassis from Morris Motors at Cowley, tuning the engines, modifying the road springs, steering column, exhaust system and so on.'* Surmounting this was Kimber's pièce de resistance, the sporty bodywork; *'a local body builder constructed and fitted a two-seater sports body on them.'* These were the first 'Morris Garages Specials' which of course presaged what was soon to follow.

'Kimber then enthusiastically had a more special car constructed, which was done by one of the best fitters and mechanics – Frank Stevens.' For this car – which in later years assumed the name 'Old Number One' – the low-slung chassis was hand-made, but as Syd wrote *'it used the Morris front and rear axles, but fitted with wire-spoked wheels. The engine was an experimental Morris 11.9 horsepower Hotchkiss engine with overhead valves, while the body was an open two-seater of torpedo form. It could exceed eighty miles per hour.'* The story of 'Old Number One' has been well-chronicled elsewhere; for Syd the chief memories were that the car was considered a success: *'from this came the beginning of the Morris Garages Super Sports and "MG" cars.'*

Cecil Kimber

The story of Cecil Kimber has passed into MG legend; suffice to say that he was chiefly instrumental in forging the path that Morris Garages and later the MG Car Company took for two decades; from his arrival in 1921 to his unfortunate departure in 1941. **Cecil Kimber** (April 12th 1888 – February 4th 1945), was born in Dulwich (London) but shortly after the turn of the century, he and his family moved to Heaton Norris in Lancashire; in due course he attended Stockport Grammar School and was subsequently employed in his father's printing business, a role it seems likely he more endured than enjoyed.

In the 1911 Census, Kimber is listed as a patient at a hospital, his occupation being 'Assistant Manager at Printing Works'. The reason for his stay in hospital was a severe injury on a friend's motorcycle, which damaged his right leg and gave him a limp. In 1913, Kimber acquired a Singer car and the following year he left the family business (which caused a rift with his father which was never healed) and joined Sheffield-Simplex. During WWI, Kimber moved to AC Cars and then E. G. Wrigley, a maker of automotive components in which Kimber was encouraged to make a substantial personal investment; when the business suffered badly Kimber's investment was lost.

In due course he joined Morris Garages in 1921 as Sales Manager and the following year was made General Manager for reasons covered in the main text. Kimber made an immediate impression, but at the same time was very careful to nurture his relationship with his 'patron', William Morris. Syd's main recollections of the arrival of Cecil Kimber at Morris Garages are described in the main text; he wrote that '*from the first, Cecil Kimber was a leader who instilled in all those around him the team spirit and endeavour in working for the prestige of the car and the Company*.' Keen to expand the Morris Garages business beyond its original sales and servicing scope, Kimber was instrumental in developing a series of 'Specials' which effectively formed the beginning of the MG marque.

Kimber became managing director of what was by then the 'MG Car Company Limited' in July 1930. Over the next few years of intense activity – a period in which the input of Syd Enever and his colleagues came to the fore – the reputation of MG grew and the factory spent quite heavily on racing and the creation of an increasingly complex model range. In 1935, Lord Nuffield sold some of his privately owned business interests to Morris Motors and MG was part of this process; this brought the factory under the control of Leonard Lord who decreed that the racing activities should cease and the costly and increasingly unique MG running gear should be discontinued in favour of more mundane Morris components from Cowley. Kimber was initially distraught, but MG continued to thrive and became more profitable in the lead up to WWII.

Kimber was married twice; firstly to Evelyn Irene (Renee) Phillips Hunt on September 15th 1915; 'Renee' was popular and artistic in temperament and would prove to be a close ally to her husband when aesthetic sensibilities became important. They had two children (Betty and Jean) but sadly Renee succumbed to cancer in April 1938; Cecil had already begun a relationship with another woman, Muriel Lillies (Gillie) Dewar and married her in June 1938, just three months after Rene's death. It was a move which was said to have given disquiet to Lady Nuffield, who styled herself as guardian of Morris Motors morals.

Lord Nuffield's deputy as War broke out in 1939 was Oliver Boden, but the latter's death the following year precipitated Miles Thomas (**William Miles Webster Thomas**; March 2nd 1897 – February 8th 1980) in his place. Thomas had most recently come from Wolseley where he had remade that business's car range as a successful series of models closely related to Morris running gear. When the main office at Cowley failed to furnish Abingdon with enough work to sustain a viable business after car making ceased with the onset of war, Kimber – aided by Propert and Cousins – began to seek out new contracts. This proved in part to be his undoing, although there had been various developments in his personal life, not to mention the petty jealousies common in the Morris Motors business, which together contributed to the extrication of Kimber from the business which he had so carefully and personally nurtured.

Nuffield Vice-Chairman Thomas visited Kimber in November 1941 and demanded his resignation; it was a move with dubious motives which in normal circumstances would have rocked the industry – and certainly drew surprise from many who intimately associated the man with the marque – but with a war on, and armaments and munitions to build, the focus was clearly elsewhere. Kimber soon found different employment but he did not live to see MG's post-war reconnaissance; he was one of just two victims of a freak railway accident coming out of Kings Cross Station on the evening of Sunday February 4th 1945.

Cecil Cousins was happy to point out to anyone prepared to listen that his time at MG preceded that of the other Cecil, Mr Kimber. (Author Archive)

Cecil Cousins

In many early MG factory or race photos, there is a distinctive tall, gangling figure with his head higher than anyone else in sight (and in early days, sporting an unruly shock of hair); that was invariably Oxford-born **Henry Edward Cecil 'Cuz' Cousins** (April 14th 1902 – February 8th 1976). In the 1911 census we see him living with his parents Henry and Fanny at 21 Walton Street, Oxford; after school, and still during the First World War, Cousins gained an apprenticeship with the agricultural steam engineering business of T. G. West, but joined Morris Garages at the Clarendon Yard in January 1920, initially as a fitter in the cycle shop under the same Bill Bailey remembered by Syd Enever (Cecil Cousins' job was described as 'Improver' on motorcycles as he was as yet not a full mechanic).

Cousins therefore arrived at Morris Garages before Cecil Kimber – something he often enjoyed explaining to any audience in later years. The 1921 Census shows Cecil Cousins still living with his parents and eldest sister Audrey at 36 Walton Crescent, Oxford; his occupation at that time was recorded in the census as 'Motor Mechanic' employed by 'Morris Garages, Clarendon Yard, Oxford'.

Showing great aptitude for mechanical work, Cousins soon moved over to motor cars, and was part of the small team that built what he regarded as the first MGs in the summer of 1923. He was also involved in the creation of the more familiar (in hindsight) 'Old Number One' (see later) – although in later years he delighted in pointing out that this undoubtedly significant part of the MG story was far from being the 'first' Morris Garages Special.

Cousins supported colleagues Frank Stevens and Jack Lowndes to build 'Old Number One' – see separate panel – and in time he not only assumed a more senior role as Foreman of the Experimental Department at Abingdon from 1929, but also fulfilled a crucial role within the MG motorsports team, running the cars and mechanics on site at various key races. He married Mabel Maude Nutt at Wandsworth in 1927, and the couple went on to have four daughters (Audrey, Jeannette, Una and Enid Jane) and a son (William Henry). Cousins was part of the small group of committed Abingdon stalwarts that built the EX120 record breaker, described in the next chapter (which he accompanied to Montlhéry in 1931, his first ever trip overseas) and he was Team Manager for the MG 'Double Twelve' races at Brooklands in both 1930 and 1931.

Being four years older than Syd Enever mattered, especially in early Morris Garages and MG days, and for much of that period there was undoubtedly a hierarchical difference between the two, stemming from when Syd was placed under 'Cuz's' wings. They were cut from a similar cloth, however; both were local men who had started in a junior capacity and were practical innovators, adept at fixing mechanical problems.

Cousins became involved in the design of the bespoke chassis for the MG 18/80 Mark I, after Kimber came and saw him one day and asked him if he could draw; as Cousins told John McLellan, his answer was that he had done some rudimentary drawing at school carpentry classes; evidently this experience was deemed sufficient as Kimber promptly handed him a drawing of the Morris overhead-valve 2½ Litre six-cylinder engine, together with some drawings of various Morris axles, and told him to draw up what became the basis for the first MG 18/80 Mark I Chassis (Chassis Number 6251), subsequently built up by Cousins, Keith Smith and Jack Lowndes. Also assisting in this process was a young MG apprentice by the name of Jack Daniels.

In some ways, the relationship between Cousins and MG's Chief Engineer H. N. Charles could be likened to the much later one between Alec Issigonis and the latter's right hand man Jack Daniels (also, as it happens, an MG man); Charles was good at coming up with bright ideas to meet Kimber's aspirations, but invariably Cousins would be the man who had to deliver these innovations, sometimes grumbling in the process. In due course, Syd would assume a similar relationship with the Chief Engineer – as explained later.

By way of example, John Thornley recalled when some bespoke new parts were needed – as parts often were – at very short notice, in this case for the chassis of the KN Magnette. *'Charles had ordered up all the chassis brackets from a firm of bronze founders in the Midlands'* Thornley told John McLellan; *'they had notification that the first set had arrived at Oxford Station. Cecil went down to get them and staggered into the office with a sack which he hurled down on the floor and said to Charles "you must be bloody daft!"* As Thornley went on to explain, there had not been sufficient time to arrange to fabricate the brackets from steel using press tools as would have been ideal. *'That was very much the sort of corrective that Cecil would try to apply'* Thornley said.

By the start of the Second World War, Cousins had risen to become MG's Works Superintendent (according to the National 1939 Register; he was recorded as living in Abingdon with his wife Mabel); throughout the next few years, as discussed later, he worked closely with 'Pop' Propert to secure war contracts, as MG's Nuffield parents appeared indifferent to the needs of their Abingdon subsidiary in terms of securing gainful employment for its workforce. When Cecil Kimber was forced to resign in 1941, Cousins was in good position to become a valuable practical help to the new man with an overview of MG, Harold Ryder. Ryder was a long time associate of Lord Nuffield; he had previously run Osberton Radiators at Cowley, which had become Morris Radiators when Nuffield bought the business; he had no time for motor-racing but was a good manager and in Cecil Cousins he had a good 'Works Manager' (reporting to George Propert).

Cousins was key to the work to get what would become the 'TC' Midget ready for post-war production, and the subsequent genesis of the TD; for the latter, he took a Y-Type chassis, cut and shut it and fitted a TC Midget body on the shortened chassis to show the way (in point of fact it was Jim O'Neill, then still at Cowley, who designed the definitive TD and its chassis). Also in 1949, Cousins was part of the Abingdon effort to resist a transfer of MG to Coventry, as explained later. In the 1950s he tried to get the Riley Pathfinder redesigned and believed he was made the fall-guy for its failure by S V Smith, although neither John Thornley nor Geoff Iley, who came in above him, believed this was true. Cousins referred to the Pathfinder as the 'Ditchfinder', which became its less than flattering nickname at Abingdon.

Cecil Cousins retired at the end of May 1967, by which time he was MG's Assistant General Manager; his main retirement gift was a reel-to-reel tape recorder, which he was keen to experiment with. He continued to live in Abingdon at 'Winthrope', 20 Abbot Road (where he and Mabel had lived since well before the War). Like Syd, 'Cuz' spoke with a distinctive Oxfordshire brogue; he once told Mike Allison in self-deprecation that he spoke one foreign language: *'the King's English, but not very well'*. Keen to regale people with his memories, one such story shared by his granddaughter Sue Mott with the author is as follows: *'Grampy was in the process of taking an MG for a test drive in Wales. He described driving up a narrow, steep, winding track up a "mountain" and coming across a farmer leaning against a wall. He stopped and commented that the farmer probably hadn't seen another car on that track before. The farmer replied "yes, there was one – it's still here" pointing with his pipe, over the wall, to the valley below, where the wreck of a vehicle lay'*.

After a lifetime in the industry, he retained justifiable pride in his career and remained a keen participant in discussions with MG enthusiasts, visiting the United States with his old comrade Alec Hounslow and dying a little short of his 74th birthday in 1976.

The First MG – Old Number One?

There has probably been more debate about the car known as 'Old Number One' than any other pre-war MG – or Morris Garages Special, if you prefer. And therein lies the rub; this hand-built one-off special was conceived by Cecil Kimber as his first bespoke sports car (as opposed to a lightly tweaked, tuned and re-bodied Morris) and he referred to it on various occasions as 'my first MG sports car'.

Cecil Kimber sits proudly in what he often referred to subsequently as his first MG sports car. Given the sobriquet 'Old Number One', the car was built over the winter of 1924-1925 and its competition debut was the Easter 1925 Lands End Trial. First registered (as a Morris) in March 1925, the original paint finish was dull 'shop grey' rather than the bright red in which it was restored in the 1950s. (Author Archive)

Others were less polite; Cecil Cousins told MG author Wilson McComb: *'Old No. 1 was a one-off bastard. I argued until I got so unpopular that I gave up; I was flogging a dead horse.'* So what is the truth?

Most historians now agree that the proper genesis of what became 'MG' took place in 1923 – the first time that the famous octagonal logo is known to have appeared in print was in Morris Garages advertisements in the Oxford Times of March 2nd 1923. By then, of course, Cecil Kimber was a few months into his managerial role at Morris Garages and was already commissioning new models which were initially very obviously still Morris-based but with an increasingly sporting bent. From 1922, there had been a series of Morris Cowleys which were dubbed the 'Chummy' body, the name derived from the compact interior space which required occupants to be 'chummy' – or sociable – and all within a four-seater body where all inside benefitted from the hood.

These were hardly sporting in character but they sold reasonably well, and Cecil Kimber modified one for the 1923 London to Land's End Trial, in which he won a gold medal. Imbued with enthusiasm from this result, Kimber went to Lord Nuffield and secured a sanction to build six two-seater sports models, with bodies by Charles Raworth & Sons of Oxford; they were named as 'The MG Super Sports Morris' but not yet with the MG Octagon. These first MGs were available to customers earlier in 1923, and the first recorded sale was on August 16th 1923. Syd's memories of them are referenced briefly in the main text.

Advertisements for these new models finally appeared in December 1923; they had already been on sale for a few months by then, the earliest known sale having taken place in August 1923. When the MG Car Company Limited was formed in March 1928, and the MG logo first registered, the date of first use was given as May 1st 1924, the same month as it also featured in an advertisement in the new *Morris Owner* magazine, edited by Miles Thomas; it is highly likely that those involved had simply forgotten that the symbol had appeared in print over a year earlier.

Then we come back to 'Old Number One' which was completed in 1925 to tackle that year's London to Land's End trial; initial work on the project seems to have started in 1924 but paused, as such exercises often do when other work gets in the way; the finished car was not registered for the road until March 1925, just prior to that Easter's Lands End Trial, in which Cecil Kimber was destined to drive. The consequence of all the above is that various claims have been made for MG's date of origins – 1923, 1924 and 1925 being the favourites. As we have seen, the badge at least was already in use in the spring of 1923. But whichever is the date favoured, Syd Enever was involved in the business at the very least three years earlier...

And what of the detail of 'Old Number One'? The body was built by Carbodies on March 13th 1925 and registered a fortnight later (March 27th) as a 'Morris-Cowley Sports' with the Oxford number FC 7900 – by Cecil Kimber himself rather than by 'Morris Garages'. It was driven by Kimber and his friend Wilfrid Mathews in the 1925 Land End Trial of April 10th and 11th 1925 and qualified for a gold cup. Soon after the event, the car was sold off and although for a while it was feared lost, it was eventually rediscovered and rescued from a scrapyard, returned to MG in 1932, welcomed like a long-lost son as 'Old Number One' – a name which stuck – and was 'restored' before becoming a mainstay of MG publicity and nowadays at the heart of the British Motor Museum collection. But although he knew about 'Old Number One', Syd Enever had little input, so the story can be left there.

CHAPTER THREE: FLEDGLING ENGINEER

At Longwall, more cars were to be built: '*Cecil Kimber detailed Cecil Cousins, from the motorcycle shop at the Clarendon Garage, to go to Longwall and look after and prepare these chassis and cars*'. According to Syd, the objective was to build on average one car per day; '*when their engines had been tuned and the chassis lowered and modified, they were driven to various coachbuilders, the majority being done by Carbodies of Coventry.*' Here the bodies – to designs conceived by Cecil and Kimber and his first wife Irene with the help of their friend the artist Harold Connolly – were effectively hand-built from scratch using an ash frame, with the bodywork formed from steel: '*wheeling up the panels from flat sheet, edge welding, hand-beating and hammer-blocking the edges. When assembled with just screws and a few components a beautiful body emerged.*'

By this time, Syd was a junior mechanic; '*I did most jobs, from complete overhauls to knocking out dents in bodies or wings. I became proficient and well known in the use of the hammer when straightening a chassis-frame. I remember I had the knack of hitting it in the right place, most times – and to the surprise of many who warned me that I would destroy or break it.*'. In contrast to later years, there were relatively few seriously damaged cars going through the Clarendon Yard business. '*I don't remember any badly crashed cars in those days*' Syd wrote, adding by way of explanation that there were '*just a few bent wings and chassis frame members; I suppose that there were few cars on the road, speeds were lower and due to the poor brakes, drivers tended to allow plenty of distance to pull up in before turning a corner.*'

When cars broke down on the road, or would not start at the owner's own garage, Syd often found himself sent out to attend: '*I had my own system of quickly running through a few basic checks, and during this I would quietly correct the trouble. I would then swing the engine and most times it ran at once, to the surprise of the owner and to my personal enjoyment and satisfaction.*'

Although Syd was never known to his family as a man with many hobbies, in the mid-1920s he and his friends enjoyed going to dances: '*we were either at the local "hops" or the ones in the surrounding villages*' he wrote; popular dances were inevitably their main pursuit; '*the Charleston, Black Bottom and quick foxtrots to a jazz band.*' For an outlay of a pound, Syd and his friends found that they could hire a car to take them out to the country dances for an evening; '*on one such excursion, I allowed my pal Arthur Cook to drive the car. This was the first time that he had driven a car, and when his employer asked him the next day to take a car somewhere, he accepted and was a driver from then on!*' It seems that he later took charge of his employer's transport department, and for the charge and maintenance of all their contracting machinery and equipment.

Someone else who worked for a brief period at Morris Garages was Syd Purves (May 2nd 1907 – March 1999), who told the author how he only got to know Syd Enever when they both went dancing at Oxford's Carfax Assembly Rooms (opened in 1925; closed in the late 1960s). Meanwhile in February 1923 production, such as it was, of the new Morris Garages 'Chummy' was transferred from Longwall to a former stabling yard round the corner in Alfred Lane. Initially this was largely the responsibility of Cecil Cousins and Stan Saunders, and soon after Jack Lowndes and George Morris joined them from Longwall. At this stage, however, Syd Enever remained gainfully employed at Clarendon Yard.

George 'Pop' Propert

Northampton-born **George Propert** (June 21st 1884 – April 22nd 1976) joined Morris Garages in 1926, and in due course was effectively Cecil Kimber's right hand man – his eyes and ears on the shop floor whilst the boss looked after the important customers and the corporate politics. After school, Propert gained an apprenticeship in the steam and gas business.

Aged twenty, he moved over to the promising emerging automotive business; by the time of the 1911 Census he described himself as an

George Propert, seen here alongside Cecil Kimber, was appropriately, as the photo subtly implies, the latter's 'right hand man'; it was Propert who effectively ruled over the factory while Kimber was responsible for the MG business as a whole. (Author Archive)

'automobile engineer' living in Banbury with his new wife Lily Victoria née Sephton (they had married on January 19th the same year). Specialising for a while in the Knight sleeve valve (one of those bits of 'new technology' which eventually became obsolete) he moved over to management of a car garage, eventually getting a job at Morris Garages in 1926 as Works Manager – the aforementioned 'eyes and ears'.

Syd Purves told the author (speaking in 1994) that he remembered George Propert living in Leopold Street at this time (1926) with his wife and two daughters; '[Propert] *worked at Bainton Road in a small wooden office on stilts, reached by a short set of steps, and it was built inside one of the two bays which had been set aside for MG production. These bays were about 160 feet long and 20 feet wide each, and the site is used [in 1994] by Unipart*'

However Propert's spell at MG was not continuous; at one point he left for AC Cars (Syd Enever recalled he also had a spell at Beans Cars, a contemporary mainstream rival to Morris) but it seems he did not stay away long, and returned to the fold and in 1930 was General Manager, staying with MG through the second world war, with his home itself in Abingdon ("The Lodge" in Caldecott Road).

In March 1934, Cecil Kimber prepared a paper called 'Making modest production pay in Motor-car Manufacture', As part of a response to questions made by the audience, Propert – who had presented the paper on one occasion in Kimber's absence due to illness – said this about the Abingdon factory:

"*I can speak with personal knowledge of the team spirit at the MG works. It is purely a matter of the right personalities, and with us it begins with the Chief himself, and, I hope, comes down through myself and the other members of the staff, and this right personality permeates the whole works. We are a large family, and I believe that, whether we paid day-rate or piecework prices, we should still Keep the team spirit, working as a family, rather than a set of workers. To my mind, the biggest factor in creating the team spirit is the abolishment of what I call "the walls of partition" between departments. It means that one department will not see another department in difficulties, but will immediately give assistance. Incidentally, having obtained such a general feeling, there is no need to worry much about piecework rates*".

Speaking in 1974, John Thornley remembered Propert as '*an irascible character*' and, commenting on Propert's departure and subsequent return, added, '*...I expect there was a puff of smoke one day, and he cleared off and went to AC, and then when tempers cooled a bit, he came back*.'

Propert's daughter Beryl married MG's Publicity Manager George Tuck, and the couple were staying with the Properts at the family home at The Lodge, Caldecott Road, Abingdon at the time of the 1939 'England and Wales Register'. He was known (seldom to his face) as 'Pop' no doubt on account of his disarmingly kindly appearance, although that friendly avuncular exterior hid a driven man who, with the aid of Cecil Cousins, was instrumental in securing vital wartime contracts for Abingdon (with consequential engineering work for Syd and his colleagues). His account of Wartime work by the Abingdon factory is referenced in a later chapter.

In November 1945, Propert entered local politics as a borough councillor (he stood until May 1949), but remained at MG until his retirement on July 20th 1949, by when the situation of MG Abingdon versus Riley Coventry (see Chapter Six) had been resolved. He remained in Abingdon, latterly at The Motte, until his death in April 1976.

Syd was clearly keen to excel at his job as a mechanic: '*I always tried to find the easiest and quickest way to do a job, and also a satisfactory job. To this end, I used to manufacture special spanners, tools, levers and devices which would assist me. For the Morris cars I even collected my own stock of ready replacement parts, such as lined brake shoes, big-end bearings prepared for easy fitment, and rear axle gears that would make a quiet pair. Brake linings were usually fitted by fixing one rivet at a time with hammer and punch. Out of angle and steel plate, I made up a small bench press which rivetted the linings on in a matter of moments and this was used for many years.*'

Sometime around 1926, Syd acquired a 3½ horsepower BSA motorcycle, with chain drive and three-speed gearbox; '*this was a powerful machine – good and reliable*' he recalled, adding '*I could go off on holidays without a breakdown*'. Later, he acquired two more of these BSA motorcycles; '*the last one had a sidecar, which we would use when going to dances, usually at the weekends. I mostly had two passengers but one night, returning late, and some of my friends were without transport home, so I came back with seven on board.*'

The side-car also fulfilled another more sporting role: '*grass track racing, both solo and side-car, started on the outskirts of Oxford, so I and my friend Arthur*

CHAPTER THREE: FLEDGLING ENGINEER

Cook entered my machine in the sidecar events, and we alternately either drove or rode in the sidecar; it was a thrilling experience, when hanging out of the sidecar, with your hand just a few inches from the ground. We were placed in a few events, but above all it was enormous fun.'

It was through his motorcycle racing exploits that Syd began to develop what would become a life-long interest in tuning: *'I raised the compression ratio by bolting a plate on top of the piston; this worked reasonably well until it melted and ran out of the exhaust pipe.'* Syd recalled this was, in his words, *'at least a start'*, adding that *'in later years I found out the correct way to go about tuning engines, and in fact I was to become most interested in engines and their development throughout my life.'*

Around the same time, a number of popular three-wheeled cycle cars entered production, and Syd decided he would have a go at building his own home-made version. *'Using the parts from a BSA motorcycle, and with a converted car frame and front axle, I made up an open body out of sheet metal. I managed to get it licensed and used it for a few months.'* Fortunately for posterity, someone took a snap of Syd and his creation, and the image shown here comes from his photo-albums. *'During this time, I learned a little about torsional stiffness of frames, as I had to remove the springs to keep it upright, which made the ride a little hard!'*

By around 1927 (according to Syd's own records) the mechanics at Morris Garages had a rota system to work on weekends; it was in such times, when the normal day to day bustle of the business was calmed, that enterprising workers can sometimes find a way to shine, and Syd was no exception to this philosophy. *'One Sunday afternoon, when I was on duty, a customer came into the garage with a Morris Cowley on which the big-end had gone'*; evidently the man was planning to embark on a long journey, accompanied by his family, and was at a loss at how he could rescue his plans.

Unfazed, Syd (still only just into his twenties) offered to see what he could do. *'I put the car over the pit and in about twenty minutes, with the aid of pre-prepared spare big-end bearings I had ready and available, the car was finished and ready to go. The customer was greatly surprised and pleased that he could go on his journey.'* Furthermore, the garage had fixed rates for such jobs: *'I charged him the full amount of £4 10s which he paid readily.'* That sum would roughly equate to around £1,750 an hour in 2025. *'When the Accounts people saw the booking the next morning on the till against a time of twenty minutes, they did not know what to make of it, and that was remembered for many years!'*

It was no real surprise, therefore, that Syd soon found himself involved in more complex and demanding service tasks; as he recalled *'I eventually found myself repairing such cars as a 4 ½ Litre Bentley, a Lancia Lambda and a beautiful Sunbeam 3-litre sports.'* Such exotica brought him experience of working on some of the more expensive and technically advanced examples of contemporary automotive practice; *'they were most interesting designs'* he recalled, adding that many were owned by graduates up at Oxford, some of them doubtless garaged at the Morris premises behind the Clarendon Hotel to circumvent the sanctions of university officialdom.

One of the cars that clearly made an impression was a Hispano Suiza: *'it was a beautiful large red two-seater, and I was allowed to deliver it to its owner, driving it up the High Street in all its glory and with a wonderful exhaust note as the massive engine burbled over.'* The Sunbeam which he most remembered from the same period was equally striking: *'it was a beautiful low car, with a small open four-seater body, wheels set well out, with cycle mudguards that turned with the front wheels, and a twin cam engine designed by Louis Coatelen'.*

Reg 'Jacko' Jackson

Reginald Cecil 'Jacko' Jackson (February 19th 1906 – September 29th 1976) became one of Syd's dearest life-long friends; the Enever and Jackson families knew each other well. Jacko – who in the author's opinion deserves a biography almost as much as Syd Enever – was born in Windsor; his father a milk vendor from Northampton aged 53, and his mother a 37-year old from London. He became chronically ill as a child and was sent to live with his aunt near Spalding, Lincolnshire, where he was brought up in a strongly religious atmosphere, there were hopes – as families often have – that he would become a parson, but his destiny lay elsewhere.

His poor health meant that he received a private education, and he developed an interest in the mechanical world at the expense of any religious convictions; he later recalled (for a 1951 interview) with some pride that his model diorama of a WWI tank set in the fields of Cambrai won him a prize in an arts and crafts exhibition. His family home remained at Maidenhead and he was fortunate to become apprenticed to a local car maker, GWK. This car maker had showed promise when established in 1920, but unfortunately for Jacko, its success was not enduring and by 1926 its car making operations had largely ceased; Jacko was at least fortunate to have secured the paperwork to prove that he had completed his apprenticeship,

Reg Jackson in the 1950s; that distinctive half-grin reveals his mischievous streak. By this stage, he was MG's Chief Inspector and as Abingdon production output grew with the introduction of the MGA, his ability to spend time on record breaking diminished. (Enever Archive)

Syd and Jacko (right) became lifelong friends – and were a more than capable 'double act' when it came to their record breaking exploits with Goldie Gardner. (Jackson family)

and moved on to manage a car business near Kennington (he would recall that he gained experience in the repair of all manner of things, from cars to wooden table legs).

Another bout of chronic illness meant he had to give this up, and when better he secured a job as a chauffeur-mechanic before going to Oxford where he worked at a garage business, until he answered a job opportunity at Edmund Road in 1928, reporting to Cecil Cousins (working on the MG 18/80). Jacko spoke of these experiences to fellow MG employee and noted historian Mike Allison, who told the author: '*the garage job was a fill-in when he first took digs near Abingdon, which was probably in Kennington, before he finally settled at Edmund Road.*' Allison also confirms Jacko's role on the 18/80: '*the story of him being the development engineer for the 18/80 was certainly told me by both the man himself, and Cecil Cousins, who employed him*'.

Jackson and Cec Cousins claimed to be in at the start of the genesis of the first MG M-Type Midget; as he told Mike Allison: "*one day I had to go to Cowley, and spotted the Minor. Cous and I were always talking about the Austin Seven racing achievements, and I was soon taken on a flight of fancy about a small MG, and Cous and I talked it over. He took the idea to Kimber, who pooh-poohed it, but I also chatted to HN about our ideas, and he took it to Kimber, who said he might get a chassis up for development work... but we had to concentrate on getting the Six ready for the Motor Show.*" As explained in the main text, the Midget proved to be a fine gamble; as Jackson told Mike Allison: "*the prototype caused a tremendous impression at the Motor Show, and Kimber told me that he had taken 250 orders for the Midget, which caused him a little heartache as he was trying to sell the idea of a luxury sports car to Billy Morris and the press.*"

Moving to Abingdon in 1929, shortly ahead of Syd, he too became intimately involved in MG racing activities; the two worked together in 1930 on the preparation of five M-Type Midgets for that year's new Brooklands Double-Twelve event (all five cars finished and MG gained the Team Prize). Jacko – who rose to head up competitions – often recalled that he achieved a peak 146-hour week, working on the MG C-Type in the Brooklands 'Double-Twelve' in April 1931. After the factory racing shop closed, Jacko was potentially one of the inevitable victims of the cull which followed, but Kimber thought sufficiently highly of him that a new outlet was found for his energies.

Mike Allison recorded the sequence of events in the wake of the events of 1935, described later, as told to him by Jacko in later years: '*his difficulty was that, as Head of Competitions, his seniority put him into the unemployable category... there were simply no vacancies! Kimber therefore created a new position for him as an itinerant trouble-shooter, equipping him with a small van and a stock of parts, and sending him off to various dealers and good customers to sort out their problems at first-hand in the field, a job he found very much to his liking. He was also always available to answer questions about the tuning of the old racing engines, which he often carried out on behalf of those still running the now obsolescent cars*'.

As Allison further explains, Jackson eventually got called back into the works in 1937: '*...when it was decided that, with the increasing likelihood of a war, ministry contracts might require a formal engineering inspection department to be set up, and Reg was given the job of organising it.*' Without looking back, he became involved in mainstream production, rising to become the Chief Inspector (a role which in later years might be termed 'Production Manager') nevertheless he maintained an interest in the record-breaking exploits alongside Syd, as we shall see later.

A keen golfer and ballroom dancer, Jacko also found time to be a parish councillor and part of the local branch of the Civil Defence Corps. According to Mike Allison: '*Syd and Jacko were something of a double act when not on public display! They were both keen gardeners, and always keen to outdo each other!*' Living in the very English setting of Kennington, Oxford, he nevertheless gave his home the very French name of 'Montlhéry' in memory of his racing endeavours at the Autodrome de Montlhéry, where the C type Midget was so successful; however his focus on production at Abingdon meant that he became reluctant to reminisce in the workplace on his time in racing. Even so, 'Jacko' sometimes shared his memories with Allison; '*indeed, the last few years before he retired, we would be treated to a "Scottish Coffee" in the morning break on 19th February!*'

Hubert Noel Charles

Another crucial influence in the development of Syd Enever's latent interest in engineering was **Hubert Noel Charles** (November 22nd 1893 – January 18th 1982), who had come to work for Cecil Kimber in 1925, just a year after having joined Morris Motors at Cowley as a production department trouble shooter. Charles was quite an unusual man for Morris Motors; he was a former Grammar School boy who had gone on to study for a bachelor's degree in Engineering, the latter qualification quite a rarity at the time. Born in Barnet, Hertfordshire to Thomas Charles (listed in the 1901 Census as a 'solicitor on his own account') and mother Constance, H. N. Charles grew up in a well-to-do Middle Class household with his own nurse.

Charles attended Highgate School, a charity grammar school in London; from there he was admitted to study at the University of London and earned a BSc with Honours in Engineering. It is said that in 1914 he was experimenting with advanced ideas for fuelling his Triumph motorcycle; his mathematical aptitude and scientific brain would serve him well throughout his career. During the First World War, he joined the Royal Naval Air Service on September 27th 1914, just days after Russia, France, and Great Britain concluded the Treaty of London (September 5th) and in March of the following year moved to the Royal Flying Corps ('RFC'), initially as 'Assistant Equipment Officer', moving up to become 56 Squadron's Head Engineering Officer, his engineering aptitude obviously being put to good use. He was unlike the stereotypical public-school-educated upper class officers in the RFC; however the more down-to-earth Charles nevertheless managed to serve with distinction and the respect between him and other officers was mutual.

H N Charles came back to visit the MG factory in 1963; he is seen here reminiscing with Syd. (Author Archive)

With the War over, Charles briefly found employment at Zenith Carburettors, where he sought to deploy some of the expertise he had built up during the recent conflict, but then moved to the business which later became Automotive Products; from there he moved to Morris Motors in 1924 where he worked under Frank Woollard, the innovative Morris Motors General Manager who happened to be a friend of the Kimbers. It is said that Charles's connection with MG also came about through friendship formed with the Kimbers, Cecil and his first wife Irene, the latter encouraging him to come over to their then home in Oxford's Woodstock Road and to spend the evening working on 'MG' designs even though he was officially employed at Cowley. Cecil Kimber was already looking towards more 'bespoke' MGs and the overhead camshaft engines that Charles favoured were broadly what he wanted. In 1930, Sir William Morris – doubtless lobbied by Kimber – sanctioned Charles's transfer to MG as Chief Draughtsman, just as production moved to Abingdon.

Thus when Syd Enever arrived at Abingdon, he found Charles was in charge of the drawing office, with, as he recalled in 1974, Adrian Squire as his assistant; Squire left in 1931 to set up his own eponymous sports car business, leaving Jack Daniels, Keith Martin and Syd in Charles's team. At the same time, Reg Jackson was already established in charge of the associated development workshop, having joined MG in 1928. A later arrival was a draughtsman, Stewart Daniels, who remembered Charles for an article in the MG Car Club's SVW Register Yearbook in 1994; he described Charles as being a: *"very clever engineer, who had been a flyer in WWI. He would go to the enormous trouble to explain technical points to anyone, like me, who showed a genuine interest in some aspect of design – although he was one of the least attentive listeners I've ever met. If I ventured some comment on something he was saying, a glazed look would come over his eyes and he would obviously not be the least bit interested in what I was saying. Hardly surprising, I suppose, as he knew it all, and I had just about everything to learn"*.

John Thornley, who arrived at MG in 1931, later wrote of his admiration for Charles' engineering brilliance during the glory days up to 1935: *'In this period a dozen different models were designed, many of them with numerous derivatives. This was achieved by Charles working with a merest handful of devoted designers and draughtsmen. To achieve so much, so much that was innovative, so much that was right – surely here was the touch of genius'.*

Whilst the credit for turning such exceptional cars as the EX120 record breaker, C-Type, K3 Magnette and the Q-Type and R-Type Midgets into reality should rightly be shared with those others, as hinted by John Thornley, it was Charles who had the inspired mind which led to their creation. In this period, the practical minds of Cecil Cousins and Reg Jackson (see separate panels for both) flourished with Charles's encouragement and the still young Syd Enever was able to shine and learn a few tricks of his own, as we shall see getting his name on automotive patents in the UK, Canada and the United States. Meanwhile Charles got married – in the summer of 1932 – to May Dardon, who was 13 years younger than him. Around the same time, he and Syd between them were responsible for the first of the classic J-Type Midgets – the classic J2 – which would form the basic pattern for most future 'Midgets' up to the mid-1950s.

With the closure of the MG racing shop in 1935, and the transfer of design work to

Taken from H. N. Charles' own photo album, this annotated photo records a Bullnose Morris car out on test in the local countryside. Charles was a great influence on Syd's interest in the finer points of engineering. (Hilary Aston)

CHAPTER THREE: FLEDGLING ENGINEER

Hubert Charles stands between his sister and wife, towering over both, in this family photo from the 1970s.
(Hilary Aston)

Cowley, Charles went there too and until 1938 oversaw the MG design programme there (he was responsible for the new SA, VA and TA MG cars); he would have liaised with his friend Syd Enever who was still at Abingdon. That year he conceived the front suspension and anti-roll bar on Morris's new 10 for 1938 before leaving Cowley and joining the newly-formed joint venture between Rolls Royce and Bristol Aeroplane Company called Rotol Airscrews as Chief Engineer (in some way harking back to his wartime aviation experience perhaps).

Rotol – the name came from an amalgamation of the "ROlls-Royce" and "BrisTOL" names – was responsible for the constant-speed propellers of such aircraft as the Hawker Hurricane and Supermarine Spitfire (both soon to become immensely important) and he appears in the 1939 England and Wales Register as 'Chief Engineer (Airscrews Manufacturing)' living in Cheltenham. Early in the Second World War he joined Austin Motor Company as a development engineer, and undertook some consultancy work during the following years for Cam Gears and Norton. At Austin, Charles designed a coil and wishbone front suspension which was destined to appear on the wholly new A40 model of 1948, and he also contributed to the design and development of that important model's new overhead valve engine – a precursor of the famous post-war B-Series unit.

In 1946, Charles fell out with Austin chairman Leonard Lord, who would obviously have remembered him from his time at Abingdon and Cowley; both as it happened had left Morris Motors in 1938. Although the full details of this disagreement are not recorded, it seems plausible that Lord, with his well-known inferiority complex, would have found it easy to take against the sharp-minded, well-spoken, urbane and highly-qualified engineer with his BSc degree. In 1953, Charles became a partner in a consultancy called Manley & Charles. H. N. Charles worked in this capacity, specialising in the petro-chemical industry, for the remainder of his career. In 1959, just after normal retirement age, he was living in Cherrywood Court in Teddington, Middlesex, but he only finally retired fully in around 1970 (according to Mike Allison, who recalled meeting him prior to that when Charles was working at Associated Octel Company). Allison notes that '*during his time with the MG Car Co Ltd, Charles filed no fewer than 18 patents relating to brakes, suspension, engine cooling and other matters*', adding that '*no less than five patents were filed relating to carburettors for cars. and in 1967 he told me that fuel injection was the way forward for lower emission levels, but that electronic control would be necessary...*'

Hubert Charles died in Oxford in January 1982. In a touching obituary in Safety Fast, John Thornley wrote: '*Charles was a jolly man. However serious the subject under discussion, however grim the prospect, laughter was never far away. And when he laughed, the whole of him laughed from tip to toe, and we laughed with him. Naturally, in the course of the years, there were many crises. The boys would work long hours, days, weeks, but on test -- bang! Morale would be shattered .... And then the door would open, and 'Papa' would come in (we called him 'Papa' among ourselves, albeit he was only 40 years of age at the time) – a rotund figure with a beaming smile and twinkling blue eyes – and he would clap his hands and rub them together, saying 'Oh well. We'll get it right next time, chaps, won't we?'.*

Jack Daniels

Oxford-born **William John Daniels** (February 8th 1912 – November 27th 2004) – better known as Jack Daniels – began his career at MG, although he is far better known for his later work as Alec Issigonis's practically-minded right hand man on the Morris Minor and BMC Mini. Daniels joined MG as its first unindentured apprentice in 1927, and immediately fell under the wing of H. N. Charles; he would soon also come up against the six-years older Syd Enever. Daniels was born to 'boot repairer' William John Snr. and his wife Edith, then living in New Marston, Oxford; Daniels told the author in 1996 that his father was '*basically of country stock, and thwarted of a farm inheritance*'.

As Daniels explained, his job at MG came about almost by chance: '*someone from MG came to my school* [Oxford Central School] *and offered a place; I am sure that the head-master thought that the offer was for something in the commercial line, and so he told me to go along.*' Daniels was met at the new Edmund Road factory by George Propert and was told that the offer was for an apprenticeship: '*without consulting my head-master, I straight away said yes. My father said that he was happy, but when the headmaster found out he was hopping mad: but as far as I was concerned, that was too bad*'.

When Daniels started at Edmund Road, a letter came from a railway company – which had been his first choice – offering him a second interview. Daniels was initially paid the princely sum of ten shillings (£0.50) per week; on his first day, he was taken to the part of the factory where the chassis for the flat-radiator MG 'Mark IV' 14/40 were brought in from the Morris works at Cowley: '*I was fascinated by how they did this: there was one tow vehicle at the front, drawing five wheeled chassis behind it, each with a man standing on a board on the chassis, steering with the wheel and operating the rod brakes; that was quite something to see!*'

As an apprentice, Daniels was able to move between departments and was cushioned against the seasonal variations in demand that caused much of the workforce to be vulnerable to lay-offs. Much like Morris Motors, for two or three months during the summer, virtually all of the men would be laid off except for the apprentices. '*One time, I had to build a road round from the front of the factory to the back, and during the second year I installed the first compressed air line right through the factory itself – from front to back.*' In the middle of this work, Daniels accidentally eavesdropped news of a new face destined for Edmund Road: '*I was up a ladder, over the door to Propert's office, installing the compressed air line, when I heard Kimber's voice; he said "Propert – there's a chap named Enever at Morris Garages in Cornmarket: I want him brought into the factory here". I thought to myself "I wonder who he is?" and shortly after he came over; it was obvious that Kimber thought very highly of him.*' Syd's own memories echoed this, for he also wrote: '*I was sent there with the remark that I was a bright boy from the Clarendon, and that they should look after me!*'

In 1928, the MG works decided to create a dedicated draughting section, and at this juncture Keith Smith joined as MG's first draughtsman. '*It was soon obvious that Smith needed an assistant*' Daniels explained. By now there were six apprentices who were identified as first choices for the job: '*Propert called us all into his office and asked us if any of us wanted to do the job. Nobody was particularly keen but I asked if I could try it on the condition that I could come back to the shop floor if*

Jack Daniels photographed at an MG 'old boys' reunion at Gaydon in the 1990s; note his MG tie. Daniels is perhaps best known for his work alongside Issigonis on the Minor and Mini' but he started his automotive career at MG, and also knew Syd from an early stage in his career. (Author photo)

> *I didn't like it. Propert agreed to this – although in retrospect he needn't have. Keith Smith started me off in the old-fashioned way – tracing drawings – which I found that I could do very quickly – and so my experience built up.'* Not long afterwards, however, Smith was dismissed after he got into the factory one weekend, without authorisation and borrowed a car [it was 'Old Speckled Hen']; *'there was then some trouble with his car and his passenger and as a result he was instantly dismissed.'* Keith Smith was also recalled by Syd Enever in his role as draughtsman at Edmund Road; Syd wrote that Jack Daniels was at this time, in his word, *'shop boy who then traced for Smith.'* Smith was swiftly replaced by George Gibson.
>
> Daniels looked up to H. N. Charles (see above) who was his senior in the MG Design Office: *'I respected him very much'* Daniels told the author, adding, *'although I attended night school, it was Charles who really got me going.'* When MG design authority was transferred from Abingdon to Cowley, Daniels went with it, and from 1942 he found himself working along Issigonis on what would eventually emerge as the 1948 Morris Minor. *'My first job at Cowley was the Morris-ised MG'* he told the author, referring to the TA Midget, *'but then in 1937 I was transferred to work with Issigonis on independent front suspension designs and, barring the War, both Morris and MG would have had independent front suspension at the 1939 Motor Show – which was of course cancelled'*. In the 1939 England and Wales Register, he is listed as *'Designer Draughtsman, Automobile Engineering'*, living with his wife Mabel and infant son Roger in Oxford; in total they would have two sons and a daughter.
>
> After the War, the front suspension would be adopted by Gerald Palmer and be used in the TD Midget and thereafter in the TF, MGA and MGB; Daniels would continue to serve in first Nuffield and then BMC and was still part of the engineering fraternity in the British Leyland era, until his retirement in 1977.

By 1928, Syd already owned his own small car – a second-hand Trojan; in his opinion it was revolutionary in its design for the time; *'it had a two-stroke motor which had four pistons fixed to only two connecting rods, and each pair of pistons had one common cylinder head; it had epicyclic gearing, chain drive and solid tyres on the most flexible of springs.'* One hazard of the time was the tram lines in Oxford and many other cities; *'if the front wheel got caught in these, it was quite interesting for a few moments!'* Syd recalled. The little Trojan proved worthy of its name; Syd credited it with providing him with many miles of useful service; he remembered that the way it would go up the steepest of hills at a regular and reliable 11 miles per hour; after twelve months Syd sold it to a country vicar.

By now, a large number of second-hand cars were being stabled at the Clarendon Garage; in 1929 Syd was given the task of looking them over and prepare them for sale. This gave him his first view of the future Abingdon-on-Thames home of 'MG'; *the Pavlova Leather Company's factory was empty, and for a short time, before MG moved there in September/ October 1929, part of the site was used for the storage of these second-hand cars, and I visited the premises a number of time whilst looking after these cars.'* At least one account suggests that it was Syd who not only recognised the potential of the empty Pavlova buildings, but suggested the idea to Cecil Kimber; his family feel it unlikely that he would have suggested the idea directly to Kimber, but it is clearly conceivable he might have sowed the seed of the idea.

At this stage, Syd was at a crossroads; had he chosen his next course differently, he might have inadvertently robbed the motoring world of the next chapters of this story. The reason was that he could see that he had climbed about as far as he within his existing job: *'I could see that before becoming a charge-hand or foreman, it would be a case of waiting for many years for people to die or retire before I could move up; pay was not good and I wanted to progress.'* Accordingly Syd went to the main Morris works at Cowley, where he says he was promised

'Old Speckled Hen', mentioned by Jack Daniels in his interview with the author, went on (much later) to inspire a new beer brewed by Abingdon's other major employer of the time, Morlands Brewery, when MG celebrated 50 years in the town. (Author Archive)

A 1927 'Flat-nose' MG sports, with neat engine-turned side panels; it is easy to see that Kimber had a good eye for fashion, and why these models flew out of the workshops. However at the time that these were being built, Syd was still working as a mechanic at Morris Garages; his MG heydays were ahead of him. (Author Archive)

Young Syd, with favoured Trilby, accompanied by his good friend Arthur Leslie Cook, drives through the streets of Oxford's St. Ebbes – where his mother Maud ran a boarding house – in his home-made three wheeler. Those houses have all gone – replaced through the tide of redevelopment which swept away much of the older buildings. Cook remained a life-long friend, later working at Kingerlees, the Oxford builders. (Enever Archive)

a job in their repair shop. Meanwhile, however, Syd's friendly boss and sometime mentor 'Copper Crease' went to see Cecil Kimber and as a result, Syd was offered a job at Abingdon within the MG business there.

Syd started in 1930, working under Cecil Cousins in the Experimental Shop. When Syd joined – under Cecil Cousins' wing – he noted that George Propert was the Works Manager at Abingdon – effectively Kimber's right-hand man there; Cousins was not only the Foreman of the Experimental Department but also over-riding Works Foreman. Alongside Cousins were Jack Lowndes (Chassis Line Production Foreman), John Bull, an ex-Sergeant Major (Body Line Foreman) and George Morris in charge of road test and rectification of the cars.

Mike Allison researched this period intensively; he explains *'Syd was never at Edmund Road, but after the Company moved to Abingdon, and being friendly with Jacko, was seconded as a fitter when extra hands were needed for the C-type 12/12 work in April 1931. He came to Abingdon permanently from Morris Cowley in September 1930, according to his personnel record, which Jack Gardiner showed me.'* In fairness it should be noted that Syd's own notes do not confirm the view that he spent time at Cowley prior to Abingdon.

Jack Lowndes, John Bull, George Morris And Other Early Morris Garages Men...

There were of course many other people who arrived at Morris Garages in broadly the same period as Syd Enever; space precludes the opportunity to cover all of them, or to do their stories justice, but a few of them – many of whom remained life-long work colleagues – included the following:

JACK LOWNDES joined Morris Garages in 1923 as an electrician in Vehicle Assembly and eventually rose to the position of 'Works Engineer'; he was recalled by John Browne and Jack Daniels as being foreman on the chassis assembly at Bainton Road and Edmund Road even before the switch to Abingdon. Browne, who reported to Lowndes, described him as 'a quiet chap' and also credits him as being part of the small group who helped shape the wooden master for the first definitive MG radiator grille. Syd Enever noted him as *'a foreman running the building of cars and engines – all engines being run in by Town gas.'*

JOHN BULL is sometimes seen in contemporary photos of the production line. Jack Daniels remembered him from the time he joined in 1927 and started work on converting Morris

CHAPTER THREE: FLEDGLING ENGINEER

chassis from Cowley to repurpose them for MG use: *'John Bull was an ex-Sergeant-Major – and he showed me how to knock out various rivets, take out the engine and strip it right down and to cut off certain brackets on the Morris chassis which were not required'.*

GEORGE MORRIS, wrote John Thornley, *'... joined Morris Garages as a fitter in 1918 ,where he assisted in the assembly of early 'specials', then became Chief Tester'*. According to his grandson Kevin Whitehead, George Morris had started out as an apprentice at a sewing machine factory in Oxford before the move to Morris Garages; *'he was one of four brothers, all huge (in addition there were four sisters), a local Oxford boy – his father managed the local Oxford Co-op'*. From Kennett Ullyett's book *'The MG Companion'* we learn that Morris actually joined the same month that war ended – in other words November 1918. From *'Nuffield Teamwork'* of January 1950, we learn that George Morris spent time at the Clarendon Yard, Alfred Lane, Bainton Road, Edmund Road and of course Abingdon. In the thirties, Morris was employed on the MG lines and occasionally got to work in the Development Shop, but in due course he settled into the important work at the end of the production sequence. As Jack Daniels recalled, at the end of the lines, each car would be taken out on road-test, followed by any rectifications required and then a second road-test. *'George Morris was in charge of rectification and testing, with Sam Nash – one of his best test drivers'*. Syd Enever's notes also record *'George Morris was foreman on rejects and tests at Edmund Road'*. Moving like his colleagues to Abingdon, Morris remained in broadly this role well into post-war years, becoming 'Superintendent B-Block'. His grandson says that the factory shut early for the day when Morris retired; *'Grampa had a long retirement, passing away at 86, always interested in what we did and the cars we drove... having said that when I turned up at their house with my first MG, a Midget and proudly showed them my new pride and joy (it was only three years old). Grampa's reaction was – 'what the bloody hell did you buy that for?' – and on lifting the bonnet told me to 'get out of the way – it's not running properly', so he then balanced the carbs and reset the ignition... much better...'*

CHARLES ('CHARLIE') MARTIN joined Morris Garages in 1921 as assistant in the Machine Shop, where he helped to build Old Number One – his principal role being to build that car's special engine. He was another member of staff who thrived at MG, ending up in post war years as the head of Progress Department, a position he held until retirement in the sixties.

STAN SAUNDERS joined Morris Garages in 1923 to assist Cecil Cousins; for the first six years he was one of the drivers responsible for delivering motorised chassis to coachbuilders, and then moved over to take charge of the Tool Stores; in post-war years he became an assistant to Charles Martin (q.v.) as a so-called 'Process Chaser', an important role which comprised making sure that all the parts needed on the assembly line remained available.

F. D. H. (FRANK) STEVENS was engaged originally as a foreman in the Morris Garages Machine Shop at Longwall in 1923, where it was recalled that he was responsible for assembly of the chassis for Old Number One. He took charge of the work in the early machine shop to make the sets of parts necessary to convert the Morris Oxford into the Morris Garages sports models. In 1929, Stevens was part of the 'advanced guard' that moved into the Pavlova works at Abingdon, helping lay out first the new Machine Shop and then the Paint Shop there. In 1935, he fabricated the chassis for what was to become the 'R' Type Midget and was later part of the team responsible for turning the factory over to war work. By the

A close-up view of the back end of Syd's home-made three-wheel car. (Enever Archive)

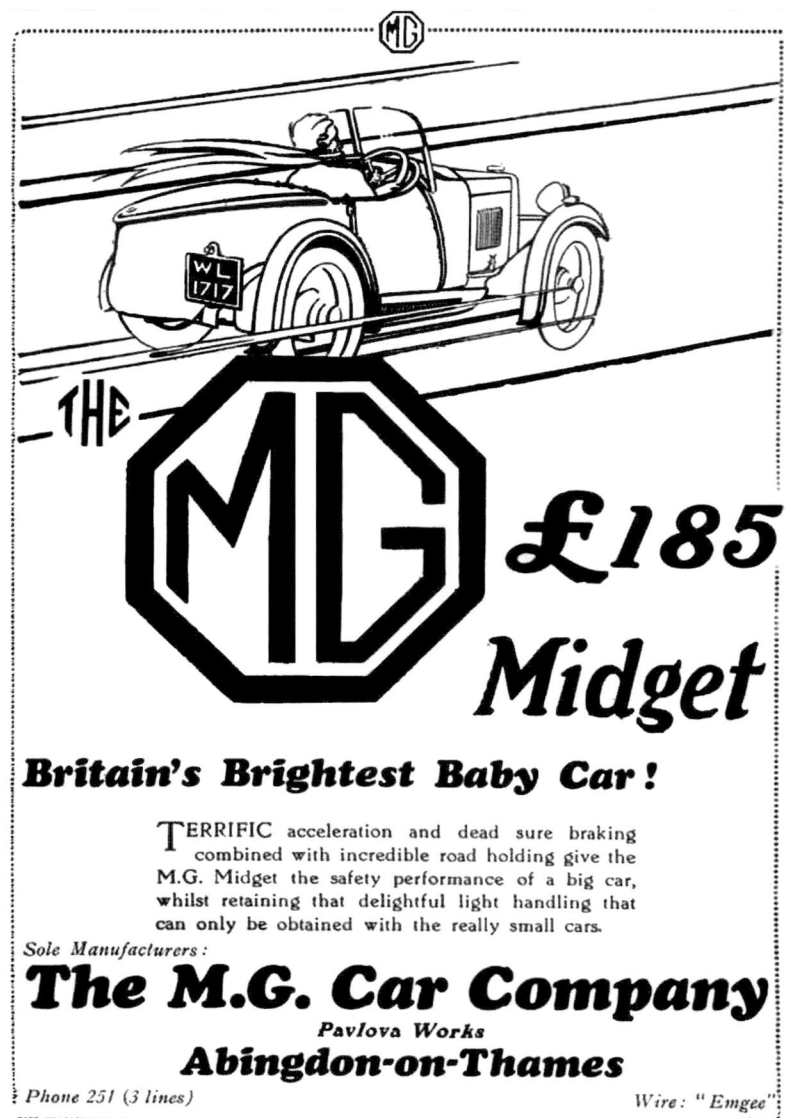

A 1930 advertisement proclaims the new Midget as 'Britain's Brightest Baby Car'. (Author Archive).

time of his retirement in the spring of 1959, he had risen to the role of Chief Ratefixer and Process Planner at Abingdon.

G. S. (JACK) GARDINER joined Morris Garages as salesman in 1921. He eventually rose to become MG's Personnel Manager. In 1924, Gardiner decided to have a 'Morris Garages Special' built for him by the MG team, and this set the tone for a series of replicas with polished bodies (by Coventry Car Bodies Ltd. – better known as 'Carbodies') with their painted wings and matching interiors.

GEORGE KING was recalled by Syd Enever as charge hand in the machine shop.

TOPPER COLLIS (not to be confused with Syd's mentor 'Copper' Crease), was the gate porter at Abingdon who greeted the majority of visitors to the plant. His father had been a porter at Exeter College, Oxford for 55 years, and Topper followed suit for nineteen, until, as Kenneth Ullyett recorded *'...he decided that the hours of six in the morning to midnight were overlong, and that portering to the motoring fraternity was a better job'*. Many of the VIPs who came to call at the factory from the earliest days *'... were welcomed by Topper with his cheery grin and College courtesy.'*

By the time he joined at Bainton Road in 1925, Syd Purves also recalled others; when he was there he said he was one of a staff of little more than a dozen – comprising George Propert; Cecil Cousins; Jack Lowndes; **George Hamilton** on paint-work; **Jim Prickett**, an electrician; George Morris; **Albert Eustace** (stores); **Pat Wright** (test driver); **Alec Hounslow** and **Frank King** (both apprentices or improvers) and two other members of staff – a second test driver and a cleaner (probably Stan Saunders and **Fred Hemmings** respectively) – although it has also been recorded that the total staff was more like fifty.

Chapter Four: Magic Midgets and Magnettes

Initial Distraction – The MG Six

It was evident that Syd's reputation preceded him when he arrived at Abingdon; his skill at servicing a wide variety of cars, and doing so quickly and with clever improvisation, meant that he was soon working at the heart of the new factory's experimental shop. As we saw in the last chapter, head designer was H. N. Charles, whose expertise was put to good use by Cecil Kimber; the foil to Charles was Cecil Cousins, a practical man who frequently clashed with the designer.

As Syd arrived, the MG marque was in full flight and whilst the production lines accommodated at various points the M-Type Midget, Mark I (previously sold as the 'MG Six'), Mark II and Mark IV, the range was moving away from its humble Morris origins, and in this enterprise, the experimental shop were the favoured team who under Kimber's direction were mapping out the future development of new cars, for both road and track purposes; young Syd was in the right place at the right time to dive in to the exciting atmosphere of hard work and development of new models.

Although Kimber aspired to make his larger cars into luxury successes, the biggest selling model at this juncture soon proved to be the new Midget – its neat little sports car body wrapped around Morris Minor chassis and drivetrain, bringing sports car ownership well within the scope of many motorists for whom the usual sports car exotica remained an unaffordable dream. There was already excitement building even before the new small sports car arrived; less than a month after the Morris Minor was announced in *The Motor*, the same magazine stated that there would soon in addition be a new '*Morris Midget, to be built by the MG Car Company of Oxford.*'

The M-Type was unquestionably a great success – 200 orders were placed at the Motor Show alone against 40 for the bigger cars – and it brought new owners to MG, amongst them a young trainee accountant called John Thornley, who acquired an M-Type on his thirtieth birthday – but as a sports car it had its limitations due to its more pedestrian origins.

In the midst of this, Kimber was casting his net to see what form his next small sports car should take; his ambition to create a junior Bentley, through the big six-cylinder MG 18/100 'Tigresse' (unveiled in February 1930) would prove a failure, with the new Midgets winning races en masse in the wake of an ignominious failure of the 18/100 on the occasion of its big debut. The M-Type certainly launched MG's great series of sporting prowess, and did so with remarkable success. The 1930 Brooklands Double-Twelve (including the coveted Team Prize) spawned a series of thirty

The MG 18/80 'Six' was a sporting car of its time, but rather more stately than the much smaller Midget which came to usurp its prominence in MG affairs. (Author Archive)

The apple of Cecil Kimber's eye was unquestionably the '18/80 Mark II', seen here before and after one was entered in the late January 1930 Monte Carlo Rally by Sir Francis Samuelson. The top photo, with Cecil Kimber second left and Lord Nuffield next, shows the car displayed for a small party of invited press (behind the car) whilst the other shows it in Monte Carlo (bearing Race Number 8), where it finished in 48th place. Reg Jackson (in Plus Fours) is at far right; he evidently drew the longer straw than Syd on this occasion! (Jackson family)

'Double Twelve Replicas' and the same year's bold but less successful attempts at Le Mans helped cement the reputation of the MG Midget.

Notwithstanding this early success, the M-Type was still very much a by-product of the Morris Minor, and there was obvious scope and potential (provided management support remained) to develop a more becoming sports car chassis. Whilst it is often held that by the thirties at least, small sports cars were the preserve of the British, the situation in the late 1920s was somewhat less clear cut; one of the better small sports cars was the Rally, which was made in France, one of the nations where development of the automobile received a clear head start.

Syd Enever recalled examining a Rally soon after his arrival at Abingdon; he believed it had first been studied when MG was still at Edmund Road. Charles pored all over it and there seems little doubt that it helped inspire the form of the first bespoke small MG sports car – indeed in his own notes, Syd recorded later that the Rally informed the design of every model from the D to K Type MGs: *'although we based our design on that of the French Rally sports car, but Charles wanted the chassis frame of our models made so we could manufacture it ourselves, and component parts could be made by motor cycle people, so we had steel tube cross members and malleable machined end fittings brazed on.'*

This accords with the words of Wilson McComb, who wrote of the Rally that it was *'a purposeful 1,110cc machine rather similar to the Riley Nine in appearance. The chassis side members were of channel section and, apart from curving up over the front axle, were straight for most of their length, the low lines being achieved by passing the chassis beneath the rear axle... the Rally had square-section cross-members, but square tubing was costly and required end-brackets that were hard to make ... it was made to extremely fine limits and allowed the use of turned brackets, pinned and brazed in place, cycle fashion. In this way, a dead-true frame could be built even with the limited facilities available at the factory.'* One may fairly imagine that this technique would have met with the approval of William Morris, based on his personal experiences of cycle manufacture.

Automobiles Rally

It is not clear whether or not Cecil Kimber attended the Paris Salon in 1927, but even if he did not, he would surely have read reports; one of the exhibits which may have interested him was the Rally 'ABC' sports car, a product of a company founded in Colombes, Paris in 1921 by French engineer Eugène Affovard Asnière. The ABC was a low, sleek sports car with a gutsy engine, and crucially, a lightweight underslung chassis frame of the company's own manufacture. As an offshoot of the earlier 'cycle car' traditions, a consequence in part of French fiscal legislation in place from 1920 to 1925, the two-seater Rally was light in weight (around 650kg) but serious in intent, and was clearly built by enthusiasts for enthusiasts; arguably a philosophy sometimes shared at MG and seldom the best recipe for enduring commercial success.

At some time in 1927, it seems that one of these gamine cars arrived at MG and, as Syd Enever recalled, was studied carefully as inspiration for a new generation of MG Midgets and Magnas which were being schemed for the enhanced production space that first Edmund Road and soon Abingdon offered. It is not recorded which model this was; possibly the Rally ABC, which was available with a choice of proprietary engines. 'ABC' was a play on words – "*châssis abaissé*" referring to a "lowered chassis".

As for Rally itself, the company – without the patronage of an equivalent to Lord Nuffield – lasted into the early 1930s but was a sad victim of that decade's recession, closing its doors in 1934, but not before its products had appeared at the Mille Miglia, Le Mans and many other sporting events, including the first May 11th 1929 Brooklands Double Twelve (where a Rally, driven by JA Driskell, finished in third place).

As it was increasingly obvious that the way forward for MG as a maker of sporting cars was to base their efforts on this promising chassis base, so the future of the Abingdon factory was mapped out, and whilst for the time being the 18/80 models remained important, it was to the new Midget four cylinder, and subsequent six-cylinder Magna and Magnette models, that Kimber, Charles and their team looked for success, both on the road and the race track. Abingdon was destined to be become the world's premier sports car factory – and rising through the ranks, just at the right time, was the former Garage Hand from Morris Garages.

'Motorsport' on the Abingdon factory

A report from Motorsport of August 1930 which summarises the sporting intent of the latest range – and states Kimber's claim that the new factory was the largest of its kind in England...

Sports Models Only

'The history of most pioneer manufacturing concerns, both in England and abroad, is much the same. From small beginnings they have grown to gigantic concerns, from tiny obscure workshops their premises have expanded out of all recognition. All can boast of a reputation and experience extending over many years. With the MG Car Company, it is somewhat different. It is not an old firm. There were no MG cars before 1925. Yet it can be truly described as a pioneer concern in that it was one of the first to specialise in the production of sports models only.

At a time when other makers were concentrating on the cheap, mass-produced utility vehicle, MG's were using their resources for building a

In Motorsport *of March 1930, it was reported 'Much interest has been caused by the announcement during February of a road racing model. This car, which is called the Mark III, is fitted with an engine of similar capacity to that used in the Mark II, but with a high compression head fitted with two plugs per cylinder and a new camshaft. Dry sump lubrication is a feature, and the crank case sump is separate from the flywheel compartment. An oil tank is carried between the front dumb irons, and is fitted with an oil cleaner. A large petrol tank holding 25 gallons is used and is provided with a quick filling device. A light four seater body complying with International Regulations is standard, and the price of the complete car is fixed at £895. This model will be raced by private owners during the coming season, and one car has been entered in the Double Twelve'... (Author Archive)*

Whilst the big 18/100 proved to be something of an igniminious failure at Brooklands, the same could not be said about the MG M-Type Midgets which dominated the smaller engine class. Here, at the Junior Car Club Double Twelve, we can spot a pair of privately-entered Midgets, Nos. 75 (Victoria Worsley / D. G. Foster) and 80 (Norman Black / H. H. Stisted) – both of which finished. There were six MG M-Type Midgets in all, versus the one 18/100, so the odds were not in the bigger car's favour from the outset; the fact that the Midgets finished fourth, joint fifth and seventh in their class was cause of much celebration back at Abingdon. (Jackson family)

In the wake of the sensational results at Brooklands in May 1930, MG offered a limited number of MG Midget '8/45' Double-Twelve Replicas; twenty were built at a retail price of £245. The distinctive MG badge and radiator grille were becoming well-known hallmarks of junior motorsport. (Author Archive)

An example of the French 'Rally' sports car was acquired by the MG works and its neat underslung chassis was studied by the engineering team. (Malcolm Green)

The MG factory in 1930, illustrating the overlapping period when both the 18/80 MG Sixes and the new Morris-Minor based MG Midgets were both in production. (Author Archive)

roadworthy, fast car for the sportsman. That was in 1925, and they have been doing it ever since. The first MG Sports, many of which are still to be seen on the road, were built, first of all, in a small mews in Oxford. They sold very well and their owners liked them; the demand far exceeded the supply, and so in 1926 a speedy removal was made to larger works in North Oxford.

Here cars were produced in considerably larger numbers, but sales increased to such an extent that a £20,000 factory was built at Edmund Road, Cowley, and production on a still larger scale was started in 1927.

It was thought that this would be the home of the MG Sports car for a few years at least, but with the introduction of the now well-known MG Midget and MG Six models, it soon became apparent that the accommodation was far too limited.

Then, by chance, the big five-acre factory, known as Pavlova Works, Abingdon-on-Thames, which had been in disuse for some years, was discovered. There the MG Company are now producing MG Sports cars by a new kind of flow production method in which each car is built with individual care as if it was the only car being manufactured, and their output is such, that they are able to claim to be the largest manufacturers of sports cars in England'.

Motorsport magazine, March 1930

A New MG Model for this Season
The 18/80 MG Six 2-Seater Sports.

The new factory of the MG Car Company at Abingdon is now finished, and the first of the Mark II models are on the erecting tracks. The range of models available for the present year is wide, and will appeal to all classes of motor sportsmen.

The Mark I six-cylinder model is unaltered from last year, and embodies an overhead camshaft engine of 2468 c.c., fitted with two SU carburettors and coil ignition, and a three speed unit construction gearbox. Drive is taken from a universal joint behind the gearbox through a ball jointed torque tube to the bevel driven back axle. The frame is of heavy section, upswept front and rear, and springing is by four semi elliptic springs assisted by Hartford shock absorbers. Lever and pedal are independently coupled to the four wheel brakes, which are fitted with single point adjustments.

The Mark II retains the good points of the earlier model, but is fitted with a four speed gearbox, embodying a silent third gear, and centre ball bearings for main and layshaft. The frame has been stiffened by a stouter centre cross girder, a front tie rod, and an additional pressing to brace the rear of the chassis. Springs are wider, and are fitted with Silentbloc shackles. 14in. brake drums are fitted to all wheels.

The Mark II, which will be available in the middle of March, costs £550, which the Mark I is available at £445.

Much interest has been caused by the announcement during February of a road racing model. This car, which is called the Mark III, is fitted with an engine of similar capacity to that used in the Mark II, but with a high compression head fitted with two plugs per cylinder and a new camshaft. Dry sump lubrication is a feature, and the crank case sump is separate from the flywheel compartment. An oil tank is carried between the front dumb irons, and is fitted with an oil cleaner. A large petrol tank holding 25 gallons is used and is provided with a quick filling device. A light four seater body complying with International Regulations is standard, and the price of the complete car is fixed at £895. This model will be raced by private owners during the coming season, and one car has been entered in the Double Twelve.

The MG Midget is unaltered, but a neat coupé with sliding roof and Triplex glass is now in production at £245.

'Motor Sport' Magazine March 1930 side panel.

John Thornley

A decade after Syd's start on his MG journey came **John William Yates Thornley** (June 11th 1909 - July 16th 1994), a larger-than-life character whose first brush with MG came when he acquired a new Midget in 1930 as he turned twenty one; he soon became involved in the formation of the MG Car Club and that brought him into contact with the MG Car Company and in particular Cecil Kimber. Thornley had been embarked on a career in accountancy, but he eventually managed to persuade Kimber to give him a job at the factory, where he started work on November 3rd 1931.

Thornley later recalled that Kimber initially told him that his job would be to run the MG Car Club and help in the service department in his spare time; he soon met the General Manager, George Propert, who said contrariwise that his job was to work in the service department and run the MG Car Club in his spare time. When there, he found himself working for a series of less than competent service managers until, in due course, his quiet diligence and efficiency led to him getting the Service Manager job himself.

In the thirties, Thornley managed the Cream Cracker and Three Musketeer teams of MG trials cars. Thornley admired Kimber and like many was dismayed when, in 1941, Miles Thomas sacked him; in an interview for 'Thoroughbred & Classic Cars' in 1986, stated: *'I admired Kimber for what he did. He had the imagination and drive to start it all. He was a visionary, and he had the ability to install his enthusiasm into others – take those two things together and that's enough, really. What Thomas did to him was shameful, the toffee-nosed bastard: I suppose he saw Kim as a chap who'd once had Nuflield's ear to a dangerous extent, so he couldn't go wrong.'*

Thornley served during the War attached to the War Office: *'I had a very hard-working war but I wasn't exposed to danger, much – bombing, of course, but we all had that. And it taught me to think big. As a Lieutenant-Colonel, General Staff Officer Grade 1 at the War Office, I had the buying of all Signals equipment for the British Army – a bill of about £200 million. And although we worked to various rules, of course, it was entirely within my purview whether the final bill was £175 million or £225 million. For that, a grateful Government paid me £918 a year'.*

After the War, Thornley returned to MG and doubtless that war-time parsimony helped; 1952 saw 'MG & Riley' supremo Jack Tatlow move out to Morris Commercial Cars and Thornley, hitherto his deputy, got the General Manager job at Abingdon. This swiftly brought him into contact with Len Lord, as Chairman of the newly-merged British Motor Corporation. Lord had history at MG, with the closure of the Racing Shop, and there was understandable trepidation at Abingdon when he was once again master of their destiny.

However, Thornley made a conscious effort to be in Lord's good books (helped undoubtedly by soaring sales); as he claimed: *'I think I'm probably the only senior executive in BMC that never had a thick ear from Lord. I never had any difficulty with Longbridge, never had any difficulty with Lord. It was a sad day for me when he went, because George Harriman was nothing of a man by comparison. A terrible dead loss. But Len Lord ... I think it was like dealing with a dog, in a way – I wasn't afraid of him, so he wagged his tail. If I'd got myself on the wrong side of him, I reckon Abingdon would have been snuffed out very soon'.*

John Thornley gained an OBE in the January 1964 New Years Honours (for his war work) remained in harness at Abingdon – working especially closely with his good friend, Syd Enever along with the other MG acolytes – although an eighteen-month long health scare from September 1966 was followed by retirement in 1969 – two years before Syd's turn to hand in his staff pass.

Five years after John Thornley's death in July 1994, Peter Thornley wrote about his father in fond reflection: *'Pop was a wordsmith – see his writings; he was an enthusiast – the product attests to that; he was an authoritarian – my posterior can attest to that! Humanitarian, artist, accountant, public speaker, engineer, father and remarkable grandfather. As a son, one is perhaps too close to fully appreciate this remarkable multifaceted man, who was very complex – an enormous personality. At times very warm and generous, at others he could be disapproving. His expectations of himself and others were always high – he was not liberal in his praise. Which made it more appreciated when it came'.*

At a reception in the mid-1950s, we see John Thornley (left) and Syd in discussion with Rodney Walkerley (Rodney Lewis de Burgh Walkerley, April 2nd 1905 – December 1982). The latter was a well-known British motoring correspondent in his time; he started at 'Motor Sport' in 1927, then joined 'The Light Car' in 1930, as Sports Editor, under the nom-de-plume of 'The Blower', but he was better known as 'Grand Vitesse' at The Motor from 1934, and like Syd, was part of the 1938 Frankfurt trip and the subsequent celebratory party at the Trocadero in December 1938, described later in this Chapter. In the sixties, Walkerley wrote a column in the BMC magazine 'Safety Fast'.(Enever family)

CHAPTER FOUR: MAGIC MIDGETS AND MAGNETTES

A New MG Midget – For a New Factory and a New Era

With the metaphorical bit between the teeth, the new MG design team soon began to plan the next step on from the MG M-Type Midget, which had been created as something of an expedient using Morris Minor bits and a re-designed engine thanks to the collaboration of H. N. Charles at MG and Frank Woollard at Morris Motors Engines Branch (the latter a good personal friend of the Kimbers). It was clear to Kimber, especially when the 18/100 Tigress proved to be a damp squib, that more effort needed to be given to a new Midget and beyond it a related range of slightly upmarket models with six-cylinder off-shoots that would eventually spawn what would become the Magna and Magnette ranges.

Although he aspired to make MGs less dependent upon humble Morris components, Kimber had sufficient restraint to keep as much of the source material 'in house' from the Nuffield family as possible; new bespoke chassis and bodywork were accepted as necessary but as far as possible the other building blocks needed to be either Morris or Wolseley based (the latter business having fortuitously joined the family in February 1927). However what Kimber wanted was to create a superior confection from all the components on offer, and in this he was supported by his enthusiastic development team.

H. N. Charles was certainly the master of the design domain, with number two Cecil Cousins, but arguably it was the up-and-coming Syd Enever, recently arrived at Abingdon and buoyed by his reputation for original thought and innovation who, working with Charles, undertook much of the practical work on developing the nuts and bolts of the new MG Midget family. The famous EX-Register, the MG factory's master list of most of the development work from 1930 to 1980, lists the early work on the new Midget as EX115. With a nod to inspiration from the Rally and other models, the new chassis was straight-through beneath the rear axle and possessed cross-tubes brazed in the classic bicycle-frame fashion. The rear ends of the springs were mounted in sliding bronze trunnions.

The exercise was bolstered by the desire – encouraged by no less a figure than Captain George Eyston, already famous in the motor racing and record-breaking field – to be the first driver of a 750cc motor car to break the 100mph barrier. Eyston had been friends since their time together at Cambridge with J. A. 'Jimmy' Palmes, a Wimbledon-based MG dealer, and the two of them were keen to plan some record chasing in a small British sports car; MG would benefit, as we shall see.

Kimber was no doubt influential in fostering the relationship necessary with the recently ennobled Lord Nuffield, and it was a canny move; whilst William Morris – seldom a man for inconsequential small talk – probably felt some kinship with the racers who bought his products, and also less out of place; he could also no doubt offer his own pearls of wisdom, whether they were wanted or not.

An Ex-Cursion into Numbers: The Early EX-Register

When the author interviewed Jack Daniels – as we have seen, at MG from 1927 onwards – amongst the things discussed were the early entries in the EX Register – the neatly typed ledger of entries for projects being undertaken in the Development Department. There is some pre-history to these EX numbers as the first use of the EX prefix was related to chassis numbers for the MG 18/80 prototypes; however with the move to Abingdon there was a decision to start again at EX101 (which dates from November 6th 1929); the entries would have been lodged by H. N. Charles, but over time responsibility eventually passed to Syd Enever.

In the case of these early EX-Register entries, Jack Daniels told the author that he was sure that most of the drawings – few of which, sadly,

A well-known photo but an illustrative one nevertheless. This shows a line of MG M-Type Midgets in 1930 exiting the factory via Cemetery Road, past the large MG administration building (nowadays repurposed as residential flats with timber cladding concealing brickwork and heritage alike). The present-day MG Car Club offices are nearby. (Author Archive)

actually survive at Gaydon – were his. The 'Tiger' headlamp assembly, for example, was EX107 (certainly Daniels' handiwork) and EX109, 110 and 114 all relate to the Brooklands 'Double Twelve' Midget, which Daniels remembered being drawn, the latter in particular: *'EX114 was for the Brooklands petrol tanks which George Gibson drew up; the tail was pointed and the tank formed part of the tail itself, and was made up by Hubbards at Basingstoke. I know that because George Gibson went over to Hubbards to discuss the tank with them, and he took Mrs Hubbard out to lunch and became involved in a fatal accident. All I can recall is that Gibson never came back to Abingdon.'*

The next number, EX115, is significant in that it denotes the all-new MG-designed chassis which Charles designed for the 1931 Midget, slightly predating the EX120 Record Breaker which became the prototype for the new MG straight-through chassis. Daniels remembered EX115 too: *'H. N. Charles was really getting going at this point, and I certainly detailed this as by that stage I was the chassis draughtsman.'*

Another project was the cross-flow cylinder head, designed for the 1932 'C' type, but before that came the excitement of the first MG record breakers: *'I was the chassis man on EX127 - the Magic Midget – and did all the drawings for that. EX127 had an inclined drive line, at an angle of seven degrees in plan to allow it to become a single-seater, with a full 'Charles' type chassis.'* There then followed work on every chassis of every MG produced between 1927 and 1935; the development team – Syd amongst them – were perpetually busy, as a glance at a list of production and racing MGs of the period will prove.

The EX-Register appears as an appendix to this book.

Around the World in an MG Midget

On August 25th 1930, to much fanfare and ballyhoo, the MG Midget (registered as RX 7367) depicted in these factory photos from Syd's album set off from the RAC Club in London's Pall Mall, ostensibly to circumnavigate the globe with the assistance of Shell Petroleum. We know that the intrepid explorers were two former RAF officers, Captain Max Hay and W. E. Wolveridge. Their ambition was to travel with the bare minimum of supplies, relying upon petrol from their key sponsor (the standard petrol tank meant in practical terms that they could not venture more than 200 miles from a fuel supply point). In a contemporary report in the Singapore newspaper *'The Straits Times'* (September 30th 1930), Wolveridge was quoted as stating *"we hope to accomplish the journey in five months, and if we are successful it will be a record. We are taking plenty of spare parts, but our personal luggage will consist of little more than a razor and pyjamas"*. From time to time there were reports from various far-flung points, but the story seems to have petered out and the final outcome, and the whereabouts of both the car and its occupants, has remained something of a mystery.

EX120: MG's First Foray into Record Breaking

Serendipity came to call at Abingdon in the summer of 1930 when George Eyston and Jimmy Palmes, with record-breaking on their minds, called to see Cecil Kimber to discuss an idea for a record breaker with the engine derived from that in the MG M-Type Midget; the thoughts were that this engine could be turned into a high-revving 750cc unit, boosted with one of Eyston's 'Powerplus' superchargers, and if assembled into a suitable chassis, there might be a chance to become the first to achieve 100mph from such a car, which would run in the international 'Class H'. Whilst William Morris was no great fan of motor sport, he could see the promotional benefits of record breaking, with the

Before embarking on a new generation of MG Midget, there was clearly mileage – literally – to be gained by demonstrating the virtues of the plucky Morris Minor-based M-Type. Here we see a 'world record' car in the course of preparation at Abingdon, in the summer of 1930 (around the time those M-Types were doing great things in the Double-Twelve at Brooklands, as we saw in the previous chapter)... (Enever family)

CHAPTER FOUR: MAGIC MIDGETS AND MAGNETTES

prestige and associated implication of a competent and reliable motor-car underneath it all, and it was hardly lost on him that his great rival Herbert Austin was interested in chasing the same targets with his popular Austin Seven.

Thus began the creation of a special lightweight record breaker under the project code EX120; although H N Charles and Syd were in notionally in charge of the technical design of the project, Eyston brought in his trusted engineering expert E. A. D. (Ernest) Eldridge – who also happened to be a distinguished record-breaker in his own right, and so someone whose advice was worthy of attention. If anyone doubted his courage, they only needed to learn how, as a result of an injury resulting from a crash during one of his runs at Montlhéry in his Miller, Eldridge had a patch over his right eye. The engine was of course specially built and whilst fundamentally based on the M-Type block, had a 54mm bore and 81mm stroke, to give a capacity of 743cc – just inside the Class H parameters. Development at Abingdon was largely undertaken by Syd and Jacko – further forging their bond of mutual trust and friendship.

Although supercharging was part of the plan, the engine was initially run without, and in this form the car was readied in the hope of achieving the goal of 100mph.

...The proud team responsible for preparing the Midget intended for a world tour – with Syd third from left, and fourth from left is Johnny Crook. At this juncture, Syd was more involved on the 'development' side than racing. (Enever family)

The Shell MG Midget on the street, registered now as 'RX 7367' – in a photo from one of Syd's own albums. (Enever family)

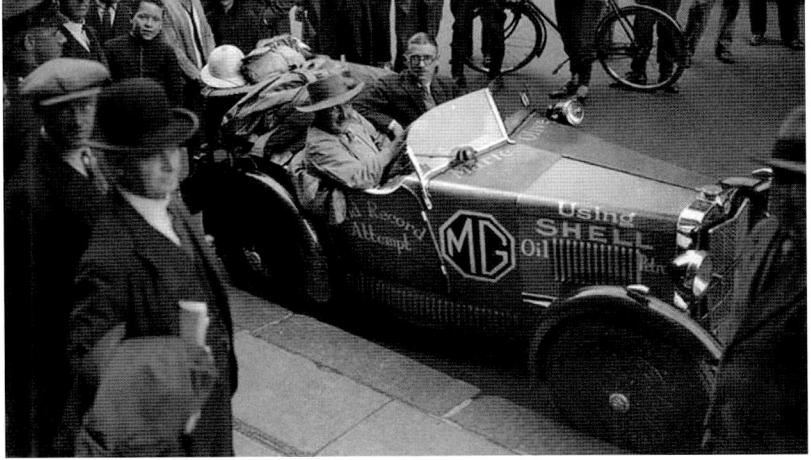

The little MG set off from Pall Mall on August 25th 1930. The pair of travellers – Captain Max Hay and E. H. Wolveridge – intended to cross Europe and then on through India, China, San Francisco and finally, they hoped, to New York. Reports appeared in sundry publications of the car in places like Athens, Egypt and Baghdad, but how their journey ended is not clear. (Author Archive)

Captain George Eyston

Captain George Edward Thomas Eyston MC OBE (born in Bampton, in those days still in Berkshire, June 28th 1897 – June 11th 1979 was a large, avuncular figure who came from a distinguished Roman Catholic family line; his father was Edward Robert Joseph Eyston, whose occupation was described as 'gentleman'. Studying at Stonyhurst College in Lancashire and subsequently for an Engineering Degree at Trinity College, Cambridge, at the latter he met J. A. 'Jimmy' Palmes – who shared rooms with him at University – the two becoming life-long friends and were linked commercially through Palme's MG dealership Wimbledon, South-west London. By the fifties, Palmes was the Managing Director of 'Jarvis and Sons' at Morris House, Wimbledon, and Eyston was his fellow director. Eyston eventually assumed a role of boys-own hero, with a series of stirring land speed record breaking attempts which rivalled those of the more famous Campbell dynasty.

Eyston started the heroics young; before

57

EX120 at speed at Montlhéry. It is important to stress that the main credit for the building and support of this endeavour belongs to the likes of Cecil Cousins and Reg Jackson; but Syd was there in the background, working closely with H N Charles. (Author Archive)

Stressing the often-forgotten fact that EX120 was privately owned by Jimmy Palmes of Jarvis of Wimbledon (Eyston was a director), this March 1931 advert shows EX120 without the distinctive nose cowling with which it is more commonly depicted, and which inspired that of the early MG C-Types. (Author Archive)

the First World War he raced motorcycles under an assumed name, and in the War he was commissioned as second lieutenant in the Third Battalion, Dorset Regiment and served in France; was awarded the Military Cross on July 18th 1917, the citation reading: '*2nd Lt. (Temp Lt.) George Edward Thomas Eyston, RFA., Spec. Res. For conspicuous gallantry and devotion to duty. He rendered most valuable service when carrying out reconnaissance under heavy fire. On several occasions he went forward under heavy shell and machine gun fire. He carried out his duties with great courage and determination, and was able to obtain most valuable information.*' He returned to Cambridge in 1919 to complete his degree, graduating in 1921 and then spent some time in France to study French, whilst there becoming entranced by the racing at Le Mans.

Eyston married American banker's daughter Olga Mabel Eyre in 1924, and they in turn had two daughters; after a brief interlude racing on water, he returned to road racing and record breaking, and in the latter field he vied with the likes of Cobb and Campbell for the ultimate land speed records, which he raised personally to a remarkable 357.5mph, at a time when air speed records were barely 50mph greater. His famous record-breakers were *Thunderbolt* and *Speed of the Wind* – the latter reproduced as a popular Dinky Toy for school-boy hero-worshippers. As an engineer he had a number of directorships, one of them being for Powerplus superchargers for which he held development patents: he met Cecil Kimber and the two agreed that there would be mileage in pursuing speed records for much smaller-engined sports cars. As explained in the main text, he was involved with EX120, EX127 and EX135 – the latter in its original 'Humbug' guise – and was a key member of the team that won the team prize with their K3 Magnettes in the 1933 Mille Miglia. He spent up to half his time in France in those days, to such an extent that he was known popularly there as '*Le Recordbreaker*'.

By 1938, Eyston had retreated from his MG endeavours; some say he was disappointed with the way that Kimber had disposed of EX127 to the German Bobby Kohlrausch, but if it was true, he said nothing – discretion being the classic hallmark of an English gentleman – and he was in any case caught-up in his ultimate land-speed-record endeavours; By then Goldie Gardner had stepped into the MG record-breaking field. In the second war, Eyston was involved in the Allied Landings and afterwards was awarded an OBE but never a Knighthood (unlike Campbell) although he claimed to be proudest of his 1938 award of chevalier of the French Légion d'honneur.

After the war, his directorship of C. C. Wakefield, producers of Castrol Oil, brought him extensive travel and no doubt time with his wife's family and friends in the USA; he also returned to Cambridge in 1950 to study geology. His travel in the USA brought him the opportunities to see how MG's initial post-war success was at risk of collapse unless what was by now BMC could be persuaded to invest. As we shall see later, he was part of the renewed record-breaking which followed Goldie Gardner's retirement, although his time in the cockpit was shared with other drivers much younger than him; unlike Gardner, he later stood back to be a guiding light rather than the man in the hot seat.

In retirement, he continued to support MG Car Club events right up to shortly before he died, on a railway journey between London and Winchester, in 1979. It is a peculiar coincidence that he left this world in a train carriage, as did poor Cecil Kimber, albeit in a somewhat gentler manner.

EX120 and C-Type Midget – Recipes for the Future

Syd played no part in the actual trip with EX120, and it is important to stress that credit for the project lay more with the likes of Cousins and Jackson, but it is salient to record what became of a project on which he had probably contributed towards, alongside his mentor, Charles. On Boxing Day in 1930, EX120 was despatched to Montlhéry; it would prove to be a crucial element in the genesis of the bespoke MG Midget. As already discussed, the key objective was to be the first small car (750 cc) to break the 100mph barrier; the pressure was on because around the same time, Malcolm Campbell was at Daytona undertaking some land-speed record breaking attempts in Bluebird and he had also taken a small 750cc Austin to try for the 100 mph record too. In different time zones the Austin and MG cars were struggling to achieve the elusive ton. Meanwhile, on February 6th 1931, Campbell drove his Austin at Daytona Beach and took the 'Flying Mile' at 94mph, still shy of the ultimate objective but giving the MG team added impetus. By now, the on-site team in France of Reg Jackson and Freddie Kindell were exhausted, and

An ignominious end for poor EX120 came in September 1931; the remains are being surveyed here back at Abingdon by Eyston and James Palmes, and clearly after Eyston had recovered. Afterwards, Eyston became well known for his asbestos racing suit; he clearly had no desire to repeat the experience of near incineration. (Author Archive)

so Kimber sent Cecil Cousins and Gordon Phillips to relieve their colleagues.

After much effort, the team got the little MG up to 97 mph – still shy of the magic hundred; Cousins decided that the nose of the car needed a streamlined cowl, and he proceeded to make one, taking an opened-up five-gallon oil drum which he proceeded to crudely hammer into shape using the curved concrete drainage gulley at the side of the circuit. With this improved nose cone in place, on the evening of a very wet, cold and windy Monday 16th February 1931, EX120 achieved 103 mph for five kilometres and cracked some other records; these tasks done, it was brought back to a great reception by Kimber, the make-shift cowling replaced by a more elegant version for subsequent appearances and track record attempts such as at Brooklands (where it took the Flying Mile in March 1931, for example).

A snapshot early in the storied life of a car: here, Syd is behind the wheel, and his associate Johnny Crook alongside, in one of the fourteen MG C-Type Midgets produced in time for the 1931 Brooklands Double Twelve. (Courtesy of Jim Cox)

EX120 – THE FIRST 750CC CAR TO BREAK INTERNATIONAL 100MPH RECORDS		
December 26th	1930	EX120 leaves Abingdon on the back of a lorry, bound for Montlhéry near Paris.
December 31st	1930	EX120 makes its first record attempt at the hands of Captain George Eyston at Montlhéry, winning some records but failing to achieve 100 m.p.h.; instead, he takes three 750 c.c. records at speeds of up to 87.30mph (100 kilometres).
February 6th	1931	Malcolm Campbell takes a supercharged Austin single-seater to 94.061mph at Daytona Beach, Florida, USA whilst making his land speed record breaking attempt in 'Bluebird'.
February 10th	1931	In EX120 at Montlhéry, George Eyston smashes all the Austin records – including 97.07mph over 5km.
February 16th	1931	EX120 is run again at Montlhéry by Captain George Eyston and achieves 103.13mph over 5km, 102.76mph over 5 miles and 101.87mph over 10 miles. The previous day (Sunday 15th), Cecil Cousins had made a crude nose-cowling for EX120 by bashing pieces of oil-drum in the track-side gully, in order to cure the problem of the carburettor icing up.
March 13th	1931	MG tries to take the 100mph record at Brooklands with EX120, but achieves 96.93mph for the Flying kilometre (still beating the Austin 750's Daytona record) to take the circuit's record for the class.

The car, bearing registration number RX 8306, is in fact C-Type 'C0263'. The race number of 74 in the photo on the previous page appears to relate to the car driven (with little success) at the Double Twelve by H Sisted; it started life as the works demonstrator; Cathelijne Spoelstra fills in the subsequent history: '..after the Double-Twelve it was used by Capt. George Eyston for a demonstration drive at Shelsley Walsh then by Victor Ferguson (main Ulster M.G. dealer) at Craigantlet, then by Hailwood and Crabtree in the BRDC 500 Miles Race at Brooklands and later for the road test which appeared in The Autocar on Nov 20 1931, during which period it was cream (body) and brown (wings). In The Motor of Dec 8 1931 however, the car was again used for a road test with the pictures showing the car now black, or dark coloured anyway. Shortly after this, on December 12th Linfield (journalist for The Autocar who executed the original road test) used it in the Gloucester Trial, in black. In 1932, the car was finally used as a recce car (still black) by Eyston for Pendine after which it was sold to the Evans Family, as their first M.G. ever. It was soon painted blue with a white stripe, which then became the Evans' (and Bellevue's) livery. They kept it until the winter of 1933/34'. Nowadays it is owned by enthusiast Chris Cadman. (Courtesy of Chris Cadman)

CHAPTER FOUR: MAGIC MIDGETS AND MAGNETTES

Some of the happy band of MG mechanics with the C-Type Midgets; we can see Alec Hounslow at back left and to the right, possibly 'Jacko'. (Jackson family)

A line-up of shiny C-Types (note the glossy tyres!) posed for the cameras. There were only a small number made, and arguably they generated little profit per unit for MG, but alongside Eyston's exploits in EX120, their prowess contributed immeasurably to MG's reputation. Bill Boddy of Motorsport Magazine wrote: '...those who sampled it described the exhaust note as sounding "like tearing calico" or just " a satisfactory crackle", the blower scream coming in only at high revs. The gear-change was a delight, roadholding good with 32/30 pounds tyre pressure front/ rear, and the ride comfortable'. (Author Archive)

The programme cover for the 1931 Junior Car Club Double-Twelve. (Author Archive)

At Brooklands for the 1931 'Double Twelve' – a gruelling event held over two days (Friday and Saturday May 8th and 9th 1931) – here Syd Enever smiles for the camera in Midget No. 61 whilst behind him can be seen Alec Hounslow in one of the other team cars. (Enever Archive)

Syd in the driving seat of Car No. 61 which was raced by H. D. Parker and G. K. Cox, who finished in fourth place. (Enever Archive)

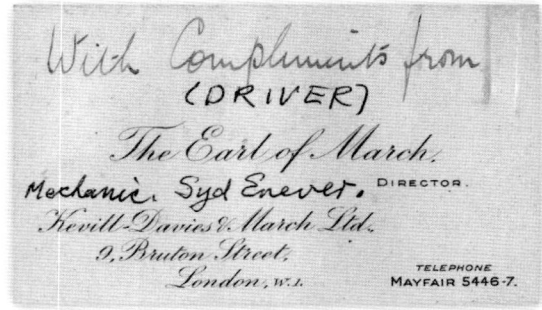

In his photo album, Syd Enever proudly added this annotated business card from the Earl of March, Frederick, 9th Duke of Richmond, Lennox, Gordon and Aubigny (1904 - 1989) (Enever Archive)

By May 1931, the EX120 philosophy had multiplied into the basis of the C-Type Midget and there were fourteen of them at that month's Double Twelve at Brooklands. In his book *Magic MPH*, Goldie Gardner related the debut of the new cars, one of which he had ordered for his own use:

'The purchasers had been warned by Kim (Cecil Kimber) that they would be able to take delivery at Brooklands on a certain date, which coincided with the first official practice period for the Junior Car Club's "Double Twelve" Race which was run on 8th May, 1931. On the day specified,

The Earl of March alongside his Midget, with Syd behind. (Author archive)

The Earl of March in the 1931 'Double Twelve' at Brooklands (note the distinctive concrete bowl of the track behind). The car is an MG C-Type (car No. C0251) and the Earl – 'Freddie' to his close friends - shared the driving with Chris Staniland, with Syd (sitting alongside the Earl in this photo) as their dedicated race mechanic. They covered 1,574.9 miles at an average speed of 65.62mph. (Enever Archive)

a most impressive line of MG Montlhéry Midgets painted in a variety of colours arrived in the Brooklands paddock led by the Earl of March'. Gardner recalled that 'the entourage' was accompanied by George Propert with what Gardner referred to as '*a skeleton office staff*' – one of whom was Syd Enever, although at this juncture Syd was not directly associated with the team formed by Goldie Gardner, Ronnie Horton and Robin Jackson (of whom more anon), their cars being painted black, red and white respectively.

Cecil Cousins was responsible for getting all of the C-Types ready for the actual race, but in the race itself, he was only responsible as 'Team Manager' for the cars run by the Earl of March; Syd was one of the race mechanics, alongside no less than 'Freddie' March himself. Spotting that some of the cars had been failing on the circuit, Kimber instructed Cousins to get the drivers to slow down, but Cousins had other ideas as he did not believe that calculations supposedly made by Reid Railton were correct; accordingly Cousins entered into a pact with the drivers and their mechanics, asking them to maintain their speed even if the pit board told then to slow down.

As the race resumed on the second day, the MGs set off and after they had warmed up, they started circulating at 65 mph. Cousins duly put up the 'slow' signal and as agreed the drivers ignored him; up came Kimber and Railton, and Kimber asked Cousins what was going on *'well, I told them to slow down'* Cousins said, meekly, showing Kimber the pit signal. A few hours later, with the cars evidently still circulating at higher speeds, the ruse was up, but by then it was too late and as the cars mostly finished, nothing more was said in the atmosphere of celebration.

The May 1931 Brooklands race is significant to the story of Syd Enever because of his support of the Earl of March in his C-Type 'C0251' as riding mechanic; in one of Syd's photo albums is a great action shot of the pair of them, out on the circuit, along with one of the Earl's business cards from 'Kevill-Davies & March Ltd' on which has been added by hand the soubriquet *'mechanic – Syd Enever'*.

Meanwhile, however, we should briefly relate the story of what became of EX120 – in which Syd had played an essential part. In the early afternoon of September 25th 1931, George Eyston squeezed his considerable bulk into EX120 and set off round the Montlhéry track, aiming for the one-hour record for an average of 100 m.p.h. Having successfully achieved 101.1 miles in the hour, Eyston continued for another lap but, to the consternation of his mechanics – Jackson and 'Nobby' Marney – he failed to reappear. They noticed that the engine noise had ceased, and quickly set off to look for him, only to find EX120 ablaze by the side of the track.

They began to kick away the side of the bodywork but swiftly saw he was not in the car; walking back along the circuit they could find no trace of him. Only later did they learn that Eyston – a man of not inconsiderable bulk, and with flames licking around his feet, had somehow extricated himself, while the car was still travelling at around 60mph, sat on the bodywork behind the cockpit, managed to steer the wheel with his feet, then jumped out and rolled to the side of the track using a technique he had learnt as a young man when hunting on horseback.

A Citroën test driver, circling the track behind Eyston, had seen Eyston and had managed to pick him up – impressive in itself – placed him into his car and conveyed him to hospital, where he was found to be suffering from a broken collar bone and quite severe burns. The remains of EX120 were shipped back to Abingdon, photographed for publicity and the car was eventually cut up. EX120 had fulfilled its primary purpose; now Kimber and the team would focus on their next tasks – road-racing sports cars based loosely on EX120 and thoughts of a second MG record breaker.

Syd Enever is centre stage in his white overalls, alongside drivers the Earl of March and Chris Staniland. Midgets took all top five places. (Enever Archive)

Syd Enever and the Incredible Race Season Of 1931 – Surrey and Ireland…

The tables of race results below, from four of the key races of the 1931 season (May, June, August and October), demonstrate the pre-eminence of the supercharged C-Type MG Midgets that year, and Syd's role at the heart of the action.

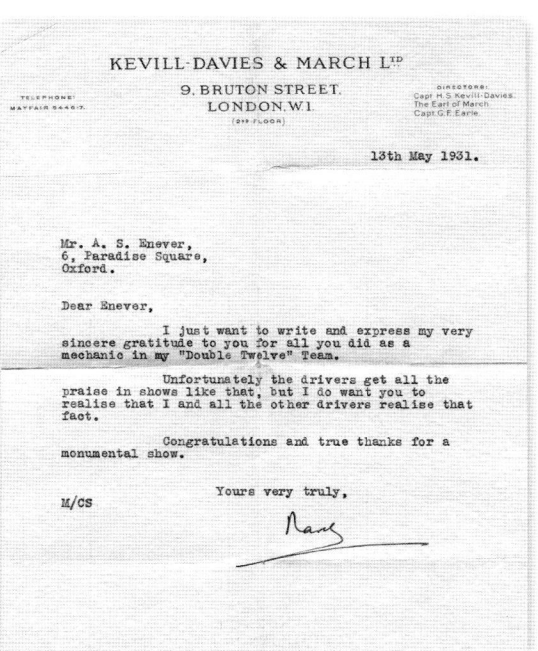

Within the family archives is this touching letter of appreciation from Lord March to Syd, dated May 13th 1931; a thank you from a true gentleman. (Enever Archive)

| 1931 DOUBLE-TWELVE, BROOKLANDS MAY 1931: CLASS 'H' MG MIDGETS ||||||
Race No.	Car	Entrant	Driver (1)	Driver (2)	Result
60	MG Midget 1	The Earl of March (Kevill-Davies & March Ltd.)	The Earl of March	C. S. ('Chris') Staniland	1st
61	MG Midget 2		H. D. Parker	G. K. Cox	4th
62	MG Midget 3		N. (Norman) Black	C. W. Fiennes	5th
63	MG Midget 4	C. (Cecil) J. Randall	T. V. G. Selby	G. Hendy	13th
64	MG Midget 5		F. M. Montgomery	R. Hebeler	DNF
65	MG Midget 6		R. Gibson	L. Fell	2nd
66	MG Midget	G. (George) Bradstock (University Motors Ltd.)	H. C. Hamilton	S. V. Holbrook [due to drive but did not]	3rd
70	MG Midget 7	A.T.G. Gardner	A.T.G. Gardner	R. C. Murton-Neale	DNF (Engine)
71	MG Midget 8		R. T. Horton	W. E. Humphreys	DNF
72	MG Midget 9		R. R. Jackson	F. H. B. Samuelson	18th
73	MG Midget 10	Hon. Mrs Chetwynd; H. H. Stisted;	Hon. Mrs Chetwynd	A. M. C. Jameson	DNF
74	MG Midget 11	D. Higgin	H. H. Stisted	J. (Fred) Kindell	DNF (clutch)
75	MG Midget 12		D. Higgin	J. F. Field	DNF (engine)
76	MG Midget	J. H. P. Clover	J. H. P. Clover	O. H. J. Bertram	Did Not Start

Footnotes: The Double-Twelve event was run for the second time at Brooklands on May 8th and 9th 1931. A team of Midgets, entered by C J Randall, had won the team prize at the 1930 event. MG announced the 750cc supercharged Montlhéry version of the Midget as the 'MG Midget Mark II' (the 'C' type Midget; also known colloquially as the 'Montlhéry Midget') on March 16th 1931. The engine stroke at 73mm was shorter by 10mm than the 850cc. standard engine, giving a cubic capacity of 746cc (bore remained 57mm). Two versions were on offer: supercharged at £345 and unsupercharged at £295. Transmission was through a four-speed manual ENV gearbox. With the supercharged engine the top speed was about 100mph. C type bodies retained the open two-seat configuration of the M type complete with an opening rear boot which now contained the rear mounted petrol tank. The body was doorless and featured two large 'humps' on the scuttle, designed to deflect air over the driver and passenger. The race was won on handicap by the Earl of March and C.S. Staniland in their MG Midget, at an average speed of 65.62mph, and covering a distance of 1,574.9miles. Cecil Cousins was Team Manager for the three 'Kevill-Davis & March Ltd.'; Syd Enever described himself as riding mechanic for the Earl (although 'Johnnie' (Jack) Crook was paired with Staniland) while Alec Hounslow and Johnnie Crook also supported the other two cars. From MG we know from photos that the factory team presence also included, alongside those already named, Reg Jackson and Frankie Tayler. The Earl wrote a brief thank-you letter to Syd on May 13th 1931, thanking him for his efforts. As the tables show, similar Midgets took all first five places in the race. All these C-Type Midgets listed above had an engine capacity of 746cc, with bore 57mm and stroke 73mm. Class 'H' covered cars with engines over 500cc and up to 750cc. The race stipulated minimum speed average of 47.5mph and minimum mileage in 24 hours of 1,140 miles.

Ready for the sea journey to Dublin's Phoenix Park for the 1931 Dublin Grand Prix. Just visible in the first car, 'RX8622', are Alec Hounslow and next to him John 'Jack' Crook; standing behind the second car is the unmistakeable figure of Cecil Cousins, whilst in the car at right ('RX8623') are Syd Enever and Frankie Tayler. (Enever Archive)

An Incident on the Way Home from The Double Twelve – Recalled by Jack Daniels...

"Alec Hounslow and Frankie Tayler were both engaged as drivers on the early test team, and acted as pit mechanics during races. I particularly recall that following MG's win on the Double-Twelve at Brooklands, where I had been doing timing in the pits, I joined Alec Hounslow on the journey back home in the winning vehicle, carrying the laurels. Alec reckoned to be home within the hour, and proceeded to drive accordingly. Around half-way home we shot past H. N. Charles (our boss) and gave him a wave. Subsequently, at Sutton Courtenay, just five miles from Oxford, with five minutes to go to the hour, we came up to a car ditherer which caused Alec to brake heavily on a freshly-showered road surface. The outcome was that we ended up at ninety degrees to the road with both front wheels locked in the ditch. With no personal damage to either car or occupants, and the assistance of passers-by, the vehicle was pulled back onto the road, at which time Charles arrived, looked at the scene but continued driving past. The front wheels of the car were splayed so wide that stability was next to nil, but somehow Alec managed to drive with tyres screaming to a garage at Iffley, where he parked it for the night. Next morning, he acquired another complete axle and wheels, which he then fitted to the car, and had it fully mobile again back at the factory".

1931 SAORSTÁT CUP – THE MG MIDGET C-TYPES – CLASS H (750c.c.)					
Place.	Race No.	Entrant	Driver	Riding Mechanic where known	Registration Number
1st	32	Earl of March	Norman Black	Frankie Tayler	RX 8623
2nd	35	Major A. T. G. Gardner	R. T. 'Ron' Horton		
3rd	34	Major A. T. G. Gardner	Goldie Gardner		
6th	31	Earl of March	H. D. (Harold) Parker	Syd Enever	RX 8621
7th	38	D. Higgin	Dan Higgin		
10th	36	Major A. T. G. Gardner	R. R. (Robin) Jackson		
12th =	39	F. J. Barnes [father of F. S. Barnes]	Frank Stanley Barnes		
12th =	41	C. J. McMullan	W. Kehoe		
15th	33	Earl of March	R (Dick) Watney	Alec Hounslow	RX 8622

Footnotes: The date of the race was Friday June 5th 1931. The Irish Grand Prix comprised two races; the Saorstát Cup (on Friday) was for smaller-capacity cars (including, on this occasion, eleven MG Midget entries) and the Éireann Cup (on Saturday) was for over 1,500cc. Syd Enever was riding mechanic to Harold Parker, and Alec Hounslow to Dick Watney (these facts confirmed by Syd in a 1959 paper about the much later EX181). Syd was soaked in fuel during a pit-stop in the race and recalled that he had to strip off his overalls whilst the car returned to the fray, simply in order to dry his clothes and try to ease his burns. The overall winner of the Grand Prix was decided by the driver who completed the 300-mile race distance from either the Saorstát Cup or Éireann Cup races in the fastest time over the two days. The Team Prize was won by Goldie Gardner whilst Norman Black, driving one of the Earl of March team cars, won both the Saorstát Cup and the whole Grand Prix on handicaps, with his winning average of 64.76mph. As the table shows, nine of the eleven Midgets finished. As with the Double-Twelve, the Earl of March wrote to Syd on June 9th 1931: *'This is just a quick line to put down in writing my thanks and appreciation for all you did in connection with the Dublin race... a little later on I am going to arrange that we have a party...'* Grateful acknowledgement goes from the author to C-Type expert Cathelijne Spoelstra for help with the details; she confirms that Frankie Tayler was riding mechanic to Norman Black; this was certainly stated as being so within an obituary tribute to Tayler in the July 1934 issue of *The MG Magazine*.

The MG team prepares to set off in their C-Type Midgets to catch the ferry from Liverpool from the Market Square in Abingdon in August 1931, ahead of the Ulster TT. Left to right, driving is Cecil Cousins, then in Car No. 42 (Norman Black's race winning car, C0253), is Frankie Tayler, then in Car. No. 43 is Alec Hounslow and last in No. 41 is Syd Enever accompanied by 'Jock' Little. The view of the square ninety years later is not greatly different. (Enever Archive)

| \multicolumn{6}{c}{**1931 ROYAL AUTOMOBILE CLUB INTERNATIONAL TOURIST TROPHY RACE**} |
| \multicolumn{6}{c}{**AUGUST 1931: CLASS 'H' MG MIDGETS**} |

Race No.	Car (S)=super charged	Entrant	Driver (1)	Driver (2)	Result
40	MG Midget (S)	S. A. Crabtree	S. A. Crabtree	C .J. P. Dodson	3rd (67.62 mph)
41	MG Midget (S)		H. D. Parker	Earl of March	7th (66.92 mph)
42	MG Midget (S)	The Earl of March	N. (Norman) Black	G. K. Cox	1st (67.90 mph)
43	MG Midget (S)		C. W. Fiennes	–	DNF (23 laps)
44	MG Midget (S)		Major A. T. G. Gardner	–	DNF (9 laps)
45	MG Midget (S)	Major A. T. G. Gardner	R. T. Horton	–	DNF (13 laps)
46	MG Midget (S)		R. R. Jackson	–	10th (65.85 mph)
47	MG Midget (S)	S. W. B. Hailwood	Stanley. W. B. Hailwood	–	DNF (11 laps)
48	MG Midget (S)	E. R. Hall	E. R. Hall	H. A. Smith	DNF (6 laps)
49	MG Midget (S)	F. S. Barnes	Frank Stanley Barnes	–	Did Not Start
50	MG Midget	F. M. Montgomery	F. M. Montgomery	R. G. J. Nash	16th (62.41 mph)
51	MG Midget (S)	G (George) Bradstock	H. C. Hamilton	G. K. Cox	DNF (19 laps)
52	MG Midget (S)	J. G. Reece	Dan Higgin (car reg. 'KF 5114')	–	DNF (4 laps)

Footnotes: The race took place on Saturday August 22nd 1931 at the Ards Circuit, Belfast; press reports suggest that conditions were wet. The Earl of March's team was managed again by Cecil Cousins; riding mechanics from the factory were Syd Enever, Alec Hounslow and Frankie Tayler (the latter was riding mechanic for Norman Black) and Jock Little was also part of the group that set off from Abingdon's Market Square. Jack Crook recalled in an interview twenty years later that he was mechanic for E. R. Hall. Note that all but one of the cars in the table was now supercharged – a consequence in part of the ever-tougher battle against strong competitors and the dead hand of the handicapper. 'Hammy' Hamilton in Car No. 51 set a new class record for the circuit. In their subsequent report, *Motorsport* magazine wrote: '*The MG Car Company have added yet another trophy to their bag, and the supercharged model has proved itself beyond all doubt a very wonderful little motorcar, and we heartily congratulate them and Norman Black on their performance, and also the R.A.C., and their willing helpers on their marvellous organisation, and on the cheerful and helpful manner in which it was used to assist competitors and spectators alike to get the best out of the race.*' The Earl of March wrote again to Syd on August 28th 1931, saying that '*such a truly marvellous result was only made possible by the very hard work which you, and the others, carried out in such splendid style.*'

CHAPTER FOUR: MAGIC MIDGETS AND MAGNETTES

	OCTOBER 1931 BRDC 'BROOKLANDS 500'				
Race No.	Car (S)=super charged	Entrant	Driver (1)	Driver (2)	Result
1	MG Midget	J.H.P. Clover	J.H.P. Clover	O.H.J. (Oliver) Bertram	DNF (39 laps)
7	MG Midget (S)	The Earl of March	The Earl of March	-	DNF (38 laps)
8	MG Midget (S)	The Earl of March	Harold D. Parker	G.K. Cox	DNF – retired (25 laps)
9	MG Midget (S)	The Earl of March	Norman Black	C.W. Fiennes	DNF – blown gasket (11 laps)
10	MG Midget (S)	Major A. T. G. Gardner	Major A. T. G. Gardner	J.R. Jeffress	DNF (60 laps)
11	MG Midget (S)	Major A. T. G. Gardner	R. R. (Robin) Jackson	W.D. Phillips	DNS
12	MG Midget (S)	Major A. T. G. Gardner	R. T. Horton	-	DNS
14	MG Midget (S)	Dan Higgin	Dan Higgin	-	DNF – engine (4 laps)
15	MG Midget (S)	E. R. Hall	E. R. Hall	-	3rd overall and 1st Class 'H'
16	MG Midget (S)	S. A. ('Stan') Crabtree	S. Hailwood	S.A. Crabtree	5th overall and 2nd in Class 'H'
17	MG Midget (S)	J.A. Palmes (Jarvis of Wimbledon	G.E.T. Eyston	P.M. Walters	Still running but unclassified – still eligible for Team Prize

Footnotes: The race took place on Saturday October 3rd 1931 at Brooklands; 'BRDC' is of course the 'British Racing Drivers' Club'. There were eleven MGs in total, plus five supercharged Austin Sevens and a single supercharged special. As Wilson McComb has written, the handicappers had set the 750cc class an impossible target of 93.97mph; Eddie Hall in No. 15 came close with a remarkable 92.17mph overall, in 5hr. 50min. 10sec, gaining himself third prize and for MG, along with Nos 16 and 17, the Team Prize, the RAC Cup and £75. The overall race winner was a 6.6-litre Bentley which achieved an average of 118.39mph over the 500 miles – above the 750cc MGs, but not that far. As reported by *Motorsport* in their November 1931 issue: *'The third car home was the super-charged 750 c.c. MG Midget belonging to E. R. Hall, who drove the entire distance single-handed and averaged over 92 mph, a feat which would have been considered impossible, but a short time ago, for a car of this size under any conditions.... MGs were out in force with an entry of no fewer than three complete teams among their eleven entries. These were entered by the Earl of March, Major Gardner, and E. R. Hall, but Gardner's team was depleted by R. R. Jackson's car being a non-starter.'* The author could find no evidence of a corresponding thank-you letter to Syd from the Earl of March afterwards; we know from contemporary photos that Syd was there, also reinforced by the note of the subsequent road collision at Clifton Hampden on Monday October 5th on the way back to Abingdon (see separate panel), but on this occasion the Earl clearly had rather less to celebrate after the race. Nevertheless, the dominance of MG in the Brooklands 500 was not a one-year fluke; a year later (September 24th 1932) first place went to R. T. Horton and J. H. Bartlett, with a speed of 96.29mph over a time of 5hr. 42min. 13 secs., and the year after that (September 16th 1933) the honours went to Eddie Hall again, but in a Magnette at 106.53mph rather than a Midget. Grateful acknowledgement goes from the author again to C-Type expert Cathelijne Spoelstra.

The Norman Black MG C-Type Midget in Ulster in August 1931; left to right can be seen Syd Enever (in waistcoat), Frankie Tayler (Black's race mechanic) at the wheel, and next to him Alec Hounslow. Team Manager Cec Cousins in the dark suit towers over everyone; finally is Jock Little. (Enever Archive)

Norman Black proudly wears the winner's garland, with his mechanic Frankie Tayler on his left, while the entrant for the car, the Earl of March (with arms folded) looks on. Motorsport wrote: 'The M.G. Car Company have added yet another trophy to their bag, and the Supercharged model has proved Itself beyond all doubt a very wonderful little motorcar, and we heartily congratulate them and Norman Black on their performance.' (Enever Archive)

As ever, Cecil Kimber was quick to promote the latest MG sporting successes; here the advertisement celebrates an admirable 'hat trick' – The Brooklands Double Twelve, Irish Grand Prix and the Ulster Tourist Trophy. Syd was an MG mechanic for all three. (Dave Robinson)

The Earl of March accompanied by Leslie Callingham (of Shell-Mex at the time) and Syd Enever as race mechanic. The event is the October 3rd 1931 Brooklands 500. The car succumbed to a big-end failure after 39 laps. In the same race, Eddie Hall finished third overall in his MG Midget, behind much the larger Bentley and Talbot in second; it was truly 'the luck of the game'. (Enever Archive)

October 5th 1931 – Syd Enever Crashes Lord March's C-Type...

There was a slight problem with the Earl of March's Midget after Brooklands in early October 1931, an unfortunate incident being recorded in a note from Syd dated October 9th 1931 to John Temple (MG's Competitions Manager). Headed *'Report of accident to Earl of March's Car Number C.0.251'* the note continues: *'On the road between Clifton Hampden and Abingdon on 6pm on October 5th 1931 five of our Cars were returning from Brooklands in line. The fourth car, the one damaged, was being towed, A. Kemp steering the car over-run and broke the tow rope. The rope being wound round the front brake cable, pulled the car up dead. S. Enever driving the car behind (Mr Crabtree's) failed to pull up quick enough and crashed into the tail of the car, smashing in the rear panels. Mr. Cannell will send you report of damage to body.'* Of those named in the note, Alfred Kemp worked alongside Syd in the Experimental section. A hand-written pencilled comment has been added to the note *'write March'* which suggests that someone had the unenviable task of reporting what had ensued to his Lordship...

The Magic Midget – EX127

With the task achieved of breaching the 100mph barrier with a 750cc engine, the next target was 120mph – the magical 'two miles a minute'; with EX120 destroyed, there was clearly a need for a new car, and as speeds got ever higher, aerodynamic efficiency became more critical. The design was started under the new code 'EX127', a car eventually to become better known as the 'Magic Midget'. Jack Daniels in his capacity as assistant draughtsman was involved: *'I was the chassis man on EX127 and did all the drawings for it. EX127 had an inclined drive line, at an angle of seven degrees in plan to allow it to become a single-seater, with a full "Charles" type chassis.'* As a result, the driver sat really low in the chassis, and in order to mate with the angled prop-shaft, both the differential and crown wheel were specially made.

The overall shape of EX127 was largely credited to Reg Jackson, who took it upon himself to build a scale model at home – ostensibly a marriage of Kaye Don's 'Silver Bullet' for the nose (which also gained a neat octagonal grille aperture), the centre section inspired by Campbell's 'Bluebird' and the tail resembling Sir Henry Seagrave's 'Golden Arrow'; evidently Kimber was impressed because Jackson's model was scaled up for the real thing. Although Syd Enever's input is seldom explicitly credited, we know from his role in the Experimental Shop that he and his small team would

CHAPTER FOUR: MAGIC MIDGETS AND MAGNETTES

The D-Type Midget was the first of the 'new generation' of MGs with the new chassis; it was a four-seater and the rear passengers were seated right above the back axle. (Author Archive)

Captain George Eyston in his asbestos race suit – something which became his trademark after the unfortunate incident with EX120 described earlier. At the time, few of the ancillary risks of using asbestos were known. (Jackson family)

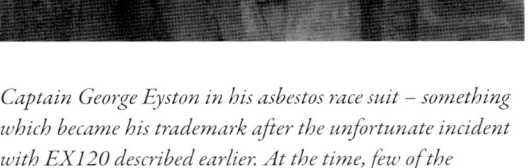

George Eyston in EX127, with Bert Denly at left, at Montlhéry. (Enever Archive)

In later years, here we see Syd, Reg Jackson and Alec Hounslow at a dinner function, with Alec's then partner, Gladys. (Enever Archive)

A contemporary cigarette card captioned as the 'MG Magic Midget'. (Author Archive)

have been involved in the engine at least, even though both Eyston and his trusted colleague Ernest Eldridge took key roles in this aspect too.

In October 1931, with Eyston recuperating from his injuries sustained in conjunction with EX120's demise, Ernest Eldridge (wearing a lounge suit and eschewing goggles) took the new EX127 to Montlhéry but due to a burst radiator (a non-MG part), the maximum speed achieved on October 17th was 110.28mph. By late December, Eyston was sufficiently recovered to drive – although he donned an asbestos suit to be on the safe side; back at Montlhéry again he raised the bar with four records at speeds up to 114.77 mph on December 22nd 1931. Then there was an alarming development with the record-breaking rule-makers; henceforth records would only be accepted as the average of a pair of runs in opposite directions; this ruled out the use of Montlhéry, not prepared to accommodate the exclusive closure of their track for the return run, and Eyston found that Brooklands was closed over the winter for maintenance.

Kimber then alighted on the idea of using the Pendine Sands in South Wales (best known in motoring circles for being the place where Parry Thomas lost his life) and so it was that the party from Abingdon convened there at the end of January 1932; there were problems on February 8th, in front of movie cameramen and the rest of the press, with the electric timing equipment (salt water got into the cables laid over the sand). Eyston made another run, timed by stop-watch at 122 mph, but frustratingly the tracer-pen in the RAC equipment had run out of ink. By the time that this fault had been fixed, the tide was on the turn, and so with his third and final attempt, Eyston had to make do with 116.48mph in one direction and 117.30 on the return leg.

69

Captain Goldie Gardner was one of the many prominent customers for an MG C-Type Midget; here he collects his car – 'C0256' - from Abingdon for the 1932 season. Note how almost ridiculously tall he appears alongside the tiny MG Midget, appropriately named. (Jackson family)

The D and F Type MGs

In the wake of the work on a new chassis frame, MG introduced new models – the D-Type Midget (a four-seater model with the M-Type engine) and, using the six-cylinder Wolseley-designed version of the same basic engine in the F-Type, which saw the use of the 'Magna' name for the first time. A number of these received special bodywork, notably from Jarvis of Wimbledon (the company behind Eyston and the EX120); gradually MG began to gravitate towards a range of smaller, lighter models whilst the old MG Six slowly faded into the background.

> ### Alec Hounslow
>
> Another of the key contemporaries of Syd and Jacko was Oxford-born **Alec Leslie Hounslow** (April 11th 1911 – October 17th 1976). He started as a 'tea boy' at Morris Garages in April 1925, (his nickname, 'The Boy' stayed with him amongst his older friends – although the younger staff would never have dared call him that). He joined the racing department in 1931, often serving as riding mechanic – most memorably for Nuvolari who won the 1933 TT. In 1935 he moved briefly to join Adrian Squire (a former MG colleague) at Squire Cars of Remenham; after that business folded he worked as a race mechanic for celebrated band leader and entrepreneur Billy Cotton and Arthur Dobson as a racing mechanic. In the Second World War, Hounslow served in the RAF as a Flight Sergeant, and later on Air Sea Rescue work.
>
> After the War he re-joined MG, initially as a service tester, but before long found his perfect niche in the Development Shop, working closely with Syd and the team. His second marriage in 1934 to Margaret brought five children; his relationship with his spouse seems to have been fractious and they separated in the 1960s.
>
> Alec Hounslow enjoyed his whiskey and seemed to have a remarkable capacity for its consumption; in a similar manner he enjoyed his cigarettes, and his daughter June told the author that her father was known by some of his colleagues as 'dog-end Hounslow' on account of his habit of smoking his unfiltered cigarettes until they were almost gone, balanced on his lips. Alec, June and her sisters often met up with 'Uncle Syd', as well as Henry Stone and Tom Haig, often on Sunday afternoons at *The Perch* in Binsey Lane in Binsey, near Port Meadow, Oxford. Roger Enever remembers these convivial occasions as well.
>
> Hounslow was responsible for the unusual transverse carburettor installation on the MGB GT V8, an answer to a problem which defied theory and had eluded everybody else, although it was the kind of lateral thinking that both he and Syd (who had just retired) were known for. Contrary to the familiar sad model for some of his peers, retirement appears to have offered little disappointment; The Hounslow family told the author that Alec was kept busy tinkering in his workshop and fixing cars for friends. He died from lung cancer at the age of 65 in Wallingford in October 1976.

In addition to the aforementioned Brooklands Double-Twelve of May 1931, the RIAC Irish Grand Prix (with the Saorstát Cup) in June and the Ulster TT in August, the busy 1931 calendar featured other outings for the C-Types, such as the Shelsley Walsh Hill Climb (July 11th), the Light car Club Relay Race at Brooklands (July 25th) and the BRDC 500-mile race at Brooklands again on October 3rd; suffice to say that the MG Midgets did well in all of these events and more besides, even if racing success did not necessarily contribute enormously to mass production sales in a time of national recession. Syd and Jacko were at the heart of this activity, but the details of which events they took part are almost inevitably rather sketchy, as their details were seldom recorded with the same diligence as those of the entrants and the drivers.

Racing continued through 1932, 33 and beyond – for a while it seemed that MG was almost unassailable, although of course the truth was that sometimes a degree of driver talent, sheer luck and the numbers of entries supported the undoubted excellence of the basic offering. In the background, however, sales were not really reflective of the circuit successes, and of course pure race cars were somewhat unsuitable (and too expensive) for road use, especially in a time of market depression. This half-decade was unquestionably one of the busiest in MG's history; a plethora of road and race models ensured that there was seldom a quiet period for Syd and his colleagues on the development side.

New Midgets and Magnettes – From J To K

In the summer of 1932, Cecil Cousins came down with appendicitis and was hospitalised; one almost immediate consequence of this was that Syd Enever was made Foreman of the Experimental Department (with Charles as the Chief Designer and Engineer); Cousins, when he returned, was made Technical Superintendent. In this period, therefore, Syd's role and seniority advanced and set him almost on a par with his friend Jacko; the two became almost a double act – where one went, the other was seldom far behind.

Meanwhile, one of the great creations of the MG Car Company arrived (in August 1932), the sublime J2 Midget – an evolution of the C-Type via the 1931 D-Type but with many of the design features which would become classic hallmarks of the small MG sports car line for the next couple of decades. Alongside the J1, J3 and J4, these models further advanced the pedigree of MG and most of the design credit should be shared by Hubert Charles and Syd as his talented protégée.

Not content with a revamp of the smaller model, Cecil Kimber also oversaw evolution of the short-lived F-Type Magna into the K-Type Magnette (the diminutive term a consequence in part of a reduction in capacity of the straight-six engine from 1,272 to 1,087cc); part of the thinking was to chase records and race victories in the 1,100cc class because the MG Midget had become so ubiquitous in the 750cc class that it was almost handicapped out of contention.

The basic components of the Magnette engine were largely the same as those in the Midget – just more of them! In his book 'Works MGs', Mike Allison dedicates a section to development of the small six-cylinder engine; in essence it seems that cooling deficiencies of

Gardner participated in his new car in Ulster's August 20th 1932 TT race; his car, No. 32, crashed seriously at Glen Hill (the car somersaulted three times, and his riding passenger, local man Oscar Paterson from Belfast, was thrown onto the road). Gardner was hospitalised for four months; he decided to refocus his energy towards record-breaking, acquiring the offset-drivetrain MG K3 Magnette of Ron Horton. (Jackson family)

The Tourist Trophy Race was one of the highlights of the late summer calendar, and by the early thirties was dominated by the buzz of MG Midgets. Syd went there as part of the MG mechanic team on at least two occasions. Two snapshots from Syd's albums of the MG convoy en route to the 1932 Ulster TT (held on August 2th 1932), taken at a stop in Lancaster. Thanks to Cathelijne Spoelstra it has been possible to identify the MG F1 Magna RX 9618 as a Vanden Plas bodied 2/4 seater (Chassis Number F0280) which was built in November 1931 for race driver Eddie Hall. RX 9540 also belonged to Eddie Hall and was a green MG F1 Magna Salonette, Chassis Number F0380, similarly built in November 1931. Cathelijne comments: 'safely tucked up on top of the transporter must have been the racing C-Type, C0268; Eddie Hall took his own Bentley to Ulster'. Standing alongside is Johnny Crook. (Enever Archive)

the four cylinder were exacerbated in the longer six. Work ensued at Abingdon to rectify this and whilst Charles was the leader in this endeavour, we may have little doubt that the inventive mind of Syd – still only 22 years old – contributed to this work.

As a prelude to the famous MG K3 Magnette entries at the 1933 Mille Miglia race, the Abingdon factory built a prototype with an unusual sloping radiator grille which was driven on Italian roads as a reconnoitre exercise. Syd was part of the team responsible for building this car; he recalled fitting the special radiator: *'I did that more or less overnight, and I remember old Kimber got in it and drove it quickly up the Marcham Road and back again, just to try it out before it went overseas'.* Syd did not accompany the MGs to Italy; that fell to his friends 'Jacko' and Alec Hounslow, who accompanied the test car on a five-week trip into Europe.

It is fair to say that the K3 would go on to become a legendary giant-killing high point in MG's pre-war racing history – class victory at the 1933 Mille Miglia and Tazio Nuvolari's outstanding victory at that autumn's TT notable within the K3 lexicon – and its prowess was down to a combination of many factors, makers and drivers included. It is also the case that, as is so often said, 'success has many fathers' and it would be wrong to lay all the credit at Syd's door; he played an important role, doubtless on the engine side in particular, but in lauding his role one should not underplay the important parts played by the likes of 'Jacko', Alec Hounslow and others, not least the drivers who brought the victories.

The Insomnia Crew

The peak period of MG factory racing activity was from 1931 to 1935, with the crescendo probably in 1934; it was not unknown for some of the mechanics to work solidly around the clock for a day and then another day beyond; the gang called themselves 'The Insomnia Crew', the title of an excellent memoir by Henry Stone published in 1983.

Two happy pals: Syd and Johnny (aka Jack) Crook at the 1932 Ulster TT. (Enever Archive)

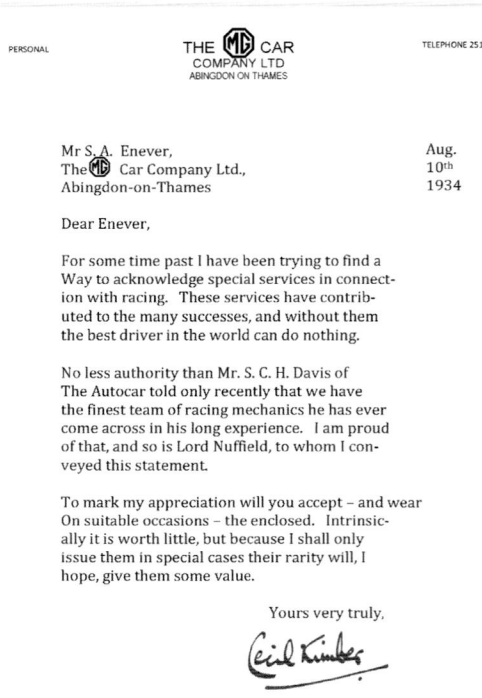

Syd – in suit and tie – sits on one of the 1932 Ulster TT C-Type Midgets. The car (No. 34) is again Eddie Hall's Midget (C0268). Car No. 33 behind was Stan Hailwood's Midget C0269. There were ten of these Midgets in the race. (Enever Archive)

Some time after the events in this section, Cecil Kimber sent this letter of appreciation to Syd for his sterling efforts. (Enever Archive)

CHAPTER FOUR: MAGIC MIDGETS AND MAGNETTES

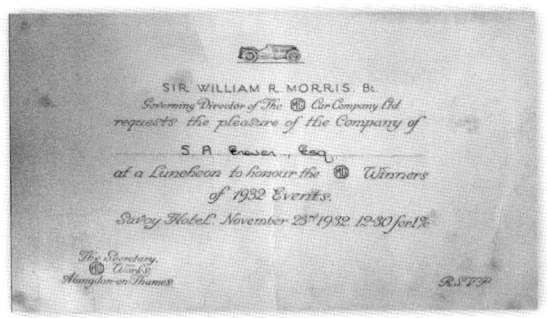

In November 1932, Syd received an invitation from 'Sir William R. Morris, Bt' to attend a celebratory luncheon at London's Savoy Hotel. (Enever Archive)

The J4 Midget was a step towards a more affordable semi-bespoke racing Midget. (Enever Archive)

What Became of EX127?

With the ongoing gentlemanly tit-for-tat between Austin and MG, records were periodically exchanged between the two marques. EX127 appeared at Brooklands in 1932 and achieved the local Class H record at 112.93mph, but it was clear that eking out speed increases from a 750cc engine was no simple matter; sometimes it was the diminutive Bert Denly in the cockpit as he was arguably a better fit. In December Eyston returned to a freezing Montlhéry and finally achieved the 120mph originally sought. Further records fell in 1933 and the bodywork was modified, with a turret roof and slimmer profile which meant that Bert Denly was passed the cockpit duties. Denly was behind the wheel again at Montlhéry on October 19th 1933, taking six International Class H records up to 128.62mph; MG's advert reported that the Magic Midget was 'again pre-eminent'

Then, in May 1934, Kimber arranged the sale of EX127 to a German racer and MG dealer, Bobby Kohlrausch; within weeks the new owner had his charge out at the Avus on May 27th 1934; he was easily the fastest in his class, but the driving position – with his legs higher than his seat – led to uncomfortable cramps and he had to withdraw. The issue was that Kohlrausch was considerably smaller in stature than Eyston, and thus the layout was no longer suitable even when adjusted as far as practicable.

EX127 was therefore returned to Abingdon and whilst some versions of the story have it that the car was rebodied, Michael Allison established that the truth was more prosaic; Kohlrausch commissioned a second car which was an amalgamation of P-Type body, J4-style body and one of the new three-bearing Q-Type engines. This process involved a new number – EX154 (see table extract below). With the cars painted in the white German racing colours, Kohlrausch took EX127 to Gyón in Hungary on May 18th 1935, where he took the 750c.c. records to 130.89mph for the flying kilometre and 130.51mph over the flying mile. Thus Kohlrausch now had a brace of very fast, very special 750cc MGs – EX127 and EX154. A contemporary MG Car Company advert proclaimed the fact that with 'the Magic Midget' in the hands of Kohlrausch, this was *'the first time a car of 750cc has exceeded 130mph'*.

Next, Kohlrausch had a cylinder head specially cast in bronze; back to Abingdon came the cars, accompanied by Kohlrausch's mechanic Artur Baldt, and then Jacko and Syd set to work to develop two parallel set-ups with differently-sized Zoller superchargers – the bronze head was intended to help cope with higher heat from the high-pressures involved. The two cars were amalgamated as one – under the later EX number, partly Allison supposes to hide the work from Cowley accountants. The car which emerged bore some resemblance to the R Type, and the engine was effectively an R Type unit with the bronze cylinder head.

In *Maintaining the Breed*, John Thornley explained what happened in the effort to meet Kohlrausch's ambitions: *'It was on one Sunday morning that the final tests were to be and it was with elation and no little surprise that Jackson, Enever and Baldt saw the indicator on the test bed run up to 145bhp when the taps were turned on. This indication was only momentary as 'everything*

This is the pre-production MG K3 Magnette which Syd Enever helped to build; he specifically recalled the sloping nose that was unique to this prototype. He was not destined to be part of the actual race entourage. (Enever Archive)

The K3 Mille Miglia team lined up for a photo; from left to right we see Count 'Johnny' Lurani at the wheel of JB1475, Bentley racer Sir Henry Ralph Stanley 'Tim' Birkin, 3rd Baronet, in JB1474 (the mechanic behind it is 'Nobby' Marney) and an empty JB1472 (behind which, with his characteristic lock of hair, is 'Jacko'). It was JB1472 which would go on to secure a class victory to the amazement of the excited Italian spectators and motoring press alike. (Jackson family)

This is MG K3 '020' fitted with a new boat-tailed body during 1934 (Enever Archive)

then lit up' and the motor banged and spat and had to be shut down. But the power was there – they had all three seen it and Baldt, particularly, would be satisfied with nothing less. It remained to find out how to sustain it.'

'With the head off, a detailed examination of valves and plugs was made and Enever came to the conclusion that the cooling of the exhaust valves had to be improved. The only simple way to do this was to extend the bronze valve guides to embrace the stem right up to the valve head, but it was Sunday, no bronze bar was available, and Baldt was due to return to Germany next day. The method adopted was crude but effective; the bronze guides were pressed out of the head, sawn in two, and short lengths of cast iron guide were then interposed as packing pieces. Next time up, the engine recorded, and held 146 brake horse power; engine speed was 7,500 rpm. and the blower pressure 39 lb! The noise set all Abingdon by the ears. Back in Germany, the engine was installed, the original single-seater body was fitted and on the Frankfurt Autobahn, Kohlrausch covered the flying mile at 140.6 mph'

This was on October 10th 1936 – by which time, as we shall see later, things were every different at Abingdon. Returning to Thornley's account: 'This was almost the end of the story of this astonishing vehicle, but in the years immediately preceding the war, Bobby parted with it to Mercedes-Benz. Whether this was done voluntarily or under Nazi duress we shall never know, but one smiles wryly when one pictures the mystification of the German designers when they stripped the engine and the valve guides pressed out in three separate little bits!'

Once again Syd and Jacko's lateral thinking had served them and MG well.

It has sometimes been suggested that the sale of EX127, and other exploits with EX135, caused something of a rift with George Eyston, although as a gentleman, such disagreements if true would not have been made public; it may also be born in mind that with the closure of the racing shop, and disbanding of many of its key members, circumstances at Abingdon were changing; meanwhile the great man was at this stage engaged in chasing his ultimate land speed record goals with his 'Speed of The Wind'. It would be another Captain who would next pick up MG's record-breaking exploits.

EX127   Single seat racing car [93 drawings for Eyston's second record breaking car – the 'Magic Midget' which achieved 120 m.p.h. from less than 750 c.c. Bobby Kohlrausch (see also EX154) later achieved over 140 m.p.h. EX127 was eventually reworked into EX154]

EX154   Special car for R. Kohlrausch esq.; specification as follows: Chassis No. EX154; Engine No. 2443A; P-type chassis frame; P-type front axle; P-type rear axle; Q-type brake drums; J4 torque-reaction cables; Straight-cut gears to back axle; rear axle nose-piece through-bolted with tubular distance pieces; J4 body, petrol tank and spare wheel carrier; J2 cycle type wings and P-type wing stays; three inch diameter prop-shaft balanced to 8,000 r.p.m. (200 series joints, four and a half inch O/D flanges, five sixteenth inch bolts on a three and 61/64 inch P.C.D., thirty six and 1/16 inch long); Q-type engine with pre-selector box and Zoller supercharger mounted between front dumb irons; P-type steering cam gears; special road wheels and tyres supplied by Mr. Kohlrausch. [72 drawings for the Bobby Kohlrausch car, eventually amalgamated with some parts from EX127. EX154 was later believed destroyed in Germany.]

MG R-Type: The All-Independent MG Sports Car ('EX147')

The ultimate incarnation of the classic MG Midget was the furiously fast but skittering lightweight Q-Type, which saw the Morris Minor-based engine brought to its apogee; the challenge for many drivers was taming the miniature beast on the track. Knowing the limitations of the Midget's front suspension, H. N. Charles and Syd worked on a more sophisticated set up but it was swiftly obvious that the flexibility of the whole chassis, often promulgated by armchair pundits as a virtue, was an obstacle to an efficient and more sophisticated independent front end.

Wilson McComb wrote in 'The Story of the MG Sports Car' (Dent, 1972) that *"some typically suck-it-and-see experiments [were] carried out at Abingdon by Jackson and Enever; they had sawn the rear end off a J2 chassis and fitted it with a home-brewed suspension using fabricated wishbones and old axle-shafts as torsion bars. Tests on Kimber's private circuit within the factory grounds met with Kimber's approval, and a similar arrangement was evolved for the front end."* This further step also worked, although rather than by theory, it was a case of turning down the axle shafts in a lathe *"until they looked right."*

The rudimentary efforts by 'Jacko' and Syd were progressive but inadequate; as Jackson told Mike Allison: *"HN [Charles] took [Syd] under his wing; he was always thinking things out from first principles... I don't think 'HN' ever used ideas without reducing them to first principles and that's probably where Syd got it from".* Charles brought with him wisdom and experience from his WWI aircraft experience, and as he said to author Wilson McComb, *"the heavy things must stand still"* meaning, fundamentally, rigidity of the engine mounting and by extension the frame on which the moving parts were mounted. It was with this in mind that Charles decided to create as stiff a chassis as possible, and came up with what was at the time a radical departure, with a rigid but light weight wishbone structure which he, Jack Daniels and Syd worked on together. Fabrication was by Frank Stevens, the man who had worked on Old Number One's chassis, barely a decade earlier.

According to Jack Daniels, Bill Renwick (see side panel) arrived in the midst of this work, but Daniels adds that work on what became the MG R-Type was already under way – but we know from his named joint patents that Syd was a key participant in this work.

The engine choice for the new model was never in much doubt; it was essentially an improved version of the Q-Type's unit, a Zoller supercharger helping deliver power of up to 110 bhp at a sizzling 7,200 rpm (although the Zoller unit gained a reputation for a slightly alarming wear rate in heavy race use).

The K3 Magnette K3002 driven by 'Tim' Birkin (with Rubin acting as riding mechanic) during the 1933 Mille Miglia. Birkin notably acted as 'hare to the hounds', driving his car in a way that drew out the local Maserati opposition even though it meant that Birkin did not finish; the classic hallmark of a great sportsman, driving for the spirit of his team even though he would not get to drive into the square at the end of the race alongside his team mates in their cars. (Enever Archive)

SYD ENEVER

Syd (looking smart, third from left) and his Experimental Shop crew at Abingdon. Fifth from left is Johnny Crook. (Enever Archive)

The sleek boat-tailed rear with integral fuel tank transformed the formerly stubby back end of the K3. (Enever Archive)

Transmission was the ENV 75 pre-selector unit already seen on the Q-Type. The light weight, alloy single seater bodyshell – a 'monoposto' in the terminology of the day – made it abundantly clear that the R Type was about as far from a luggage carrying and passenger-friendly sports car as could be imagined; Kimber was going out on a limb, and he took space in the motoring sports press to seek support for his proposed monoposto Midgets and a promised (but, as we shall see, never delivered) Magnette equivalent.

Ten R-Types were built, with the intention to follow with further batches, and these were sold to specially selected customers, among them Eyston and Campbell. The new model was unveiled on April 25th 1935 and had its race debut a fortnight later at Brooklands on May 6th 1935, with six R-Types taking part. Sadly this was not the most auspicious start; only one car finished, and that one was in sixth place. Drivers complained that the novel suspension demonstrated peculiar characteristics on the track, but the MG design team had plans to address this. Unfortunately, as we shall shortly see, they never got the opportunity to put these into practice.

Extract from *The MG Magazine* of March 1935

MG Magazine of March 1935 carried the following statement:

'As in the past, any MG's that race will be a standard product that anyone can purchase, except for modifications their respective owners subsequently may have carried out. Both the existing 'Q' Type Midget and the 'K3' Magnette, which have been so successful during the past season, will be considerably modified and improved, and instead of being produced as a two-seater road-racing model, as for the 24-Hours Race at Le Mans, will appear with monoposto or single-seater bodies. At this juncture it is not considered advisable to release any further information, but provisional orders will be accepted for delivery in strict rotation commencing April of:
- MG Monoposto Midget 750 c.c. approximate price £600
- MG Monoposto Magnette 1,100 c.c. approximate price £950

Needless to say, they are being designed and produced worthily to maintain the great reputation MG's have already established'

The reference here is clearly to the 'R' Type Midget and the proposed (possibly 'S' Type – the name is less certain) larger Magnette.

William 'Bill' Renwick

A new sparring partner for Syd Enever, arriving at Abingdon in 1935, was Glasgow-born **William ('Bill') Somerville Renwick** (February 4th 1889 – December 20th 1962), who would eventually work alongside Syd on the MG R-Type, and even shared credit for UK, US and Canadian patents on suspension developments. He had travelled to New York in 1912 as a mechanical engineer, and subsequently served in the Air Force during WWI, then marrying Joan Lesley Bayly in Chelsea on July 31st 1918, before the end of the war. Renwick worked briefly for Enfield-Allday, a short-lived car maker in Sparkfield, Birmingham and in due course Renwick – who inherited a substantial sum of money from his father when the latter died in November 1923 – and an Anglo-Italian colleague, Augustus Cesare Bertelli, left that business after it collapsed that same year in order to build their own car, which they called, naturally enough, the 'Renwick and Bertelli' or 'R&B'.

Aston Martin fell into financial difficulties in 1925, and the 'R&B' was conveniently taken on to form the basis of a new model; A C Bertelli remained with Aston-Martin (and his is a name well-known to historians of that great sporting marque) but his partner Renwick, alongside as his business partner as they rebuilt the Aston-Martin business at Feltham, Middlesex, is less well known in Aston Martin circles despite his evident genius; for example, Renwick patented a wedge-shaped cylinder head combustion chamber which was used in the Aston's 1½ litre engine.

Little was known about Renwick's business affairs, even by most of his relatives; family rumours suggested that he had been swindled by his business partner Bertelli, but with little concrete evidence, although it was known by his relatives that, at one time, an apparently impoverished Renwick spent some time riding the railroads in the USA after he left Feltham. Bill Renwick had married Joan and they had two daughters – the first of whom, Anne Barbara Renwick, was born on September 11th 1919; she married Peter Scott and they had eight children, the youngest of whom is Andrew Scott. Research has also thrown up the fact that Renwick fathered an illegitimate child, born in King's Norton in 1926 – on his other daughter's birthday; perhaps it is not too surprising therefore that Mr and Mrs Renwick separated around this time.

In 1929, Bill Renwick inherited shares in the Great Western Railway which must have helped with his finances; even so, in 1932 Aston Martin was sold (Bertelli, whose brother styled many of the cars, remained with the business until 1936. Bill was soon working under H. N. Charles at MG, although remaining at Abingdon for a while, but would eventually leave at some point – although not before registering suspension patents jointly with Syd Enever. By 1939 Bill Renwick was recorded as a 'Motor Engineering Draughtsman', by then living in a house in Marner Crescent, Coventry; his family do not know precisely when he left MG.

When the author interviewed Jack Daniels, Bill Renwick came up in the conversation a number of times, even confirming the family rumours about Renwick having ridden the US railroads. *'Bill was a clever mathematician and joined us late in the development of the 'R' Type'* where, Daniels says, Renwick's analytical skills were used on the

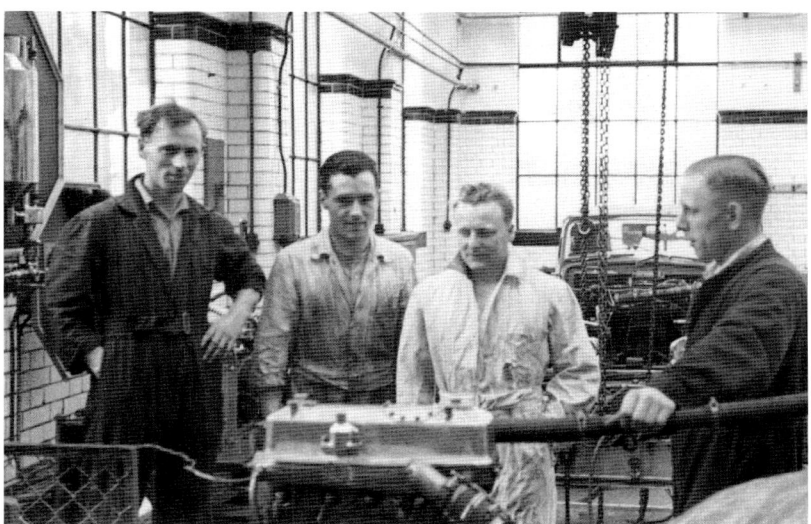

This 1934 photo from Syd's album is captioned by him simply as 'testing Magic Midget engine' – note the existence of what looks like an 'SVW' MG in the background. At the right is Artur Baldt, mechanic to Bobby Kohlrausch. The engine of EX127 had been returned to Abingdon to try to extract more power. This is probably the 'Sunday morning' referred to by John Thornley in his book Maintaining The Breed, *described in the text. (Enever Family)*

Once the career as record breaker of the famous 'Magic Midget' was over, it was updated and rebodied, with a 146bhp 'Q' Type engine and bigger brakes. It was later sold to German Bobby Kohlrausch's. Syd is seen here in the cockpit and Artur Baldt, Kohlrausch's mechanic, is standing at the right. (Enever Archive)

suspension. *'When he had left Aston-Martin, he had disappeared for a while: he told me that he had spent some time as a 'hobo' – travelling across America on trains! He also loved playing poker; he got himself into Frilford Golf Club to play poker, and would get me to pick him up in his car and drop* him there. I would then have the use of his car for the whole weekend, and I just had to pick him up on the Sunday evening after he had spent the whole weekend playing poker!'

Someone else who remembered was Stewart Daniel, whose recollection of H. N. Charles we saw earlier; he described Renwick, his immediate superior at the time, as a 'larger-than-life character'; "by 1935, Bill had obviously seen better days. But he was a superb technician, and he taught me a lot about such things as stressing when applied to motor-car design. Whilst not intolerant of suggestions from a junior designer, he was a master of the gentle put-down. Bill always smoked cigarettes through a long black holder, and was certainly not averse to a few sherbets at one of the local pubs. I was driving him home one night in a P-type and must admit I did slightly misjudge a sharpish corner, involving a certain amount of tyre squeal but no actual departure from the intended route. Bill uttered not a word, but a flurry of sparks on the floor indicated that his cigarette holder had landed there. In fact, he had bitten the end off of it..."

The patents that Bill Renwick and Syd Enever took out for the independent suspension would eventually prove highly beneficial to the British car industry; as Jack Daniels explained to the author: 'We were aware of a patent taken out by Maurice Olley on behalf of General Motors, which talked about the roll centre being raised only marginally above ground level, thus needing the inclusion of an anti-roll medium. Now, with parallel wishbones, the roll centre is at the ground; that was why the 'R' Type had rolled so badly, although we didn't know that at the time. By the time of the Mosquito/Minor, being aware of this patent, we decided to make the torsion bars stronger and avoid using anti-roll bars. Subsequently, we had a request from a number of companies – Singer, Daimler and Standard – who, with independent front suspension vehicles in the field, were having trouble with GM litigation – and they paid us to take Bill Renwick's anti-roll patent and seek legal counsel for an opinion on it, as GM were asking £100 per car against their patent!'

Daniels found himself accompanying the Cowley Patent Agent to brief the engineering lawyer, '... who eventually opined that the Renwick patent predated five out of the six points of the GM patent – the exception being that Renwick's patent failed to define its total function. In the meantime,

The MG R-Type was a distinctive looking sports car, with an aerodynamic front body-colour cowl and, befitting its pure motorsports guise, no mudguards or extraneous lighting equipment. It was technically brilliant, if initially flawed, but it was doomed to an early death. (Dick Knudson)

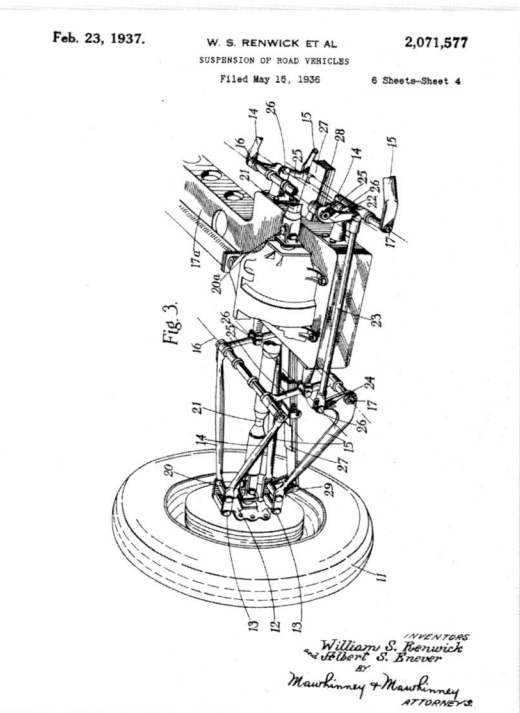

Testament to the undoubted genius of both Syd Enever and Bill Renwick is the existence of a number of patents, of which this example – relating to independent suspension – is just one. (Enever Archive)

CHAPTER FOUR: MAGIC MIDGETS AND MAGNETTES

> *GM had rescinded and cut the claim to two cents per hundred dollars cost of each car, at which everyone was happy! Bill Renwick's work had saved the day in the end.'*
>
> In more recent years, Renwick's grandson Andrew Scott approached Aston Martin and the company's modern-day archivist (Alan Archer), trying to establish what had become of the small fortune his grandfather had obtained when the family estate in Scotland had been sold. Upon further investigation, Archer uncovered the sums of money inherited and also spent; Andrew Scott soon saw the evidence he feared: *'the prosaic truth was that my grandfather had never been swindled; it was simply that he was a great engineer and a poor businessman and had sunk the family fortune in racing fast cars.'*

Lost Letters of the MG Alphabet

The period from 1934 to 1936 would prove to be a turbulent time for MG; for the Abingdon team the great successes in motorsport seemed to be their guarantee of a golden future, and with that in mind the work on ever more exotic cars did not let up. Clearly when one talks of prototypes and concepts, then there is often some degree of uncertainty about the intended model names – hardly a surprise before the eventual baptism. Of the EX147 R-Type, there is little doubt, because as we have seen, that model made its debut, but in the immediate aftermath of that independently-suspended race-car, there were a number of almost-rans.

There was the aforementioned MG Monoposto Magnette, the six-cylinder model intended to sit above the R-Type; logic suggests that this might have become the S-Type, or at a pinch the RB if the R-Type became the RA. The EX Register entry for EX148 covers fittings for the P-type Le Mans car, whilst this is followed by an 'unallocated' number – EX149 – which might conceivably have been originally considered for the new Magnette, but as no car was made, this has to remain nothing more than speculation. Then there was further work on the R-Type itself, intended to address some of the shortcomings of the original design and its tendency to roll in a peculiar manner in corners; this would appear to be EX152, described as *'R.A. experimental chassis (anti-roll experiments)'* which was cancelled.

Next entry was EX150, which is most interesting, as it refers to '3½ -litre independent car' with something referenced as 'banana type rear suspension'. This car was reputedly a large saloon which was nicknamed

A rare family photo of Bill and Joan Renwick, courtesy of his grandson Andrew Scott; for some reason the photo was cut out and mounted on a piece of wood. Due to Bill and Joan's divorce, it seems that quite a few old photos of Bill were destroyed; this is consequently one of few survivors, treasured no doubt by their daughter Anne. (Andrew Scott)

Gardner and his Magnette, K3007, at Brooklands for the September 21st 1935 500; behind in the crowd is the ever-present figure of the Hon. Freddie Clifford (holding a programme). This was the ex-Ronnie Horton Magnette. (Jackson Archive)

The 'Magic Magnette', as it was sometimes known, was also irreverently dubbed 'Humbug' due to its resemblance to the eponymous mint sweet. (Author Archive)

Reid Railton (with glasses, left) in conversation with 'Jacko'. (Enever Archive)

The Nuffield delegation for the 1938 Berlin Motor Show (an event opened on February 18th 1938, amidst great pageantry, by Adolf Hitler) included Syd Enever (at far right) and next to him Stan Westby, Chief Body Draughtsman at Morris Motors. (Enever Archive)

This beautifully finished scale model was useful for wind-tunnel testing as well as fund-raising. (Enever Archive)

the 'Queen Mary'; Syd Enever referred to it in passing in his autobiographical notes, although he sadly did not elaborate. Again the intended model name for this grand vision of Cecil Kimber's is not known; it might well have been an S-Type or a T-Type, but again this is speculation.

Logically if it was to have been a 3.5 litre, then an engine candidate might have been a Wolseley straight six. In period, the top Wolseley was the 25 hp 'Super Six', with a 3,485cc straight six engine. Despite being derived from a Morris-Commercial truck unit, Kimber had persuaded the engine suppliers to achieve miracles in the past, and it had the benefit of having a capacity that was not far off that of the Bentley, with its 3,669cc – and hadn't Kimber once aspired to build the "poor man's Bentley" previously with the ill-fated Tigress?

Stories have circulated that the engine was in fact a special V8 which Kimber had commissioned, whilst others suggested that it was a Blackburne straight six. Daniels drew up the chassis, but could not recall anything about the engine of this saloon; he always thought that the car was intended to be a two litre; *'We built one – and it was scheduled for the 1935 Motor Show at Olympia. The car was built on the lines of the R-Type, but to overcome the problem of the roll angle, Bill Renwick sat down and designed a pre-loaded anti-roll bar – which I drew up for him – which had a torsion bar concentric with a torsion tube, with one hundred pounds pre-loading, so that when the car went into roll mode there was already a force restraining the roll action.'.* Daniels added that the car had what he called a *'classy, typically MG look'*.

The next EX Register entry was EX151, which covered the Morris 10/4 engine as fitted to the real T-Series Midget – the story of which follows shortly.

The End of the First Beginning

On July 1st 1935, Lord Nuffield announced that he was relinquishing his personal hold of MG and Wolseley and intended to pass them to Morris Motors; he still held the two businesses as privately owned companies and he was encouraged to move Wolseley – which supplied many engines across the whole Morris empire – under the same umbrella as Morris Motors, the latter a public company. It certainly did not help that for the first eight months of 1935, the MG Car Company Limited posted a thumping loss of £28,156.

There were undoubtedly tax benefits of changing the corporate arrangements too, and Nuffield had painful memories of past 'super-tax' cases. As with Wolseley, so the argument went, MG should follow suit. On July 10th 1935, a transfer took place of shares in MG from

Morris Industries Ltd. to Morris Motors Ltd. Cecil Kimber now became a director of Morris Motors Ltd. but was now only General Manager at MG, Leonard Lord becoming Managing Director. Even so, Kimber was more than compensated by also being made a director of Morris Motors Limited, at that time the largest car maker in Europe.

Just as MG was sold to the main business, it did not take long for less emollient management to descend upon Abingdon – not least, Leonard Lord himself, by now a powerful figure within the Morris Motors business who had unquestionably boosted that business significantly and so enjoyed the trust and support of his master. The absorption of Abingdon into the Cowley way of doing things led to two immediate casualties – the racing and design shops. It was later recorded by Sir Miles Thomas that Lord took one look at the Abingdon racing workshop and said *'that lot can go for a start.'* Morris historian Peter Seymour believes that the aforementioned loss (which became £30,248 with tax) was the key reason why Lord closed the Racing Shop. Thomas was no more a fan of MG or Kimber than was Lord; the latter also expressed a further view that future MGs needed to be nothing more than *'tarted up Morrises and Wolseleys'.*

Just as this bombshell struck, the Abingdon team had been working on the R-Type, with Charles and his little team proposing improvements which should have cured some of the deficiencies experienced up to then; parts had been made or ordered, and optimism had been high. Reg Jackson told Mike Allison: "*H.N. told me afterwards that he and C.K. had tried to talk to [Len Lord] sensibly about independent suspension, but Lord had said he didn't want any of this suspension nonsense on any of his cars!*" The big 3 ½ Litre saloon mentioned earlier, with its proposed all-independent suspension, also fell victim to this purge; fortunately the elegant bodywork for it, which Kimber had commissioned from Mulliners, would survive largely unscathed for the big MG saloon which Abingdon was permitted to make, the SA, first seen at Olympia in October 1935.

The end of factory racing activities, and the degree of design autonomy which Kimber and MG had hitherto enjoyed, was an enormous blow at Abingdon just as it was a surprise to the rest of the motoring world; MG's reputation as a feisty, furious sports car racing hub was legendary and it seemed incomprehensible that Lord Nuffield would countenance the destruction of this enterprise. *The Autocar* was one of the first publications to report the news: '*The decision that the MG company is to cease racing forthwith has come as quite a shock to a lot of people.*'

However, notwithstanding Kimber's supposed

The chassis of the Gardner record car was derived from the earlier K3 Magnette which had previously been raced by George Eyston. (Enever Archive)

The light weight of the 'Duralumin' aircraft-alloy space frame for the bodywork of the rebodied EX135 record breaker is clearly demonstrated here. Syd Enever – complete with papers - is third from left. (Enever Archive)

financial acumen, motor racing was a very expensive business – and one that was becoming ever more so – and whilst Nuffield enjoyed some of the trophies and the approbation, he had always been somewhat wary of what he saw as the extraneous expenses and wastefulness of motor racing, especially when he was being expected to underwrite the costs of ever more specialised products, far removed from those emerging from his other factories. Kimber's idea of promoting the concept of a highly specialised brace of bespoke Midgets and Magnettes was a risky path to take.

There were also without doubt some internal

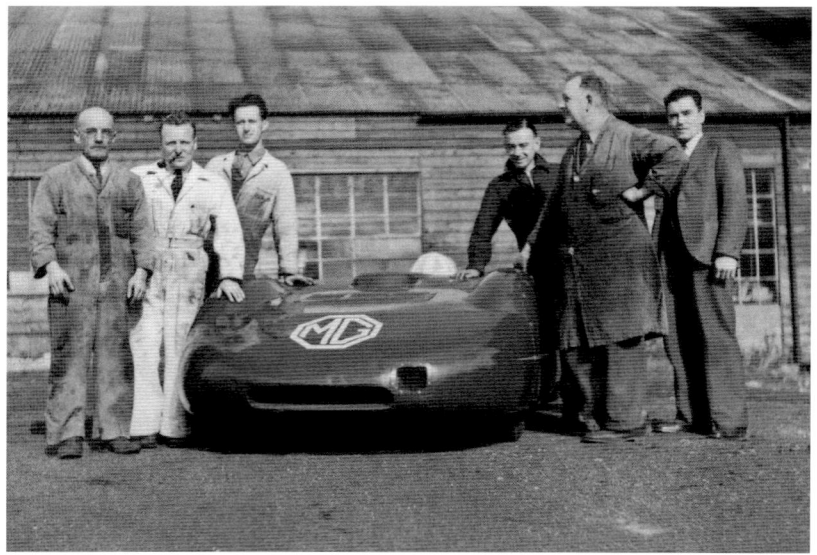

The Gardner record car awaits its great adventures, here parked in the compound of the Abingdon works. Syd stands at far right, while Johnny Crook leans on the car. (Enever Archive)

The wooden body buck for Gardner's record car ready for forming the alloy panelwork. Standing to the right are MG General Manager George 'Pop' Propert, Publicity man George Tuck, Syd Enever and Cecil Cousins. (Enever Archive)

'Jacko' gazes quizzically upwards whilst looking on behind are Leslie Kesterton (SU), Syd and, at right, Robin Jackson, the Brooklands-based race-car specialist who collaborated with the MG team on the Gardner car. The setting is the so-called 'Robinery' – Robin Jackson's workshop at Brooklands. (Enever Archive)

A slightly over-dressed Reg 'Jacko' Jackson with the Gardner car engine during testing at Brooklands in 1938. (Enever Archive)

jealousies – both of Kimber himself, the personal connections he had carefully forged with Lord Nuffield himself, and the special treatment given to MG as a private business owned by Nuffield outside the main Morris Motors company. Furthermore, the overtly sporting nature of MG sports cars had resulted in a sharp increase in insurance costs for the motorist, which made the prospect of ownership less affordable for everyday use. Furthermore there was the recent death of Francis Leonard Cyril 'Frankie' Tayler on May 29th 1934, prior to the second Isle of Man RAC 'Mannin Beg' race. The accident had involved Kaye Don, partnered by Tayler as his mechanic.

Don was tired, having been called from an evening bridge match, when he and Tayler took their MG out on the public highway the night before the race, drove it without lights, and collided with a Buick taxi – with a number of passengers on board – before crashing badly. It might reasonably be speculated that Don had quite possibly 'had a few sherbets' before the fateful events which ensued. Don was hospitalised but recovered, whilst poor Frankie Tayler, aged 27 and only recently married, died in hospital as a consequence of his injuries.

Until then, there had been no publicised fatality involving an MG; with their motto of '*Safety Fast!*' this tragedy was also an obvious embarrassment; when Don was brought to court, public scrutiny was uncomfortable, not least for Lord Nuffield, already developing a reputation as a philanthropist in the medical arena. Nuffield was especially upset at the death of poor Tayler, who had joined Morris Garages in 1923 and moved to Abingdon in 1929; H. N. Charles later said that following that tragic incident, Lord Nuffield no longer wanted to be involved in motor racing. Reg Jackson told Mike Allison that the unpleasant task of calling on Mrs Tayler was delegated to him.

As far as the design function at Abingdon was

concerned, it was cut back to a minimum; H. N. Charles was decamped to run MG design affairs from Cowley, some of the more fortunate staff either followed suit, found other gainful employment at Abingdon, or left; Syd Enever remained at Abingdon as a 'liaison man' (Bill Renwick, who as we saw earlier, had worked alongside Syd on the MG R-Type). H. N. Charles was ripped from the fabric of Abingdon and despatched to Cowley, becoming a fish in a bigger pond; he did not stay there long.

Jack Daniels told the author that the move to Cowley was fairly uneventful from his perspective: *'we just got called in and together given the instruction that we were going to Cowley. There was me and George Cooper, together with Eric Selway, Geoff White and another named Lewis. We just transferred; only George and I stayed together, and the others were dispersed throughout Cowley, although I don't think many lasted there long.'* Their initial task was principally to re-cast the MG range – both sports car and saloon – to utilise more of the prevailing Morris running gear – including the overhead valve engines. There was a section leader called Jack Grimes who, Daniels said, showed no more interest in MG affairs than many of his other Cowley colleagues; provided they stuck to Nuffield components, Jack Daniels on chassis and George Cooper on bodywork were given fairly free rein.

It was a considerable let down after the excitement of the racing exploits culminating in the R-Type and tentative plans for yet more beyond that, but the very fact that Syd was retained (as head of the experimental department), no doubt with the support of Kimber and Cousins, speaks volumes for the esteem in which he was clearly held. Syd's modest Experimental Shop continued to work on more modest testing work, and no doubt supported some work in connection with customer demands for the older models; by maintaining a liaison role, Syd could keep a pragmatic foot in both Abingdon and Cowley camps, and of course support the local technical needs associated with the introduction of new models, such as the T-Series Midget (the 'TA') which arrived in 1936, and the MG VA (EX159), a year later.

In hitherto unseen correspondence of September 1972 with MG author Wilson McComb, Charles shared part of his design philosophy for the TA: *'when I left Abingdon and designed the TA in the Cowley drawing office, I decided to use a four-point rubber block engine mounting to reduce engine noise; it was a good mounting, mathematically designed from the point of view of engine frequencies and so on.'* He also related the detail of a conversation he had with Syd during a visit to Abingdon around 1970: *'Syd pointed out to me that my TA chassis*

Syd (looking very dapper in three-piece suit and trilby hat), with Reg Jackson, Robin Jackson (no relation) at Robin Jackson's premises at Brooklands. By all accounts, the relationship between the MG men (with what they saw as 'their' engine) and 'RR' Jackson (commissioned independently by Gardner) were not always the easiest – perhaps no great surprise. (Enever Archive)

Goldie Gardner discusses engine details for his record car with Syd, who is holding one of the minuscule pistons from the 1,100 cc six-cylinder engine. In the garage behind is the light blue MG WA saloon generously loaned for the trip by Cecil Kimber. (Enever Archive)

frame layout had never been substantially altered in thirty years. He also pointed out to me that the "phased suspension" I designed into the TA had never been altered over the same period apart from adjustments for changes in body weight.'

As far as HN Charles was concerned, when he arrived at Cowley, engineering was in some turmoil as several senior staff under Robert Boyle left, and then when Boyle also departed in turn, A. V. 'Vic' Oak was placed in charge of engineering; one of Oak's early actions was to place Jack Daniels alongside Alec Issigonis, thereby initiating what would become a career-defining union of engineering minds. As we saw earlier, there was only room for one genius in this endeavour, and H. N. Charles left for pastures new in 1938. In the meantime, there was yet another twist with the arrival at Cowley of Gerald Palmer, who told the author how he had been able to meet Cecil Kimber and before long, thanks to that meeting, found himself in Vic Oak's office at Cowley.

Oak was evidently impressed by Palmer's unique 'Deroy' sports car prototype that Palmer brought with him, and Oak offered Palmer – aged just 27 – the chance to take over the MG Drawing Office at Cowley: '*Prior to me there hadn't really been a special MG chief at Cowley – any MG work required was done in the Morris drawing offices. Previously, of course, sports car design had been done by H. N. Charles and Syd Enever at Abingdon, but when it came to saloons, Abingdon were*

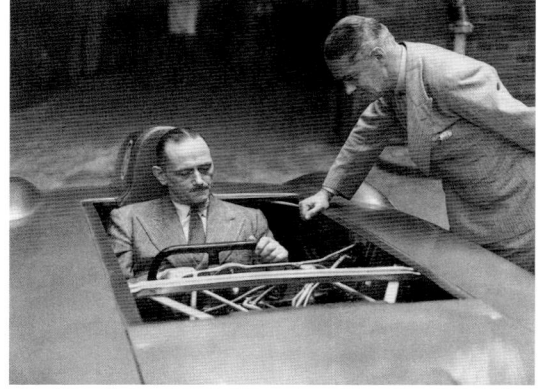

Lord Nuffield looks into the cockpit of EX135 for the cameras as Goldie Gardner grips the wheel at the project's formal debut in July 1938. (Enever Archive)

An overhead view of EX135 with Lord Nuffield and Goldie Gardner, at the University Motors depot. (Enever Archive)

not as experienced as Cowley, which is why they wanted me there.' Among the work that Palmer worked on was the beginnings of a new MG 1 ¼ Litre saloon which in the event would only see the light of day in 1947. In the meantime, Palmer had left Cowley to work at Jowett, but as we shall see, he would return.

Looking back in 1974, Syd himself recalled the events and consequences of the events of 39 years earlier: '*they took the design office away from us, so we had no design office of our own; they put me as 'liaison man' – the liaison engineer with Cowley... so I was working with Cowley all the time: although they were drawing it, we had to have someone between the two.*' The MG VA 1½ Litre of 1937 was viewed by Cecil Kimber as a rival for the upstart SS Cars model of similar capacity; to set it apart from the competition, he was keen to exploit the famous octagonal badge to the maximum.

Speaking in 1974, John Thornley noted of the VA: '*Kimber got hold of it and started to put octagons on it, and in the end, there were 47 octagons on that bloody motor car, at an average cost of 6s 8d each, and it priced the thing completely out of the market...purely on 'MG' [octagonal motifs]; MGs on the door handles... special door handles inside and out, boot handle, you name it; there were MG octagons all over the place...*' On the same occasion, Syd added (speaking to John Thornley): '*...he even wanted octagonal headlamps, do you remember? We kept them on the door handles for quite a while after that...*'

EX135 and Goldie Gardner

With the Racing Shop closed, and with George Eyston somewhat distanced from Abingdon, there was a hiatus in the saga of MG record-breaking. However, where one chapter had ended, a new one was about to open up. Eyston sold EX135 and its two bodies to Ron Horton, who had been part of the Goldie Gardner équipe at the Brooklands Double Twelve and Irish Grand Prix back in 1931. Horton had sold his MG Midget after a lack of success at that time but over the following years had both a Midget and Magnette specially built with unusual offset single-seater bodies, the Magnette being of particular interest and relevance to this story. By all accounts, Horton had very little help from the MG works (Kimber occasionally sold him parts at cost) and so Syd and Jacko would have had no direct involvement, even though they would undoubtedly know about Horton and his unusual cars.

Goldie Gardner later bought the offset Horton car and, **à la** Frankenstein, the best bits were eventually merged within a new body for 1937 to form the first iteration of what would become the 'Gardner Record Car', still bearing the factory code of EX135.

CHAPTER FOUR: MAGIC MIDGETS AND MAGNETTES

Gardner was keen to chase circuit records, which he did at Brooklands, but his zeal for ever higher speeds eventually brought him to Germany and the new roads there.

Lord Nuffield and Gardner with EX135; the semi-matt paint finish at this point was a silver-green metallic (Enever Archive)

Captain Goldie Gardner

Lieutenant-Colonel **Alfred Thomas Goldie Gardner** OBE MC (May 31st 1890 - August 25th 1958) developed an interest in motorcycles when he was at school at Uppingham, aged 14, and asked his father for a loan of thirty shillings, to which his father retorted that it depended upon the quality of his school report. The latter must have been adequate because soon afterwards, Gardner acquired his first motorbike, and gradually traded his way up the ladder to a twin-cylinder 5Hp Rex. In 1910 he left the UK for Colombo in what is now Sri Lanka, and continued to enjoy the pleasures two-wheel motorised transport, even driving through jungle on one occasion. Back home in England in 1913, he visited Brooklands and was especially entranced by the aerobatics he witnessed there.

Although he set out for Burma in 1914, circumstances conspired to send him home again on sick leave, just before War was declared. He joined up almost immediately; in August 1917, his reconnaissance plane was shot down and his right leg and hip were badly damaged, necessitating twenty operations and meaning he was discharged from his post as Major in the British Army as medically unfit for service. In 1924, he acquired what he classed as the first car that satisfied his urge for speed, an Austin Seven Gordon England Special; thereafter he hardly looked back, getting behind the wheel of a succession of ever faster and more potent race cars.

Over the summer of 1930, Gardner got to know Cecil Kimber and began his long association with the MG Car Company Limited; he participated in the 1931 Brooklands Double Twelve described in this chapter, as well as the other races that season. He was back again in 1932, but suffered a serious crash in his C-Type Midget (C0256) at the 1932 TT which meant he was hospitalised and his already injured leg further damaged; he recovered in due course, and was successful again, but the risk and discomfort of his leg probably helped his shift of emphasis away from competitive circuit racing towards one of striving for records, which whilst undoubtedly still a dangerous occupation, requiring a mix of bravery and dogged determination, at least made him free of the risk of crashing on a circuit busy with other race cars. His visit to see Sir Malcolm Campbell undertaking land speed record breaking at Daytona in 1935 only excited his interest further; the previous year he had acquired a special offset-drivetrain MG Magnette from Ronnie Horton – it had had to be modified with a blister in its diminutive bodywork to allow Gardner to squeeze his six-foot-three frame into it.

In 1936, he pursued the first of many records, initially using the circuit at Brooklands; soon he heard about the new roads being built in Germany and made enquiries through Jack Woodhouse, the MG distributor in Köln (Cologne), to see if any of them could be made available for his use in 1937. He was in luck; Woodhouse replied that the Germans would be only too pleased to help, and suggested the new Frankfürt-to-Darmstadt Autobahn; two sessions ensued, in June and October, and it was here the first time that Gardner met Reg 'Jacko' Jackson, Syd's colleague and racing ally.

From the luncheon at University Motors on July 27th 1938, this cartoon pokes gentle fun at Lord Nuffield apologising for arriving a little early: 'it's this new MG I've just delivered to University Motors' his Lordship explains to bemused caterers. (Enever Archive)

How, the following year, his car evolved into the basis of the familiar 'Gardner Record Car' is related in the main text, and his further exploits – most of them now with Syd as well as Jacko on board – follow in subsequent chapters. As we shall see, he returned to the fray after the second world war, but it was obvious he was finding it more of a challenge as he entered his sixties and the speeds involved got ever higher. He was unquestionably a brave man, and inspired much hero-worship; but he was not a technical man himself, and put enormous faith in his engineering team. John Thornley wrote touchingly in *Maintaining The Breed* of the tall English Major, who even the Germans admired (mainly for his manly fortitude and military bearing; before the second world war, it was not unknown for him to disappear with his jackbooted hosts for a spot of revolver practice):

'*...he enjoyed his successes. He enjoyed the preparations for them. But as the time came near to start, he tightened up inside. To the casual observer – even to those with whom he spoke – he preserved an appearance of phlegmatic calm, but those who knew him well were aware that, as the minutes ticked away to the time when he must get* into the car and move off, he suffered the tortures of the damned. "Careful, chaps. The Old Man's on edge" was a not uncommon comment in the équipe at these times. This, indeed, was the measure of his sheer guts. Had there been neither apprehension nor fear his performances would have merited but a tithe of the credit which was accorded to them. About every run there was an element of the unknown. Remember, for instance, that nobody else ever drove this car at 200 m.p.h. and, whereas every precaution was taken which calculation and wind-tunnel tests could devise, there could be no absolute guarantee that the car would not aviate or flip at some critical I speed. With a distinguished military career behind him, a long history of suffering with a leg originally smashed in a war-time flying accident, and subsequently "modified" a little by the crash in the TT [1932], he was, by any standards, a brave man*'.

Somehow alongside all this record breaking, Gardner found the time to marry, on March 10th 1936, an American heiress, Mary Eleanor King Boalt, the nuptials taking place at Daytona Beach, followed by the couple setting up home in the UK, but that relationship was not destined to last; by 1938, when Gardner was at Frankfurt, Eleanor had run off with another racing driver and Gardner's affections shifted to a young woman, Hester Jackson (no relation to either Reg or Robin, and about twenty years younger than Gardner) who was referred to as his fiancée, following an engagement announced in The Times in December 1937. That relationship evidently did not last long either, for in 1940 he married a Yorkshire woman, Una Eagle-Clarke, 24 years his junior and the daughter of a celebrated artist Eleanor Eagle-Clarke, and they went on to have a daughter, Rosalind.

Gardner's injury in 1952, described later, soon lead to his retirement from record breaking and he spent the last six years in relative quiet, illness finally achieving what two world wars, race crashes and the associated injuries had collectively failed to manage. His widow, Una, went on to be Mayor of their adopted home of Eastbourne two times (in 1982 and 1983) and died on January 4th 2008, nearly half a century after her husband, aged 93. For anyone keen to learn more about Gardner's life, the brilliant book by John Mayhead (*Goldie* – published by NMM Publishing in 2023) is highly recommended.

Goldie Gardner began chasing records in his special MG Magnette in 1937; towards the end of that year, following some successes in Germany, he met with Cecil Kimber and discussed his ideas to pursue further records but with a more aerodynamic car, taking cues from the impressive state of the art race cars he had seen in Germany. In *Magic MPH* Gardner wrote: *'I had a long talk with Kim re the possibilities of his being able to produce a really fast 1,100 c.c. record breaker and the proposition was put up to Lord Nuffield. Lord Nuffield's reply was prompt and very much to the point – briefly – it was to the effect that my proposition was a good one, and that he would be only too pleased to authorise the MG Car Co. Ltd., to do as I had suggested. Would I please settle all details directly with Mr. Kimber? As a result, I handed over my "offset" single-seater to the MG Car Co. and the construction of my present record car commenced in their factory'.*

Although Gardner did not in his book explicitly attribute Syd's initial role in this, we know that he was part of the team which built the car into its new form – albeit with specialist bodywork designed by Reid Railton under Jaray patents – and engine construction was entrusted to Robin Jackson, who we saw earlier had formed a racing alliance with Gardner before the latter retired from circuit racing after the major accident at the 1932 Ulster TT, which was described earlier.. However, this was not all, for as Gardner wrote: *'Whilst the remainder of the car was being constructed at Abingdon, I arranged with Kim that Robin Jackson should prepare and test the engine taken from my old car at his Brooklands Depot. Early tests of the engine were satisfactory to a point, but still that intermittent misfire persisted at high revs, and it was therefore decided that MG's should carry out further tests in their Experimental Department at Abingdon. Here the engine was slightly modified (the cause of the misfire having been located as mentioned earlier on), rebuilt, and retested with most satisfactory results'.*

The key point here is that the engine wizard at Abingdon was none other than Syd Enever, who Gardner would shortly come to know and appreciate better once the record car began its career in earnest. What was to be achieved from the basis of the 1,087 cc MG Magnette six-cylinder engine would be little short of remarkable. The bodywork was made up using an alloy frame, built at Abingdon, to which were attached alloy panels made by E. G. Brown & Co. Ltd. Of Northumberland Park, Tottenham in North London.

In June 1938, the reborn EX135 ('K3023' – but arguably sufficiently different from earlier incarnations that a new code would have been justified, but it was Gardner's property rather than MG's, and so '135' stuck) was ready for a formal introduction like a debutante's coming-out ball. On July 27th 1938, Cecil Kimber hosted a party at University Motors for the press and key personnel who had been involved; Lord Nuffield was in attendance, along with Reid Railton (who a few months later moved to Berkeley California, as described in the side panel). The exact finish of the car is a little difficult to discern accurately with only black and white images, but we can see that the colour appeared much lighter than it would become in later excursions.

Alongside the reveal at Abingdon, Gardner announced his intention to take the new car to Germany for a crack at the Class G records; it was clear that with all the work since his last excursion the previous year, and in particular the smooth new bodyshell, he saw there was unfinished business in Frankfurt. Shortly after the unveiling, Gardner received an invitation from the Brooklands Auto Racing Club for a number of demonstration runs at the August Bank Holiday Meeting; he was pleased to accept as it was obvious that he could try the car out before it was transported to Germany.

However, this proved to be quite an uncomfortable experience, as Gardner related in his book: *'It was arranged that I should cover two laps at any speed I liked. At the end of the second lap I had had enough! A combination of almost solid suspension, almost lying in the cockpit and the famous bumps round the track gave me one of the most uncomfortable and painful rides I have ever experienced in any car! I was shaken up and down like a sardine in a tin throughout the whole of these two uncomfortable laps, being kept in the car only (a) by the flat underneath portion of the steering wheel hitting my tummy, and (b) the*

Here with the new car are, left to right, Cecil Kimber, Lord Nuffield, Goldie Gardner and Reid Railton. The livery was very simple at this stage; uniform green with Union Jacks on both sides. The white lightning flashes were added before the first outing to Frankfurt in late 1938. (Dick Knudson)

top of my head cracking up against the top of the Perspex blister over the cockpit! When I came in, my goggles were lying on the back of my neck, having been shaken off my head by a "bump" and I was bruised and sore all over. The real reason for all this punishment I discovered afterwards was due to Dunlop Mac (McDonald of Dunlop); having decided to guard against any possible tyre trouble, he had accordingly put each of my tyres up to 60 pounds pressure, no doubt under instructions from his boss, Bill Freeman (N. W. H. Freeman, Dunlop's Racing Manager).

The candid snapshots of EX135 at Brooklands seen here are again from Syd Enever's albums. Gardner continued: *'All those drivers who used to compete at Brooklands can imagine the painful discomfort of a ride round the outer circuit in a fast and light car with practically solid suspension and 60 pounds pressure in the tyres! Nevertheless, this ride gave me real confidence in the car, because if it had shown no signs of becoming uncontrollable round the Brooklands outer circuit, it should be perfect on a German Autobahn – this turned out to be an accurate forecast'.*

Reid Railton

Often sought after in the pre-war racing and record-breaking world were the services of specialists, and few were more respected than Cheshire-born **Reid Antony Railton** (June 24th 1895 – September 1st 1977). Having benefited from a sound education – school was Rugby, followed by a degree from the Victoria University of Manchester – he first joined Leyland Motors near the end of WWI, where he worked alongside J. G. Parry Thomas on a luxury car called the Leyland Eight. Throughout his life he was plagued with migraines and poor eye-sight, but these did not prevent him securing a Royal Aero Club Aviators' Certificate, flying a Caudron Biplane from Hendon on August 9th 1915 and much later becoming a highly respected designer in his field.

In 1922, Railton set up his own business, Arab Motor Company, where he was not only the proprietor but also the Chief Designer. Five years later, soon after Parry Thomas died whilst testing the Leyland racing car nicknamed 'Babs', Railton closed the 'Arab' company and joined Thomson & Taylor, born out of Parry Thomas's business at Brooklands, as Technical Director and Chief Designer, which truly brought him to the heart of the British motor racing fraternity. Whilst there he was largely responsible for the designs of a series of record-breaking cars which would each go on to be as famous in their own right as their pilots – in particular Cobb and Campbell, both 'Boys Own' heroes of their day.

On February 11th 1928, Railton married Margaret Hensman. The Napier-Railton, an aero-engined race car first create in 1933, became a watchword for the best of British motorsport engineering in its day. It was through the Brooklands connection that Railton was persuaded to consult for MG on a number of occasions, most famously in terms of the design of the new aerodynamic aluminium alloy body for Goldie Gardner's record breaker, first unveiled in the summer of 1938, although it is less well known that he (with engineer John B Perrett) had also briefly offered consultancy work with MG in the period leading up to the great schism of 1935. There seems little doubt that Reid Railton and Syd Enever would have crossed paths in the creation and running of the Gardner record car.

Railton could see better prospects for his talents in North America and left for California via New York on the Queen Mary in July 1939, just two months before WWII, settling there with his wife and young children Timothy and Sarah. During the war he worked on a variety of important marine engine projects for the Hall Scott Motor Company of Berkeley, living nearby for the rest of his life.

At the 1938 Brooklands August Bank Holiday meeting, Ivy Enever stands in front of the car in which her husband had expended so much effort. Gardner demonstrated the car for the crowds, but later wrote how uncomfortable the experience had been on the pockmarked Brooklands surface: 'I was shaken up and down like a sardine in a tin'. (Enever Archive)

CHAPTER FOUR: MAGIC MIDGETS AND MAGNETTES

> **Building the Gardner Car**
>
> The new body shape may well have been designed by Reid Railton, but actual build relied upon a marriage of talents between the MG team at Abingdon and a specialist body maker. In 1975, Ted Eves of *Autocar* interviewed Syd about the work. *'Syd told me that the body was very much a derivation of the Auto-Union body. They built a wooden frame to Railton's lines and sent it to a body-maker, Brown Brothers in Tottenham, to make the panels. It's a measure of costs in those days that the panels cost less than £100. The Abingdon experimental department built the frame from light alloy sections riveted together and Brown Brothers laid on the panels. New ground was broken by causing the driver to lie down to his job. The radiator was ducted and the wheels were housed in close-fitting boxes. Frontal area was only eleven square feet. Even in those early days Enever appreciated that the body was effectively a lifting airfoil and mounted it on the chassis with a negative angle of incidence.'*
>
> As we shall see, with an engine that was hardly different in terms of the 1937 tune, the new aerodynamic body would furnish an increase in speeds of some 40mph later in 1938.

Frankfurt 1938

In 1938, the Berlin Motorshow was a big European draw as much as it had been in recent years; in February that year, as had been usual since 1933, it was opened by Adolf Hitler, a sign of the importance he placed in German displays of automotive superiority – although only weeks previously, poster-boy and Aryan icon Bernd Rosemeyer had lost his life (January 28th 1938) whilst trying to raise the upper echelon of car speed road-records. Five years earlier, at the 1933 event, Hitler – fresh from taking power – first announced tax benefits for car owners, the major road construction programme which brought the beginnings of the extensive Autobahns and state-funded motorsport events which saw Mercedes-Benz and rivals Auto-Union vying for supremacy as German 'supercars' of their day; by 1938 this programme was at its apogee.

With his new sleek-bodied MG record breaker ready, Goldie Gardner naturally settled on Germany for his next outing, although at the beginning of September, it was initially declared that the Speedweek event was going to be cancelled, as the roads were said to be unready, and Gardner started looking for an alternative venue, such as the Italian Autostrada or the road at Gyón between Budapest and Kecskemét; however the original Frankfurt plans were soon reinstated, perhaps after some intervention from the senior echelons of the Nazi Party. Gardner's initial preference was to try for a new autobahn being built near Dessau; however it became obvious that the new road would not be ready until sometime in mid-November 1938. Indeed the matter was confirmed through a telephone call on October 31st 1938 to Gardner from Cecil Kimber, in Berlin, literally hours before the group were due to leave Dover; it was agreed that the party should divert to Frankfurt.

The Gardner car had a starring role on the cover of the week ending September 8th 1938 issue of 'Modern Wonder', a regular comic aimed at British boys interested in the latest in mid-thirties technology. (Author Archive)

The very next day (i.e. November 1st) the MG party travelled (the car in its MG-badged lorry) by ferry from Dover to Dunkirk and then through France and Belgium (pausing in Brussels for lunch) and ultimately to Frankfurt. Syd, Jacko and Kes evidently had time during their trip to stop at a few places en-route, as the photos from Syd's photo albums show – an opportunity that less than a year later would not have been possible. The big draw remained 'Speedweek' on the outskirts of Frankfurt, an event that had been concocted at least in part to proudly show off German prowess in the world of automotive engineering.

At Frankfurt, Gardner took the car out for several practice runs on the arrow-straight autobahn on November 4th 1938 and took the two-way average flying mile at 187.62mph and the flying kilometre at 186.567mph, which Gardner was delighted to observe bettered his previous year's results (in the older body) by 38mph. After the return of the group to the UK, Lord Nuffield was pleased to celebrate their success in Germany; one of the guests at the event that was laid on at London's Trocadero on December 15th 1938 was motoring correspondent Rodney Walkerley (earlier Sports Editor and by 1938, 'Grande Vitesse', of 'The Motor') who had accompanied the trip.

Walkerley looked back on the occasion in 1977: *'Nuffield gave a very sumptuous and very select luncheon in Gardner's honour, and there presented him with a silver-gilt model of the "Magic Magnette" which he had ordered secretly, confident of the results. That was the sort*

'Jacko' (with typical mischievous grin) and Goldie Gardner take the air on the cross-channel ferry to Dunkirk on November 1st 1938; perhaps the empty seat next to Gardner is ready for Syd, the presumed photographer, to resume his place after this candid snapshot? Gardner wrote in his book 'Magic MPH' how '...this was the first occasion on which Kim had included Syd Enever in my party'. (Enever Archive)

The Morris Commercial three-ton lorry on the Dover-Dunkirk chain ferry (Enever Archive)

Dunkirk and the 'Douanes Francaises' – French Customs – where the MG party hopes to be swiftly on their way to cross Belgium. Gardner wrote in Magic MPH that 'by 8 am we had been cleared by the customs and were on our way to Brussels for lunch.' (Enever Archive)

'Kes', 'Jacko' and Syd pause for refreshments in Belgium in 1938. (Enever Archive)

of party he enjoyed, relaxing in the company of friendly and eminent men assembled to celebrate an MG success. Among them were Sir Malcolm Campbell, John Cobb, George Eyston, as well as all Gardner's MG mechanics and Les Kesterton, the SU carburettor expert. No one who had contributed to the records was left out. On such infrequent occasions Nuffield revealed an urbane charm which few realised he possessed and rarely showed.' The small trophy referred to by Walkerley and shown here is now part of the British Motor Museum collection.

We are also fortunate that amongst Syd's treasured papers is his personal lavish invitation to the Trocadero, and even the seating plan; it is fitting that diagonally opposite Lord Nuffield, Goldie Gardner and Cecil Kimber, on the far side of the tables laid out in a kind of circular horseshoe, were Syd and Jacko (and next to them, equally appropriately, Les Kesterton and Chris Shorrock – see panels). Gardner, in his speech of thanks, predicted that '...on the next occasion he sought a record with the car, the speed would be nearer 210 than 200mph; this prophecy turned out to be a fairly accurate forecast.'

The MG lorry at rest in Cologne (Köln). (Enever Archive)

Jacko (left) and Syd praise the virtues of German beer; Mainzer Aktien-bier was a famous beer from a brewery in Mainz. (Enever Archive)

Gardner seemingly has closed his eyes in deep thought as he contemplates what is on the paper that perhaps Syd (at left) has handed him, while meanwhile Jacko, right, looks on. (Enever Archive)

Les Kesterton – The Carburetor Man

Alongside Syd Enever and Reg Jackson were two other invaluable members of the record breaking team – Leslie 'Kes' Kesterton and Chris Shorrock, respectively carburettor and supercharger experts, who supported these record breaking exercises and to whom Gardner was also greatly indebted. **Leslie Gilbert 'Kes' Kesterton** (January 30th 1896 – September 13th 1970) was born at Tendring in Essex and later moved to Willesden, Northwest London, where he appears in the 1911 Census as a Motor Mechanic, aged 15, living at 13 Priory Park Road with his parents and two older brothers Thomas and Herbert. From the previous year, 1910, for the next four years, he was working at the Warrington Garage in Maida Vale, London on 'motor car testing and racing'.

From early 1914, he was soon in the thick of the First World War and became 'Cadet Leslie Gilbert Kesterton' in the Royal Flying Corps – precursor to the RAF – having joined on March 24th 1914, qualifying at the Central Flying School, Upavon. By 1915, he was in France where he was awarded various medals. He evidently told John Dugdale that he had shot down one of the so-called 'Richthofen Circus' during the conflict. In August 1918, flying an Armstrong Whitworth FK8 reconnaissance biplane, Kesterton crashed and although he was injured, his observer was killed. Kesterton left the

RAF in 1919 and was recorded in 1920 as still living at 137 Castellain Mansions, Maida Vale.

On December 29th 1920, he joined The Auxiliary Division of the Royal Irish Constabulary (ADRIC), a paramilitary unit of the Royal Irish Constabulary (RIC) that operated during the Irish War of Independence, and which had been founded in July of that year by Major-General Henry Hugh Tudor. The so-called 'Auxiliaries' was made up of former British Army officers, most of whom, like Kesterton, had fought in the First World War. Less than two months later, on the February 2nd 1921, two lorries carrying seventeen of these ADRIC 'Auxiliaries' – one of them Kesterton – were travelling in two lorries between Granard and Ballinalee. In what became known as the Clonfin Ambush, the IRA exploded a mine under the first lorry, wounding all the Auxiliaries in that lorry and killing the driver; the second lorry – driven by Kesterton – ran into the ambush and its occupants were also attacked by the IRA.

The Auxiliaries surrendered when their ammunition ran out. The IRA commander Sean McEoin gave orders that the wounded were to be cared for and that survivors should not be executed. One of the Auxiliaries got away and managed to summon reinforcements from the 'Black and Tans'. Les Kesterton was subsequently awarded £1,500 compensation – a considerable sum at the time (worth around £74,000 in 2025). In July 1921, Kesterton was discharged from the RIC as 'unfit for service' and was awarded a pension of £146 5

Cecil Kimber (in trilby and light checked overcoat, at right) looks on as an ONS official shares the result data. (Enever Archive)

Cecil Kimber at left and Laurence Pomeroy at right look on and take photos of Gardner. (Enever Archive)

Syd (left) and Jacko – both in white MG overalls – aided by carburettor expert Kes Kesterton in suit – attend to the engine in EX135. (Enever Archive)

Goldie Gardner almost glares at the camera; John Thornley later wrote 'as the minutes ticked away to the time when he must get into the car and move off, he suffered the tortures of the damned. "Careful, chaps. The Old Man's on edge" was a not uncommon comment in the équipe at these times. This, indeed, was the measure of his sheer guts.' (Enever Archive) shillings for the following year.

He then moved to Berlin, working as an engineer during 1922, and returned to the UK before going to Australia in 1924, where he had thoughts of emigration; his photo album, referred to by Bill Boddy in Motorsport in June 1974, included photographs taken in New South Wales of a pair of Bugattis. However in April 1925 he was back in the UK again, where he remained, joining SU Carburettors. Here his early background in tuning cars for motor-racing meant that he became the go-to man for the upper echelons of racing and record breaking, and he forged a strong rapport with the team at MG; there was a letter from Cecil Kimber to T. C. Skinner of the SU Company expressing gratitude for Kesterton's help in Italy in 1933, on the famous Mille Miglia event, endorsed with a cheque in appreciation.

In 1936, he was called on to assist with the carburetion of a racing Delage owned by famous racing driver Dick Seaman. Kesterton's involvement in the 1938 and subsequent Goldie Gardner record breaking is told in the main text; by the time of the 1939 England and Wales Register, he was living in Solihull (aged 43) at 1 Marsham Court Road, with his wife Jessie (also 43), and is listed as an Engineer.

After the war, as well as helping out with Goldie Gardner's renewed record-breaking, he was often called upon by the cognoscenti to assist in tuning cars intended for motorsport use, such as a Jaguar XK120 used for record-chasing at Montlhéry (average 100mph over seven days) in 1952 and a Bentley in the 1953 Monte Carlo. Retirement came in 1961; he died at Newhaven, Sussex aged 74 in 1970.

Chris Shorrock – Supercharger Supremo

Another key member of the Gardner record breaking team was **Christopher Shorrock** (May 6th 1901 – July 3rd 1978) who was born in Darwin, Lancashire and attended the Manchester School of Technology. In 1920 he joined the motorcycle firm of Toreador at Preston and worked there, becoming Senior Partner in 1922, until 1928. Along with his brother Noel, Chris Shorrock took part in side-car racing and the pair won many long-distance events.

From 1932, he described himself as a consultant in the field of internal combustion engineering

Wheeling the car into position for a run at Frankfurt. After the first leg, Gardner wrote how 'Syd Enever and Jacko had presented me with a highly concentrated packet of dynamite.' (Enever Archive)

Three figures in close consultation at the Frankfurt venue; opposite Gardner is Eberan von Eberhorst and between them, Otto Langsteiner, head of the Auto Union racing shop at the time. (Enever Archive)

Syd talks to Goldie before a warm-up run. Gardner later noted the ambulance in the background was there 'just in case'. (Enever Archive)

'Jacko' in action beneath the Gardner car. (Enever Archive)

Here we see Syd and 'Jacko' and between them Leslie Kesterton of SU. A decade older than the others, Kesterton had seen distinguished service as a fighter pilot during WWI in the Royal Flying Corps (predecessor of the RAF) during which had shot down several accomplished German pilots (Enever Archive)

and supercharging, and this included design and development of the Centric supercharger as used on many MGs before the War ('Centric Superchargers Ltd' was founded in 1934, with Chris Shorrock described as 'Technical Director and Chief Designer'). In the 1939 England and Wales Register, he is recorded as an 'internal combustion engineering specialist' living with his younger brothers Noel and Ernest and their widowed mother at Moorlands on Garstang Road, Preston.

During the War itself he was involved with the amphibious Sherman Tank, developing superchargers for tanks and even submarines; from 1945 he reverted to the automotive supercharger world, although by then 'Centric' no longer existed, having gone out of business in February 1939, before the war had even started. Meanwhile he had married – to Doris Eaves – at Preston, in October 1940. Both before and again

Early in 1939, MG produced a special celebratory booklet called 'The Greatest Achievement of the Year' which covered Goldie Gardner's exploits at Frankfurt the previous October... (Enever Archive)

A magnificent and long-remembered luncheon took place at the Trocadero on December 15th 1938; this is Syd's treasured copy of the official menu card. (Enever Archive)

CHAPTER FOUR: MAGIC MIDGETS AND MAGNETTES

after the War, it was Shorrock who built all the superchargers used on EX135, and eventually went on to offer superchargers for MGs with the XPAG engine such as the Y-Type, TD and TF; meanwhile he also designed and manufactured his own oil-firing equipment. Shorrock Superchargers, a partnership between Chris and Noel, was incorporated on June 12th 1947.

In 1950, Chris Shorrock joined Harry Ferguson as part of the development team on the latter's prototype for his own car; Harry Ferguson Research Ltd. was formed with the intention to design a four-wheel drive family car and to sell the manufacturing rights to a major car maker, but the idea was eventually dropped, even if the 'Ferguson Formula' for 4WD continued. Shorrock left Ferguson after two years.

Meanwhile, in September 1954 Shorrock Superchargers Ltd became a subsidiary of the Owen Organisation at Wednesbury in Staffordshire. As set out later, he became involved with MG record breaking again with EX181 and EX219. In the following decade, Shorrock superchargers became popular with the owners of a range of British cars, including BMC and Ford models. In 1961, Allard became worldwide distributors for Shorrock Superchargers, but during the ensuing decade the appeal of supercharging waned and the company ceased trading in 1966, although 'Peco-Shorrock Developments Ltd.' was listed that same year – and in the *Who's Who In The Motor Industry* of 1967, his home address was still listed as the same as it had been in 1939. Widowed in 1977, he died the following year at Lytham St. Annes.

Dessau 1939

As political storm clouds brewed over Europe, the MG record breaking contingent returned to Germany to build on their impressive portfolio of engine-class speed records. As before Goldie Gardner was the chef d'équipe, with Syd Enever and Reg Jackson his trusty Abingdon mechanics. Also with the group again were Les Kesterton of SU and Chris Shorrock, of Centric (the supercharger manufacturers). The trip out through France and Belgium was much as the previous year; the terrible conflict which would rip through both those nations was yet to come. Whilst Syd and his colleagues accompanied the record car, Goldie Gardner went with Alan Bicknell of Lagonda (in his V12 Lagonda) along with MG Publicity Manager George Tuck and John Dugdale, then at *The Autocar*; the whole party met

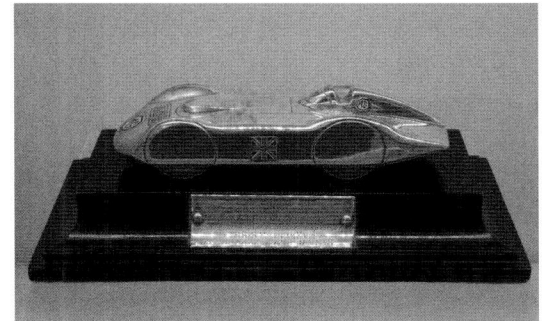

This silver trophy was presented to Goldie Gardner by Lord Nuffield at the Trocadero luncheon in December 1938. (Author photo)

Syd makes a local friend on the streets of Frankfurt; he appears to be buying a badge as a consequence of being cornered by a so-called 'can rattler' collecting for charity as part of the annual 'Winterhilfswerk des Deutschen Volkes' (literally 'Winter Relief of the German People'), ostensibly aimed at helping people on welfare. (Enever Archive)

Squeezing the van through a medieval arch by the Schloss Stolzenfels in Koblenz, by the left bank of the Rhine; nowadays the castle is part of a UNESCO World Heritage site. (Enever Archive)

up at the '*Goldener Beutel*' (literally the 'Golden Bag'; regarded at the time as the premier hotel in Dessau, with a distinctive 'lamella' conservatory roof designed by Hugo Junkers himself. Commonly used by the nearby Junkers works to host important visitors, the hotel was destroyed during the subsequent 1945 bombing and was replaced post-war by a block of flats).

Syd, Jacko and Chris Shorrock (the supercharger wizard) with the V12 Lagonda of Alan Bicknell. (Jackson Family)

'Jacko' in characteristic pose attends to one of the wheels on Goldie's car – possibly after Gardner had applied the brakes rather too hard and cooked the linings on the Friday session, as related in the text. (Enever Archive)

Jacko and Syd (fourth and fifth from left respectively) are heavily outnumbered by onlookers and hangers on. (Enever Archive)

Of course there were ample signs within Germany of the growing prominence of the Nazi Party and its proud banner of choice, the red and black Swastika, but naturally the local officials were still at their efficient genial best, and despite the inevitable bluster of the occasional officious Nazi, there was no obvious hostility – mostly curiosity tinged with some respect for the Major – to his hosts, the archetypal military Englishman. This time, the party descended on Dessau, where, since their last trip to Frankfurt the previous autumn, the German government had at last formally opened a so-called 'record route', built with ruthless efficiency as the '*Dessauer Rennstrecke*' between Bitterfeld and Dessau South.

The record route section was 10km long and 25 metres wide – ideal for record breaking by all major categories, notably the larger Mercedes and Auto Union cars which represented the pinnacle of German engineering. Enthusiasm about Gardner and his MG had been boosted by the 1938 results, and so this time there was more interest from the British and even German press. It seems likely that the German officials tolerated the British contingent at least in part because of the desire to show that 'everything is normal' and after all, the 'amusing' MG was competing at a much more modest level in engine capacity terms.

Geoffrey Iley recalls the efficiency of the local NSKK, as related to him by Syd and Jacko: '*when they went to reconnoitre the site, they found it was this dual carriageway autobahn, and there was a German senior officer in charge of arrangements, and they said 'well, we can't really do it on here, because it's too narrow...' and he gave an order, and in the centre reservation there were all these trees in planters, and the planters were all got up as one and moved to the side of the road by soldiers, and suddenly they had a full-width track...*' Furthermore, as Gardner wrote in popular weekly motoring magazine '*The Light Car*', in the next issue after the event (June 9th 1939), '*all the cables and timing points are permanently on the Autobahn; the timing was in the hands of Herr Schäfer, Germany's Number One timekeeper.*'

Having arrived in the back of its lorry, with Gardner and his entourage travelling separately, EX135 started off at Dessau on Wednesday May 31st 1939 (coincidentally Gardner's 49th birthday) and took a slew of under-1100cc records, including the two kilometres at 203.5mph, one mile at 203.3mph and the five kilometres at 197.5mph.

With such stunning speeds under their belt, the MG team decided to extend their reach by re-boring the engine cylinders in EX135 in-situ just enough to raise the capacity over the 1.1-litre threshold, and to allow the car to pitch for the 1.5-litre class. Gardner relates in his book how he advised the local ONS (*Oberste Nationale*

Sportbehörde – Germany's Motorsport body of the time) representative of his plans; Gardner noted that, '*Herr Dienemann, impassive as usual, replied that this would be quite in order, but I could see that he was wondering how we proposed to do it.*' As described in the side panel, Syd Enever and Jacko worked on this overnight – not without problems – and all under the watchful gaze of uniformed onlookers; they successfully raised the capacity of the engine – still in the car – to 1105.5cc.

The Van Norman Boring Machine

When you are working without the direct backing of a vast organisation, it becomes inevitable that innovation is called for; this was very much the case for Goldie Gardner's équipe, because even if Lord Nuffield had largely underwritten the cost of building the record breaker, that was about as far as his largesse extended, beyond 'loaning' the likes of Syd and Jacko. In the process of chasing records, a wealthy outfit might be expected to have at its disposal a considerable array of equipment, including a number of engines for different category attempts, but that clearly was not the case in this instance. On the trip to Dessau in 1939, Syd and Jacko brought with them a set of 0.020 inch oversized pistons and a Van Norman cylinder boring machine, of a type often seen in many competent automotive workshops, albeit seldom in a factory.

The Van Norman boring machine was a product of a company in Springfield, Massachusetts which had its origins in a nineteenth century watchmaking business founded by two Van Norman brothers; in 1890 they built their first milling machine, and by the 1930s their portable engine boring equipment was in use across most of the world. Syd and Jacko told colleague Geoffrey Iley many years later, both assumed the other knew how to use the machine, but found that neither had used it – but at least Syd had had the foresight to bring the instruction manual. Mike Allison adds in 'The Works MGs' that Syd told him that as he only dealt with new parts; '*in his view it was Jackson, now the officially accepted expert in reconditioning MG cars who should know all about the machine*'. However the plan depended upon using the device; the next day would be the acid test.

The engine as it stood was suited to the Class G category for up to 1,100cc; therefore, by a modest increase in capacity, it was reasoned, further records could be pursued in the next category up (Class F; 1,100-1,500cc). The plan was for Gardner to run the car on one day with the smaller capacity, enlarge the bores overnight (from 57mm to 59.5mm) with the engine still in-situ, and then to run straight away the following morning in the next category. It was a bold plan, but typical

Jacko (left of the three in white overalls) clearly relished being the centre of attention; next right is Syd and then Chris Shorrock. (Enever Archive)

In the white overalls are, left to right, Chris Shorrock (of Centric Superchargers), a Dunlop representative and Syd. (Enever Archive)

Speed data was relayed by telephone. Gardner noted 'magnificent support' from the ONS and NSKK, in effect Germany's motorsports and breakdown assistance organisations respectively. Syd (at left) with Jacko next to him discuss the data with interested onlookers. The uniformed official at right is crouched alongside one of the temporary trestles used to line part of the route. (Enever Archive)

Jacko in typical playful mood 'performs' for the camera. (Enever Archive)

of the cunning and endeavour for which Syd and Jacko were already famous. They set up inside the local military police barracks at Dessau, with many personnel about – most of them either engaged almost continuously in posturing martial parades or poring curiously over the work of their English guests.

John Thornley recorded in *Maintaining the Breed* what happened the morning when the pair were due to try the machine for the first time. The first problem was that the machine needed a three-phase electricity supply, whereas only a 110 volts single-phase was on offer at the police station: *'accordingly, the authorities called in a unit of the German Army signals, who ran a cable on poles several hundred yards to the police station from the nearest three-phase supply. This done the two boys sat on a box and began to figure out how the darned thing worked: there was plenty of time and, in any case, they were probably a little slap-happy from the success of the morning. The machine lay on the floor in front of them, and they succeeded in connecting it to the supply. To verify this they switched it on, whereupon the torque reaction of the motor took charge and trundled the device all around the room. As the switch was mounted on the motor, it was quite a job to catch it and switch it off again, and they were quite convinced that they had ruined it for good and all'.*

'Detailed examination failed to disclose any damage, and so they erected it on number one cylinder, set the cutter, switched it on and hoped for the best. A beautiful bore, dead to size, resulted. Between each bore it was necessary to sharpen, and therefore reset, the cutter, and there was a great deal of apprehension when the cutting noise in number two bore was very different from what it had been before. The explanation of this proved to be that the cutter had been put back to front, and number two cylinder exhibited all the qualities of a fine screw thread. It was within size, however, and responded well to the judicious use of a hone. Extreme care with the remaining bores ensured that they resembled number one, and reassembly of the engine, now 1106c.c., proceeded.'

The tall urbane figure at the rear of this 1939 photo is Count Lurani of Italy, another distinguished record breaker and motoring sportsman. Lurani's own 0.5-litre record car 'Nibbio' (Italian for 'kite') was also present at Dessau, and shared the autobahn as well as the expenses for closing it) with Gardner; the two became personal friends. Nibbio broke eight records in Class 'I', at speeds up to 172kmph from half a litre. With sunglasses (second right) is John Dugdale and alongside him in turn, Alan Bicknell. (Enever Archive)

The Chief Engineer at the Junkers factory at Dessau, Herr Iserante, made the MG engineers welcome in June 1939 – provided that they did not look too closely as they passed through the busy assembly shops, where new fighters and bomber aircraft were being built – and of course would be used extensively within months. Note the tiny, enamelled Swastika lapel badge. (Enever Archive)

A photo from Dessau, full of interesting details. Second left we see Captain Gardner in conversation with Count 'Johnny' Lurani, whilst behind and between the two of them, Autocar correspondent John Dugdale, complete with his ever-present camera, listens intently as part of his task of reporting of the event. Dugdale had travelled to Dessau along with Goldie Gardner and MG's George Tuck in Alan Bicknell's V12 Lagonda. In the foreground is a tripod-mounted anemometer, a device designed to measure wind-speeds. (Enever Archive)

Even after overcoming the challenges of the re-bore, however, the team's troubles were not over; in the process of refitting the cylinder head, it was found that the front camshaft bearing had somehow fractured across one of the stud holes, and there being no spare on hand, the only recourse would be to find some means of repair. Here they were in luck as the local ADAC official, there to ensure fair play in terms of dimensional compliance with the categories, also happened to be the engineering director of the nearby Junkers factory (under Nazi control since 1935); there is a photo in one of Syd's albums captioned simply 'Herr Direktor', showing a sports-jacketed bespectacled man with a small Nazi pin badge on his jacket lapel.

Herr Direktor (Gardner records his name in his book as 'Herr Iserante') offered to have the necessary repairs undertaken in his factory – and bearing in mind the time, not long before war, the security implications were not inconsiderable; Syd would later recall the instruction not to look either side as he walked through the factory. The reasons for this were in hindsight obvious; John Dugdale, then (in 1939) part of the party and reporting on the record-breaking trip for *The Autocar*, wrote subsequently in 1975: '*this was rather remarkable in that the same outfit was in that time developing Germany's latest twin-engined bomber, a hot secret at the time, the JU88.*' Better known as the deadly 'Schnellbomber' or 'fast bomber', destined to become one of Germany's most important offensive aircraft of its type, Dugdale saw one fly fast and low over the record road early one morning; '*I snapped it on my Leica, bringing back a useful record of its profile for the RAF reconnaissance against the*

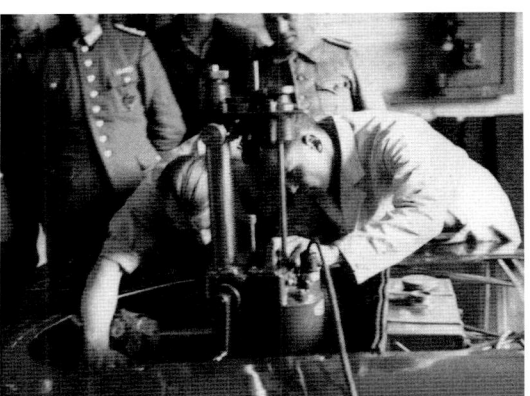

Jacko and Syd apply the Van Norman boring machine to enlarge the cylinder bores of EX135's engine to allow a further run under the larger racing class. This work was undertaken over the night of Thursday June 1st and Friday 2nd 1939. Boring the engine in-situ, with an audience, was an impressive achievement – increasing capacity to just over 1,100cc to allow EX135 to tackle the Class 'F' records the next day at Dessau (the kilometre at 204.2mph, the mile at 203.9mph and the five mile at 200.6mph) (Enever Archive)

In this photo Syd (with magazine firmly in his grasp) is second left and Les Kesterton of SU Carburettors is on the right. In the background is the Herzogliches Hoftheater in Dessau (literally the 'ducal theatre') originally built in 1798, then burned down twice, in 1855 and 1922, after which it was rebuilt as a café. It was destroyed five years after this photo was taken, during the wartime bombings....
(Enever Archive)

We know from Goldie Gardner's book that after the May/June 1939 record breaking at Dessau was finished, the local military and civic dignitaries laid on a lavish spread for their English guests. (Enever Archive)

mass bombing to come.' The JU88 first saw service during the invasion of Poland.

Meanwhile, as John Thornley records, with his inimitable style, in *Maintaining the Breed*: 'Herr Direktor having pressed innumerable buttons and having instructed a cavalcade of heel-clicking Ober-something-or-others, a very passable repair was made and in a very short time.' Final assembly of the engine was completed later that night in readiness for record breaking to resume the following morning. Thus at six in the morning on Friday June 2nd, EX135 was back out on the Dessauer Rennstrecke and, some alarming brake problems on the outward run notwithstanding, proceeded to break the equivalent suite of records (the two kilometres at 204.28mph, one mile at 203.85mph and the five kilometres at 200.60mph, with a fastest one-way speed of 207.37mph). Gardner, by his own admission, had applied the brakes a little too hard at the end of the five kilometre run; as he later explained in '*The Light Car*': '*on this car there are no front-wheel brakes. Heavy use of the back brakes caused one nearside shoe to distort, and Jackson decided that it would have to be removed. So, I made the return run with brakes operating on the offside rear wheel only*'. Remember

...here is the cover of the magazine which Syd is seen holding in the image above; 'Der Adler' (translated it means 'the eagle') was a fortnightly propaganda magazine for the Luftwaffe which had only recently entered publication; this issue is dated May 31st 1939, which means that it was the latest one when Syd got it at the beginning of June... (Wartime Press Archive)

EX135 is proudly displayed with the results of the Dessau runs. (Jackson family)

that this was at speeds of over two hundred miles per hour...

After the event, Gardner recalls, his hosts were amazed at what 'der Englanders' had achieved; as he subsequently wrote in *The Light Car*, '*it was a fine engineering achievement; the Germans were greatly impressed*'. In his account in *Magic MPH*, Gardner acknowledges the importance of his team-mates: '*I would like to pay my tribute to Syd Enever and Jacko and their assistants, Chris Shorrock and Kes [Kesterton] for their brilliant rebore of my engine in situ. To be able immediately to run an engine up to and over 7,000rpm after such an operation without any means of "running it in" speaks volumes for their technical skill and initiative.*'

Shortly after the MG record breaking was over, and some separate records having been taken by Count Lurani in his car 'Nibbio', the celebrations began, and the German hosts did not stint on their hospitality; '*two large vans appeared on the Autobahn from one of the official parking places, both of which appeared to be loaded up to their roofs. As soon as they were in position, half a dozen Germans in some sort of uniform – every German wore a uniform of some sort in those days – swarmed in and out and in a very few minutes, two long tables had been set up on the Autobahn which were soon loaded with all sorts of attractive things to eat and drink.*' Speeches were given by the Bürgermeister of Dessau and from Gardner in reply, and evidently a great time was had by all, including of course Syd and his friends.

After the main party broke away for the trip back, Gardner records that Syd and his colleagues returned separately: '*Syd, Jacko and Kes left to make their own way back and spent that night in Berlin. Under the guidance of [Artur] Baldt, Bobby Kohlrausch's mechanic, they were shown the town, and the three of them agreed that Berlin was not at all bad.*' According to Jacko, the two of them had a visit organised discreetly by Robert Eberan von Eberhorst to see the Horch factory at Zwickau (part of the *Auto Union* since 1932) before returning homewards. Meanwhile, a formal lunch was laid on at a hotel at Würlitz, the former residence of the Hertzog von Anhalt, organised by MG's George Tuck, to which all the local officials who had helped – from the ONS, Junkers et al – were invited. One of the honoured guests was Herr Iserante, the Technical Director of the Junkers factory who had been so sportingly helpful.

Wrapping up after the event, Gardner wrote his postscript for the '*The Light Car*': '*I still feel confident the car has not reached its limit. I found that certain fairings could be altered to give a slight reduction in height, and thus reduce windage. Also, I think I was a bit over-geared; I actually ran on an axle ratio of 3.09:1*'. He went on to muse about the future: '*what next? I am already being asked if I am planning to go still faster. I write from Germany and at the moment I have no plans. I shall have to have a word with "Kim" about it when I get back. The engine is in perfect condition and could be run again in the smaller class if a new block were fitted.*'

Back in London, a cocktail party was arranged at the Rembrandt Hotel for around a hundred guests, with Lord Nuffield and Cecil Kimber at the heart, to celebrate the successes; one hopes that Syd and Jacko were invited; both could be suave and debonair when the need came. Naturally much was made of the affair that summer, and work began on a new engine, but of course by September, focus and priorities would swiftly be turned to arguably less frivolous matters.

As for Dessau itself, the town was decimated, less than six years after Syd and Jacko had departed, by Allied air raids on March 7th 1945, six weeks before American troops occupied the town. Afterwards it was subsumed into East Germany and became a major industrial centre of that now communist nation; it was rebuilt, but with what is recorded as '*typical GDR concrete slab architecture*'. John Thornley made tentative enquiries about the potential availability of the old Autobahn in 1957 (see later chapter) but it became clear that the record-breaking role of the great road was long past.

An MG advertisement in the issue of 'The Light Car' of June 9th 1939, featured, naturally, with the exclamation 'Major Gardner scores again!' Elsewhere in the same magazine there were optimistic comments about returning to Germany in pursuit of further records later in the year: 'What next? I am already being asked if I am planning to go still faster. I write from Germany and at the moment I have no plans. I shall have to have a word with "Kim" (Cecil Kimber) about it when I get back. The engine is in perfect condition and could run again in the smaller class if a new block were fitted...'. Come September 1st 1939, such ideas would clearly be off the table... (Author Archive)

Goldie Gardner's speeds in EX135 at Dessau				
Distance	Times (seconds)	Mean	Speed (kmph)	Speed (mph)
Wednesday May 31st 1939; 1,100cc Class G				
1 kilometre	10.84	10.99	327.570	203.5
	11.14			
1 mile	17.36	17.72	326.254	203.2
	18.07			
5 kilometres	55.44	56.62	317.909	197.5
	57.79			
Friday June 2nd 1939; 1,500cc Class F (actually 1,105.5cc)				
1 kilometre	10.84	10.95	328.767	204.2
	11.05			
1 mile	17.46	17.65	328.065	203.8
	17.85			
5 kilometres	55.10	55.75	322.869	200.6
	56.39			

Footnote: Source of this table is the June 9th 1939 issue of *The Light Car* magazine, in which Goldie Gardner wrote of his record breaking at Dessau. Gardner wrote that he had thought of trying for the five-mile, ten-kilometre and ten-mile records in both classes but '…I felt the car had done marvellously and did not proceed with this plan. The wind would have been very troublesome for the longer records and the course is not straight for the necessary distance.' It seems likely that Syd and Jacko would have been relieved too – especially after the incident with the brakes referred to in the main text.

Chapter Five: War Years at Abingdon

With the declaration of War against Germany in September 1939, it was immediately obvious that British industry would be obliged to turn over shop floor capacity to the machinery of combat; all thoughts of new MGs for 1940 were put to one side and the factory floor space at Abingdon, as at Cowley and elsewhere, was swiftly cleared, with valuable parts and manufacturing equipment placed in storage, most of it off site at a former clothing factory at East St. Helens Street on the other side of town. Many of the critical parts of the Gardner record car were also stored there. Meanwhile, thoughts soon turned to very different production opportunities, although it soon became clear that MG came somewhere down the order of priorities when it came to Nuffield allocating war work.

What this meant for a bright 33-year-old man like Syd – most recently (since 1938) 'Foreman of MG's Experimental Shop' (according to the 1939 England and Wales Register) was a change of focus but an opportunity to use his many talents in new projects and other opportunities. Whilst formal engineering design functions had been vested in Cowley for the past four years, Syd had been one of the key liaison men between

In the period immediately before the outbreak of World War Two, the situation at Abingdon was pretty healthy. Here we see a parade of managerial staff in 1939; Front row has Cecil Cousins at left (with a smiling Reg Jackson two behind him), George ('Pop') Propert fourth from left, and then we see Cecil Kimber (in the light suit); last two in the front row are John Thornley and George Tuck. Syd can be seen in the back row, ninth from left. (Author archive)

Goldie Gardner married for the second time in September 1940 to Yorkshire-born Una Eagle-Clarke, the only daughter of a talented artist and puzzle designer (Elspeth Eagle-Clarke); here they are about embark for their honeymoon in Gardner's MG WA, complete with the mandatory war-time headlamp mask. The couple had a daughter, Rosalind, and in later life Una was the Mayor of their adopted home of Eastbourne on two occasions. (Enever Archive)

Syd in his Home Guard Uniform stands alongside his sister Florence.(Enever Archive)

Abingdon and its larger neighbour; now with the War begun he became MG's Chief Planning Engineer. Syd observed that having started at MG in 1920 for 'ten bob a week', by the onset of War and his new role, he was earning five pounds a week.

Solving engineering problems remained one of Syd's well-regarded fortes, and since H. N. Charles had moved on to pastures new in 1937, leaving his protégée behind, Syd had flourished in his own right. Although the masters were based down the road, there can be little doubt that Cecil Kimber positively encouraged the independent spirit that Syd and his colleagues were only too keen to recapture; whilst George Propert and Cecil Kimber busied themselves trying to secure gainful employment for the Abingdon works, it was Syd who focused on the engineering applications that ensued.

A superb booklet, '*War Time Activities of the MG Car Company Limited, Abingdon on Thames*' was produced after the War describing the MG factory's work and experiences; it was not a regular publication from a conventional print house, but a booklet of 59 duplicated pages. For many years it was not generally known who had written it, but it is now believed to have been the work of George 'Pop' Propert. Copies are available from the MG Car Club, and it is well worth reading for a comprehensive account of the war years. The book goes into some detail about the impressive range of work undertaken, but understandably does not single out individuals for praise; to focus on the work by Syd Enever it is necessary to cross-reference the details in the booklet from what is known through other sources, notably Syd's own words and the knowledge of his family.

The booklet relates how the factory floor was effectively cleared, noting that '*our expensive paint plant and all other motorcar producing equipment was removed and put into cold storage... fortunately we were able to acquire a very dilapidated dis-used local factory, which at some considerable expense, we were able to put into suitable condition as a stores... so at the end of 1939, we had a completely empty factory, and no work to do, because our idea that as soon as the works was empty, the Ministry would be rushing a job along to us was erroneous.*' Cecil Cousins told Wilson McComb that Cowley seemed indifferent about Abingdon: '*they completely ignored us – just left us with nothing.*'

The MG factory would nevertheless become extremely busy on war-work, and Syd Enever was at the heart of much of it. Among the exercises that Syd oversaw was work on development and production of the Crusader tank, modifications to the American Medium M4 'Sherman' Tank to create an 'OP' (Observation Post') version, and the successful application of a bulldozer blade to a British Centaur Tank, both of which are referenced in the 'Wartime Activities' booklet. The 'OP' conversion of the Sherman involved the creation of an armoured mobile post for controlling artillery. The tank's normal 75mm gun was removed (and a dummy barrel fitted outside in its place) making space inside for map tables within the turret. Three radio sets were fitted inside and two more were carried for portable use outside the tank.

The Centaur bulldozer, meanwhile, was created as a faster vehicle needed within Europe in the aftermath of 'Operation Overlord' of June 1944 that could keep up with the regular tanks; the turret was removed and the front was equipped with a winch-operated bulldozer blade. These were used as armoured obstacle-clearing vehicles and were mostly issued to the 79th Armoured Division in Belgium during the latter part of 1944.

Abingdon's role is also acknowledged in the book 'Calling All Arms' by Ernest Fairfax (a pseudonym for Sir Miles Thomas) which, like the Propert volume, was published just after the War; although again Syd's name is understandably absent from the book, he must have taken some pride in the role he played. In a section concerning the war-work at Abingdon, the book records how the bulldozer came about '... *a Centaur prototype was, at urgent request of the Army, completed in seven days, and after being tried out in the "doodle-bug" ruins of London, was declared the best bulldozer ever.*'

The book also quotes from a message from the Ministry of Supply, received by the Nuffield Organization received just days after Field-Marshal Montgomery had advanced over the river Rhine (part of Operation Plunder, in late March 1945): '*...your effort on Centaur bulldozers has been absolutely magnificent and fully justifies the waving of the flag. The reports we have had on Centaur bulldozer after crossing the Rhine have been first-class and indicate the effort was well worthwhile*'. The armoured bulldozers were used to clear paths through bomb-damaged rubble whilst at the same time ensuring that the drivers were not capable of being picked off by snipers or blown up with similar ease; as *Calling All Arms* recorded: '*the armoured Centaurs with the wide bulldozer blades swept thousands of tons of rubble aside to make way for tanks and then transport vehicles.*'

In addition to the bulldozer conversions, tanks were also waterproofed (and tested) at Abingdon, and some were converted into 'tugs' to tow 17-pounder anti-tank guns. 'Fairfax' wrote: '*These Crusader gun tugs were on the secret list for months even after D-Day. Not until Monty's daring plan for crossing the Rhine was put into operation was their use disclosed. It will be recalled that the Rhine crossing involved the landing of the 6th Airborne Division behind the Germans holding the east bank. The task of the Crusader armoured anti-tank gun tugs was to cut right through the enemy and reach the airborne troops.*'

In addition to tank conversions, there was also work to equip Rolls-Royce Merlin engines with mounting frames to allow their used in aircraft; this and more tested the skills of Syd as Planning Engineer.

It would have been during this period that the MG works was temporary home to a young engineering apprentice called Roy Haynes, who in 1942 was seconded from the 'Directorate of Tank Design' at Chobham, Surrey to work on the design of Centaur and Churchill tanks being manufactured at Abingdon; many years later this young man would meet up again with Syd Enever, by which time the former was BMC's new

'Bitsy' was specially created by the MG engineering team to fulfil a need for a vehicle capable of moving plant, equipment and supplies in and around Abingdon, in the place of the usual lorries and similar machinery which had, understandably, been requisitioned by the military authorities. (Enever Archive)

As well as 'Bitsy' there was this one-off pick-up truck, also photographed in 1940. (Enever Archive)

Director of Styling and Syd had risen to become MG's Chief Engineer – but that is a story for a later chapter. The factory also became involved in refurbishment of smaller but higher volume throughput equipment including Bofors anti-aircraft guns (Morris Commercial made a Bofors mounted on an articulated motorised carriage and called it the 'Bofors Quad', doubtless these would have come through Abingdon for repairs) and, more esoterically, army rifles.

While the hefty tanks were logically dealt with safely on *terra firma* within the factory, the upper floor was largely given over to assembly of the intricate front sections of the fuselage of the Armstrong-Whitworth Albemarle aircraft, the prototype of which flew on its maiden flight on March 20th 1940. Initially conceived as a bomber, the Air Ministry soon re-purposed it for transport and reconnaissance work, the associated redesign delaying series production. MG were not the only car maker involved – Rover built the wing centre section – but Abingdon's work was arguably the most complex and impressive. The nose cones were shipped from Abingdon to A.W. Hawksley Ltd of Gloucester, a subsidiary of the Gloster Aircraft Company, which was specifically formed to construct the Albemarle.

The Albemarle work came about partly through lobbying by Kimber, Propert and Cousins, but also assisted by Kimber's close friendship with John Howlett, founder of the important company Wellworthy, who made piston rings and other components much in demand, and who with the onset of war had become 'Southern Area Emergency Services Chairman' and had set up a shadow factory at Abingdon, situated in the Pavlova Works – an idea from Cecil Kimber, whose sister-in-law took on a managerial role there. The work on the Albemarle nose section undertaken by the MG factory was one of the more complex aspects on this nowadays largely forgotten aircraft, and it required Syd Enever's ingenuity; in the end some 900 units were built at Abingdon (in the end only 602 complete aircraft were ever delivered), and the speed and quality astonished the client; in due course a dozen of the aircraft were sent to Soviet Russia as part of a subsequently cancelled order for 200; perhaps some of the first and few MG assemblies ever seen in Moscow.

The Albemarle Bomber, nose-cones for which were built in significant volume by the MG factory. (Enever Archive)

The 'Wartime Activities' book makes reference to this voyage in what was uncharted territory for MG: *'quite unexpectedly an aircraft contract came our way, the Parent Company having in mind, we assume, that as we were builders of really high-class motor cars, we could successfully handle aircraft. Little did they know that at that time, our knowledge of aircraft work was just nil... the days that followed, when we got hold of some drawings, were simply terrific. Had it not been for the fact that a number of the senior staff were such grand people who were prepared to have a go at any job, however difficult, and once started, never give in, I doubt very much if we should have been brave enough to tackle this, our very first aircraft production job.'*

The work on the Albemarle proved to be something of a mixed blessing; while its complexity challenged but was rewarded by the admirable design and production capacities at Abingdon, it was also in part the recipe for Cecil Kimber's departure from MG. In a shock move in late 1941, following a visit by Sir Miles Thomas, Kimber announced his resignation; the reasons were several but ostensibly securing such large contracts without relying on the handouts (if any) from the central Nuffield Organisation was seen as the last straw, and Kimber was encouraged to 'pursue his energies elsewhere'.

An important achievement which was worthy of celebration at the MG works – we can see 'Pop' Propert next to the lady with the striped dress, and Cecil Cousins standing third from the left; those two individuals did much to bring work into Abingdon during the war years, whilst colleagues like Syd Enever excelled at the engineering problem-solving at which the factory excelled. (Author Archive)

Meanwhile, Syd also worked on the delicate tracery of a blood analysis centrifuge for the Royal Navy.

Bitsy

Even though proper car production was no longer on the cards in 1940, the activities at Abingdon not only included some conversion of regular cars (often requisitioned for war use) but also involved a great deal of moving about of parts, materials and equipment. Whilst trailers were simple enough to fabricate, there was a parallel need for a kind of 'tug' suitable to pull them after it, which needed to be simple, functional and reliable, and ideally based on spare parts that were reasonably close to hand. Thus was the premise of 'Bitsy', recorded in the EX Register as EX167, which took the form of a functional tractor-like vehicle which used a TB engine ('XPAG 529') as its motive force. Three trailer trucks were towed behind the short wheel-base prime mover.

We can see how 'Bitsy' – its name an obvious evocation of its mix-and-match origins – was regarded with some affection by the Abingdon workforce by the photos in Syd's photo albums; it even warranted a mention in the aforementioned 'Wartime Activities' booklet; *'Bitsy... had one or two things in its favour. Its track was quite wide and its gearbox ratios had been so arranged that with the ten horsepower engine with which it was equipped, it could tow an eight-and-half ton load.'* Bitsy was often called upon to trundle back and forth through the centre of Abingdon, to and fro over the roughly two miles between the factory in Marcham Road and the stores in East St. Helen's Street.

Albert S Enever in the 1939 England and Wales Register

Name:	Albert S Enever
Gender:	Male
Marital Status:	Married
Birth Date:	25 Mar 1906
Residence Date:	1939
Address:	2 Albert Place
Residence Place:	Oxford, Oxfordshire, England
Occupation:	Foreman Experimental Dept M G Car Co Production Liaison Officer
Inferred Spouse:	Ivy M Enever
Household Members	Age
Sarah E Davis	53
Albert S Enever	33
Ivy M Enever	29

After Kimber

With the departure of Cecil Kimber, responsibility for oversight of MG fell to Birmingham-born **Harold Alfred Ryder** (September 23rd 1888 – October 10th 1950). In the 1911 Census he had been recorded as a *'clerk in the manufacture of gas fittings'*; three years later in WWI saw him managing Doherty Motor Components, suppliers of brass fixtures to William Morris. In due course became a partner in Osberton Radiators at Osberton Road, In a move typical of his style, when the business could not match Morris Motor's expanded delivery requirements in a timely manner, Morris bought the business in 1923 and set about making it more effective, helped by his greater capital and clout, and he kept Ryder in charge; he became a Director in 1926.

No doubt viewed benevolently by Lord Nuffield as

One of Syd's key tasks during the War Years of 1939-1945 included the conversion of tanks into armoured bulldozers and transports. (Enever Archive)

Perhaps not the most flattering photo of Syd, as it shows the back of his head; however the man directly across the table, holding centre stage, is Sir Stafford Cripps, during the War the government's Minister of Production, visiting the Abingdon plant in 1945 to discuss some aspects of wartime production. To the right is seated George Propert, MG's General Manager at the time, and on Syd's left is Mr Duffield of the MG Joint Committee, thus representing the workforce. (Courtesy of Abingdon Museum)

a man who owed much of his status and success to his benefactor, and therefore a safe pair of hands unlikely to rock the boat, Ryder became one of Nuffield's few trusted associates. Oliver Boden, Lord Nuffield's Vice Chairman, died of a heart attack in 1940; although some betted on Ryder being Boden's successor, Miles Thomas got the Vice-Chairmanship. Thomas, aged 42, took Boden's place as managing director and vice-chairman of Nuffield, at a 1940 salary of £10,000 a year (equivalent to in excess of £480,000 in 2025) Meanwhile Ryder was put in charge of Cowley and, by association, MG.

Being a Victorian in a new century meant that Ryder could come across as conservative, and he certainly had little interest in either sports cars or motorsports, but he seems to have had some fondness for his charges at Abingdon (some of the men he would have remembered from their time at Bainton Road) and he did his level best to ensure that the factory was productive; he was also instrumental in getting MG going again after the War. Planning for post-war production in March 1943, Miles Thomas asked all of the heads of department for their suggestions, and Ryder suggested the 1¼ litre MG saloon (a prototype of which Thomas had been driving) would be a logical candidate.

In October 1943, Ryder wrote to Miles Thomas: 'because MG is a small factory, it makes sense to put Nuffield Mechanizations at Cowley, and reinforce the policy of all MG design to happen at Cowley under Mr Oak and the Drawing Office and Experimental Department at Cowley. If MG is not allowed by government to make cars after the war, the factory can be used to make parts for other cars.' Then on February 2nd 1944, Ryder wrote again to Thomas, stating how he had had a very productive meeting with the 'Executives' at MG: *'I must say, they made a very good case for the introduction of a Midget'* he said, adding *'I think you will appreciate that this company was built up on a Midget car, and I feel that provided we run a "bread and butter" line, which is an improvement on the standard, we could economically produce a Midget car: at least for a few years after the war in order not to give the public the impression we were falling out of the market which had given us such a good name. I have therefore contacted Mr Oak, and he informs me that the chassis of the 1¼ litre can be readily used for a Midget, and he is investigating the possibility of body styles and types, using as much as possible the standard panels.'*

With the end of the conflict in Europe approaching, plans could begin to be formulated for post-war MG assembly, and in the subsequent years of his involvement, Ryder supported the entreaties of Cecil Cousins and others who had cause to speak to him, to build up towards introduction of the MG TC Midget and the Y-Type Saloon, and even to experiment as suggested with the creation of a 'new Midget' as a blend of the Y-Type's new chassis and the traditional Midget body style. Syd Enever and his reconstituted Experimental Section were instrumental in this process; Ryder's memo does not record names but it would seem reasonable to suppose that Syd Enever would have contributed to that encouraging conversation.

That the TC and the later TD went on to become major export successes can be credited at least in part to Harold Ryder, as we saw, a former Morris Radiators man. However time was not on his side; by December 1947, when he was finally 'retired' as a director, he was seen by a younger Morris Motors Board as part of the 'old guard' which newcomers such as Reggie Hanks wanted to pension off. Ryder's place was assumed by Sydney Victor Smith; meanwhile Harold Ryder did not work again – he died at his home in Yarnton in 1950.

CHAPTER FIVE: WAR YEARS AT ABINGDON

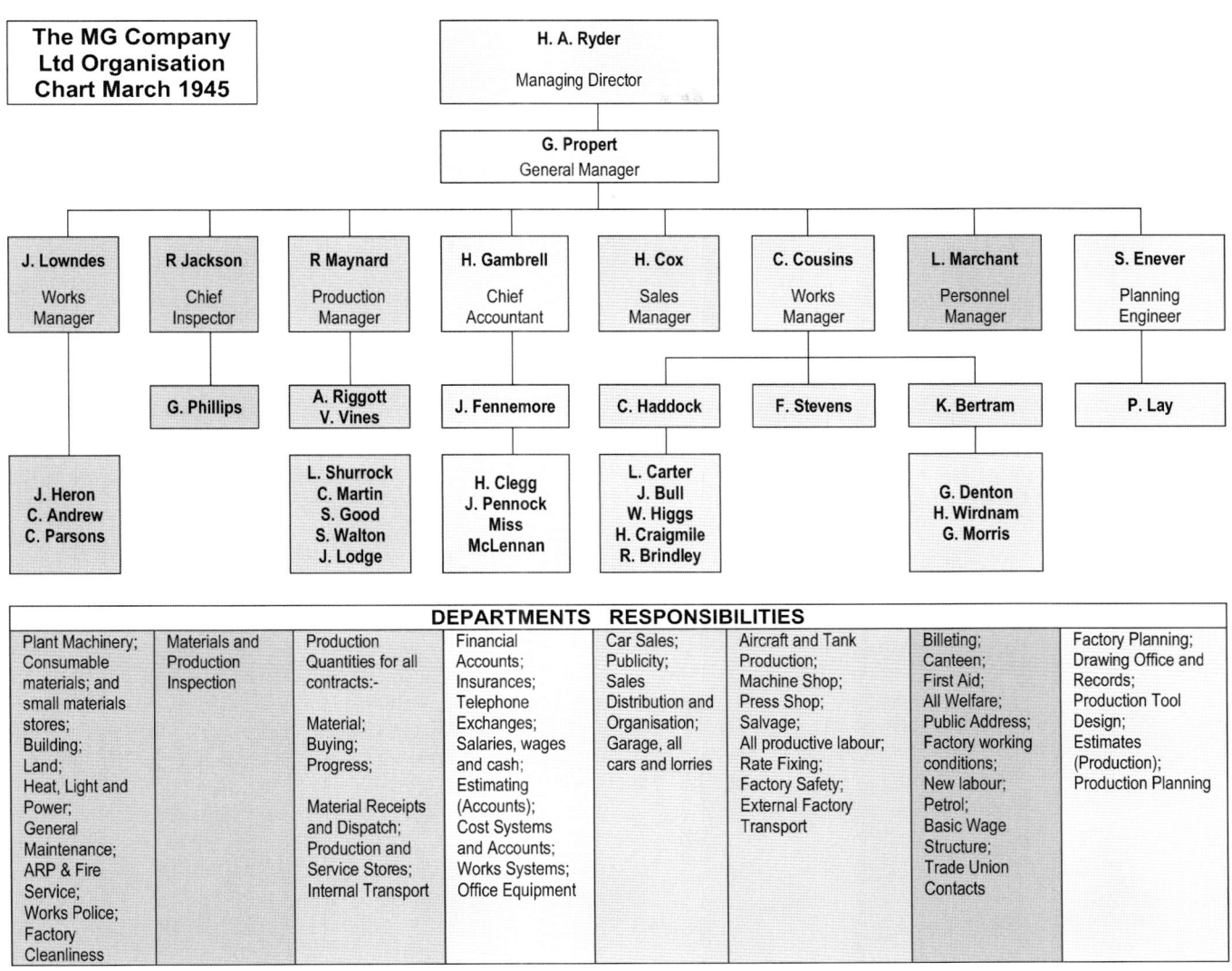

Chapter Six: Export Or Die

As we have seen, plans for post-war MG activities were already being given serious thought from at least 1943; almost as soon as the war had ended, the race was on to get the Abingdon lines running again. Wartime damage had been fairly limited from MG's perspective; some jigs and tools had been lost, and parts of Goldie Gardner's record car had been consumed by a fire, but it was not too hard to rework the MG TB Midget of 1939 into the MG TC of 1945.

The task of drawing up the new TC Midget was undertaken by Jim Stimson, who had been part of the Cowley team working on the Morris Minor, but in due course (in 1960) would move to Abingdon. '*I produced the quarter scale for the TC to Syd's requirements, using the general arrangement of the TB Midget as the base*' Stimson told the author. The first production prototype of the new car was completed at Abingdon in September 1945, with the appropriate '251' chassis number suffix ('Abingdon 251' was the factory main phone switchboard number); there were a few changes suggested by Cecil Cousins and Syd, such as a slightly wider body, and suspension improvements, although it seems likely that other alterations, such as the single 12-volt battery on the scuttle in lieu of twin 6-volt ones near the rear axle were more Cowley than Abingdon inspired.

It was obvious from the onset of peace that exports would be essential as part of the drive to rebuild the shattered UK economy, and accordingly senior Nuffield executives undertook fact-finding trips to North America in 1946 and 1947; their findings were mixed: the Americans in particular were rather taken by the MG sports car, but could see less obvious merit in the Morris and Wolseley offerings on the table at that point (the Morris Minor was not due until October 1948, for the 1949 model year). Jack Daniels told the author that both MG and Wolseley versions of the Morris Minor were conceived, but in the event as related later, neither materialised, although there would be Wolseleys based on the larger Morris platforms.

Vic Oak was still the Cowley-based engineer in charge of MG design and in tandem with Harold Ryder he gave the order to Syd Enever and Cecil Cousins to create their first slightly crude prototype. Working to Syd's direction, Alec Hounslow, Henry Stone and Billy Wilkins in the MG Experimental Shop at Abingdon proceeded to chop a foot (300mm) out of the wheelbase of a Y-Type chassis and mounted a TC body on it (the Y-Type saloon was launched in May 1947, but like the T-Series, had distinctly pre-war styling). After initial review by Oak, a few minor changes were made, and the basic concept approved.

The next step was to develop a buildable production car; Syd and his colleagues later scoffed at how long it took Cowley to 'draw up' what they had created, but in fairness there was a lot more to making a sound, safe, buildable and saleable series production car. Jim O'Neill, at Cowley, reported to Assistant Chief Draughtsman Tom Ramsay and was given the task of developing

MG returned to its sports car strengths with the TC Midget – effectively a reworking of where it had left off with the TB in 1939, although the production of bodies at Coventry required new jigs, many of the old ones having been lost in wartime bombing. (Author Archive)

the new MG sports car, under a new Cowley Design Order Number DO 968 (the MG YT was DO 967). O'Neill – who as we shall see would later become one of Syd Enever's trusted lieutenants at Abingdon – told the author that the only person who seemed to take an active interest in what he was doing was, John Thornley, who came over from Abingdon and made some modest suggestions to improve the lines of what would in due course be the first all-new post-war MG Midget. However there would be a lot of activity, both in the boardroom and on the record-breaking front, before this new sports car would come to fruition.

EX135: 1946, Monte Carlo and Italy

During the early part of 1946, Goldie Gardner made plans to pick up his pre-war record breaking exploits, with eyes on existing smaller capacity records established at Frankfurt in 1935 by Bobbie Kohlrausch. It was by no means an easy feat, however; the fire at the MG depot at St. Helens had resulted in the loss of many valuable parts of the Gardner car, although miraculously the body and chassis and the 750cc engine had survived. Obviously Cecil Kimber was no longer there to lend his irrepressible enthusiasm; as Gardner wrote in *Magic MPH*, '*in the MG Factory there had been changes, although Syd Enever and Jacko were still there and as keen as ever. All the manufacturers were faced with the seemingly impossible job of reverting back to peacetime production, in spite of the fact that much space in the factories was still occupied producing war materials*'.

The MG factory was clearly part of the wider story of gearing up again for the post war economy, and interestingly it seems that the factory lacked – or simply could not make available so soon – testing equipment, for Gardner wrote '*MGs were unable to bench-test the engine owing to the appropriate apparatus not being available, but offered to do all that was necessary in its preparation as a normal service job*'. Mike Allison notes that Lord Nuffield provided, privately, a contribution and agreed that Syd and Jacko's time would be paid for by the factory; Gardner owned the car and obtained some sponsorship from Jack Duckham of the eponymous oil company. The new supercharger was the independent work of Chris Shorrock, as 'Centric', the makers of the pre-war unit were no longer in business. Eventually the set-up was found to deliver around 130bhp at 8,000 rpm with a boost of 30psi.

Gardner's next task was to find a road that was both suitable and available; as noted at the end of the last chapter, Dessau, now lay in Eastern Germany whilst the Frankfurt road was being actively used by the American Army of Occupation. Gardner cast around various nations with little success, until Count Giovanni 'Johnny' Lurani got in touch to say that he had found a possible candidate in the Brescia-Bergamo road.

Plans were put in place to make a run on or around July 27th 1946, and by Monday 21st July a party embarked from Dover; amongst the group were what Gardner fondly termed his 'faithfuls' – '*Syd Enever and Jacko, both of whom had most sportingly decided to make this trip count as their annual holiday, and Les Kesterton with the lorry, Kenneth and Alec Baines in their Vauxhall, Reuben Rutter Harbott and some of his friends in my old 2·6 litre MG, and Chris Shorrock*'. The convoy – including Gardner in his MG TC, Rutter Harbott's Ford lorry, the MG WA and Jean Simons in a Standard 8 – went through Ostend and thereafter by road. As Gardner wrote: '*The trip to Brescia was a long one, so I*

Syd and Chris Shorrock at right amongst the party relaxing en route to Italy in 1946. (Enever Archive)

Dinner with Varsi; at the far left we see Jacko and Les Kesterton; at far right is Goldie Gardner, then to his left are Count Lurani and Chris Shorrock; Syd is across the table from the latter. (Enever Archive)

decided that we should make Monte Carlo in three days from Belgium, stay there for a day's rest and make Brescia on the following day after an early start – all four vehicles running more or less in convoy, but with definite stopping points each night.'

It was a very long trip, with the need to secure petrol coupons to sustain their journey. Fortunately for posterity, cameras were on hand – no doubt simple Box Brownies or similar – as photos of this trip are found in Syd's albums, including the convivial accommodation at Monte Carlo, where Gardner had arranged a 'stopover' for his exhausted party, especially those like Jacko and Kes in the lorry.

At the border into Italy, the team were met by with Count 'Johnny' Lurani and his associates Corrado Filippini and Luigi Villoresi, who smoothed the passage through customs. Once inside Italy, there was still a considerable drive to Brescia. First impressions upon arrival were mixed, according to Gardner: '*It was nearly 11.30 p.m. and just on the outskirts of Brescia that I noticed a thick white line painted along the middle of the Autostrada. Having arranged that such a line should be painted on that portion of the Autostrada I would use, I gathered we were then travelling along the actual site for the record attempt; what I could not understand was why the road appeared to be so rough, and why there was quite an acute bend in it?*'

That was not all for this first taste: '*On arrival at the Hotel Vittoria in the town, we were greeted with the news that the whole staff of the hotel were on strike and that the restaurant was closed. We were too tired to worry much about that so retired to bed*'. Out on the Autostrada, Gardner found his initial concerns on first sight to have been warranted; the quality of the road surface was poor, there was an appreciable bend in it and, just as bad, a humped bridge at one end. But many of the great and good from British and Italian motorsports world were there – including Lord Howe as official RAC Steward, 'Johnny' Lurani and Piero Taruffi.

In the event, the problems with the road were sufficient to limit the speeds which could be obtained, and to compound matters their problems with the timing equipment and mechanical problems led to the trip being curtailed, and it was decided to regroup and try again in October, but at Jabekke in Belgium rather than Milan. On the trip back, it seems that it was Syd and Jacko in the lorry, whilst Gardner and the others travelled a different route: '*The lorry with Jacko and Syd still kept to the lower road, but Jean Simons, with Chris Shorrock as his passenger, and I in my MG decided to take the road from Cannes through Grasse, Digne, Sisteron and Grenoble, and to spend the night at an excellent little hotel just south of Macon on the N6 road, which we had discovered on our way down*'. The party then regrouped at Ostend.

The in-house publication 'Nuffield News Exchange' reported in the September 1946 issue that Gardner had arrived in Italy with his 750cc Gardner-MG, stating that he planned '*... in the near future to make an attempt on the 750cc (Class H) international record which stands at 140.6mph, held by the German driver Robert Kohlrausch with an MG Midget... the record attempt will be made on the Autostrada near Milan, and a speed of over 150mph is to be attempted.*' By the time of the report, the actual attempts in late July had finished.

EX135: Jabekke, Belgium October 1946

The summer 1946 disappointment in Italy was more than compensated in October during the trip to the Jabekke highway near Ostend, a popular long straight road originally built before the War as part of a proposed European continental expressway. The first indication of the possibility of this road being available stemmed from a helpful inside information through the MG works; as Gardner wrote: '*... within a few days Jacko gave me some*

Syd has simply captioned this 1946 photo in his album as 'on the way to Monte Carlo'. (Enever Archive)

Syd, Goldie and 'Jacko' behind the record car at Monte Carlo. (Enever Archive)

quite startling news. It appeared that an ex-member of an M.T. Branch of the A.T.S., Margaret Wills, a sister of one of the staff of the MG Factory, had sent a message to me via Jacko that a motor road near Jabbeke... might be suitable for what I had in mind. Margaret Wills had during the war been attached to a prisoner of war camp in the vicinity, and had motored her truck up and down this road many a time in the course of her duty'.

Once again, the trusty Rutter Harbott lorry was pressed into use, and Syd and Jacko were the lynchpins of the party, of whom Gardner said he had *'once again been fortunate to borrow from MGs.'* In addition, there were Leslie Kesterton, Alec Baines, Dunlop "Mac," Mr. and Mrs. Chris Shorrock, Dick Benn and E. L. Midgeley (both of Brighton and Hove Motor Club) and a significant press contingent. George Tuck and Sidney Hornblower came on behalf of the Nuffield Organisation, accompanied by their wives.

The key objective again was the 750cc Class H record; scheduled for October 27th the attempt had to be deferred due to bad weather until Wednesday the 30th. In a report in the January 1947 'Nuffield News Exchange' headed *'Safety – Very Fast!'*, it was recorded that *'the car was out on the road for a short period on the Tuesday and did a trial run for final carburettor tuning'*. In *Magic MPH*, Gardner added: *'conditions* [on the Tuesday] *were still bad – a gusty wind, and the road very wet. Late afternoon I decided to take the car out, to give the photographers, who had been waiting so patiently, a chance of taking some pictures. It was therefore unloaded on to the road, and after fitting soft plugs and practice wheels, I ran the car down to the far end and back. There was far too much water on the road for any sustained high speeds, but I managed a few bursts on the drier portions and on my return to my starting point, I decided to pack up for the day again.'*

Apart from one drive down the course to warm up, Goldie Gardner did only two runs, breaking three records. The results are summarised later; highest speed was 164.722mph (265.095kmph) on the return run of the flying kilometre – all from 750cc. Having achieved the 750cc Class H results, Gardner resolved to try for the 500cc Class I records, but with less success; Nuffield News Exchange recorded that *'Gardner made a preliminary attempt on the Class I (500cc) International record, using the same car with modified engine, but after several runs at over 160kmph (the record stands at 172kmph) abandoned the attempt for the time being as the road was no longer available for record purposes.'* This was a disappointment because once again, the genius of Syd Enever had been involved; he had prepared two pistons, the domes of which had large holes in them; thus, as Gardner wrote *'by immobilising the appropriate valve gear and by substituting these two pistons for the*

A convivial group in Italy; Count Lurani at far-left converses with Reg Jackson (third from left) whilst Goldie Gardner puffs on his pipe; then are Les Kesterton. Chris Shorrock and Syd at right. (Jackson Family)

In October 1946, it was back across the Channel – in this case to the Jabekke Highway in Belgium. The services of Rutter Harbott were once more very welcome; we see the lorry at Ostend en route. (Jackson Family)

occupants in number two and five cylinders, we had a four-cylinder engine of 496 c.c.!'

The conversion on the ground in Belgium was undertaken as usual by Syd, Jacko and Chris Shorrock; Gardner made three runs on Sunday November 2nd 1946, but the speeds obtained were not enough to crack the existing pre-war 'Class I' figures. *'As a result of these runs it was evident that it would be necessary to alter the induction manifold, do away with those two dummy pistons altogether and to fit "bobweights" to the crankshaft instead.'* Needless to say, that would be part of the 'homework'; ahead of the next year's attempts – with, as we shall see, better results.

Isla Watts was sister to other well-known members of the MG family – her brothers Doug and Mick. (Hilary Watts)

Isla's retirement presentation in December 1975; left to right are Don Hayter (by then her boss), Syd (who had popped in to join the send off), Isla and lastly Roy Brocklehurst. (Hilary Watts)

Isla Watts – Behind Every Good Man…

Hilary Watts has very fond memories of her aunt, Isla Evelyn Watts (December 10th 1916 - January 19th 2001) who was also sister of MG's great Doug Watts, an important member of the post-war motorsports team. *'My Auntie Isla was Mr Enever's secretary. She never called him by his Christian name – for maybe 35 years'* Hilary explains. *'She loved her job so much and had the greatest respect for Mr Enever. I suppose by today's working standards she would be known as a PA but in those days, she was "a secretary" and worked very hard. He travelled all over the world and it was her job to arrange hotels, flights etc as well as doing all his typing, receiving guests to the office, even celebrities of the day. A real jet-setter in those days'.*

Isla Watts was born in Abingdon-on-Thames during WWI to Hilda May Watts (née Williams), and father John Urry Watts, known as Jack Watts. Jack became an MG storeman after his own butcher's business – of which more anon – went bankrupt. Later Isla had two younger brothers, Doug Watts and Mick Watts. All lived in their home at 56 Swinburne Road, Abingdon. Hilary relates that when Isla's father had his own butcher business, her mother helped with cooking faggots and peas with gravy. Meanwhile young Isla wound the handle on the sausage machine. Hilary remembers them as *'a very happy, laughing, close and loving family throughout their lives'.*

Isla was educated at Abingdon Council Girls' School; she told her niece how she loved school and was a good learner: *'she did well and I have inherited some of her school reports which show she was a star pupil and would do well in the world. She was a good writer, speller and excelled in her three Rs.'* Isla had swimming lessons in the River Thames allocated waters and along with her brothers, became an excellent swimmer. *'She was good at art and cookery and these interests stayed with her, along with swimming'.*

On leaving school, Hilary understands that Isla worked in some capacity at "Chivers", a large drapery in High Street, Abingdon. *'Then In the mid-1930s her cousin, who was approximately the same age as Isla, was killed in a tragic accident whilst living in North London. Isla then went to London to help her Aunt cope with her bereavement. In London, her uncle, a headmaster, encouraged Isla to go to evening classes and she would do well learning Pitman Shorthand Typing, popular at the time'.*

In London, Isla settled into a new life; *'she worked at "Stephens" Drapers in Stoke Newington; here she made lots of friends and enjoyed her shorthand typist job'*; this was the employment listed on her entry in the 1939 'England and Wales Register'. She later got a job in a major Kensington High Street store, "Derry and Toms" [1853-1971], once again in the offices. *'She loved living in London, she loved the fast pace, excitement and fashions. She was romantically linked to a man from Wales'.* Sadly, the onset of War upset everything: *'Her family were worried about her in London, travelling on underground tubes,* bombing etc. Her three brothers were by then in the RAF, and Army. Back Isla went to Abingdon, lived with her parents and eventually got her job at MG in 1940, where the factory was building tanks'.

Although she may have started as a typist, Isla wanted more responsibility: *'I think she originally wanted to get out of the typing pool and knew she was capable of more responsibility. In doing so, she had a wonderful, interesting job that she loved'*. Meanwhile the wider Watts family as a whole were one of many whose working lives became entwined in the busy sports car factory on Abingdon's Marcham Road: *'Her brother Doug Watts, after the war, worked in The MG Competition Department as foreman; Isla's eldest brother Don worked in the paint shop until getting his own business; Isla's nephew John Watts also worked at MG and her nephew Mike Watts at BMC Cowley'*; as Hilary says, they comprised *'a real family hub at MG'*.

There was a side benefit of the MG connection, according to Hilary: *'in the early days, I believe a great deal of the blueprint designs were on Draughtsman's' Linen. These linens were later disposed of or rescued. The linens rescued were excellent, white, soft, good quality fabric. When washed in my grandmother's old copper, which always boiled over on a Monday, they made amazing pillow cases – maybe we slept on what was once an MG car design!'*

Naturally Isla, working for Syd, was in the Design Office *'...where those gorgeous MGs evolved, from bits of paper scribbles to worldwide, fast, shining sports cars. What an achievement, she loved the cars as much as her family! Syd Enever was her boss for most of the thirty five years and she always called him Mr Enever. Even at home she always respectfully called him Mr Enever. At work, my aunt was a good organiser, hard worker and meticulous secretary. She was well respected, as so many people told me later'*.

Like many preoccupied geniuses, Syd could occasionally be absent-minded: *'my aunt used to tell me Mr Enever always lost his pens. He would never have a notebook or paper with him when away from the office, and so he would often scribble and doodle on scraps of paper, a cigarette box or table napkins, some design of a car, or car part that came into his head. Perhaps some of the MGs started out on a scrap of paper that ended up in the wastepaper bin...Isla used to say, "how I wish I had kept those bits of paper with details on"*.

Both Syd and Isla's brother Doug used to send Isla postcards from their trips; Hilary Watts still treasures some of these, inherited from her aunt: *'they were posted from so many locations, whilst they were abroad on rallies and business. It is a shame because the stamps and some dates from the various countries have been removed, probably for stamp collecting purposes'*. Although on some it is difficult to be certain what year and what rally the cards are relevant to, one of Syd's cards from the South of France mentions 'Sputnik', visible in the sky where he was (the famous Russian satellite was only in orbit between October 1957 and the beginning of the following January). One card was even written in pencil because Syd had mislaid his pen, and there is one from Utah in 1959 when Syd was there with EX181.

'My aunt loved her job at MG and I never, ever heard her complain of work, going to work, anyone at work or bad words about anyone in general. She was a very private woman and like her boss wasn't keen on being in the spotlight for whatever reason; she was

The prototype for what eventually became the new MG 'One-and-a-Quarter Litre' – better known to many as the MG Y-Type (Author Archive)

One of the Cowley concepts (in which Syd and his Abingdon colleagues took no active part) was this so-called 'MG Midget Major' ('DO926') which might have been based on the Morris Minor. The men from Oxford clearly thought this was just what the modern sports car customer wanted; their colleagues down the road – and their counterparts overseas – were less convinced. (Author Archive)

Another Cowley MG concept from 1947/8 – prior to the arrival there of Gerald Palmer; this was coded DO965 and was conceived in the context of the ideas to group MG and Riley operations with Morris Motors Bodies Branch, at Coventry. (Author Archive)

In this page from the January 1947 issue of Nuffield Exports publication 'Nuffield News Exchange', we see Syd depicted as MG's 'Chief Planning Engineer' and one of the people 'supporting the export drive'. Note also Jack Gardiner, also of MG, at top left – one of the early customers for an MG. (see Chapter Three). (Author Archive)

a very loyal person, clever, and so kind to her family and anyone she met. I would say she always put others before herself'. Hilary expresses the relationship between Isla and Syd as rather like '*Miss Moneypenny to a real James Bond 007 car designer*'.

Discretion was Isla's watchword: '*she never talked much about who came to the office. I know that she made coffee for George Lazenby – the tall, handsome model and actor at the time. The "Big Fry" chocolate man and later James Bond; I know that Isla liked meeting him.*'

The following is an extract from a news item in the 'British Leyland Mirror' dated December 17th 1975 on Isla's retirement, headed 'Thirty Five Years later':

"*Isla Watts didn't like the idea of working in a factory typing pool. She intended staying only a few months when she accepted the job. But the enthusiasm of the place caught her imagination. For Isla had joined MG at Abingdon. And the professionalism of the men who built some of the finest sports cars spilled over to the tanks the factory was constructing for the war effort. That was in 1940. Isla stayed and became secretary in turn to some of the men who led the production of MGs. Syd Enever, Reg Jackson, Frank Stevens, Roy Brocklehurst and her last boss, Don Hayter*".

Most of them can be seen in the photograph of that occasion on page 114.

Hilary remembers her aunt with enormous affection: '*Isla will always be remembered with love by her family. She always had the greatest of respect for Mr Syd Enever, his wife and boys. She missed him very much after he retired*'.

Isla's hobbies when not looking after her family and others included travel: '*she went to Australia, and Dubai for holidays, along with Europe. We went to Ibiza, Spain, France and Greece, Malta together, sometimes with other family. She loved a cruise in the Mediterranean with Doug Watts and his son John. Isla loved the sunshine and always loved her swimming. Although good at tennis, she never carried on with it after her twenties. She had many medals for ballroom dancing. She loved her cars and always pleased she learnt to drive. She was an amazing organic gardener, with rows and rows of vegetables in her garden. She was a fantastic cook and everyone adored her Sunday Roasts. If not on holiday in the sun, she loved her home. She was born there and was to end her life there at 84, passing away in her sleep and independent and healthy always*'.

CHAPTER SIX: EXPORT OR DIE

Having found the Jabbeke road so suitable and relatively easy to reach, it was natural that Gardner would plan a return there in 1947; his prime objective was to complete the 'unfinished business' from the previous October. However, it appears that the MG factory was unable – or perhaps less willing – to undertake the necessary engineering work; there had been changes in senior Nuffield management, with R. F. 'Reggie' Hanks and S. V. Sidney Smith appointed to the Morris Motors Board; both would soon have a great deal of influence over MG affairs.

With the factory facilities evidently being 'off-limits', Syd and Jacko offered to go to Gardner's premises in Croydon and build the engine there. Bench-testing was also seemingly out of question at Abingdon, but Gardner made alternative arrangements with Harry Weslake for this, and also arranged with Thomson & Taylor at Brooklands to undertake final preparations – but despite these grand names, it was still Syd and Jacko who would be primarily responsible for the engine. One small difference for 1947 was that the cockpit of EX135 was fully enclosed for the first time.

Despite the problems with MG, the Nuffield Organisation clearly remained keen to bask in some of Gardner's glory; a request came from their Swiss distribution agents Keller AG to have the record car for display at the 1947 Geneva Salon; *'With the proviso that the car must arrive back at Croydon not later than 1st April, I agreed, so off it went on another of its long journeys'*. Once returned from Switzerland, the car was taken in to Gardner's Croydon workshop where Syd and Jacko set to and built the engine. Once the car was ready, it was shipped off in a lorry once more (this time provided by Martin Walter of Folkestone) via Dover on Tuesday July 22nd, 1947; and although the entourage was a large one, at first it did not include either Syd or Jacko; they had been unable to get away from work for the initial runs and arrived on the Saturday for a weekend only.

Jabekke, July 1947: Flying Kilometre at 118·043 mph; Flying Mile 117·105mph; 5 Kilometres 114·105; 5 Miles 110·531mph. Later that year, Count 'Johnny' Lurani beat these records by over ten miles per hour.

For 1948, enthusiasm within some of the management for supporting Gardner's efforts seems to have been waning; he was keen to revisit the two-litre records, but he needed a new engine for this. *'I first asked the MG Car Co. Ltd. Whether a suitable two-litre engine existed within the Nuffield Organisation, and much regretted to be told that no such engine was available'*. It seems curious in hindsight that this goodwill should be discarded, when the positive publicity had been seen by various parts of the Nuffield Organisation as beneficial, but as we shall see shortly, there were changes of attitude at the top and once more it seems that the decision-makers at Cowley took a rather jaundiced view of racing and record breaking.

Meanwhile, Gardner was not kowtowed; he went off to Jaguar and secured agreement from William Lyons to have use of an experimental two-litre four-cylinder version of their new XK engine; the MG badges on his car would have to be removed and replaced with Union flags. Syd and Jacko would not be involved. Nevertheless,

The new MG TD Midget effectively married the chassis structure and front suspension of the Y-Type saloon with the classic Midget sports car layout – and for the first time, export models were offered where appropriate with left hand drive. The concept was conceived at Abingdon, but in reality much of the detailed engineering work still had to be undertaken at Cowley – with a leading role by Jim O'Neill, yet to make his subsequent move to work at Abingdon with Syd. (Author Archive)

The lorry carrying EX135 all the way from the UK to Belgium reveals its precious load. (Enever Archive)

the Nuffield News Exchange issue of November 1948 sportingly reported how on September 14th Gardner had established new Class 'E' records *'using a 2-litre unsupercharged Jaguar experimental engine in his record car in place of the MG power unit fitted for previous records.'*

Turmoil Inside the Nuffield Organisation– The Battle for Abingdon

By the time that peace had returned, as we have seen, the pressure was on at Abingdon to get production back underway. There were many sound and obvious reasons why those who actively cared about MG and the factory would want to see sports cars going down the line, and not simply because they had a passion for the cars themselves.

The war years had seen many changes across the parent organisation behind the MG Car Company as well as within the marque itself. War work had led to major re-organisation of everything from factory layout to management – and of course the loss of Cecil Kimber meant that MG could no longer rely on its most passionate defender.

The MG TB Midget had just entered production before the war and as we have seen, its simple structure and ease of manual assembly made it simpler for the MG works to start where they left off, and work towards the new TC Midget. Some of the jigs and tooling had been lost during the recent conflict, but the ever-resourceful team of Cecil Cousins, Reg Jackson and their development supremo Syd Enever, all under the watchful eye of George Propert, were able to get the production lines working again.

The pressure for exports to secure vital foreign currency helped MG and Abingdon enormously, not least because the rest of what was now the Nuffield Organisation was woefully ill-prepared for exports to the United States of America, unquestionably the export market with the biggest potential. Whereas Leonard Lord's Austin Motor Company hit the post-war export market running in 1945, the relative numbers of Morrises sold in the USA were almost insignificant, and Wolseley sales there practically non-existent. By January 1947, when his photo appeared in that month's issue of in-house magazine *Nuffield News Exchange*, Syd Enever – who was shown as one of the key people supporting the corporation's export drive – was referred to as 'Planning Engineer, the MG Car Company.'

Success notwithstanding, it was a source of great embarrassment in the corridors of power at Cowley that their most popular US export was a comparatively crude and old-fashioned sports car with distinctly pre-war origins; the annoyance at Cowley was all the greater because the new range of post-war Morris and Wolseley saloons launched in October 1948 proved to be a hard sell in North America. Various high-level fact-finding trips were undertaken there by senior Nuffield executives from 1946 onwards, and it is clear from surviving records, including internal correspondence, that many of these executives were frustrated that virtually all their North American hosts seemed to be interested in were the MG sports cars.

Many within the wider Morris organisation had long looked at the feisty factory at Abingdon with a jaundiced and often jealous eye; these messages from America probably only reinforced some of those

Goldie with cockpit canopy secured awaits the off. (Enever Archive)

George Tuck's wife in the fur coat and head scarf glances back to the camera as Syd, in immaculate white MG overalls and flat cap smiles. (Enever Archive)

Syd leans into the engine bay for some fine adjustments. (Enever Archive)

prejudices; many thought, like Leonard Lord, that sports cars were frivolous distractions at the periphery of the core business; Lord had once suggested that in his view, MGs were (or should be) little more than 'tarted up Morrises and Wolseleys'.

> ### MG Minor?
>
> Although there is no evidence that Syd Enever was directly involved, it is worth mentioning the slightly bizarre interlude of the suggestion – stemming from Miles Thomas – that the new post-war Morris saloon, developed using the Mosquito code name, should be given the MG badge instead of (or in addition to) the obvious 'Morris Minor' name. Thomas wrote in a memo *'MG owners are not averse to paying a little more. In return they expect novelty, which the "Mosquito" would provide.'*
>
> Harold Ryder was aghast at the idea – but mainly from a production capacity issue; he argued that with the TC in production and the Y-Type imminent, there simply was not sufficient space at Abingdon to build this new car as well; we imagine that the likes of Propert and Cousins would have been whispering in Ryder's ear, and even if they were not necessarily part of the discussion, John Thornley and Syd Enever would have heard the chatter. Next, it seems, Thomas went over Ryder's head and spoke to S. V. Smith, then production director at Cowley (but whom we shall see again shortly) and asked him if it would be feasible to build the MG derivatives of the Mosquito (including, by now, a roadster with a planned new 1,100cc engine) at Cowley, but have them driven to Abingdon where they would be road-tested and marketed from there as 'MG' models; the idea was tentatively approved to start from January 1st 1948.
>
> By the autumn of 1947, however, the government's intervention in steel supply and its attempts to influence car production led to the decision by Lord Nuffield to suspend all but the core Mosquito work; the sole remaining element, more or less to the familiar rounded shape, was christened the 'Morris Minor' in December 1947; by then, however, as explained in the main text, both Thomas and Ryder had gone. Whilst MG's stalwarts such as John Thornley and Syd at Abingdon had 'lived another day', the rocky ride was far from over.

Irrespective of those hostile thoughts, it was clear, in simplistic impartial manufacture planning terms, that any expansion of the MG business that was warranted might justify changes in factory infrastructure – and it is a short step from such thoughts to contemplating the shuffling of production between different factories; no doubt there were some within the Nuffield Organisation who would have quietly relished the prospect of silencing those independently-minded upstarts at Abingdon, if the responsibility for making MGs could be taken away; the overall design and engineering functions were in any case vested in an often indifferent satellite office at Cowley. As Abingdon's MG Liaison man, Syd Enever as 'Planning Engineer' often walked the tightrope of diplomacy, although his balance was no doubt steadied by his good friend and colleague, John Thornley.

But there were even more factors at play in this new post-war Nuffield world. A year before the war broke out, Lord Nuffield had acquired the Riley business, and its premises at Coventry. With the interruption of the war, Riley had been allowed to continue on a broadly self-contained path of development and production, but in the post-war world, there were moves to start bringing Riley closer to the heart of the Nuffield business. Victor Riley had remained as a Director of Nuffield until December 1947 when, along with many other 'old retainers', he was removed on what was known by some insiders as a night of the long knives.

Shortly before this, Sir Miles Thomas had left the business, his place as Vice Chairman filled by Reginald Hanks, who was keen to accelerate the pace of change and level the balance with Austin, who meanwhile had been manoeuvring for 'collaboration' with their Morris rivals, with overtures still in play at this time.

John Thornley has a careful hand on the shoulder of Rosalind Goldie Gardner whilst her father in his distinctive white race cap and her mother Una watch Syd and Jacko as they peer into the EX135 engine bay. Just to right of centre is Chris Shorrock. (Enever Archive)

> **Austin and Nuffield Talks of 1948**
>
> *The Motor* of October 13th 1948 carried a news item inferring that Nuffield and Austin were thinking of combining some of their operations: *'Lord Nuffield and Mr L. P. Lord (Chairman and Managing Director of the Austin Motor Co. Ltd) have recently had a series of talks which have resulted in an announcement whereby there is to be a constant inter-change of information on production methods, costs, purchases, design and research, patents and all other items which would be likely to result in manufacturing economies. The object is to effect maximum standardization coupled with the most efficient manufacture and, by the pooling of all factory resources, a consequent reduction in costs.'* The assets of the Nuffield Organisation were quoted as being £24 million; those of Austin 'exceeding £10 million'. The magazine concluded its brief report by stating that *'it is understood that the new working arrangement will be put into effect immediately, but current production will continue as planned for 12 months.'*

> There seems to have been little real appetite below the levels of Lord Nuffield or Len Lord for this dialogue, despite its logical intent of stemming losses of market share; however its failure would have a subsequent effect as we shall see, with ramifications even for MG projects and ambitions shared by the likes of John Thornley and Syd Enever.

Whilst the Riley business, with its own distinctive styling, engineering, chassis design and engine range, was more self-contained than MG had become since the great purge of 1935, it was clear that the new management was keen to change the Riley business model as part of a broader process of rationalisation which would bring the 'specialist' MG, Riley and Wolseley marques closer together whilst still aligned to a newly resurgent Morris.

After the TC Midget, MG's next product was the 1¼ Litre Saloon – the Y-Type Saloon (and a Tourer off-shoot). Launched as a new model in 1947, the new four-door proved popular in some markets but it was effectively a product that, as we have seen, had been lined up before the war with input from Gerald Palmer for an intended 1940 launch; although it shared the TC Midget's doughty XPAG engine, it was another narrow-bodied upright and old-fashioned pre-war car in character, but without the same sport-car appeal. An 'MG Ten' (the working name for the new model) had been used by Sir Miles Thomas during the war, and a car (possibly the same one – a black car, registered KWL 200, was recalled by Jim Cox as a 'garage car' run by MG's 'Tubby' Reid.

Like MG, Riley depended upon Morris Motors Limited Bodies Branch ('Morris Bodies' for short) as the primary source of its timber-framed bodywork, at a time when other newer body-making divisions, such as Nuffield Metal Products (under the dynamic management of George Dono) were supporting the more modern monocoque coachwork of the new generation of Morris and Wolseley saloons, including the aforementioned models introduced at the end of 1948. John Thornley and Syd Enever were not blind to this; they wanted to modernise the MG sports car line because they could already see that a philosophy of upright bodyshells made from, as Thornley jokingly put it, *'sheets of tin and a bundle of fire-wood'*, was not a recipe for survival in the post-war world. But they had to walk before they could run; what became the MG TD Midget would have to be the first step towards the modernity that they craved.

Morris Motors Bodies Branch was located, like both the Riley plants, in Coventry: the production planning logic of bringing MG and Riley assembly under one roof and near the body factory was simple enough to see; the fact

We know from the fact that this image appears in Goldie Gardner's 1951 book 'Magic MPH' that it depicts the record car in Belgium in the summer of 1950, in perhaps its most remarkable guise – with an engine capacity of less than 350cc, using just two cylinders of the venerable K3 six-cylinder. Gardner wrote how '...cylinders four and five were fitted with dry cylinder liners giving a bore of 57.25mm. Thus the capacity of the engine finally worked out at 332cc... on the bench test, Syd Enever and Jacko were quite satisfied with the results'. The run took place on July 24th 1950; the final outcome was new Class J records of up to 194.809kmph (121.048mph) for the one mile. That little engine revved up to 8,200rpm and had a 'bob-weight' fitted to the unused crank journal of number six. (Enever Archive)

that Riley also had a 1.5-litre engine in production made the idea all the more tenable to the Nuffield bean-counters and Cowley-based production engineers.

Thus, the Morris Motors Board began to make plans for changes right across the organisation. With the MG factory effectively a satellite of Cowley, with most managerial, engineering and other directions driven from within the Morris Motors HQ, it was perhaps no great surprise that at first these grand plans remained unknown at Abingdon – although unsurprisingly, news would soon have reached the MG works, most likely via George Propert, who would have been advised 'as a courtesy'. Confidential or not, bad news often travels fast, and before long the threat was surely known by the likes of Cousins, Thornley, Jackson and Enever.

The plans were formally discussed at Morris Motors Board level at a meeting a few weeks before Christmas 1948, with a confidential memo tabled by Hanks. An extract from the Board Minutes is illuminating:

Also part of the 1950 record-breaking run, almost as an adjunct to it but one which had closer ties to the MG that could be bought by the average customer, Gardner drove this supercharged MG Y-Type saloon. Some of the people in the upper photograph can be identified; from the left we see Chris Shorrock (whose supercharger was on the car); the tall figure fifth from left is 'Kes' Kesterton, next to him is Goldie Gardner and then Gardner's friend Freddie Clifford. On the other side of the car, John Thornley has his foot nonchalantly perched on the wing; then we see Syd Enever, Jack Crook (of MG), and the final two figures are respectively Reg Jackson and Dick Benn, whose car it was. The car had some rudimentary aerodynamic work underneath and larger rear tyres than normal. It was later recorded by Russell Lowry, writing in the Nuffield publication 'Motoring' that Dick Benn was subsequently able to drive the car back to Brighton afterwards with no problems. There is further coverage of the event, and how it fitted into Gardner's other efforts, later in this chapter. (Enever Archive)

Morris Motors

Minutes of Meeting held at Cowley Wednesday 1st December 1948

Present:
  Mr R. F. Hanks – in the chair
  Mr G. E. Dono
  Mr D. Harrison
  Mr W. Hobbs
  Mr A. E. Keen
  Mr S. V. Smith
Absent
  Mr H. C. R. Mullens – en route from Australia
  Mr A. V. Oak – sick

1. Re-organization Scheme
The Vice Chairman tabled his confidential memorandum, which detailed the various phases of this scheme, which will not necessarily be carried out in the order in which they are listed. A copy of this memorandum is attached. He notified that Mr. Richardson had been put in charge of the detailed planning work, and advocated that he should be given an opportunity of seeing and initialling all future capital expenditure and disposal sanctions until the scheme was complete. This was agreed.

It was further agreed that Companies and Branches concerned should book all re-organisation expenses to a separate account.

Mr Harrison stated that he had prepared a preliminary scheme under Phase 6, and gave an outline of its salient points. It was decided that this be deferred until the next meeting, when Directors would have had an opportunity of studying the scheme in detail.

2. Co-operation with the Austin Company
The Vice-Chairman reported on a talk he had had with Mr Lord on the 29th November. Both of them were of the opinion that the matter should not be pursued with extreme urgency, but be allowed to take its course for perhaps a year. Earlier stages would consist of interchanges of ideas on manufacturing methods and costs.

Note the presence of George Dono, mentioned earlier, who was in charge of the Nuffield Pressings Division; Gerald Palmer (yet to join the party at this juncture) told the author that Dono was a help to him when he arrived – because, as explained later in this chapter, Palmer saw Dono as driving the restructure of Nuffield's specialist car making from within. Tom Richardson, mentioned in the note above, was Morris Motor's Chief Planning Engineer but destined for greater things. The confidential memorandum is reproduced here in full:

> **Strictly Confidential**
>
> **Nuffield Factories Re-Organization Scheme**
>
> **Phase 1**
> The Wolseley Motors Limited assembly line, and all its ancillary services, will move down to Morris Motors Limited Cars Branch, Cowley, and will be administered by Cars Branch.
>
> **Phase 2**
> Morris Commercial Cars Limited assembly line, and all its ancillary services, will move to the Wolseley Motors Limited factory at Ward End. The M.C.C. control will eventually cover the assembly of their own vehicles, the Nuffield Tractors, the Oxford Taxicabs, and the odd W.D. types we have in hand. The M.C.C. Design and Engineering Department will retain its identity at Ward End and will take over Tractor and W.D. vehicle design.
>
> **Phase 3**
> The whole of the Nuffield Organization machining resources will be co-ordinated, so far as is practicable, in two main locations, viz. Courthouse Green, Coventry, which will cater for all Group Engine production, whilst the present Wolseley works at Ward End will look after all axle production. It may prove to be expedient to close down the existing S.U. Works and absorb their production either in the Birmingham Machine Group or at Coventry. The progress made in regard to Phase 3 is dependent, to some extent, upon the development of the Nuffield-Austin co-operative system.
>
> **Phase 4**
> Radiators Branch in North Oxford will be dispersed to Birmingham (Messrs. Nuffield Metal Products Limited) and Llanelly [Llanelli] respectively.
>
> **Phase 5**
> MG Car Company and Rileys will combine production resources at the Riley factory in Coventry. This will create a tidy bloc comprising our two "specialist" cars with Bodies Branch on their door-step. All three factories will be under common Management.
>
> **Phase 6**
> The Sales Departments of Morris, Wolseley, MG, Riley and Marine and Industrial Engines will be brought together at Cowley under the direct control of the Sales Director. The same thing will apply in the case of all Publicity work. N.B. Mr D. Harrison is preparing his own scheme covering the detail of these changes.
>
> **Phase 6a**
> The Service Departments of Morris and Wolseley will be combined at Cowley. Those of MG and Riley will join forces at the Riley Works, Coventry. The M.C.C. Service Department, after its move to the Wolseley Works location, will take over Nuffield Tractor and Taxi-cab service.

As soon as the news of this plan reached Abingdon, the alarms were sounded within the small group of faithful MG people, among them Cecil Cousins, Reg Jackson and Syd Enever. As far as the author knows, neither Jackson or Enever ever spoke publicly of this interlude, but Cousins – by the time well into his retirement – became less reticent; you can be sure that if he was involved in the ensuing battle to save Abingdon, so were the other two – and John Thornley at the fore.

Cousins spoke to author John McLellan in around 1974 about the interlude: '*I give Propert full credit. He was due to retire in July 1949 but he argued that Riley had no real production methods*' Cousins said. '*The original plan by the Nuffield Organisation was that MGs should be built at Riley to make Foleshill more viable. The MG place at Abingdon could be used for something else. It was only a shed out in the country in any case. But Propert wanted to use Foleshill as part of Morris* [Motors] *Engines* [Branch] *and let Abingdon build assembly-line Riley cars and MGs. They were still building Rileys the old way with gangs of men, one at a time, in Coventry.*'

Cousins said that Propert called on him to help convince the Nuffield planner Tom Richardson (referred to above in the December 1948 minutes) that Abingdon was much more than just a shed in the country: '*Propert sent for me and told me he wanted me to stop for lunch that day- I usually went home. It turned out he had this Richardson coming in. He was quite a knowledgeable man, chief planning engineer at Morris Motors, later general manager of Nuffield's toolmaking company.*

Propert told me to take him round the factory.' Cousins recalled this event as taking place in November 1948 – thus very shortly before the aforementioned Board Meeting; Cousins took Richardson on an extensive tour of the Abingdon works; '*I kept telling him how clever we were, how we were getting high production out of the place. Richardson had been sent in as judge and jury but in the end, he voted for us*'.

Cousins told McLellan that Propert had confided

'...he had a paper in his desk: as from March 1949, MG was to cease to exist. I was to be the sole person to go from MG to Riley.' Whether or not the Cousins 'guided tour' was the true catalyst for a change of heart – and it seems likely that others played their part – the proposals under 'Phase 5' were changed – more or less a reversal of the plan, with Riley destined to decamp from their traditional home at Coventry and move down to the MG factory, under what would become the 'MG and Riley' business. The changes were formally ratified at the Morris Motors Board meeting of January 19th 1949 – thus roughly a month and half from the discussion by the same directors.

> **Morris Motors**
>
> **Minutes of Directors meeting held at Cowley, Wednesday 19th January 1949**
> Present:
> Mr R. F. Hanks – in the chair
> Mr G. E. Dono
> Mr D. Harrison
> Mr W. Hobbs
> Mr A. E. Keen
> Mr H. C. R. Mullens
> Mr S. V. Smith
>
> Absent
> Mr A. V. Oak – sick
>
> **1. Re-organization Scheme**
> Consideration was given to a further memorandum tabled by the Vice Chairman. This drew attention to certain unavoidable variations in the plan adopted at the meeting held on the 1st December 1948, due to the inexpediency of moving Morris Commercial Cars to Ward End in its entirety and transferring MG to the Riley Factory.
>
> The following amended scheme was therefore adopted again on the understanding that the phases would not necessarily be carried out in the order in which they were listed.
>
> a). M.C.C. Ltd to remain at Addersley Park but all machinery activities to be transferred to Ward End in Coventry.
> b). Tractor production and assembly to continue at Ward End. Marketing and Service to be moved to Adderley Park.
> c). Riley to move to the MG premises at Abingdon where assembly of the two marques will be combined.
>
> The chief reasons for this reversal of the original plan are:
> (i). Lack of space at Riley plant.
> (ii). Need of Engines Branch for some accommodation.
> d). Future deliberation to be given to the prospect of transferring Bodies Branch to the Cowley region.
> e). The transfer of Wolseley assembly to Cowley, now almost complete, to be followed by a similar transfer of Wolseley Sales and Service, MG and Riley Sales and all Publicity activities. The latter moves to be made as soon as office accommodation becomes available, enable the departments concerned to be grouped in one centre under the control of the Sales Director.
> f). MG and Riley Service to be located at Abingdon as a preliminary measure. It is envisaged that all the Sales and Service departments of the Organisation will ultimately be grouped in one factory.
> g). Complete re-organisation of the Engineering Department in congruity with the major plans. The Vice Chairman exhibited a chart illustrating the details of this re-organisation, which was approved in principle.
>
> **2. Re-naming Factories**
> It was agreed that following the transfer of Wolseley activities to Cowley, the Ward End factory will be described as 'Morris Motors Ltd., Machining Branch, Wolseley Works, Ward End, Birmingham'. After the transfer of Rileys from Coventry, the present Riley factory to be described as 'Morris Motors Ltd., Engines Branch, Riley Works, Foleshill, Coventry.'
>
> **3. Riley (Coventry) Limited – Change of Name**
> It was resolved that the name of Riley (Coventry) Limited be changed to Riley Motors Limited, and the Secretary was instructed to arrange accordingly.

The revised plan was reported two days later, somewhat obscurely, in the Manchester Evening News of Friday January 21st 1949; two thirds down the front page, under a small headline 'Riley- MG merger' the paper reported that *'Riley (Coventry), Ltd., is to join forces with the MG Car Company at Abingdon (Berks), the Nuffield Organisation announced to-day. The characteristic MG and Riley features will be retained, it is stated'.* MG at Abingdon had emerged victorious; we can be reasonably sure that John Thornley and Syd Enever would have quietly celebrated the outcome, but were sanguine about the implications of such a near miss; after all it was not that long since voices at Cowley had discussed ideas like an MG-badged Morris Minor. Although they had to continue to grin and bear rule from Cowley, they were both keen to wrest as much control away to Abingdon as they could. Meanwhile, the 'MG Planning Engineer' had survived in his role.

George Propert retired from MG on July 20th 1949 – he continued to serve in local politics. Perhaps in part as compensation to Riley, that company's Jack Tatlow came south from Foleshill to manage the new joint 'MG and Riley' facilities, which soon started building Riley saloons alongside the TC Midgets and Y-Type saloons. In the midst of this, with the backdrop of the growing US export business, came the final development of the TD Midget.

The TD Midget and the Arrival of Gerald Palmer

Around the same time that George Propert retired, and Jack Tatlow arrived to take his place at Abingdon, there were other changes in MG design management – still centred at Cowley. MG design was still managed – as it had been since 1935 – from a small office at Cowley, reporting to Chief Engineer Victor Oak. There had been some tentative ideas for new MGs related to Riley parts and body construction methods – copies of photos made it into Syd Enever's photo albums – and it is clear how the logic of bringing MG and Riley under one roof near Morris Motors Bodies Branch had been seen by Hanks as a good idea. As the dust settled on the revised plans for MG and Riley discussed above, it was clearly seen as logical that if MG and Riley were both going to be built at Abingdon, next door to Cowley, that fresh impetus should be given the design of new models for both marques that it was hoped would be better fitted to post-war sales.

After casting around for suitable candidates it was Gerald Palmer – already looking to come back to his home in Iffley from his spell at Jowett in Bradford – who got the job. Palmer told Graham Robson that his brief from Reginald Hanks was a remarkably loose one: *"All I had to do was produce new cars for Riley and MG"* he told Robson in 1977; *'there was no product planning, nothing: all I had to do was to come up with new ideas, which I hoped would be accepted. Luckily they were!'* This was not quite the whole story; Palmer told the author that whilst initially his brief was to develop a new range of MG and Riley models, for the time being the intention was that 65-year-old Harry Rush, the Riley Chief Designer, would initially retain some input. Palmer was obviously aware of the sensitivity of Riley feelings: *'Harry and I never spoke about this: he worked mostly at Coventry, where he was involved with the remaining Riley side and then the Morris Engines function which took over at Foleshill. He was nearing retirement age, and he knew I was working on future Rileys, but we never discussed the future.'*

However, Rush died at hospital in Banbury following a road accident on the way home two days before Christmas 1949; Palmer therefore took over Riley design completely. Palmer soon extended his influence to the Wolseley marque too, for as he told the author: *'Vic Oak also wanted a new small and large Wolseley, and so it seemed to me that they needed two pairs of bodies – what would become the MG Magnette and Wolseley 4/44, and the bigger full six-seater Wolseley 6/90 and Riley Pathfinder.'* As the Z Magnette and Wolseley 4/44 took shape, the former became the first car to receive the BMC 'B' series engine. The Wolseley was launched first, with the old Nuffield 1,250 c.c. engine instead of the BMC unit. However, Palmer says that it was the Magnette design which came first, the Wolseley form being developed from it – but from the perspective of 1949, these developments were still over three years in the future, by when there would be other major structural changes at the head of the Nuffield Organisation.

Before Palmer arrived, however, as we have already seen, there had already been design work on what would appear within a few months as the new TD Midget. Although originally envisaged as benefitting from a 1949 Motor Show launch, this was inevitably deferred when the Earls Court event that year was cancelled; in the event the new MG TD Midget was unveiled to great fanfare on January 18th 1950 (production started on November 10th 1949 and the last TC went down the line on the 29th).

The new TD arrived in time to support the export drive as the British Government devalued the Pound against the Dollar. Over 90% of the 4,767 TDs built in 1950 were exported, more than half for the USA. As production at Abingdon began to ratchet up, the plant celebrated the completion of its 10,000th car in February 1951. Competition activity in the new TD led to production changes with a 'Mark II' version, and a team of TDs were raced by Ted Lund, George Phillips and Dick Jacobs. John Thornley and Syd Enever were bursting with new ideas and ambition, and they wanted nothing more than some of the independence that Abingdon had lost in 1935. However, at this stage, Syd's formal title was still 'Planning Engineer' rather than 'Designer'; he would have to wait a little longer for that change of status to be realised.

Gerald Palmer was alive to the sensitivities; those events of 1935 were still raw memories for many people, even if they had preceded a more profitable era. *'The sports cars were Syd Enever's babies, and he was mostly involved with them'* Palmer told the author. *At first, I had little direct involvement with the MG sports cars, with the exception of trying to solve the problem of scuttle shake which came up during development of the TD Midget.'* Even so, with his role as Chief Designer, it was perhaps natural that Palmer would dabble in sports car ideas; we will return to this topic later in this chapter.

'MG' Record Breaking Again

With the embarrassment of seeing Goldie Gardner's record car having been shorn of its MG badges, and using a Jaguar engine in 1948, it seems that wise heads eventually intervened; it seems highly likely that Lord Nuffield himself would have had something to say on the matter, having been largely responsible for underwriting the car's original creation in 1938. With a more modern MG range on the way, it was clear that despite its pre-war origins, the sleek record breaker could still be worthy of the right kind of headlines. The first step back to MG identity came with fresh efforts to pursue records with the smaller engine classes. What brought this to a head was the news that some of Gardner's records were being pursued by Piero Taruffi in a twin-boom record breaker of his own design. When Taruffi secured three of the 500cc class records, the gauntlet was laid and Gardner decided to respond with his car, confident on the basis of the previous efforts that his own car still had more to offer.

To plan the next steps, Gardner consulted Syd, Jacko and Chris Shorrock and their remarkable solution was typical of Syd's creative mind; they would convert the engine (still essentially the pre-war K-Series block) to a three-cylinder with 120-degree crank throws and using just cylinders 4, 5 and 6; with a new crankshaft from Laystall, re-boring of those three cylinders and fitment of a Shorrock supercharger, the end result was a 497cc supercharged 64.3mm stroke three-cylinder, and another demonstration of the combined genius of Syd and Jacko. It was agreed that Abingdon facilities could be used to build the engine, and once more Thomson & Taylor were to prepare the car, with bench-testing in Dunstable. At Abingdon, recently appointed MG & Riley General Manager Jack Tatlow and his second-in-command, John Thornley, supported further work on the car and agreed to formally loan Syd and Jacko to accompany Gardner on the trip.

The completed car, in new three-cylinder trim, left Folkestone on Monday 12th September 1949 and suffice to say the trip was a great success, with several records broken. After the record car returned, Gardner and his MG friends did not rest on their laurels; by reassembling the engine with one less cylinder, it was possible to create a two-cylinder 330cc engine but still using a six-cylinder block. Once again it was the ingenuity of Syd Enever who had achieved something of an unlikely engine miracle, contrary to conventional theory; it was typical of him to show the theoreticians what, often, only experience and original thinking can deliver. In his seminal book *'Maintaining The Breed'*, John Thornley devotes much of a chapter to the creation and testing of this engine, and with some justice, because there is no doubt that it was a theory-busting miracle.

Thornley wrote about the debate in the experimental shop – with Syd, Jacko and Chris Shorrock at the heart of it; there was an argument about the induction pipe: *'the engine has two cylinders working on a three-cylinder 120-degree crank and therefore fires irregularly at 240 and 480 degrees of crankshaft revolution. Shorrock considers that the spasmodic gas flow calls for a reservoir adjacent to the inlet ports, but Enever doubts it. Anyway, one is made. Finally, engine, blower, fuel and a Saturday conspire together to make a run possible, the engine is switched on, the fuel pumped up, the starter pressed and – wonder of wonders – it fires on both and ticks over quite merrily but with the anticipated erratic sound. After a while, the throttle is opened, but the engine fails to accelerate. Everyone waits patiently while Enever juggles with the butterflies and, after a minute or so, the note changes, the engine seems to shake itself, increase speed and, finally, away it goes straight up to 7,000 revs'.*

'At the first sign of life, those present take up their stations; Jack Crook at the brake with a streamlined left hand ready to pounce on the switch; Enever at the carburettors; Jackson standing back with a hand on the air pump and an eye on the gauges; nobody, it will be noted, in the plan of the cranks or flywheel. The power is low, the blower pressure very high – 37 pounds – obviously Chris Shorrock has done a very good Job. The fumes from the dope get In Enever's eyes and temporarily blind him, and he runs, on a sudden, out into the open air, forgetting in his pain that there is no return spring on the throttle. The engine skies and Jackson makes a dive for the carburettors just as Syd comes dashing back – and they bang their heads together'.

The story continued; how the supercharger gearing had to be altered, vibrations tackled, packaging sorted, bob-weights fitted, and the choice of twin cylinders resolved as numbers four and five, with six sealed off. Early in 1950, the car was crated up and shipped off to New York to be displayed on a rotating turntable centre stage on the Nuffield stand at the New York Motor

Show, which opened at the city's Grand Central Palace on April 15th 1950. John Thornley and others were on hand, but Syd was not part of the happy throng on this occasion; he was far too busy back at Abingdon supporting the new MG TD Midgets now on sale and receiving a sales boost from their Eastern US show debut in New York.

The Gardner car returned to Jabekke again that July to tackle the 'Class J' (sub 350cc) records.

Although blighted by problems with the timing equipment, the équipe gained further glory, but not without some weather challenges; for as Thornley wrote: *'as the day wore on, the wind freshened and by the time all was set again around six in the evening, it was blowing more strongly than Goldie liked. For at 120mph or so the road does not seem to be very wide. Nevertheless, the decision to make the attempt was taken and the east to west run was made in fine style, though Goldie found it somewhat difficult to keep the car aimed at the far end of the road. On the return, however, things were not so good. Goldie entered the five kilometre stretch at 8,000 rpm and the mile at 8,200, but at the start of the kilometre the cockpit filled with white smoke, and, by the end of the stretch, the revs had dropped to 7,600 rpm, so he switched off the motor and coasted for the rest of the run'.*

To the author's mind, the simple fact that a high-pressure two-piston engine within a six-bore block could operate at over 8,000 rpm in such circumstances serves to illustrate Syd Enever's counter-intuitive, rule-breaking engine-building brilliance.

Gardner was content that he had beaten Lurani's old record of 106mph and by a fair margin. However, the fact that the record car still had a pre-war MG engine at its heart was a topic sometimes swept under the carpet when the topic was raised; perhaps to assuage this the summer 1950 trip included a specially adapted MG Y-Type owned by Dick Benn (of the motoring dealer and distributor, Brittains Limited), with its 1.25-litre XPAG engine supercharged by Chis Shorrock. Benn's car was driven by Goldie Gardner – after the main record-breaking had been concluded – on the timed section at Jabekke at speeds of up to 104.725mph for the kilometre and 104.68mph for the mile. Next year, it was surely logical the XPAG engine would also find its way into the record breaker; Gardner's target there would be 210mph to eclipse his own 204.3mph kilometre record for the 1.5-litre record from 1939.

The Morris Motors Board made a decision on future MG and Riley and competitions policy on October 16th 1950 (to only support third party owners of their products), but they further resolved on November 15th 1950 to continue to support Goldie Gardner's efforts – for the time being at least: *'...it was agreed, in broad principle, to continue to co-operate with Colonel Gardner in his record-breaking activities. It was understood that these were unlikely to continue for more than a year. It was emphasised that there must be the closest possible liaison between the Competition Committee and the Technical Director's Department, particularly because it was already envisaged that certain of Colonel Gardner's future projects would be incapable of realisation on technical grounds alone. Mr Tatlow, who joined the meeting during the discussion of this item, expressed his understanding of the position and undertook that no plans would be discussed with Colonel Gardner without prior reference to the Board'.* Reading between the lines one may deduce that the plans needed to include contemporary powertrains at their heart.

On January 3rd 1951, the Morris Motors Board discussed the motorsports proposals further; amongst them was support for an *'...attack by L. Col. A.T.G. Gardner on International Class F One-hour Record and one other record yet to be selected using basic TD power units... preparation of chassis and three TD engines, packing and shipment to New York and return. Return air passages for Col. Gardner and two mechanics to New York, insurances and expenses... £1,500'.* A few days later (January 9th 1951) Gardner went to Abingdon, where the good news was confirmed, and plans began in earnest. It was a dramatic volte face and showed that Goldie Gardner (now entering his sixties) and MG were back in harness; and of course, Syd was happy if the Board was kind enough to authorise him to be flown out at company expense...

Days later, the EX-Register recorded the first entries under a new code, EX173, described as 'TD engines for Record Car' with a total of 36 drawings listed. At the beginning of February, EX174 was ascribed to 'Two-litre converted Wolseley 6/80 engine for Record Car' – effectively a smaller-capacity version of the overhead camshaft 2.2-litre six-cylinder used in the Wolseley. Although much work was done on the latter, subsequent events would mean that it would never be utilised to the extent intended; as we shall see, there were changes coming in both the motor industry and Goldie Gardner's personal circumstances; it is perhaps ironic that the idea of this two-litre engine had not been countenanced a couple of years earlier when Gardner had felt obliged to turn to Jaguar for help...

MG Records in 1951: Salt Lake, Utah

Goldie Gardner's record car was now given a new lease of life – with a contemporary MG engine at last, albeit one that had been supercharged. The engineering work on the latter naturally fell largely to Syd and his team –

notably Jim Cox – in conjunction with Chris Shorrock for the supercharger. The fact that the project had the blessing of Lord Nuffield is immediately evident from a photo of him at Cowley, smiling alongside a small group including Gardner, Jacko ('Chief Inspector, MG Works) and Syd ('Chief Planning Engineer, MG Works'), shortly before they were due to set off for their autumn 1951 trip to the salt lakes. Before then, however, the car was once more summoned to become a show star; it appeared at the Festival of Britain from May 4th and although that event ran until September 4th, a request was made (with much negotiation and no little reluctances on the part of the organisers) to withdraw the record breaker nearly a month early on June 15th; in the event the actual extraction did not take place until the beginning of July, just in time for a press reception at Abingdon with Goldie Gardner, Dick Benn, Jacko and Syd in attendance; they called in at Cowley for the photograph of them flanking Lord Nuffield.

The Minutes of the Morris Motors Board (which were referred to earlier, in terms of the £1,500 grant for Goldie Gardner of January 3rd 1951) also record the fact that various attempts had been made – apparently without initial success – to secure sponsorship from an oil company (an entry from March 28th 1951) but we know from the subsequent publicity that Gardner was able to draw upon a beneficial relationship with Duckhams; indeed Jack Duckham attended the runs at Utah.

The car and entourage went with two 1,250cc engines; one – a Stage III unit with a 10psi boost, which was fitted in the car, and the other in a separate crate, boasting a supercharged boost of 30psi and, with alcohol fuel, capable of achieving 213bhp at 7,000rpm – Enever's brilliance at work again. The plan was that the car, initially ensconced in the hold of the *Queen Elizabeth*, would arrive at Wendover on August 7th and Goldie, Syd and the others on the 14th – although the crates were initially misdirected to Salt Lake City, and their arrival delayed. Syd, Jacko and Dick Benn (referred to in the publicity as 'Governing Director of Brittains Limited, Nuffield Distributors in Brighton') accompanied Goldie on a BOAC Monarch flight (Boeing 377 Stratocruiser) instead of travelling with the car on the ship. Travel arrangements were aided by American Express and publicity on the US side was largely handled by Hambro, Nuffield Export's US partners, whose Vice Chairman C. B. Webb was on hand to share the congratulations.

Meanwhile Syd was bothering himself with the considerations of running the record car in the special circumstances on the Salt Lake, which required the course to be carefully cleared and marked out in a vast file-mile diameter circular course and was at a higher altitude. Syd had to contemplate the balance of wind load and rolling resistance and drag levels; as Thornley wrote these were not properly known with accuracy on a conventional sea level concrete road (Belgium) in a straight line, let alone on salt at 4,000 feet above sea level and in a big circle; '*in this matter Enever therefore, was feeling his way through a vast mas of information, much of it conflicting, which had been supplied to him by the cognoscenti and previous visitors to Utah.*' Among the latter, most likely were the likes of David Abbott ('Ab') Jenkins known for his pre-war record breaker, the 'Mormon Meteor', who along with his son Marvin met up with the MG team during their trip at the invitation of Gardner.

A happy party just prior to setting off to seek more records in the USA in 1951; Jacko, Goldie, Lord Nuffield, Dick Benn and Syd. (Enever Archive)

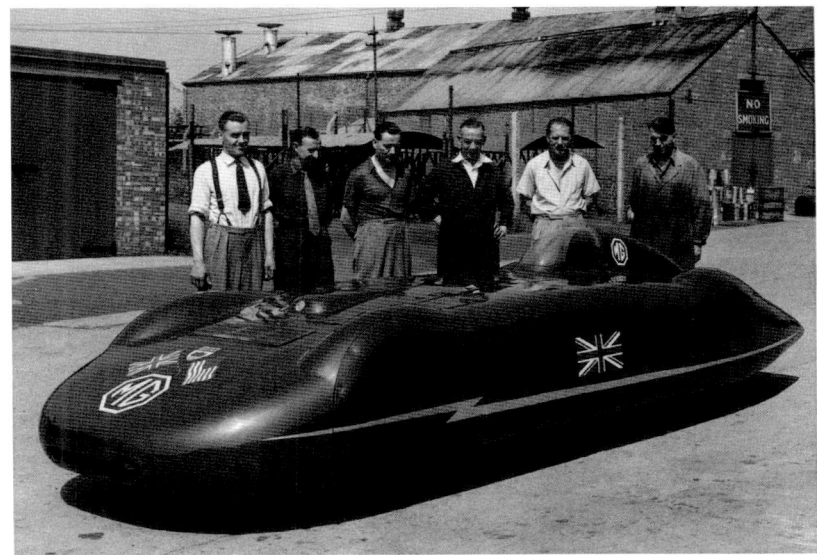

Syd Enever stands alongside some of the key members of the team who were involved with preparing the Gardner car for 1951; in turn, next to Syd, are Henry Stone, Alec Hounslow, Jack Crook, Reg Jackson and R Avenall (the latter referred to by Syd, in his caption, as being a charge hand in the machine shop). A version of this photo also appeared in The Autocar of August 17th 1951. (Enever Archive)

Gardner's main aim was the Class 'F' standing start one hour record, which was duly taken on August 20th 1951, Gardner's figure of 137.4mph easily eclipsing the existing record (by a Bugatti) of 119.01mph; he took a total of Sixteen International and American National records up to 139.3mph. For the one-hour effort, an alternative cockpit cover was used, not fully enclosed, the idea being to admit more fresh air into the cockpit. For the high-speed short distance records, a straight 14-mile course was marked out; a change in the weather disturbed this final stage for 1951, and while the car went on a publicity tour around the USA, Syd, Jacko and the rest of the team returned home. As a related exercise, meanwhile, *Motor Trend* magazine drove a 'showroom stock' MG TD Midget around the circular course for a twelve-hour run on August 22nd 1951, the outcome being a record for such a car in the same Class 'F' capacity as Gardner's main efforts; the average was 75.34mph over the twelve hours.

But for the moment, before continuing the record breaker saga, it is necessary to rewind to early 1951 and another important project for Syd which also relied on the XPAG engine.

Jack Crook

By the time he was interviewed for the *Nuffield Teamwork* magazine issue of October 1951 (a copy of the typed draft manuscript is in the Enever archive), Jack Crook had been working in the MG Experimental Department for 21 years, and was 43 years old. He said that he had worked on every racing car that MG had ever built, including the Gardner record cars covered earlier. Crook's first memory in the MG racing world was serving as E. R. Hall's racing mechanic in the TT race of 1931.

In the USA, a MG TD was plucked from a local dealership and subjected to a high-speed run on the Bonneville Salt Flats, the obvious idea being to link the contemporary TD, complete with its Nuffield 'XPAG' engine, with the similarly-powered Gardner record car. Here we see Syd (in dark glasses) with Ab Jenkins of Salt Lake City. (Enever Archive)

Out on the salt flats in 1951, with EX135 and the MG TD Midget running with the support of Motor Trend, are – left to right – Jack Duckham, Dick Benn, Goldie Gardner, Syd Enever and a helper. Note the drum of Duckham oil strategically placed just within the photo at right. The TD had been taken from a Salt Lake City showroom just hours beforehand; the car had then been checked by the American Automobile Association to ensure it was genuinely to stock specification; the AAA also undertook the timing. (Enever Archive)

A happy party on their Monarch flight to New York; left to right Dick Benn, Reg Jackson, Syd, Goldie Gardner and an American Express man. (Enever Archive)

CHAPTER SIX: EXPORT OR DIE

According to *Nuffield Teamwork*, 'his vast experience in interpreting the ideas of the designers, make him an essential member of any team working on record bids. To Jack, record breaking bids mean long hours and working every weekend. "It's always a rush for us to prepare the cars in time" he says.' Crook lived in Spring Gardens, Abingdon, and treasured amongst other things an engraved cigarette case given to him by Eddie Hall after the latter had come third in the Brooklands 500-mile race.

Jim Cox

There is a fairly well-known photo of Syd Enever standing attentively alongside one of the B-Series engines under development testing prior to the 1955 Le Mans race; alongside him, almost in tandem, is Jim Cox. Like Syd, Jim Cox started at the bottom and through his skill and aptitude worked his way up, becoming of Syd's trusty development technicians; the respect was mutual and strong throughout. Jim Cox, born in 1931, is really Sydney John Cox; he started at MG junior office/messenger boy in 1945, as a 14-year-old fresh out of St. Edmund's school, and was told he would move from section to section after six months. When this did not happen, and Cox began to get restless, he was summoned to see Cecil Cousins: '*he called me in to his office and the first thing he said was "sit down lad – now what's your problem?" I said that they had told me that I would only have to do six months as messenger and there I was, still doing it after eight months. "Is that all your problem is?" he replied, and added "take your satchel upstairs and come with me" whereupon he took me to see John Bull and said, "here's your new tea boy for the chassis line".*'

At this stage, MG was just starting up the TC production line, and Cox recalls the works well from seeing it on the chassis line. At the same time, the factory was still making Neptune amphibious tanks (which, he told the author, were built, inspected, tested and duly scrapped – mainly because the contract had not completed its course!), Bren-gun carriers and Rolls-Royce engine frames. Jack Lewis was Cox's first foreman: '*he asked me what my name was and I started to say Sydney John, but he interrupted me almost as soon as I had finished saying the Sydney and said "we've got too many Syd's and Cissies (Cecils) here so we'll call you Jimmy". Before I could protest he had called out to the line "here's our new tea-boy – JIMMY" – and so Jimmy stuck!*'. Funnily enough, this misnaming became compounded many years later when Jim moved to Cowley in 1980, where 'Jimmy' was not felt to be respectable enough, leading to Jim becoming James.

Meanwhile, however, Jim Cox found himself getting to know the intricacies of production, not least when occasionally he would fill in to cover absentees or illness. In May 1949, Jim went into the Army for his National Service – just as the Riley production line was starting up at Abingdon. When he came back to the factory in June 1951 (after time in Hong Kong and Malaya), through his friend and mentor Bert Wirdnam, he managed to secure a place in the Development Shop, initially working under Jack Crook, from whom he learned the rudiments of engine building.

Syd with Jim Cox working the factory's DPX2 engine test bed. (Author archive)

Ab Jenkins – the 'Mormon Meteor' – with Goldie Gardner on the salt flats. (Enever Archive)

'Henry Stone was Alec Hounslow's right-hand-man; he had been educated at Abingdon School and therefore had a better academic background than Alec; Henry was thus a very good assistant to Alec, while Jack Crook did the engine and test-bed work, and Harold Wiggins did welding and fabrication. They asked me if I would like to stay in Development and I said that I would, becoming their tea-boy'. This was far more than the job name implies: '*I quickly learned – particularly from my mistakes. I remember one time when Syd Enever came in and an engine which I had rebuilt was making a strange noise. Syd asked me what was wrong, and I replied that I didn't know. So I went back to the bench where I found a plate; I didn't know what it was for and Syd said "you know what you've got to do? Find out!" It turned out to be a thrust plate for the camshaft [XPAG engine]*'.

Cox was never an apprentice, which created its own challenges: '*It is very difficult if you learn the theory after the practice – but I had it that way round. But if you wanted to do something, someone would show you – e.g. lathe work – and that way I soon picked up the rudiments of engine work from Jack Crook. We even had a K3 Magnette in one time, and I had the job of rebuilding the engine in that*'. Cox says that he had a sort of 'apprenticeship by default'. When Jack Crook (q.v.) left in the early 1950s to work for Esso Research near Abingdon, and this gave Jim Cox the opportunity to take over responsibility for building racing engines at Abingdon; that included the George Phillips car [UMG 400 – EX172] '*... that was Syd's idea and most of the basic body was by Wally Kimpsey*' he says. '*Syd always wanted to turn EX172 into a production car, and so he managed to get a further prototype [EX175] built*. According to Cox, '*Syd managed to get the body for HMO 6 done on the quiet at Bodies Branch*'.

In due course he would be involved in many of the special projects which feature in this chapter; as well as EX172 and EX175, he worked on EX135, EX179, EX181 and EX182 amongst others. It was hard work much of the time, but enjoyable with it: '*The basic working week was eight to six, Monday to Thursday, and then eight to five on a Friday, but we often did eight till nine – except for Friday, when we still finished relatively early. We often worked Saturday and Sunday and one year I recall that we only had Christmas off. I was courting at the time and couldn't get Saturday afternoons off. I would go up to Alec and he would say "but you had a Saturday afternoon off a couple of months ago – how many d'you want?"*'

EX172 – An Aerodynamic TD for George Phillips

When, in January 1951, the Morris Motors Board discussed sanctioning the investment in Goldie Gardner's record-breaking efforts with the XPAG engine fitted to his record breaker, they also considered a separate request to finance a unique MG TD special, using both chassis and engine, to provide a chance to win the Rudge-Whitworth Biennial Cup at that summer's Le Mans 24-Hour race. George Phillips, and his friend and co-driver Eric Winterbottom, were eligible for the cup on the basis of their 1950 success. The Board agreed to supply **£850 for** '*...preparation of one TD Midget Mark II, to be driven by G.E, Phillips and E. Winterbottom. Weight to be reduced as far as possible. Return transport of vehicle to France, insurance, expenses etcetera...*'

John Thornley and Syd drew up a list of essential specifications – Wilson McComb reproduced it in one of his books, showing it to be a single hand-written sheet – and the Development Shop at Abingdon set to in order to build their 'TD Special' – Thornley originally conceived it as a narrow-bodied car like Phillips' earlier MG TC special, but he and Syd soon switched to a full-width concept. Phillips himself would later claim that he had suggested the Sunbeam Alpine for inspiration, but to the author a better match would be the shape of the Jaguar XK120, still fresh and exciting; the car was however very much a product of Syd Enever's own fertile mind rather than being simply derivative.

The outcome of this was 'EX172' a smart curvaceous sports car although obviously unknown at this stage, resembles the later MGA of a few years hence. The low cockpit sides had no separate doors, making it easy for the occupants to get in and out, although the narrowness of the TD chassis frame meant that the seats were quite high, so the driver's head projected well above the scuttle line and into the airstream. The car was duly inspected by the great and the good from

Alec Hounslow in the driving seat and Syd alongside, at Abingdon part way through the build of EX172. (Enever Archive)

Cowley – including local director S. V. Smith – and was handed to George Phillips for his Le Mans attempt.

Sadly, the engine expired in the race – MG and Phillips had unkind words for each other – and the prototype was eventually destroyed. However, Syd was sufficiently pleased with the concept that he began to make plans for a more realistic production sports car, using a new chassis with a perimeter chassis frame which would allow the driver and passenger seating to be set lower. But he had to develop this in the knowledge that MG design responsibility was still centred a few miles north in the Oxford suburbs; there were still a few hurdles to overcome.

Within the MG Design Office at Cowley, Jim O'Neill – whose work on what would become the TD Midget we touched on earlier – worked on new models under Palmer's direction, and saw several projects in their infancy, including the MG Z Magnette, Riley Pathfinder and a neat proposal by Palmer for a new open monocoque MG sports car; the latter could have been produced in multiple versions with a choice of exterior body panels to cover both the 'traditionalist' and 'modern' sports car markets. *'I had my head in the clouds at the time – I wanted to do an all-steel monocoque two-seater sports car'* Palmer told the author; *'I had to get Vic Oak's agreement to start off development of the twin cam engine, although he was on the point of retirement, and it was really as a corollary of that that I did the monocoque sports car.'*

Of his 'Midget' concept, Palmer said: *'the car had a patented form of folding windscreen, which could be wound forward, and the 90° twin cam engine which I designed, based upon the B-series block, could have been used'.* We will return to the subject of the Twin Cam engine later, because that took on a crucial role in some of Syd Enever's future projects. *'The car body would have been built at Nuffield Metal Products (NMP) at Birmingham, and because of their non-involvement in the design, MG at Abingdon were against the car.'* Palmer added *'I had much encouragement by getting the drafting of the monocoque done at NMP – their director George Dono was very supportive. Dono had also supported me with the Pathfinder – I suppose he was empire-building, and the Pathfinder bodies were actually built at NMP.'*

A selection of the team involved in the creation of EX172, the car for George Phillips to take to Le Mans in 1951. Alec Hounslow is behind the wheel; standing alongside are, left to right, Gerald Wiffen, Henry Stone, Syd Enever, Wally Kinsey (who crafted the body), Reg Avenall, Johnny Crook and an unknown. Alec Hounslow is behind the wheel. (Enever Archive)

Here EX172 is being admired by a number of onlookers – many of whom are involved in MG in some way; we can see Syd towards the far right (with jacket and tie) whilst 'Jacko' (fifth from right) has his arms folded, and roughly in the centre is Alec Hounslow. (Enever Archive)

Sidney Victor Smith

When Reggie Hanks swept into position as the new Deputy Chairman to Lord Nuffield, a number of older directors were pensioned off, amongst them Harold Ryder, who as we have seen had presided over MG affairs in the wake of Cecil Kimber. Taking over Ryder's role as far as MG were concerned was S.V. Smith – like Ryder, a long-serving employee although in Smith's case he had started before the first War at Wolseley. **Sidney Victor Smith** (March 27th 1896 – September 1968) was slim and almost handsome; in a favourable light he was occasionally compared to the actor Errol Flynn. However, many of S. V. Smith's staff often referred to him behind his back as 'Hitler Smith' because of his neatly trimmed moustache. Geoffrey Iley says of Smith that the foremen at Cowley used to hide from him when he was on the way; '*he was an absolute tyrant*' but that he was amenable when it served his purpose; '*when I was at Cowley after my time at Abingdon, Smith used to come into my office most mornings for a chat*'.

Like many of his Nuffield Peers, Smith had risen through the ranks; first coming from Wolseley to Morris Motors at Cowley in 1933, he was Works Manager three years later (and would have been well known to Leonard Lord) and in the second world war years was recorded as Technical Director of Morris Motors. In 1947, Smith undertook a fact-finding trip to the USA with Sales Director Donald Harrison and one consequence of this was the creation of the MG YT Tourer – Cowley conceived of course by Abingdon built, with learning opportunities for Syd Enever in the process. The Morris Motors Board purge of December 1947 did Smith (a director since August 1947) no harm; with the departure of Harold Ryder it was Smith who gained overall responsibility for the MG works, and he was sometimes part of the team who ventured overseas on fact-finding missions which tended to reinforce the message that international customers – particularly North American ones – generally wanted more MGs rather than much else in terms of Nuffield's car lines.

By the time of the creation of EX172 at Abingdon for George Phillips, Morris Motors Board member Smith was the 'Director of Assembly Facilities', overseeing the factories at Cowley and Abingdon; he would come over to Abingdon at least once a week to inspect production and progress, and for his sins he was a regular recipient of memos from John Thornley and Syd Enever. Following the BMC merger, Smith soon rose to become Technical Director for the whole of the Corporation, with a seat on the joint BMC Board – a measure of the respect from Leonard Lord among others; it was in that capacity that he was delegated the task of giving the good news to Abingdon when the go-ahead was received for the MGA.

By 1959, Smith was recorded as 'Engineering Co-ordinator, BMC', a position from which he retired, handing the baton to Alec Issigonis, on October 28th 1961.

Before long there were ructions in the British car industry when it became known that the Austin and Nuffield organisations were to merge; the news came on Friday November 23rd 1951 and the shock waves reverberated at Abingdon as much as they did at Cowley. It was obvious from the outset that the new man at the top would be Leonard Lord, the same person who had swept into Abingdon in 1935 like a tornado, ended MG factory racing and shifted design to Cowley. John Thornley later recalled being at an industry event and being teased by someone asking him if he would be returning to Abingdon or Longbridge; Thornley said he did not appreciate the joke.

Roy Brocklehurst – The Boy from Didcot

Less than seven miles south of Abingdon-on-Thames is the railway town of Didcot, and near the latter is Harwell, home to the famous energy research establishment. In the summer of 1947, fifteen-year-old **Roy Brocklehurst** (June 18th 1932 - April 29th 1988) cycled from his home in Didcot looking for work opportunities; he found that there were no vacancies at Harwell; he cycled north from there to the MG works in the Marcham Road and was more fortunate: he was interviewed by Syd and started work in June 1947. Brocklehurst's father was originally from the northeast of England, but had brought the family south to Didcot for work, and so that was where young Roy grew up.

George Phillips drove EX172 at Le Mans; look how prone he looks, a consequence of both the low build of the sleek body and the fact that it sits on a TD Midget chassis. The entry was not a great success and there was something of a mutual blame-game between Phillips and MG afterwards. Sadly the unique car was later cut up. (Enever Archive)

Roy Brocklehurst soon found himself designing engine components intended for the Gardner Record Car, whilst still studying design at night school at the Oxford College of Technology; he was also jointly responsible for drawing up the chassis for EX175, although in the midst of this he was called up for his two years of National Service in 1952. Syd was very fond of Brocklehurst and saw him as the heir apparent – indeed, according to some colleagues, Syd encouraged Brocklehurst to believe this, which occasionally caused a little frustration when the younger man felt he was being left behind by some of his older colleagues. Even so, by 1956 he was Chief Draughtsman and by December 1964 had risen to become Syd's deputy, as Assistant Chief Engineer, aged thirty-two.

Sadly, from Abingdon's perspective, the presence of Roy Brocklehurst as Chief Engineer would be short-lived; at the heart of British Leyland, as described later, MG's importance was subsumed by politics and, as Brocklehurst's reputation preceded him, he was soon drawn to Longbridge in 1973. By 1987, Brocklehurst was working at Gaydon on advanced group projects and planning to retire to the south coast; tragically he succumbed to a fatal stroke aged 55.

The Last Laps for Goldie

Having returned from Utah in late 1951, Goldie, Syd and Jacko soon began to formulate plans for 1952; the team considered going after the 1.5-2.0 litre Class E records – already held by Gardner's car, albeit with the Jaguar engine. Meanwhile the Morris Motors Board agreed to authorise (on December 12th 1951) a further grant of an even more generous £5,000 for the 1952 attempts – and this was less than a month following a major upheaval in Nuffield affairs, also described later in this chapter.

EX135 at Bonneville in 1952 – which proved to be the old stager's (and Goldie Gardner's) last escapade. (Enever Archive)

The only engine available that was vaguely suitable for the two-litre class was the 2,215cc six-cylinder overhead-cam unit from the contemporary Wolseley 6/80 saloon ('DO 934'; 1948-1954); shortening the stroke from 88mm to 77.5mm solved the capacity issue; then Syd had to find a way to achieve the power output required, with supercharging; Thornley says in *Maintaining The Breed* that '*certainly nobody had made a determined effort to blow this one to pieces yet. It might have possibilities: Enever would try.*'

This was certainly no simple task, however; in *The Works MGs*, Mike Allison describes how, even though high power was achieved, it was not initially without problems: '*it took some time to realise that the misfire was a direct result of the cylinder head having siamesed exhaust ports, which of course none of the MG engines had... in due course the engine was found to reach 249bhp at 5,400 rpm, and it was decided this was sufficient for the job at hand.*'

LATE ENGINE DEVELOPMENTS FOR THE GOLDIE GARDNER CAR		
MG EX-REGISTER ENTRIES		
EX173	TD engines for Record Car – Job No. ZM.13366; Cowley DO1008 [36 drawings]	January 10th 1951
EX174	DO1009 2- litre converted Wolseley 6/ 80 engine for Record Car [62 drawings]	February 1st 1951
COWLEY DO-REGISTER ENTRIES		
DO1008	1¼- litre racing programme	1951
DO1009	2- litre racing programme	1951

On board the RMS Queen Elizabeth en route to New York as first leg of the 1952 record breaking session at Bonneville. Soaking up the sun are, left to right, Dick Benn, Reg Jackson and Syd. (Enever Archive)

The second engine was one of the XPAGs from the 1951 attempt. The car and both engines were again shipped to Utah; Gardner – accompanied by the familiar retinue including Syd and Jacko - set off on the Queen Elizabeth on July 30th 1952 and the trip began with a party on board the ship, given by the Cunard Steamship Company in the Observation Bar; distinguished guests included Captain George Eyston, who clearly enjoyed catching up with his pre-war record-breaking associates.

During these efforts, Gardner secured another slew of records, but in a freak accident, he spun on one of his runs and a marker posts was flicked out of the salt and it shattered the Perspex canopy and struck the great man on his head; it was a shock for all concerned – not least Goldie himself, of course, but the next day the high-output XPAG engine was fitted and the process continued, although a piston collapse put an end to that part. Next the two-litre supercharged Wolseley unit was fitted and achieved 202mph; Mike Allison recalls speaking to Syd some years after the event and learning that Syd had realised that the Gardner car, still essentially of the same shape as had been built in 1938, was reaching the limits of what were possible aerodynamically; what Syd was already angling for was a new record breaker entirely.

Plans were laid for further record-breaking in 1953, this time the intention being to run in Belgium again at Jabbeke on September 16th 1953; Gardner planned to take two International records for the Flying Mile and Kilometre for Class 'E', using a 1,517cc bored-out supercharged XPAG engine, the existing records – both held by Piero Taruffi – being 180.50mph and 185.41mph respectively. However, it was not to be; illness – possibly lasting effects of Gardner's accident – led to the reluctant decision in July to finally retire – he was, after all, sixty-three years old; it is suggested that the impact had been more severe than initially thought and resulted in a cerebral haemorrhage.

The in-house magazine *Nuffield News Exchange*, which had assiduously followed Gardner's exploits since its first year in 1946, published a brief note in the October 1953 issue: *'we regret to state that Lt. Col. A.T. "Goldie" Gardner recently underwent an operation following an attack of sunstroke and has been ordered a complete rest. His doctors have advised him not to run on the 16th September and consequently the record attempts which had been planned for that date have been cancelled. We extend our sympathy to Col. And Mrs. Gardner and wish "Goldie" a quick recovery to full health.'* Gardner never did get to run at speed again.

The car was bought by MG and, its record-breaking days behind it, Johnny Lay was given the task of letting in Perspex panels to allow it to become an exhibit, in which form it still exists as part of the British Motor Museum at Gaydon. Sadly, Gardner experienced declining health and died five years later in Eastbourne.

Merger Between Austin and Nuffield

For years there was intense rivalry between two dominant players in the British-owned automotive field – Austin of Birmingham and Morris, centred on Oxford. One aspect of the rivalry was the saga of the purchase of the assets of Wolseley, for whom Herbert Austin was the original UK lead and so had an understandable emotional attachment: when the business went bankrupt in 1927, it was Morris who determinedly outbid his rival and acquired Wolseley.

The two empires were rivals in many ways, but they had been built up through fundamentally different operation models; Austin preferred to own and make most of their output in-house – growing their own facilities – whilst Morris had a knack of buying up formerly independent businesses to remodel them and mould them to his requirements. Perhaps the biggest unintended thread that linked them was one man – Leonard Lord – who rose to near the top of the Morris Motors business and then left in a hurry in 1938, only to re-emerge shortly at Austin. Whilst there was grudging mutual respect between Len Lord and Lord Nuffield, there was also an under-current of revengeful thoughts which underpinned the eventual merger of the two businesses.

There is insufficient space here to explore all the machinations, beyond stating the obvious fact that MG – and with it the likes of John Thornley and Syd Enever – were firmly linked to

CHAPTER SIX: EXPORT OR DIE

the Morris Empire, and could see problems ahead when first the Austin and Nuffield businesses had talks in 1948 about 'collaboration' (see Morris Board Minutes earlier in this chapter) and then, in November 1951, with the announcement of a marriage. The union was announced on the evening of Friday November 23rd 1951, to the effect that the two organisations were planning to work together, under the umbrella of an as yet unnamed holding company (the internal working name was 'British Motors Limited').

The first four named directors were Lord Nuffield, Leonard Lord, Reginald Hanks (of Nuffield) and George Harriman (of Austin). Whilst it was stressed publicly that this was intended to be a partnership of equals, nobody had any doubt that it was Leonard Lord who would soon rule the roost.

were hardly likely to warm to any fresh opportunities that could lose it; with the influence of Longbridge in the mix (see panel on the merger), they were even more nervous of losing MG's centre at Abingdon. When they found out about the project that Donald Healey was cooking up to use Austin 'big four' engines from the unsuccessful Austin Atlantic, they were even more nervous.

EX175 was, as John Thornley put it, 'the George Phillips car put right'; it had a new bespoke chassis (which lowered the centre of gravity as well as the driver), proper doors, windscreen and bumpers, and represented Syd's vision for a new modern post-war MG Midget. But due to the arrival of the Austin-Healey 100/4 in the BMC family, the project was turned down. (Enever Archive)

EX175 – Syd Enever's Aerodynamic Sports Car

Just weeks after the news of the BMC merger, and no doubt encouraged by Thornley, in the New Year of 1952, Syd Enever booked the next available project code – EX175 – and started scheming a layout on his dining room table at Westminster Way, Oxford. The chassis, using a 'perimeter frame' arrangement like contemporary US chassis design (also adopted by Palmer for the Riley Pathfinder) was passed to Roy Brocklehurst to draw up; the master drawing was EX175/ 2. By the end of the active work on the project there had been 44 EX175 entries.

Obviously both John Thornley and Syd Enever were very much aware of Gerald Palmer's idea for a new 'Midget and Magna' (see Thornley's January 1953 memo below) and had their reservations about the construction methods; it seems highly likely that they were equally concerned that the proposal not only perpetuated design authority remote from their influence, but – mindful of the NMP interest fostered by George Dono – that it was not hard to envisage Morris Motors moving the final assembly of the car elsewhere. Jim O'Neill told the author that as far as he was concerned, the Palmer Midget/ Magna was a brilliant concept; '*at the time I was absolutely sure it was a winner. Many years later when I was working with Syd, I asked him why Abingdon had rejected Palmer's Midget. He had no answer.*'

Having only recently seen off two plans that might have lost MG assembly from Abingdon, the team there

John Thornley and Syd really wanted the go-ahead for a new aerodynamic sports car, based on their EX172 Le Mans car of 1951, but in the event they were forced to progress this instead – what became the 1953 MG TF Midget, seen here in prototype form. (Author Archive)

EX175 was built with the help of several parts of the Nuffield empire; Eric Carter of Morris Motors Bodies Branch was only too happy to collaborate with Syd Enever on the body for the new model, which was fully finished with metallic maroon coachwork and tan leather interior; it was, John Thornley told the author, *'a beautiful car'* and it was very much Syd Enever's creation, at a time when he was in his mid-fifties, but still bursting with the energy first seen at Morris Garages in 1920. A model was made (which happily survives as part of the wonderful British Motor Museum collection) and from it can clearly be seen the evolutionary lines that link the 'EX172' TD-Special and the eventual EX182/ DO1062 'MGA'.

On the flanks, there was a brace of neat tetrahedral grille apertures on the front wings, with lines of horizontal grille bars, and to fit the XPEG engine it was necessary to provide a slightly unsightly bonnet bulge (not the last time that Syd would be faced with such a consideration). The model was tested in the aircraft wind-tunnels by Syd's friends (from record-breaking) at Armstrong-Whitworth. By the time that it came to build the full-size shell, however, those side grilles had been replaced with distinctive oval apertures on the tops of the wings. *'I doubt if we seriously tested the effect of those side ducts at Armstrong-Whitworths'* Syd later recalled; *'as far as I recall we just didn't like the look of 'em and so we drew the ones on top. If they were tested at all, they were tested after the event'*.

Eric Carter (see side panel) told motoring writer Doug Nye of the time that Syd came to see him at Coventry with his plans for EX175: *'Syd visited us at Quinton Road with a sketch of a proposed style for the outside shape plus some proposed details for a chassis. We made a start the following day with a full-size drawing and on the third day, details were issued to our experimental department in the form of tracings or slip sheets to start work on preliminary wooden formers to produce the panels. Within three months that prototype was finished. Bodies Branch being a small company with a maximum 1200 employees and cooperation between its various departments being first-class, no time was wasted'*.

Syd naturally called in frequently at Quinton Road as his creation was brought to life; *'Syd was a regular visitor during the building of this body when cooperation was absolutely essential to marry the body and chassis together while they were being built at different plants. In fact, on receipt of the chassis from MG, we had no trouble with the mounting'*. The chassis was strong and resistant to the dreaded scuttle-shake, and the body structure – especially the internal panels, was designed with the likelihood of low-volume production in mind, as Morris Motors Bodies Branch, unlike Pressed Steel, lacked the massive presses normally seen at Cowley; the idea was that these panels could if necessary be formed by folders, fly-presses or be hand-formed.

The finished article was beautifully finished in a deep metallic maroon with saddle leather trim and a matching beige hood. The bumpers were quite substantial in appearance, as were the squared-off over-riders, but the lowered driving position made possible by Syd's new chassis was a revelation. The car was road-registered as 'HMO 6' and everyone who saw it was impressed – including MG & Riley director Jack Tatlow; the car was made ready for presentation to the BMC Combined Board of management with the hope of approval.

Unfortunately for the MG men (and their Nuffield overlords) by the time that the BMC Board got to see EX175, Leonard Lord had already committed to support what became the Austin-Healey 100; Morris Motors and MG were told to drop the proposal and focus on improving their existing products, in particular the TD Midget.

Was this Cowley concept from 1949 – now thought to be part of the evolution of an idea by Gerry Palmer - an influence on Syd's thought process? We may never know... the model was sensitively restored by the MG Car Club. (Author Photo)

Eric Carter – The Man from Morris Motors Bodies Branch

Eric Carter (February 4th 1907 – April 8th 1980) was an 'old school' bodywork 'jack of all trades' who had worked throughout the Midlands, and could turn his hand to both body styling (perhaps more accurately 'detailing'), prototype manufacture and body tool design. Don Butler, who later got to work on MG projects with Carter, told the author: *'Eric had worked at Riley and Daimler and could turn his hand to almost anything, working everything out from the basic rolled sections through to the finished pressings.'* Carter's small unit was based at the former Morris Motors Bodies Branch at Quinton Road, Coventry – a stone's throw from that city's famous cathedral, which had been bombed to a shell by the Luftwaffe but rebuilt in modern guise as a symbol of post-war recovery.

As a part of the legacy of the Nuffield business, and with strong links to that organisation's Midlands body production plants, Carter and his team operated in a similar vein to his better-known, but 13-years younger Austin counterpart Doug Adams of the 'Body Experimental' shop at Longbridge (whose role in MG work increased in the late 1960s). In the fullness of time, it would be the Longbridge facility which survived the longer, but back in 1952, Austin and Nuffield affairs remained sufficiently discreet that it was Carter to whom Syd Enever would go in search of body design work; Jim O'Neill, who got to work with Carter on the MGA and MGA Coupé, told the author that the Morris Motors Bodies Branch man was *'a very competent body engineer'*.

Peter Neal adds some detail: *'Before he went to Bodies Branch, I think he'd worked at Riley and at one stage for the Humber as they called it. Eric was a kind of itinerate body design guy who had gone round various body coachbuilding companies; he was a good draughtsman, good designer, good engineer; he was a very practical man and he had a wicked sense of humour. He would do pranks to make life as uncomfortable as possible and have a good laugh at the end of it. I think that Don Butler learnt some of it from Eric, really, because even he was a bit the same when he was at Abingdon; he'd do things like staple my coat to the drawing board, or hide my lunch – it could get a bit wearing after a while...'*

It was clear that Syd and Eric were good friends with much mutual respect; they were both highly talented 'doers' rather than esoteric theoreticians. Carter is recalled in one article (for January 1991's *'Automobile Quarterly'*, by Jonathan Stein) as being over six-foot tall – which may help explain why his later MGA Coupé has generous headroom. Carter's role in EX175, DO1062 (the MGA) and the MGB is told in the main text; Morris Motors Bodies Branch closed in 1970 and with that, Eric Carter took retirement.

Then both slightly at a loose end after their life-long careers, Syd and Eric (the latter a year Syd's junior) would collaborate briefly on a project at Jensen, as related later. Eric Carter was remembered by several MG designers, as we have seen (other examples of his work were the interior door locks for the later MG Midgets, and the distinctive MGC GTS 'Sebring' wing blisters). He was interviewed in 1978 – just a few months before his death – by Doug Nye, for a brace of articles the following year in *'Automobile Quarterly'* (January 1979) and a short-lived UK magazine, *Collectors Car*; quotes from those are included in the main text with grateful acknowledgement of their source.

Gerry Palmer conceived a new sports car with monocoque bodywork – which would have aligned it fairly logically with his Z-Magnette. It was a clever concept, with the potential for different exterior panels to suit a conservative sports car clientele (upper image - principally the USA) or a modernist one (mostly for Europe). However it came around the time of other turmoil in MG's parent organization, and both John Thornley and Syd Enever were rather nervous of it. (Author Archive)

Austin-Healey and the MG TF Midget

Cornishman **Donald Mitchell Healey** (July 3rd 1898 – January 15th 1988) was a remarkable man who built his own business and survived in a specialist sector of the car industry that saw many casualties. Like many such businesses, Healey depended upon the supply of third-party engines and other key mass-produced components for his otherwise largely bespoke chassis and bodyshells. By 1949, when Healey came to call at Cowley to see new Chairman Reggie Hanks, Healey cars were largely reliant upon the supply of modest numbers of Riley engines; when Hanks turned down some of Healey's requests for new joint ventures, it did not take long for the man from Perranporth to knock on the door at Longbridge, where he received a warmer welcome.

Working at home, in order to maintain utmost secrecy (he understandably did not want any news of an Austin-based project to get back to Riley Engines) the Healeys – mainly Donald and his son Geoffrey – worked on a new sports car concept that would make use of the Austin 'big-four' engine that had been used in the Austin Atlantic, a plush two-door car designed with a great deal of personal input by Leonard Lord but which struggled to sell in the USA, its intended market.

A deal between Austin and Healey for the supply of key components for the latter's new Healey-badged sports car was signed on November 27th 1951 – less than a week after the announcement of the 'BMC' merger described earlier. Just less than a year later, the end result would emerge as the 'Healey Hundred' at Earls Court; Leonard Lord immediately made a big splash of announcing that henceforth this would become the 'Austin-Healey 100' and be built at Longbridge; for the time being, however, between Christmas 1951 and October 1952, as far as Len Lord was concerned, he had signed up to the basis of a new Austin-powered sports car aimed at the North American market. John Thornley and Syd Enever probably did not know this at the time; their focus was on developing the MG sports car line.

John Thornley on the Palmer and TF Midgets

John Thornley regularly wrote memoranda to S. V. Smith setting out 'thought pieces' for the director to consider. These extracts are taken from one dated January 5th 1953:

'... there is a marked clamour from the USA for a larger engine in the TD. Tests have shown that more power from the TD engine do not provide the answer. The shape of the car is such that at 80mph one can pile on more power to very little advantage. This means, therefore, that coincident with the introduction of the larger engine there must be an improvement in shape.... it is probable that the American market can be held with the existing TD through the summer of 1953, but unless there is some change of model it is doubtful whether the present rate of sale can be maintained through the succeeding winter...'

Thornley went on to sow doubts about the wisdom of abandoning the XPAG engine in favour of the new BMC B-Series in the USA; this may explain the retention of the XPEG. He then referred to the mock-up for what would become the MG TF:

'In order to be able to derive maximum advantage from the increased power of the larger engine, and attempt has been made to improve the shape of the TD without destroying its essentially characteristic appearance, and the blue car which is to be submitted for scrutiny by the joint boards on the 8th January is an example'.

Next he turned his attention to the rival Cowley sports car designs:

'A new series of small MGs has been designed by Mr. Palmer. From the fact that these are at the present moment not beyond the drawing-board and rough mock-up stage, one would be entitled to draw the conclusion that they could not be in production before September 1954. A statement has been made, however, that they could be ready by March 1954.

Undoubtedly these motor-cars, or something like them, provide a very suitable long-term development from the TD, but bearing in mind what was said about the need for sending to the USA only well-tried designs, we must be extremely careful not to place ourselves in the position where we are utterly dependent for a continuation of the market upon the premature introduction of an untried motor-car'.

Perhaps rather subtly seeking to score a point against Palmer's designs, Thornley continued on his theme:

'Without wishing to be unkind, one must, based on one's recollections of the introduction of the 4/44 Wolseley, express grave doubts as to whether; (a) this new motor-car could be ready by March 1954, and (b) If it were, whether it would be, from its inception, a thoroughly reliable and satisfactory vehicle (one must bear in mind that the design is to a very large extent unorthodox, and is a complete departure in many respects from existing small MG

practice)'.

'If credence is given to the suggestion that this car could be ready in March 1954, it might well be decided that the existing TD, or the existing TD with the 1½ litre engine in it, could run on until that date. If then the new model proved to need more extended development, we should be forced into a position either where we were sending an unsatisfactory vehicle for sale is in the USA, or where we were leaving a big gap in the continuity of our supplies to that market, either of which would be disastrous'.

'The sensible answer to these potential problems would appear to be to introduce the re-designed TD (the blue MG which has been tentatively called the TF) in September 1954, or even earlier if possible, and allow it to run for at least a twelve-month, or perhaps even 18 months, during which time Mr Palmer's new motor cars can be fully developed and tried and "all the bugs taken out of them".

However, Thornley had not lost sight of Syd Enever's masterpiece alternative, EX175, which he cannily sought to re-cast as a limited-production special to sit above the TF (which was EX177):

'As a separate issue altogether, there arises from the USA a demand for what, for want of a better term, may be styled a competition vehicle. There undoubtedly exists a very fruitful market between those of the TD and the XK120 Jaguar. To fill this market the fully-streamlined car, which has been tentatively called the UA, is submitted. Produced in limited quantities, its price need be of no great concerns, and if introduced at or about the time of the Series TF, would not lead the market to believe that it represented the ultimate shape of the quantity-produced MGs of the future. It would, however, have wide acceptance for competitive purposes, in the course of which it would undoubtedly acquit itself well, and would, in addition, have a wider appeal, to those who require a really fast British car for use in long-distance travel.'

In a concluding series of paragraphs about the much-discussed 'buzz box' (eventually to materialise as the Austin-Healey Sprite – of which more anon) Thornley – who expressed little enthusiasm for such a car – threw a kind of back-handed compliment to the Gerald Palmer cars, saying that if they were as light as anticipated, *'it may well be that the basic framework and tooling of these could be utilised, incorporating the AS3 [A-Series] engine or equivalent...'*

On February 12th 1953, the Morris Motors Board duly reviewed the EX177 project proposal and gave it the nod, formally authorising the necessary tooling budget of £27,000. Thus, the MG TD gave birth to a production MG TF, and in due course the EX175 concept gained a second life as the basis of the MGA; the Palmer cars, Cowley rivals for Abingdon's sports cars, were abandoned... John Thornley and Syd Enever won that particular battle. As for Gerald Palmer, he formally resigned from BMC on October 4th 1955; a month later, Alec Issigonis was back.

The deal between Donald Healey and Leonard Lord for what became the Austin-Healey 100 came at just the wrong time as far as John Thornley and Syd Enever were concerned; as Thornley later explained, in Lord's mind he had no need for two brand new sports cars and he had already signed up to the Healey venture. That is true, of course, but interwoven in that must have been the delight of Lord at having done another deal at Nuffield's expense; just as Reggie Hanks had turned Healey away, so he had turned away Nash Kelvinator President George Mason who instead did a deal for a small saloon and open tourer which became the Austin Metropolitan.

The consequence was a bitter pill for Syd Enever to swallow; everyone had loved his EX175 and yet it seemed that his grand project had been side-lined by the Healey deal. The MG men were told to review the MG TD and see what they could do to update it; EX177 (the MG TF Midget) mentioned in the adjacent panel was the result. Syd recalled that the blue prototype was done in the workshop: *'we took a car and chopped it about... Cousins looked after it, and old Bert Wirdnam – a foreman in the 'shop – took on the job.'*

The production drawings were then produced at Cowley, using outlines from Abingdon; Jim O'Neill (still at Cowley at the time) recalled their arrival: *'some very dark brown drawings with barely discernible lines came over from Abingdon, showing their requirements for the new radiator and wing lines. Taking these crude efforts as a basis we persevered and eventually achieved what Syd wanted'.* O'Neill confirmed Cousins' input; Terry Mitchell added that the drawing work at Cowley on EX177 was undertaken by Keith Matthews. Once approved, this still avowedly old-fashioned sports car was readied for a launch at the October 1953 Earls Court Motor Show – where it shared stand space with the new-generation MG Z Magnette saloon. Also at the show were the Austin-Healey 100 and the new Triumph TR2 – both sleek modern sports cars.

A New Era on the Salt Flats

The end to Goldie Gardner's record-breaking exploits left, in some people's eyes, a sense of business that was incomplete. To fill that vacuum, MG's old friend George Eyston – who as we saw was part of the send-off party for Gardner in 1952 – reconnected with MG in 1954, his US business interests through his Castrol directorship meaning that he could see that MG sales were faltering. There is no doubt that Eyston fell firmly among friends when he resurfaced at Abingdon; Kimber may have gone, but the old guard of Thornley, Cousins, Jackson and Enever were all known to him, and the respect was entirely mutual. Eyston met with Nuffield management and evidently succeeded in impressing upon them the need to rekindle record-breaking, using recognisable current engines rather than any curious cocktail of pre-war components. Clearly there was neither justification or prospect of re-using the ageing Gardner car (which in any case had been linked to Duckhams rather than Castrol sponsorship), and so something new would be needed. This was music to Syd's ears.

The first investigations by Syd and his team involved fitting aerodynamic spats and a Perspex canopy on the sole running EX175 prototype, but it swiftly became evident that this was unsuited to record breaking at speeds in excess of 200mph – certainly no improvement on the sixteen year old EX135. Fortunately, the second chassis that Enever had shrewdly commissioned was at hand, so the solution adopted was to design a new shell and build it onto the second chassis, suitably lightened in the process. The shape ended up being quite similar to EX135; Syd turned to Terry Mitchell, part of the Cowley based MG design team, to undertake the detailed design. The chassis itself was lightened by the simple expedient of MG Development's Henry Stone and Harold Wiggins drilling hundreds of holes, while the body was crafted by Midland Sheet Metal at Nuneaton.

Captain George Eyston poses for the press in the cockpit of the new EX179 record breaker, the product largely of Syd Enever's genius. (Dick Knudson)

The powertrain was a bored-out (72mm instead of 66.5mm) 1,466cc version of the XPAG engine – dubbed the XPEG in accordance with Nuffield engine code practice, and before long offered in a facelift for the MG TF Midget which became the 'MG TF 1500' (the Midget name being dropped). Given the project code EX179, the new record breaker was ready by the summer of 1954 (by which time there were, as we shall see, other developments at Abingdon) and it was shipped out to Utah for its first record-breaking attempts in August 1954, 57-year old George Eyston wisely delegating some of the driving to 36-year old Ken Miles, the British ex-pat in Los Angeles who was a good friend of MG who much later would become famous for his experiences with Ford and Shelby American. EX179 achieved 154mph on the salt.

The following report of the 1954 record breaking run appears in the Enever family archives

THE M.G. CAR COMPANY LTD.
JWT/GEVC/CIR/IO.
23.8.54
RECORDS – UTAH, 1954.

This is a summary of what has happened on the Salt Flats, so far as we are able to reconstruct it from information available at the moment.

The car is fully streamlined, very similar in general shape to the Goldie Gardner car, but somewhat shorter. The chassis, however, is a new one, the frame being experimental, and in orthodox left-hand drive 2-seater form, as distinct from the oblique transmission single seater lay-out of the Gardner car.

The drivers were: Capt. G.E.T. Eyston, who first broke records on M.G. in 1930, and Ken Miles, one-time Wolseley apprentice, now Service Manager to Gough Industries, M.G. Distributors in Los Angeles, and very successful racing driver in U.S.A. on M.G.

Three engines were taken, all XPEG. One was only moderately tuned, giving 80 B.H.P. at 5,200 r.p.m., and arranged to be dead reliable. The second was a spare to this, slightly more ambitiously tuned. The third, tuned to somewhere near the limit of our current knowledge, gave 97.5 B.H.P. at 6,500 r.p.m.

The original plan was to run for twelve hours on Engine No.1 at around 110 m.p.h. Engine No.2 was then to be installed, and a further twelve hour run made at the highest speed at which consideration on the spot led us to believe the engine would be reliable. Lastly, with the sprint engine, one lap of the ten-mile course, i.e. ten miles, was to be covered as fast as possible with Engine No.3.

It would appear that, from preliminary tests, it became apparent that 120 m.p.h. was well within the capabilities of Engine No.1, and therefore this distance was run off at a set speed just in excess of 120 m.ph. It is apparent, from the extraordinary consistency of the speeds returned at the various distances, that this was well within the capacity of the engine, that the pit control was first-class, and that the whole thing was completed as a very workmanlike job. The records and speeds attained are shown below.

Having achieved two miles per minute and taken the records by a fairly handsome margin, there was no point in going out again to raise these same records by ten miles per hour or so. The second run did not therefore take place.

The remainder of the story, covering the run with the third en fine in which the International 10 miles and the American National 16 miles records were both taken, is best told by the following two cables, received on Friday last:

Wendover 19th 9.35 P.M.
Thornley emgee
Eyston sportingly offered stand down for miles
Propose to attempt as planned crack dawn aug 20
Jackson

And

Wendover 20th 8.30 A.M.
Thornley emgee
Ken (Miles) did 153.69 Miles per hour for ten Miles as planned proceeding to pack confirm O.K. And congratulate syd (Enever)
Reggie (Jackson)

International Class E (1100 - 1500 C. c.)
Standing Start.

500 miles	120.30 (114.29)
1000 kilometres	120.92 (115.69)
1000 miles	120.13 (107.30)
2000 kilometres	120.19 (105.47)
3 hours	120.91 (114.52)
6 hours	121.42 (114.74)
12 hours	120.74 (105.48)

American National Class I (67 - 91.5 cu. in.)
Flying Start.

300 miles	121.02 (103.24)
400 miles	119.98 (100.97)
500 kilometres	121.08 (not known)
500 miles	120.62 (99.48)
1000 kilometres	121.22 (64.83)
1000 miles	120.30 (64.84)
2000 kilometres	120.34 (not known)
3 hours	121.38 (65.82)
6 hours	121.63 (65.69)
12 hours	120.87 (65.08)

Meanwhile, whilst the MG record breaking was under way, the Healeys were also running their own 'Streamliner' on the salt and when they experienced problems during one of their runs, their Abingdon friends diagnosed the problem; as Geoff Healey wrote: *'... there were signs of the cylinder head joint leaking. We were fortunate that Syd Enever and Alec Hounslow of MG were there, with their vast experience of this sort of trouble, and between us we decided what action to take.'*

John Thornley on Leonard Lord:

John Thornley told the author how he forged a fresh relationship with Leonard Lord, a man he would have occasionally seen at Abingdon in the pre-war years:

'When Len Lord put his foot down on the MGA prototype it was a perfectly rational thing for him to do; he had just 'bought' the Healey 100 and, to his eyes, it and the EX175 were clearly aimed at the same market and it didn't make sense to him to have to tool two cars. It wasn't until I had pestered the life out of him, supported strongly by the screams from the USA, that he saw the point.'

The MG Drawing Office at Abingdon and the MGA

In the summer of 1954, John Thornley – with the support of George Eyston – managed to persuade the top management to sanction the setting up of a dedicated MG Design Office at Abingdon, under Syd Enever's leadership. The new drawing office opened on Jun 1st 1954; the first drawing listed was 'DO1062 – New MG Midget' (what would become the MGA) on June 3rd. At the same stage, Vic Oak retired as Technical Director at Cowley and Alec Issigonis left

BMC to pursue a dream at Alvis; as a consequence, Gerald Palmer was made Technical Director of design at Cowley, and therefore began to concentrate on other more mainstream Morris affairs.

As Palmer told the author: *'I became Chief Body and Chassis Engineer BMC, in addition to which I was a local director at Cowley (but never at Austin). I found myself spending half my week at Longbridge and half at Cowley and became involved in the development of the Morris Minor and a new 900 c.c. V4 engine which I schemed out for a new small front-wheel-drive car, although neither the engine nor the car were ever built'.*

Harry White.

Coventry born Harry White was working at Cowley in 1954 when, aged 28, he came across to Abingdon to take up the role of Chief Chassis Engineer. Unusual amongst his BMC peers, White was a graduate – intensely clever and of a rather sensitive disposition.

Henry Stone told MG historian Dick Knudson: *'Harry was nervous in a motor car, and had to take his driving test some five times. So, Harry changed the venue to another testing venue for the next attempt, Cruel fate, it was the same bloke. But the story has a happy ending: Harry passed!'* The story of Dickie Wright's job interview with Harry White is told later.

Peter Neal says of White: *'he was quite a character – but a very clever chap, nevertheless. I was often spending time with Harry as he concocted graphs of performance. He used to work out all the spring rates and things like that as that was something he knew quite a lot about, but eventually he left and joined the new team working on what would become the Rootes Hillman Imp... I think that Harry's wife wanted to go back to the Midlands ... I think that Harry liked the idea that he could start on a bigger project in a company where he hoped he could do more of the things that he wanted to do.'*

In a Rootes Group Press Release about the new Hillman Imp in 1963, it was stated that *'the remarkable road holding characteristics of the Imp are largely a result of White's ability.'*

Extracts from John Thornley Memos To S. V. Smith, Dated August 10th and 14th 1954

Here we see, set out, John Thornley's (and by inference, Syd's) thoughts about the new sports car which would go on to become the 'MG Series MGA' and the subsequent MGA Twin Cam...

August 10th: *'DO1062, despite reductions as compared with "Magna" will be longer in overall length and larger in general appearance than any MG "Midget" so far produced.'*

August 14th: *'DO1062 is now so far advanced that, as a policy matter, it may be disregarded. However, as it is necessary that all future projects should be integrated, it is desirable that early approval should be obtained for our intentions... a special series (50 or 100) competition version of DO1062 incorporating the twin ohc B-Series engine with, possibly, fuel-injection, five-speed gearbox or overdrive, disc-brakes, aluminium panelling, etcetera... price (guessing) of the order of £1,250... although DO1062 may be expected to run for three years, its successor may have to be something quite different... my view is that we should start to build – in the manner in which 'Magna' was produced – three or four different versions of our ideas...'*

Left to right with the all-new EX179 record breaker, pictured in 1954, are John Thornley, Syd, Captain George Eyston, Alec Hounslow and Reg Jackson. The engine is derived from the familiar 'XPAG' Nuffield unit. Spot the BMC Rosette on the wall at the far right. (Enever Archive)

Jim O'Neill & Terry Mitchell

Syd knew he needed designers of the right mindset to support him at Abingdon in his new design office; the Nuffield Organisation in particular and the car industry in general was well-staffed with many engineers and draughtsmen but the kind of people needed for a modestly resourced specialist sports-car factory clearly had to be of a particular calibre; resourceful, youthful and enthusiastic. He picked well...

James Edward ('Jim') O'Neill (March 13th 1922 - December 12th 2015)

Jim O'Neill started work in 1936, in the Drawing Office at the Pressed Steel Company in Cowley.

In an Austin Rover newspaper of November 1986, we learn that *'he has also spent time in Abingdon (designing MGs), Longbridge, and Japan – he was the main liaison engineer with Honda for the introduction of the Rover 200 models. Jim retired recently from his post in Specification Services, at Cowley'.* Inevitably there was a lot more to the story, although there is not really sufficient space to do it proper justice here.

Jim moved briefly from Pressed Steel to Austin (where he worked on the body design of the Austin Atlantic) before returning to Oxford to take up a post at Morris Motors Body Design Office, where he soon found himself working alongside designer Gerald Palmer; projects there included the DO1010 MG Z Magnette. Perhaps his first real connection with Abingdon was his work on what became the TD Midget, which led to him meeting John Thornley, who came to inspect the prototype body.

Jim was pleased to come to Abingdon to join the new design team in 1954, and he became Syd's body designer, liaising with Eric Carter at Coventry on what would become the MGA. Thereafter, he headed a growing team of body engineers and draughtsmen, and was the responsible department head for all the new models and concepts which ensued – including the MGA Coupé, EX186, Sprite/ Midgets (including the Jacobs Midget coupés), MGB and MGC ranges. Jim was a key part of the exercise to keep the MG range on sale in the USA, continuing that work long after Syd retired.

Terence Henry ('Terry') Mitchell (September 9th 1921 - October 22nd 2003) was a typical schoolboy train enthusiast; after school, he set his heart on working at the GWR engine works at Swindon as an engineering draughtsman, but when that plan faltered he took an exam and began work at Maidenhead rail station on April 26th 1937 as a junior clerk. During the War he served in the RAF as a Flight Mechanic and Fitter – a great experience for a fledgling engineer in circumstances where timely and effective solutions were always of the essence. In the spring of 1950, he saw an advertisement for a job at Cowley's 'MG & Riley' drawing office; he was duly interviewed by Gerald Palmer and started work in June.

His early work with relevance to Abingdon was on the Riley Pathfinder, but his key connection with Syd came through his work on the EX179 record breaker, while he was still working at Cowley; he told the author that he was the first to effectively start at Abingdon, working for Syd, from February 1954. Once the formal office was in place that June, Terry found himself reporting to Harry White, until the latter left for Rootes Group to work on the design of what would become the Hillman Imp.

Mitchell was often, like many engineers, more enthusiastically engaged on a project during the early conceptualisation phase, but he could lose interest when all the problem-solving seemed to him to have been done; he was also keen on building his own specials (he eventually created about ten of them), a habit which sometimes brought him close to conflict with more senior management at Cowley.

Peter Neal told the author how Terry Mitchell was often badgering Syd to do more testing, but the answer would usually be *'there's not any money for it Terry; I have to justify the budget...'* but, according to Neal, *'...Syd was sympathetic to Terry's ideas and he recognised Terry's talent, which was really why Terry replaced Harry White as Chief Chassis Engineer when Harry left in 1958.'* It was Terry Mitchell who was in charge of the creation of MG's own V8 MGB, although the story of that car is slightly outside our scope as it only really became a serious exercise soon after Syd had retired.

Meanwhile, it seems, Roy Brocklehurst was at first slightly perturbed at the design team influx in 1954, but according to Neal: *'Syd always suggested to Roy that he would take over eventually, and that meant that Roy was a little put out when Terry and Jim and the others came over from Cowley – it sort of put his nose out of joint... but Syd always said not to worry about it as he planned that Roy would succeed him, and of course in the end he did...'*

Being about fifteen years younger than Syd, both Jim O'Neill and Terry Mitchell stayed the course at Abingdon to more or less the end, finally doing work on projects like the 'BL Bounty' (Triumph

> Acclaim) and in O'Neill's case Rover Group work at Cowley – but they always looked back on their time working with Syd Enever as the heyday of their careers.

> **Ted Martin – The Model Engine Man**
>
> One of the less well-known people who worked with Syd Enever for a while in the 1950s was Ted Martin (January 19th 1924-May 22nd 2010) who is better known in other fields, notably for his crucial role in creating what became a highly-popular small engine used by model aircraft enthusiasts, and later for the creation of his highly respected eponymous automotive race engine. In January 1952, he went to Canada and took up a job with the local General Motors engineering division; whilst there he gained an interest in motorsport and according to Terry Mitchell, he was a member of the MG Car Club and through this gained an introduction to John Thornley, as a consequence of which he spent some time on consultancy work at MG Abingdon..
>
> While still at GM Canada, he had started his own company 'Alexander Engineering' in the UK, the core purpose being to tune racing engines, typically Ford 109E-based Formula Junior units. He designed his own single overhead cam three valve cylinder head for Ford four-cylinder engines and after that famously progressed towards a series of bespoke 'Martin' racing engines culminating in a three litre V8. In the fifties, however, Martin worked on certain aspects of the MGA Twin Cam but seems to have departed soon afterwards.
>
> Someone who knew Ted Martin and his sons, one of whom he was at school with, was Philip Whiteman, who told the author: *'Ted had a large gauge live steam railway running around the garden, with an elevated section leading to a hole in the wall so he could service the locos in the kitchen. Tony's elder brother, Robin kept reptiles including a Cayman (one of those little alligators) that grew too large for its tank and ended up living for a while in the bath (Anne Martin had to have been so understanding). Ted also had a Colchester lathe in one of the bedrooms and there was a constant worry that it might come through the ceiling...'*
>
> Ted clearly respected Syd, apparently one time recalling an occasion where the latter had swiftly solved a pit-stop problem: *'he up-ended a toolbox to quickly find a spanner whilst all others were bumbling around in disarray'* but his views of some other celebrated engineers was often less complimentary, and certainly not appropriate to quote verbatim in this book.
>
> According to Terry Mitchell, Syd had Ted Martin working mostly on experimental engine ideas in the wake of the Suez Crisis; Mitchell's candid view, as he expressed to the author, was that although they evidently worked well together, Syd was slightly nervous of Ted Martin, a brilliant engineer in his own right, who had been brought in without his request; engines were always seen as Syd's forte, which may in part explain why he kept Martin busy as far as possible on more esoteric projects. The two must have had a good working relationship, however, because Roger Enever remembers visiting the Martin's home and being amazed at the various model aircraft engines he saw there.

Jim O'Neill was one of the small team who came over the Abingdon to help make Syd's new Drawing Office reality: *'our first task was to beg, borrow or steal as much equipment as possible. Two 18-foot layout tables were made up by the works carpenters, improvised wooden sweeps also made up in the carpenters' shop. Drawing boards were 'borrowed' from Morris Motors'.* At the same time, Syd Enever received the go ahead to turn EX175 into a new sports car intended for production – under the Cowley master code of DO1062 (not EX182 as is often written – as we shall see, that was a tandem project).

How the news was conveyed was related to author Doug Nye in interviews that both Syd Enever and Eric Carter gave him in 1979. As Syd recalled: *'when the 'T' sales fell off and Lord told S.V. Smith to get on with what became the 'A' he stopped first at Bodies Branch to tell them, and then he got back to Abingdon and told us. We had been sitting on the thing for two years, and suddenly it was all panic and scurry. Huh! Management...'* Carter noted that as well as being director at Morris Motors in Cowley, Sydney Smith also had responsibility for Bodies Branch in Coventry: *'he told me to go ahead urgently, and he would send Syd up... a new full-size sheet of paper was put up on the Friday and was squared up with ten-inch squares. Syd dropped by and told me of the changes from prototype; they weren't much at all, only larger bonnet and trunk lids, the deletion of the rear number plate mounting and slightly slimmer front wings – though this change was hardly noticeable.'* The allocation from the Morris Motors Board was reported by Syd as being £80,000, and he wanted £50,000 of that for the chassis – both figures a fraction of modern costs for such work.

Carter continued in his explanation to Doug Nye: '*on the next day, the Saturday, we started the skin lines, and on the following Tuesday tracings and prints were being issued to the experimental shop to start work on wooden formers, metal-edged, to produce the first few production bodies. Next day, the Wednesday, a delegation from Pressed Steel at Cowley arrived ... They had come up to discuss details and to quote on the job and since they were then interested in plastic tools and wanted the work they offered to produce the tools – for the skin panels – free of charge. They said if they did not stand up to production requirements, they would then produce metal tools at an agreed price*'.

This is interesting in itself, as it suggests that the prevailing plan was still broadly as set out by John Thornley in his memo of January 1953 (i.e. 18-months prior) referred to earlier; a 'limited production' MG sports car to test the water, sell at a premium and pave the way for a higher-volume successor if the new style caught on. In the event, the plastic tools were not found to be adequate, and so Pressed Steel had to swallow the considerable cost of conventional tooling – a major boon for MG.

The Pressed Steel men from Cowley took away tracings of what skin lines were available to start their production drawings. '*After a fortnight the workload was very high*' Carter said; '*pressure from Pressed Steel for information was kept up, and we had to keep the experimental shop busy, and we had all the usual queries from the production departments on current models which included things like the Morris Taxi, Travellers, vans, Riley saloons and the MG TF... everything was compressed into a very short time span to get the MGA into production. Just one example ... the seats were designed and drawn-up in one day, using a totally new method of construction at that time, and no modification was made to them during the whole production of the model, except to suit the Coupe version when the squab was raised a and narrowed at the top*'.

Another challenge for Carter was the MGA's folding hood, which '*...caused some headaches due to the long rear deck. The idea of a double fold to tuck under the deck occurred at about 8pm one evening and an hour later the scheme was roughed out on paper and turned out to be a neat and acceptable solution, with the side curtains stowed in front of it ... there was no interference from above. They were not interested until there was something to see, consequently snap decisions were made, and they remained for the life of the vehicle...*'

The prototype body was delivered to Abingdon

Midland Sheet Metal were proud to advertise their involvement in the EX179 project; their skilled workers created the record-breaker's alloy bodywork. (Author Archive)

by lorry, was made into a running vehicle by Alec Hounslow, and then taken out on test by him; according to Eric Carter, when Hounslow returned, he said 'we'll sell a hundred thousand of these' which as we shall see was a prophecy which came true. Carter added that he learned some years later how Hounslow ran out of road with Syd as his passenger in the prototype MGB; he said he could not hold it but '*...it wouldn't have happened with the MGA*'.

Syd Enever certainly remembered that incident with the MGB prototype when Nye related what Carter had told him: '*the car turned over on us in a ditch with our heads hanging down just above the water. It's quite right what Eric says. With the monocoque B we were exploring a new field unknown to us and quite honestly the early problems we had with it were a bloody nuisance. In contrast the A was quite one of the best little cars we ever made. It performed very well first time out; it handled well and was very predictable and controllable. We had a nice car in the MGA. It was always good to us ...'* We will return to the MGB later; it would, as we shall see, be even more of a success than the MGA and a fitting finale to Syd's MG career.

Meanwhile, as far as EX175 ('HMO 6') was concerned, its main functions over, and the brief attempt to make a record breaker out of it abandoned, Wilson McComb wrote that *'it was returned to road-going trim and passed over to Cowley for a full road test. The report, dated May 26th 1954, said that on the bypass north of Oxford, the car had reached a mean maximum of 99.8mph with hood and sidescreens in place. Its one-way best was a timed 100.5mph. Carrying two occupants, and with gearchanges made at 6,000 rpm, it had accelerated from 0-60mph in 15.8 seconds.'* As McComb commented, *'by T-Type standards, this was pretty good going.'* As we have seen, that test took place just six days before the opening of Abingdon's new design office. It is believed that EX175 ended its days as a brake testing vehicle before, almost inevitably, being scrapped; by then the car it had inspired was heading for new frontiers.

EX182 and Le Mans

From the outset, John Thornley – aided and abetted by Syd – wanted to enter their new creation at the Le Mans race – they saw the frustrating failure of EX172 in 1952 as unfinished business, and in line with the philosophy set out in the January 1953 memo, racing was seen as the way to give the new 'limited edition' sports car the pedigree it warranted, and encourage would-be customers to buy and perhaps race replicas. Both of them also knew, however, that they were playing with fire when it came to abandoning the old-school MG T-Type design, which was one of the reasons for the racing approach.

As it happened, the delays with the tooling meant that John Thornley's original plan to unveil the MGA in April 1955 had to be postponed, and the entry at Le Mans re-purposed as one of 'prototypes of a possible production car' rather than simple racing derivatives of a new production model. In the event, this proved to be beneficial because of course criticisms of the new shape from die-hard MG traditionalists were naturally undermined by the sight of the sleek new MG models out on the circuit, demonstrating levels of performance the owners of older more upright MGs could only dream of.

The race cars were built largely by hand at the MG factory, with alloy bodywork in place of the steel intended for production (although, at Syd's insistence, production MGAs would have alloy doors, bonnet and boot lids to save weight). As ever, a key focus for Syd was in the development of the engines, and here we was moving into new territory as he worked on the BMC B-Series, creating the first motorsport biased versions of an engine really intended for more moribund use. In the background, too, he made plans to adopt the twin-cam engine which Gerald Palmer had conceived for his own sports cars, but which Syd's friends James Thompson and Eddie Maher at Morris Motors Engines Branch turned into reality.

As Jim Cox told the author, once everyone had got over their natural prejudices over the Austin developed B-Series, they – led by Syd, naturally – soon moved on to embrace the possibilities: *'We put a full-flow filter on it – for which we drilled through the block – and we developed the camshaft for more lift. Then we worked with Harry Weslake on the combustion chambers and before long we found ourselves working on what would become the Le Mans engine specification for EX182'*. The EX182 team – three race cars and a fourth for practice – were taken to Le Mans in June 1955 and the tragic incidents in that event are well known and need not concern us in detail here, beyond commenting on the fact that one of the MGs crashed and burned (and its driver, Dick Jacobs, was badly injured) and that the negative publicity of the major crash involving Pierre Levegh's Mercedes, where he and many spectators died, was one aspect that shaped BMC's subsequent attitude to motor racing in Europe.

Awaiting for the departure from Abingdon, via the Dover ferry and onwards into France for the 1955 Le Mans race. Syd is fourth from right, between Alec Hounslow and Jim Cox. (Cliff Bray)

MGA – The Aerodynamic Sports Car

The production 'MG Series MGA' was given its international debut on September 21st 1955 at the Frankfurt Motor Show, the main Orient Red show car being flown out to Germany, carried inside a special cargo-pod tucked under the wing of a TWA passenger aircraft. Syd supported the London reveal at the showrooms of University Motors; he is seen in one of the photos chatting amiably with UM Chairman George Bradstock. Even as this was going on, the 'EX182' lightweight cars continued their racing exploits, most notably at Dundrod, four days before the Frankfurt launch, where two of the cars were to be powered by experimental twin-cam engines – one the latest iteration of the concept initiated by Gerald Palmer (and developed further by Morris Motors Engines Branch) and a rival concept from Austin. The story behind these rival engines is covered in the panels here.

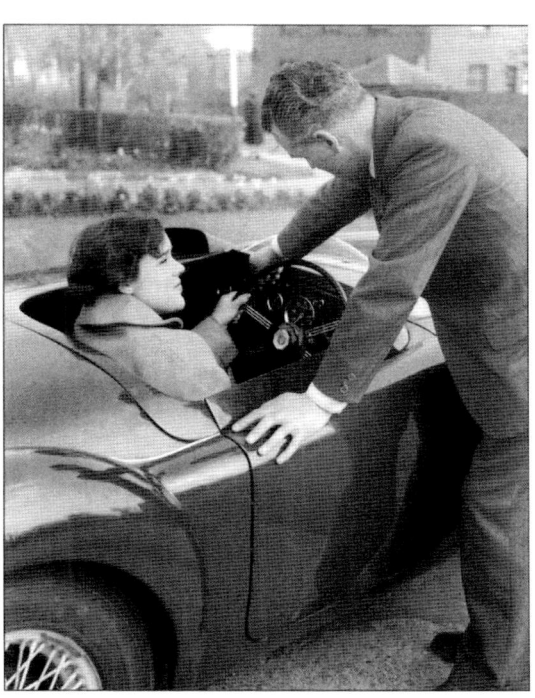

Pat Moss, sister of Stirling, raced an MG TF in 1955; here she is seated in the cockpit of one of the Le Mans EX182 cars while Syd looks on. (Author Archive)

BMC Engines: Bill Appleby, James Thompson and Eddie Maher

Whilst it was Syd Enever who defined the brief for the engines he required for his record breaking (and indeed for road use too), he turned to a triumvirate in the heart of what was now the BMC engines business – effectively a union of Austin (Longbridge) and Morris (at Courthouse Green, Coventry). As engines had always been Syd's forte, relationships were generally cordial, although sometimes there were the almost inevitable signs of old Nuffield loyalties in play.

At the top of the tree was **William Victor Appleby** (August 10th 1903 - March 1984, Cheltenham) who is described in the 1939 Register as 'Internal Combustion Engine Designer, Austin Motor Company', living then at 1766 Bristol Road South, Rednal, Birmingham. Appleby had been senior draughtsman in 1935 on the famous twin-cam Austin 750cc race engines of the time – contemporary rivals for Kimber's Midgets – and later became Austin's Chief engine designer (from 1941) and was part of a design team (which for a time included Hubert Charles) responsible for what became the Austin A40 and subsequent BMC B-Series engine. After the BMC merger, Austin's engine design function was given the senior role, and in 1953, Appleby was made 'Chief Designer, Engines and Gearboxes', for the whole BMC Group.

Meanwhile, however, the Morris Motors Engines Branch, which had evolved in part from the former Riley Engines business at Courthouse Green, was directed by **James 'Jimmy' Rochester Thompson** (October 13th 1903 – October 6th 1987), as Chief Engineer, and under him in turn, Eddie Maher (see below) as Chief Experimental Engineer. Thompson was born at Alnwick, Northumberland and began his career in nearby Newcastle as an apprentice at Armstrong-Whitworth, the famous heavy-engineering giant; much of his work there involved such works as the installation of triple-expansion marine engines and gun mountings for battle ships. He later moved over to the sister business of Armstrong Siddeley on aero engines, then to Blackburn Aviation in Leeds and finally arrived at Morris Motors Engines Branch as a Senior Draughtsman in 1929. By the time of the 1939 England and Wales Register, he was a 'Chief Draughtsman – Internal Combustion Engines' living on Kenpas Highway, Coventry. By the time that Bill Appleby was placed in overall charge of BMC engines, Thompson was the Morris Motors Engines Branch Chief Engineer down the road at Coventry. Whilst Longbridge was the source for A and B Series engine design, Morris Motors Engines Branch was also involved in gearboxes for the BMC group, the new C-Series six-cylinder BMC engine of 1954, and the twin cam versions of the B-Series relevant to EX179, EX181 and the MGA Twin Cam.

Edward Joseph ('Eddie') Maher (August 5th 1910 – September 27th 1976) was born in Southern Ireland (now Eire) and went to the Cistercian College, a Catholic Boarding School in Roscrea, Tipperary. He set out to become a civil engineer, studying to that end at Thurles Technical School (also in Tipperary). However his future would not be set in concrete; when he went to Dublin's Phoenix Park on July 12th 1929 to watch the Irish Grand Prix, he witnessed Riley racer Victor Gillow in the first Saorstát Cup. He decided there and then that he wanted to work at Riley (he said later that he came to Coventry, prepared simply to sweep the floors if necessary). His parents were perhaps understandably unimpressed, but the 19-year old followed his dream and secured a job at Riley that same year; he became Riley Motor Company's first 'Premium Apprentice', and trained further at Coventry Technical College. In due course he gained the impressive letters 'C Eng MIMechE' (Chartered Engineer, Member of the Institution of Mechanical Engineers) and 'ARAeS' (Associate of the Royal Aeronautical Society). *'I've never regretted it'* he told the Coventry Evening Telegraph of September 17th 1975; *'the friends I met while studying civil engineering built bridges and roads, but they never went out of the country – I went all over the world'*.

Riley being an avowedly sporting car company, Maher soon moved to the experimental and racing department, taking charge of engine testing, engine production and in due course Riley Motors' entire engine design and manufacture side. Maher was at the forefront of Riley's racing efforts throughout the marque's 1930s heydays, often being found at Brooklands and other circuits in support of Rileys racing there. The financial collapse of Riley and its purchase by Lord Nuffield was just before the War; after the conflict began, Maher was seconded to Rolls Royce, where he worked on carburettors for that company's Merlin engines in the famous Supermarine Spitfire, returning to Riley after the war ended. Riley Engines was an important employer in Coventry (the author had an uncle who proudly worked there) and under Nuffield ownership became the base for Morris Motors Engine Branch.

In 1953, Maher contracted polio, suffering extensive paralysis in his legs, but despite this he continued to thrive in a senior role. Despite his need to walk with the aid of sticks, he upheld a cheery and positive disposition despite his illness. Eddie Maher remained at Courthouse Green until his retirement in 1975, by which time Jimmy Thompson was long since retired, and Maher had become Chief Engineer. He was always a strong friend of Syd Enever's, the two having enormous mutual respect; Syd contributed towards a brief bio of Eddie for the 1957 record breaking efforts, saying of his friend: *'he has risen*

In 1955, The MG Car Club celebrated its Silver Jubilee, culminating in a dinner towards the end of the year. Here we see, left to right, Alec Hounslow, Syd, Freddie Crossley, Dick Jacobs (note the crutch – he was still recovering from his crash at Le Mans the previous June), Andy Collinson, Ken Wharton and Reg Jackson. (Enever Archive)

Syd took an active part in early post-launch testing into Europe in the new MGA; here he grins for the camera from under his crash-helmet. (Enever Archive)

above his handicap and directs his essentially Irish temperament towards the production of horsepower, with great, good effect'.

In the midst of all this, as set out in a separate panel, there was some work on a 'rival' twin cam engine, overseen by the Austin Engines branch and using a more radically different structure than the Gerald Palmer concept; the Austin unit was largely bespoke and featured a narrower angle between the cylinder heads. Views on how good this alternative engine was in practice have varied over the years; some claimed that the extra expense of a unit designed from the outset as a 'Porsche rival' would have been worth considering – and of course in light of subsequent events, the overall costs might have still been comparable. Others maintain that testing showed that the performance of the Austin unit barely exceeded that of a well-tuned conventional B-Series with Webers, and that this was why the only known prototype was removed from one of the cars destined to race at Dundrod in September 1955, crated up and returned to Longbridge.

Within Morris Motors Engines Branch, in the period of interest, there were many largely unsung heroes who also contributed to both the Twin Cam engine, in all its forms, and the record-breaking work in particular. Amongst them was Basil Wales (perhaps best known for his later role as head of Special Tuning) as well as Jack Goffin, Bill Andrews, Jack Yorke, Derek Frost, Derek Lowe, Bob Smart, Bill Clarke, Dennis Stevens, Tony Jennings, whilst the SU Carburettors were sometimes in the tender care of that division's Don Law.

The new MGA was revolutionary – controversial too, in the minds of many more conservative MG enthusiasts, but Syd had realised the need to move with the times – and of course by this time, the MGA – 'first of a new line' – was a BMC stable-mate of Donald Healey's creation, the Austin-Healey 100/4. (Author Archive)

The Rival Austin Twin-Cam Engine

The initial phase of the twin cam story was complicated by the fact that alongside the Morris Engines prototype of 1955, there was a rival Austin Engines design (with 66 degrees rather than 80 degrees between the camshaft planes, and largely bespoke).

It was typical of Leonard Lord to set two rival teams off – especially one from 'Austin' and the other from 'Nuffield' – with broadly the same objective. The Austin engine, see in this photograph, was received at Abingdon and tested at MIRA once fitted in one of the lightweight EX182 cars by Tommy Wellman; it seems there was little enthusiasm at Abingdon for what was clearly a rival to the engine developed by Syd's old friends at Coventry.

John Thornley wrote a mildly scathing report (dated October 14th 1955) which stated that *'the maximum rpm of the 66° engine restricted the performance to much the same as that of a standard Le Mans car. It was therefore decided, as there was little prospect of being able to correct both engines in the time available, to substitute a further Le Mans engine for the 66° engine, and to pursue correction of the carburetion difficulties on the 80° engine'.*

Here we see the Austin Engines design – in one of the only known photographs of it. (Author Archives)

In practical terms, what happened was that Syd told Alec Hounslow to remove the Austin; Hounslow in turn caked Tommy Wellman at his home (he had finished his supper and had been making plans for an early night before an early start the following morning to set off for Belfast and the TT at Dundrod). At ten o'clock Alec Hounslow called Wellman and Henry Stone to back to the factory, to remove the Austin engine and substitute a Le Mans pushrod unit. The job was completed by four in the morning, the Austin engine was placed in its crate, the lid nailed down, and the package was shipped out at the first opportunity, never to be seen again.

Car No. 35 (LBL303, EX 182/ 40), photographed at Dundrod during the 1955 TT, has a conventional B-Series engine in place of the Austin Twin Cam unit (despite the hump in the bonnet, which had been created to help the Austin engine fit). Interviewed for the MGA Twin Cam Group's celebratory book for that model's 50th anniversary, Peter Neal said that Ted Martin (see earlier in this Chapter) claimed to have contributed in some way towards the Austin engine and said in hindsight that it would have been a superior option over the Morris Engines version. Whatever the qualities of the Longbridge-designed twin cam unit, one can imagine the old loyalties between MG and Morris Motors Engines Branch must have played some part in all this, coupled with the pressures for the record breaking in 1956 and beyond.

Even so, however the Morris Motors Engines Branch twin cam proved to be a challenge from an early stage, as Jim Cox told the author: *'at Dundrod, there were all sorts of problems with the twin-cam Ron Flockhart was driving and after practice he said that he wouldn't go out in the car as it was. We sat in the garage and tried to sort out what to do – we had the car in pieces with Syd Enever looking over it; we took the carburettor to pieces and everything but we never did really find out the problem'.* Cox also remembered that one of the Dundrod cars was fitted with an experimental alloy fuel tank: *'it got split when the car went over "Deer's Leap" and that was the end of that'*

As for the ultimate fate of the Austin engine, or indeed if it might have proved a better choice, we may probably never know the truth.

The definitive MGA Twin Cam engine, with the distinctive square-edge camshaft covers, seen in the engine bay of Car No. 34 (LBL 301 - EX 182/ 38, was the one which started as an idea by Gerald Palmer, and was then developed by James Thompson, Eddie Maher and their team at Morris Engines, and became an important part of both the EX179 and EX181 record breaking programme from 1956 onwards. (Author Archives)

Sadly, Dundrod also saw fatalities on the circuit – thankfully not involving the MGAs – and this, combined with the Le Mans incidents, led BMC to announce a sanction on factory-backed racing (although racing outside Europe was considered a different issue, and eventually reliability-focused road rallies were deemed acceptable). Coupled with wider public concerns about the safety of spectator motor sports, the planned Alpine Rally was cancelled, and tentative plans for a repeat visit to Le Mans in June 1956 by the MG team were abandoned.

However, the gap in the motorsports programme opened a window of opportunity for extended testing in Europe, and Syd Enever and Alec Hounslow found the opportunity to combine this with convivial trips to

France and Switzerland, visiting alpine passes and race circuits where they could refine the new MGA, sending reports back to Abingdon, and enjoying fine hospitality from the Keller family in Zürich, who were the main MG distributors in Switzerland. October 22nd 1955 also saw MGA prototypes shipped to Montlhéry alongside some other BMC cars for a sport of endurance runs around the circuit.

Meanwhile, however, whilst the production lines began to see MGAs going down them, Syd and Alec were experimenting with new derivatives – a hardtop option, a fixed-head Coupé, a Cabriolet (never produced), a cheaper version (EX195, started on November 11th 1955) and a version with the new twin-cam engine, the latter aimed at motorsports applications. John Thornley would later say of the period from 1953 to 1958 which saw massive expansion of the MG factory output as *'this marvellous period that I could live over and over and over again, really... not easy though; we were designing over the other side; I was trying to produce more and more motor cars all time...'* Thornley told Geoffrey Iley, his deputy in roughly the same period: *'your job is to get cars out of the door: I'll deal with design, development, competitions, the press and everything else'*. At the same time, it was Syd Enever who had to cope with the development work and see, in the midst of it all, responsibility for Austin-Healey sports cars added to his portfolio as Riley moved away from Abingdon.

Extract from John Thornley Memo to S. V. Smith, Dated November 7th 1955.

As the memo shows, the 'MGB' name was loosely applied at first to a derivative of the MGA, although of course the production use of those initials would be very different:

'...we are already building a prototype of the MGB, which is the MGA fitted with the twin camshaft B-Series engine, and with disc brakes on one or both axles as may be found necessary when more is known of the probable performance. The intention is that this model will be sold alongside the MGA, again with a substantial price differential, and provide the prestige and competition vehicle for USA and elsewhere....'

The story of the production MGA Twin Cam is covered in the next chapter.

Facelifts were one aspect which seemed to elude the MGA, with its classic curvaceous lines; this was not for want of trying, and there are sketches and photos which show that Syd in particular was not averse to trying such things as duo-tone colour schemes and stainless steel trim pieces; there was even an effort to create a larger 'trunk' (boot) at the back, but nearly all seemed doomed to failure.

John Thornley explained the dilemma that he and Syd faced to Kenneth Ullyett for the latter's book *'The MG Companion'* (Stanley Paul, 1960): *'We were thinking in terms of giving the MGA a facelift; after all, the car had been in production from 1955 to 1959, and there comes a time when the designer is called in to give a car extended currency, no matter how successful is the basic conception. As the MGA doesn't wear out, anyway, it was necessary to consider a change even if only to interest the potential buyer going into the showroom.'*

'As nobody likes changes merely for change's sake, our design team was set the problem of ascertaining what really could be an improvement. We played about with alternative fronts, But bearing in mind the MGA is an idealised design, conceived as an entity, it is hardly surprising that no matter what we did to the front, the result was less satisfactory, and usually less aerodynamic.

We experienced the same not-unanticipated disappointment when we experimented with the back end. Each of the alterations seemed to have a stuck-on look. It did not take long to realise that worthwhile improvement was not to be had this way'. This helps explain why just about the only visible changes to the MGA of any note over its seven years in production were to some aspects of the exterior lighting and to the detailed form of the radiator grille.

Putting a Lid on Syd's Baby: The MGA Coupé

John Thornley always wanted to see a fixed-head coupé sports car; his enthusiasm was shared by Syd, who could see the practical advantages, including structural integrity; when Syd eventually retired, it would be an ex-development MGA Coupé that he took with him – but that is a story for later. The task of developing the prototype fell again to Eric Carter, working to Syd's brief (Jim O'Neill told the author that whilst he oversaw its development, he personally played no part in determining the original shape. Inspiration surely came from the Jaguar XK120 Coupé), as much as the open version of the Jaguar probably influenced Syd with the MGA roadster.

When he first saw it, O'Neill was not especially enthusiastic; *'I remember going to Coventry with John Thornley and Syd Enever to view the car. At the time I felt that it was too round and lumpy and told Eric so. He informed me that production tooling was already underway although the cost had not been cleared, and implored me not to 'rock the boat'. In retrospect I am sure*

The MGA Coupé was originally envisaged as a low-volume offshoot of the MGA roadster; Jim O'Neill and Eric Carter (the latter at Morris Motors Bodies Branch) worked on the design on behalf of Syd. (Author Archives)

that the MGA Coupé is a 'Classic' shape...'; it seems likely the Syd and Eric had been talking about the project and doubtless with the encouragement of John Thornley (who sometimes enjoyed showing management a 'fait accompli'). The tooling budget according to the Minutes of the Morris Motors Board was a paltry £5,000 – a tiny fraction of what even a low-volume project like this would cost in modern times.

The prototype was ready for viewing by March 1956; the project was formally approved by the Morris Motors Board on May 7th – nine days before the 100,000th MG (not to be confused with the later 100,000th MGA of 1962) went down the line at Abingdon. The MGA went on to receive a larger engine in two stages; firstly in May 1959 at 1,588cc producing 79.5 bhp (the capacity now matching that of the Twin Cam; at the same time, front disc brakes were fitted to the MGA 1600, but drums remained at the rear) and then to 1,622cc, with a larger bore (up from 75.4mm (2.97inches) to 76.2mm (3.00inches) for the MGA Mark II in 1961 (the latter engine change was prompted chiefly by wider BMC engine changes, with a new block and other key differences; by now the Twin Cam – described in the next chapter – had been discontinued).

The penultimate MGA landmark came with the 100,000th example of this model, built in March 1962 only a matter of weeks before the MGB started to go down the line as its replacement. The story of the process of superseding the MGA – and Syd's role in the process – is covered in the next chapter.

Chapter Seven: Final Furlongs

Sharpening the Pencil: Following on from the MGA

Having laid out the chassis of what was to become the MGA on his dining table at home in Westminster Way, it seemed likely that such recourse was neither necessary nor practicable for Syd once the new drawing office had been established at Abingdon, in the year prior to that new model's official launch – although there is testimony from his son Roger that Syd continued to take plans home with him to pore over in the evenings and weekends; old habits die hard. The difficulty of enhancing the basic MGA shape was touched on in the last chapter; it was clear that more substantial changes would be needed to avoid just an ugly facelift.

At first, in the immediate aftermath of the arrival of the MGA, both Syd and his manager and mentor John Thornley maintained that whatever followed would need to retain a separate chassis. It seems likely – and this is conjecture on the author's part – that their nervousness about going for a monocoque method of sports car construction was probably just as much about the potential of such a direction of travel to remove the essential role of Abingdon in the assembly (or indeed the design) process as about any fundamental objections to the very principal of chassis-less construction. In the case of the MGA, chassis assembly took place at Abingdon using components brought in from an outside supplier, John Thompson Pressings, and there was nervousness about eroding this capacity.

> **From a November 1955 Memorandum to S.V. Smith from John Thornley and Syd Enever**
>
> Hindsight is a wonderful thing, but both John Thornley and Syd would later be able to laugh about this many years later:

> *'The great disadvantage of the monocoque form, particularly in the case of relatively small production rates such as our own, is that, unless the general construction of the car is to be very orthodox, one must of necessity tie oneself to a body design too far ahead of production. By using a self-supporting chassis (even though this may ultimately be welded or multiply-bolted to the body) development of chassis and body can proceed independently. The complete design then enjoys the benefit of flexibility, such that the style may subsequently be changed without interfering with the chassis, and vice versa. We consider therefore that all future Abingdon products should have chassis frames.'*

It was, after all, still not long since the painful interlude of 1949, described earlier, when there had been the possibility of MG production going to Coventry, and Abingdon being turned over to some kind of Cowley outpost. In November 1955, therefore, both John Thornley and Syd put their name to an internal BMC paper which recommended that separate chassis should remain the order of the day for the next generation of open-topped MG sports cars. Furthermore, as we saw earlier, the fact that the 1953 MG sports car concept by Gerald Palmer, only recently departed from Cowley, was proposed as a monocoque – encouraged by George Dono of Nuffield Metal Products, who was touting for internal business – only added to their nervousness.

In the meantime, John Thornley lobbied BMC management to make Abingdon the logical heart of the Corporation's sports car manufacturing enterprises, and the cold logic of his argument was undeniable; the Healey family were well-regarded consultants who had a contractual arrangement forged with BMC and earned royalties that meant that money went outside BMC's orbit, yet MG was a fully-owned integral asset very much under the hat.

Both the Healeys and MG enjoyed good relationships within BMC (Donald Healey's links went straight to the top) and ran semi-independent record-breaking and racing enterprises, but as there was pressure to contain costs and rationalise these as well, the logic of Thornley's case was obvious. The consequence of this in due course was that Austin Healey manufacture – the Big-Healey and, in short order, an Austin and Healey designed smaller sports car – came to Abingdon, and responsibility in engineering terms for all of them now rested firmly on Syd Enever's shoulders.

The Buzz Box

The story of what became the Austin-Healey Sprite is covered later; it arose almost as a side-show to the concept of the small sports car which arguably MG had called its own, with the original M-Type described earlier. At the same time, perhaps those in the Austin camp with long memories were looking fondly back to the days of the original Austin Seven as well as the later trend for home-built sports cars based on the Seven chassis and suspension.

Both John Thornley and Syd were keen to at least be a part of this discussion – Thornley referred to it jocularly as 'The Buzz Box' – although as Thornley often pointed out, there were question marks over quite how essential such a car was to the all-important North American market, where many enthusiasts, not to mention the distributors, were clamouring for greater performance, space and engine size rather than less.

We are fortunate that there is reference to the buzz-box in some of John Thornley's memos which he wrote – in this case to the long-suffering S. V. Smith. The Thornley memo, dated December 26th 1956 (in other words, the memo was written on Boxing Day!) begins: '*In a recent conversation with Mr Woodcock* [J.R. Woodcock was the Deputy Director in charge of Morris Motors] *he mentioned that the question of "Buzz-box" was still very much alive, and he suggested that I have another look at it and write "another one of my things". This is it!*'

In the memorandum, Thornley made reference to a visit to Abingdon by Sir Leonard Lord (whose interaction with the factory 21 years earlier was still remembered by many still there), as well as the fact that Syd Enever shared his doubts about the merits of a smaller sports car. Thornley also declared that he and Syd were progressing a concept using the 948cc A-Series engine, '*...primarily because both Longbridge and Healey appear to be doing something of the kind, and we have no intention of being left out of the race*' but then went on to set out, in six detailed paragraphs, why he did not feel that the idea was a good one.

What we also now know is that the idea of this small sports car had been discussed between Lord and Donald Healey; as Geoffrey Healey wrote in one of his books about the Healey story: '*The Sprite was first conceived in the winter of 1956, the result of a meeting between DMH (Donald Healey) and Leonard Lord ... During a discussion on the sports car market both men agreed that sports cars were becoming expensive... Len Lord then commented that what was needed was a small, low-cost sportscar to fill the gap*'. So the Healeys were in at the forefront of this dialogue, whilst the men at Abingdon were prevaricating.

The MG design team, under Syd's direction, experimented with various MGA facelift ideas, including this one aimed at improving rear luggage capacity; the general consensus however was that none of them made a positive improvement. (Author photo)

In Thornley's view, the new MGA was already being viewed in its primary market, the USA, as a small car (it had, after all, replaced the old 'Midget' line, even if that name had not been continued), and he also doubted the ability to manage costs down to facilitate a 'cheaper' sports car. In his concluding comments, Thornley said: *'I hope in the foregoing I have made out a case for a pause to take stock of the situation, and try to make up our minds what it is we are really aiming at. I do not think that MG, using existing BMC units, can enter the market of "really cheap transportation". This is the big boy's job, but in any case the A35/ Minor 1000 already represent just about the minimum based on current techniques.'*

In other words, the view from Abingdon as of the winter of 1956 was that a smaller sports car below the MGA was not necessarily the right thing to consider; it is worth appreciating that this was some months before the exercise of creating a small saloon car was handed to Alec Issigonis (who had recently returned to BMC, in the wake of the convenient departure of Gerald Palmer) by Sir Leonard Lord. That project would lead to the revolutionary ADO15 Austin Se7en/ Morris Mini Minor which was launched in August 1959. The Thornley and Enever duo were more interested in an eventual replacement for the MGA; there would be a few steps in that direction, but even if they were lukewarm on the idea of the 'buzz-box', the outcome of that other work on the Austin-Healey side – referred to by John Thornley in his memo – would certainly have an important bearing on their future workload.

BUZZ BOX – ABINGDON 'EX' REGISTER AND COWLEY 'DO' REGISTER	
EX188	New Midget with [Austin] A30 ['A'-series] engine – MGD [no previous mention of MGB or MGC in register! No drawings or anything else listed, but this may have been related to Cowley's DO1035]
DO1035	New 'Midget' (small) with AS.3 engine ['AS.3' was the Austin A30 saloon, launched in October 1951. This shows that Cowley gave some thought to using this engine for a true small sports car, as did Austin and, later, BMC]

The Frua Exercise

In 1957, George Harriman had Abingdon ship out an MGA chassis to Frua of Turin to have the Italian coachbuilder create a concept for a new sports car in the vein of the alluring Ferraris and Maseratis that the BMC Deputy Chairman had seen at various European Motor Shows. The outcome of this exercise was universally admired as a testament to prevailing Italian design skills, but its bulk, weight and overly ornate nature meant that most who saw it agreed that it was not an MG sports car in spirit. Syd admired it enough to have it photographed in Kodachrome, the car itself closely examined, measured precisely, a fastback top made for it, plans and elevations drawn up and then a scale model made by Harry Herring, but in the end the hand-built prototype was cut up with an acetylene torch in order to avoid the company having to pay the temporary import Bond against it.

Even before the arrival at Abingdon of Big-Healey production in late 1957 (see later), Syd's design team was already rapidly becoming ever busier, with such projects as the MGA Coupé, Twin Cam, Magnette and Riley Pathfinder in the mix, so it quickly became obvious that more staff would be needed; this led to the arrival of Richard 'Dickie' Wright to join Harry White and Terry Mitchell on the chassis side, and Don Hayter to support Jim O'Neill and Denis Williams on the body design side. The fact that they also engaged in record breaking and some more clandestine projects, mostly out of the sight of local Nuffield Director S V Smith, simply added to the workload, whether over or under the radar.

> ### Denis Williams
>
> One of the often-unsung heroes of the MG Design Office was **Denis George Williams** (August 7th 1925 – April 26th 2022). Aged 14 shortly before WWII began, Williams had hoped for an apprenticeship to the Marshalls Flying School of Cambridge, a body responsible for the University Air Squadrons, however the airfield at Kidlington where he was expecting to work was requisitioned by the RAF and the apprenticeship was cancelled. As some compensation, his enrolment at the Oxford School of Technology was honoured and so he began his studies there in September 1939. Eighteen months later, he secured a position at Pressed Steel, working on a number of wartime military projects, including the creation of templates including some to check the wing ribs in Lancaster bomber wing ribs.
>
> As he told the author: *'the end of my time in the drawing office was also the end of my years as an apprentice. I attempted to get a permanent post*

in the drawing office but at that time there were no vacancies and so I was offered a job in the Press Shop inspection, which did not appeal to me at all, and during a conversation with the engineer I was working with in the drawing office he suggested that I try for a post at Morris Motors and gave me the name of the Chief Chassis Engineer; so I contacted him and arranged an interview'.

The Morris Motors Chief Chassis Engineer at that time was Stan Westby; 'at that time he did not have any vacancy, so he took me along to see Les Hall, who was the Chief Body Draughtsman who, after a brief interview offered me a job which was gratefully accepted. At that time the two companies had a gentlemen's agreement not to poach labour from each other, but I had made the first move and Morris Motors agreed to take me on – although the personnel manager at Pressed Steel left me in no doubt that if I left he would ensure my immediate call-up for military service!'

Work followed on projects such as the Morris Minor and Oxford; 'I did the detail drawing for the radiator grille for the Oxford, which at that time was the largest air zinc alloy casting produced in the UK'. In due course, Williams found himself working in the small 'MG and Riley' drawing office at Cowley, working under Jim O'Neill for, in turn, their manager Gerald Palmer; much of his time was spent working on the DO 999 Riley Pathfinder. In 1952, an opportunity to work in Coventry at Carbodies drew his eye and he spent a year there, although a shortage of housing helped prompt a return south to Cowley the following year.

'I saw an advertisement for draughtsmen required at Morris Motors Radiators in Oxford I applied for and was offered a job with them starting in October 1953. As its name suggests the plant manufactured a range of car components including Radiators, exhaust Systems, Radiator Gilles etc. and I worked on one or more of each during my stint here including the MGA Radiator Grille and one MG Saloon'. Williams soon got bored with radiator grilles: 'one day Jim O'Neill who was then Chief Body Engineer at Abingdon walked through the office so I said to him that if he wanted any good body engineers to let me know. A few days later he rang me and asked if I was serious about MG's and, confirming I was, we then arranged an interview with MG's Chief Engineer, Syd Enever, who offered me a job which was gladly accepted. Morris Radiators declined to let me move to Abingdon until, after I had a job interview with Ford (that had been arranged before the MG offer) when the Radiators Chief Engineer called me into his office and informed me that rather than lose me to a competitor my transfer to Abingdon would be arranged effective from March 1955'.

'At that time the Body Section was in a small office with just Jim O'Neill and me, we had one full size layout table and two drawing boards for detail work, although we soon moved into a new larger office which housed all the design team. My first jobs were on the MGA which was due for release, and was mainly on a check layout for the body shell and some minor trim items, and later with detail items, and later with detail items on the MGA 'Twin Car'. Also, a "cheap" MGA that came to nothing. Another project was the EX202, Magnette with the 'C' series engine for which I laid out the front-end body lines incorporating a new wider radiator grille, one vehicle was built that in my opinion was a very pleasant car to drive'.

Other work of note included the body layout for EX186 described later, the MG Midget in all its forms and various hard-tops, ADO34 and the detailed design work on the so-called 'harmonic' bumper for the Triumph TR7 convertible. As the Abingdon factory came towards the end, Denis Williams worked with several of his colleagues on the Triumph Acclaim, and later moved to Cowley where he was involved with the Rover 213/216 and Rover 800; he finally retired in August 1990 and lived in retirement in Witney until he died in April 2022.

Don Hayter and Dickie Wright

Don Hayter (January 24th 1926 - October 9th 2020) was born in Maidenhead but his family moved to Abingdon, where he attended the Grammar School and was awarded a scholarship to Pembroke College, Oxford. However, instead of the degree he took up a post at Pressed Steel where he worked on a number of wartime projects including the Avro Lancaster. After Pressed Steel, he moved to Aston Martin, then at Feltham to the southwest of London. He responded to an advertisement from MG; Jim O'Neill was looking for a new layout draughtsman to work alongside Denis Williams, and around the same time, Dickie Wright (see below) joined on the chassis side. Hayter's start date was February 1st 1956; both men were to become key members of Syd's design team, expanding along with the workload, now that the MGA was already in production, and much of the work already described was under way. In due course, Hayter would be the person most often associated with the MGB, although as he himself pointed out, he was part of a great team led by Syd.

Richard Neville ('Dickie') Wright (April 11th 1921 – January 4th 2012) joined the MG team at Abingdon in March 1956 to work as a chassis draughtsman. Wright told the author: '*Syd Enever interviewed me to work under Harry White. Harry White came up to London to interview me and we went to the pub; then he said, 'we can do better than this – MG are paying!' and so we went to the King's Head at Harrow-on-the-Hill. I was living in Harrow at the time with my parents. It turned out that he hadn't got any money and so he asked me to lend him some. He had arrived in an old Riley Pathfinder with a flat battery which I started on the handle. So, I paid, and he said, 'you'll have to work at MG now to get your money back!'* After Harry White left to work at Rootes, Wright reported to Terry Mitchell.

Austin-Healey Comes to Abingdon

On November 27th 1957, BMC announced the transfer of Austin-Healey production to Abingdon:

'Assembly of the Austin-Healey, one of Britain's sports car dollar-earners is being transferred from the works of the Austin Motor Company at Longbridge, Birmingham, to the British Motor Corporation factory at Abingdon, Berkshire, home of the MG and Riley. The transfer to be completed by the end of the year, is part of BMC's rationalization policy and will concentrate sports car production at Abingdon'.

In his book 'More Healeys', Geoff Healey comments how he and his father had initial misgivings when it was announced that Austin-Healeys were to be built at Abingdon instead of Longbridge. '*We had great respect for Austin and at that time had not had much experience of working with MG. John Thornley called us down to Abingdon to assure us that his company would do as well if not better than Austin, and these assurances were to be borne out by MG's performance. Often when a company takes over a design, it treats it with a "not invented here" attitude, sometimes going to extremes to prove it to be inferior to its own creations. This was never the case with MG. Syd Enever and his men did everything possible to improve the various Healey marques they produced, no doubt spurred on by the challenge to turn out a better product than had Austin with their much larger facilities*'.

Syd forged a good relationship with Donald and Geoffrey Healey through their shared objectives and interests in areas such as record breaking, and time after time Syd's ingenuity would save the day for many an Austin-Healey issue just as much as for MG ones. For example, when the Austin-Healey 3000 gained a larger windscreen, quarter-lights and wind-up windows in 1962, a scuttle shake issue was only resolved when Syd came up with the idea of fitting a heavier gauge diaphragm at the tunnel bulkhead junction; bear in mind that at the same time, the Abingdon team were wrestling with the finalisation of the new MGB – which also saw a scuttle-shake remedy fashioned by Syd. Later still, for the Mark III version of the Big Healey, Syd developed a more efficient exhaust system, with separate runs for the front and rear three cylinders; another example of clever lateral thinking that achieved remarkable results – with low power loss and good silencing.

Geoff Healey echoed the common view that Syd always preferred to slightly over-engineer

The Frua-bodied MGA was quite admired if perhaps felt to be rather large and heavy for an MG sports car. (Enever Archive)

> something rather than risk early failures; as he told Jon Pressnell: *'he was a very practical engineer, aware that he had to make things strong enough for the people at Abingdon not to break them when assembling the cars. He wanted things to be right first time – and if anything failed, he'd probably make it three times as strong as necessary and it would never fail again.'* Meanwhile, out on the salt, as far as Syd was concerned, MG and the Healeys were on the same team; Geoff Healey told Pressnell: *'When MG and Austin-Healey were both at the Salt Lakes, he helped us, although he wasn't officially working for the same outfit. There was no 'side' to Syd. If you wanted help, he'd give it'.*

The arrival of Austin-Healey enthused Syd to the extent that he began – no doubt with Thornley's encouragement – to scheme the latest Morris Motors Engines Branch C-Series '100/ 6' six-cylinder engine into various projects and proposals. The C-Series had made its debut at the 1954 Earls Court Motor Show in the new Austin A90 Westminster and Wolseley 6/ 90 and a year later featured in the Morris Isis; in 1958 the unit would be added to the facelifted Riley Pathfinder as the 'Riley Two Point Six'. Syd had it fitted into a modified MG Z-Type Magnette with a bespoke slightly wider radiator grille but few external signs that this compact sports saloon was now almost a rival for the Jaguar Mark II. For some time, the six-cylinder MG Magnette (EX202) doubled as family transport for the Enever family, and Roger Enever remembers many happy outings from Oxford to such places as the famous Hellfire Caves at West Wycombe, Buckinghamshire, a fast drive there and back via the A40 that was the main thoroughfare in those days between Oxford and London. *'We used to get to High Wycombe in no time in that car!'* Roger Enever remembers.

	MID-FIFTIES EX CODES LINKED TO C-SERIES ENGINE	
EX202	Magnette with 'C' series engine [5 drawings, of May 1956, covering respectively: rear axle scheme, rear shock absorber, scheme showing 'C' type rear axle, radiator casing grille and radiator block]	May 8th and 9th 1956
EX206	Three Litre Riley [no entries]	n/a
EX207	Twin Cam [Riley] Pathfinder (DO1067) [Note that there is reference to 'Chassis No. EX207/ 1 – Export Car'. Presumably drawings were done by Cowley, and all booked to DO1067. The engine was designed by Gerald Palmer as a twin-cam conversion of the 'C' series six. Work began in November 1955 but was abandoned in March 1956]	1955-1956
EX210	2.6 litre MG (4-seater sports) [6 drawings detailing, respectively; EX210/ 1 – quarter-scale body general arrangement – dated August 28th 1957; EX210/2 – described as for previous but annotated 'H. Harris' and dated February 28th 1958; EX210/ 3 – quarter-scale 'schematic layout' dated May 28th 1958; EX210/ 4 – sketch showing installation of pedals – also dated May 28th; EX210/ 5 – isometric sketch of front end and EX210 /6 – quarter-scale frame (the last two both also dated May 28th). The concept assumed use of the 'C' series engine	1957-1958

> **Geoffrey Iley on Syd's Six-Cylinder Magnette**
>
> *'John Thornley and I were chatting one day; we sometimes had a sherry of a lunch time, and I said that Syd Enever and the chaps had put together this car, and would he like to run it round the block to see what he thought. And what they had done, because of their success with the Austin Westminsters in Production car racing, they'd shoe-horned one of those engines into a Magnette. That meant losing a steering rack, but what they had discovered with the Westminsters was that in order to make the steering work as it should, the smart thing was to reinforce the bulkhead, because the problem was that the bulkhead wasn't rigid enough, even on the production cars: and in competitions, you really wanted to know where you were going! So, what they did on the Westminsters was they put a quarter inch plate or something to really beef up the support, and so they used a similar trick on the Magnette.'*

> *Of course, the engine and gearbox did come back into the passenger compartment a bit, and they had to do things about the radiator grille, making it wider. But didn't it go! The problem was that there was so much power there, that you could stand on the gas from relatively low speed, but you got really quite violent rear axle tramp: so, the rear suspension really would have needed completely re-designing to make it work properly.*
>
> *Nevertheless, it was really, really impressive, and I remember that one of the things that I did was that Vic Vines, who was our buyer at Abingdon, and I rather think he wanted to visit one of our suppliers such as Cox's of Watford – they made seat frames – and so I drove him there and back again, and he said, 'I never want to come in a car with you again – ever!'*
>
> *But when I went on the actual test run, I came back into the factory – I had just turned in from the Marcham Road – and in my driving mirror, I saw an Army Major – he had some pips on his shoulders – just driving out of Abingdon in an Alfa Romeo Giulietta. I thought 'ooh, interesting!' and so I did a three-point turn, and we had rather a splendid ding-dong going out towards Kingston Bagpuize; I took him on the outside on one of those curves, very much faster than the speed limit that would have been appropriate. That never went into production; I don't know quite where it would have lined up in the product range: but my goodness, the power to weight ratio was something pretty awesome!'*

The engine was also looked at enthusiastically by Gerald Palmer, who conceived a double-overhead-camshaft version of the C-Series on the lines of the B-Series Twin Cam, as a next stage on from the Riley Pathfinder, which still used the venerable 2.5-litre Riley high-camshaft four-cylinder. The theory was that this engine, in an updated Pathfinder, could have taken the luxury sports car saloon fight to Jaguar, with that marque's by now legendary twin-cam XK six-cylinder, and S V Smith issued an edict for the new Riley Pathfinder twin-cam six to be ready to show at Earls Court in 1956.

Syd and his team scoped it as a three-litre Riley, EX206, and Denis Williams told the author that he remembered the prototype with its tri-tone colour scheme. '*it had a new rear end design incorporating large fins, not unlike those on the later ADO9 series of Austin and Morris models. The prototype was painted in three shades of blue, each colour being separated by a chrome moulding. One day I was driving this car, and, whilst stopped at traffic lights, another car pulled up alongside, the driver wound down his window and asked me where he could buy such a 'wonderful' car. He was most disappointed when I told him that it was just a prototype'.* However, the poor early record of the Pathfinder, the travails of the MGA Twin Cam, and not least the departure of Gerald Palmer himself, meant that the twin-cam C-Series was scrapped early in 1956. The Pathfinder was eventually superseded by the Riley Two-Point-Six with a twin-carburettor C-Series in October 1957, but production moved from Abingdon to Cowley to free up space for the Austin-Healey 100/6.

In a similar vein, the smaller Riley One-Point-Five was originally worked on in part at Abingdon according to Peter Neal ('*Syd had a hand in the front end style of this*' he says), but like the larger Riley was switched to Cowley: '*the new Riley 1.5 was initially put into production at Abingdon but was then switched to another location within the group after only 150 cars had been completed.*'

More so perhaps than the MG and Riley saloon projects, Syd harboured a desire to create a new luxury MG Coupé, the project being ascribed the code number of EX210. Peter Neal was asked to turn some of Syd's hand-drawn sketches into artist's impressions of what this new fastback might have looked like; this initial

Syd and Roger Enever alongside the one-off six-cylinder MG ZB Magnette 'EX202' (recorded in the EX Register as 'Magnette with 'C' series engine, with five drawings, of May 1956, covering respectively: rear axle scheme, rear shock absorber, scheme showing 'C' type rear axle, radiator casing grille and radiator block). The smooth powerful saloon, like a scaled-down Jaguar Mark II, was a popular choice for Enever family run-outs to places like the Hellfire Caves at West Wycombe. (Enever Archive)

concept was hardly classically elegant, and it is not clear if any of the sketches got anywhere near the Boardrooms at Cowley and Longbridge. More promising was a refined version of this concept, which was translated into a scale model by Harry Herring based on a body design by Jim O'Neill. For Syd (and John Thornley) this initially seemed to offer a way forward for a new joint Austin-Healey and MG to lock sports car development even tighter into Abingdon's orbit.

However before long, it became fairly obvious that, from Abingdon's perspective, the MGA replacement was rather more important, and with new V4 and V6 engines envisaged on the horizon, it was clearly going to be realistic to create a six-cylinder variant of the MGA replacement than try to get the budget and resources for two new entirely separate sports cars over and above the forthcoming baby BMC sports car – the Austin-Healey Sprite.

Syd's Baby SLR – EX186

In the wake of the MGA, and the Le Mans EX182 cars which had marked the new model's public debut, Syd had two cracks at creating new racing versions derived from Abingdon's newest sport cars. The first was EX183, *'Experimental 1956 Le Mans Car (Tubular Chassis)'*, which was a lightweight EX182 shell mounted on a tubular chassis and with new-fangled Dunlop disc brakes. One car was built in Development by Harold Wiggins and 'Bunny' Hillier and although run a few times on the road, it was swiftly cut up to avoid detection by the BMC big wigs. Hardly less risky in such terms was the next, rather more ambitious one-off, the more bespoke-styled EX186, listed in the EX Register as *'Twin Overhead Camshaft "Le Mans" Type 1956 – MGA Type Chassis'* with the first entries in the summer

The ambitious plan with EX186 was to create an MGA-based bespoke Le Mans race car with the new BMC Twin-cam engine and other unique features like DeDion rear suspension. Styling was the responsibility of Jim O'Neill and the chassis work was largely down to Terry Mitchell – both Enever lieutenants. (Enever Archive)

of 1955 – weeks after the fateful Le Mans race.

Several of the MG design team pitched in on EX186; all working to Syd's brief, the body design was down to Jim O'Neill and Denis Williams, while the chassis work was the responsibility of Terry Mitchell (whose predilection for De Dion suspensions was well known) and Dickie Wright. Denis Williams told the author: *'it was proposed to build and race a team of three or four special racing versions of the MGA at Le Mans. I was given the task of laying out the full size body lines and all the structural details required for the completed body. In the event only one car was built, the body being made by Midland Sheet Metal of Nuneaton with whom I liaised closely during its construction'*.

Meanwhile, work on developing the chassis aspects of EX186 was one of the first jobs for Dickie Wright after he arrived at Abingdon in March 1956: *'little had been done on it at that stage, only the odd drawing. Terry Mitchell and I set out the layout with ten-inch lines. It started as a 'hospital job' then suddenly it had to be finished. It was Syd's baby and Ted Lund wanted to drive it'*. Wright confirmed that Syd's hope was that EX186 might have been sanctioned for a small series of cars for racing. Interestingly the MGA Twin Cam, EX187, also began to take shape from as early as June 1955. The work in the design office on EX186 was under way in 1955 and before long, Harry Herring's model making talents were called upon to turn the concept into three dimensions.

Unfortunately, the edict from Longbridge that there were to be no new MG factory attempts at Le Mans temporarily put EX186 on hold, although as Peter Neal recalled, Denis Williams simply kept the plans in a drawer beneath his drawing board, where they stayed for about three years. By 1959, John Thornley decided to build the car 'on the quiet' in the hope that once revealed it could be entered by some semi-independent means, through MG Car Club enthusiast and racer Ted Lund, who was as keen as anyone to see MG return to Le Mans to tackle 'unfinished business'. It was also hoped there might be a softening of approach on the back of the goodwill earned through the record breaking with EX179 and EX181. Cliff Bray, a member of the Development Team who had been involved with the 1955 Le Mans trip, recorded in his diary that EX186 was built in a flurry of activity between March and May of 1959, but hopes of entering it at Le Mans were soon quashed.

Roger Enever remembers his father bringing EX186 home to show the family: *'that was a beautiful car; I remember he took me out in it – he came home one day, and I was playing tennis – I must have been about sixteen or so – and he took me up the Southern Bypass... I seem to remember doing about 120mph with me in the passenger seat as he gave it a good going up the bypass. You certainly couldn't do that there now! But I always remember it as such a beautiful car.'*

Originally, Syd was interested in fitting the car with retractable headlamps (bear in mind this was several years before the Lotus Elan made the idea popular on a sports car) but complications and weight considerations meant that this idea was dropped fairly early on. Roger agrees that his father originally planned a more adventurous nose: *'he designed some flip-up lights for it, but they just went for the faired-in glazed headlamps'.* The EX Register does indeed record a number of entries for a system of retractable headlamps but also that the idea had been dropped. As Roger Enever states, with justification: *'altogether it was a lovely car, with its De Dion rear axle and the twin-cam engine... my father built it – on the sly – in the hope that something might come of it, but they killed it and ended off selling it to Kjell Qvale'.*

The unfortunate fact was that the BMC Board was unmoved; an in-house race car project aimed at Le Mans was contrary to the diktat from Longbridge at the end of 1955 – and wise counsel at Abingdon decided that it was better to ensure that the evidence ceased to be discoverable. Terry Mitchell recalled John Thornley received a phone call which made it clear that Longbridge had 'got wind of' the prototype and acted quickly to remove the evidence. *'John Thornley told us to crate it up and get rid of it'* Mitchell told the author in 1994. Consequently, as Roger Enever's comment above says, EX186 was spirited away to Kjell Qvale in San Francisco on January 31st 1961 and remained largely out of sight until 1966 – when it had a brief outing as a road car – although thankfully it survived and was subsequently rescued and lovingly restored by US enthusiasts Joe and Cathy Gunderson. The Gundersons spotted a small ad in the back pages of the October 1982 issue of 'Road & Track' which explained that the unique prototype, missing its engine, had been off the road since 1967.

The rear suspension on EX186 (as with EX181, because of Terry Mitchell's fondness for the design) was a De Dion set-up; a spare left over at Abingdon intended for EX186 was cut up, partly to remove further evidence but also because that seemed to be a standard approach with prototype parts whose primary purpose had passed; as Roger Enever says ruefully: *'that spare De Dion rear axle was in the stores at Abingdon, and everyone remembers how they never kept anything; they cut it up!'*

The dream of John Thornley and Syd to build on the EX182 debut with a new MG 'special' may have been shattered, but they did provide hefty support for the

Denis Williams took a series of photos of the finished EX186 prototype. (Denis Williams)

entries by Ted Lund over three years – but that had to be ostensibly at one remove without too overt factory 'ownership' of the project. Racing in North America was thankfully not such an issue and equally record breaking was deemed acceptable to BMC – which led to more work on EX179 and thoughts of a second new record breaker. The eventual loss of EX186 was a bitter pill, but meanwhile there were other projects that would be allowed to fly.

Experimental Engines for Record Breaking – and the Roaring Raindrop

As we have seen, EX179 was in effect a new record breaker broadly in the image of the Goldie Gardner car, but designed from the outset to use contemporary power-units and a new chassis (the spare one from EX175) rather than essentially pre-war drivetrain. The debut of EX179 in 1954 had seen great things from the last vestiges of the Nuffield engine range, but as engine rationalisation took hold at BMC, and the B-Series family usurped the XPEG, the obviously something new would be needed. Fortuitously the twin-cam version of the B-Series was already in development, and so spring 1956 saw Syd and Alec reworking EX179 to take the new unit.

In Syd's papers is a copy of a letter from him dated February 20th 1956 to J. R. Thompson at 'Morris Motors Ltd. Engines Branch' at Courthouse Green, which sets out his engine requirements for EX179 for 1956 and EX181 for the following year; it is almost possible to imagine the letter being dictated by Syd, almost staccato fashion, to Isla Watts who, from years

```
                                    COPY.

                                            ASE/IW.

Messrs. Morris Motors Ltd.,                 20th
Engines Branch,                             February,
Courthouse Green,                           1956.
Coventry.

For the attention of Mr. J. R. Thompson.

Dear Mr. Thompson,
                    EX 179 M.G. Record Car 1956.
                    EX 181 M.G. Record Car 1957.

Mr. Appleby has verbally confirmed it is O.K. to proceed with
The 80° O.H.C. engines for the above purpose, and no doubt he
will contact you soon.

For 1956 we shall require for the 12 hr record, two engines
(1 for spare) capable of approx.. 105 B.H.P. at 5500 R.P.M. and
to be tested for 12 hours at 75 B.H.P. at 5300 R.P.M
We should like a gearbox rear extension (suggest a few inches
shorter and keeping the same engine mount ring) with a ball
race at rear and a flange to take a 1300 joint. 'B' series box
and gear lever as for Magnette with latest 3/8" engine plate with
oil groove and latest oil seal in front cover to suit 3/8" plate.
Clutch suitable for job. No. fan. Details of front engine mount
to be sent by us. Short upward stub exhausts and sump will be supplied
by us, dynamo is required standard low output and starter.
S.U. carbs. If possible, plugs Champion. Oil :- Medicinal Castor,
Connection 1/2" gas for oil cooler. Distributor with auto advance
(No vacuum control).

Fuel should be Shell Premium, and could be either of :-

    AM/M Methanol          33.1/3    20    50

    Benzol                 33.1/3    20    25

    Shell Premium
    I.C.A.                 33.1/3    60    25

    Plus 60 c.c.              1%     1%    1%
    Castrol oil per gal.

providing consumption figures are what we require for minimum pit
stops.

                        (Cont'd).............
```

```
                                    - 2 -

Also for 1956, one engine similar to previous two, (for a sprint
run at 165 M.P.H. for 10 miles), but to give 130 B.H.P. at 6700 R.P.M.
and tested for 10 mins. at full power.
Starter and distributor, but no dyno required.

The fuel may be Straight Methanol + 60 c.c. of Castrol oil per gallon,
or any of the above fuels.

For 1957 (to break the present 1500 Record, which stands at 204 M.P.H.)
we should like two engines (1 spare) and both complete with blowers.
1 gearbox only to give 280 B.H.P. at 7100 R.P.M. on any fuel.
(Shell supplied, reference Mr. Beveridge Roundtree, Shell Mex House,
London). Engine to hold full power for 1/2 minute minimum.

We suggest this engine should have a gear driven Shorrock pre-compressor
type supercharger 28 lbs. boost. R.H. side mounted with two 2.1/2" S.U.
carbs. Fitted with suitable clutch and 1.1/2 Litre Riley type gearbox
with no tail extension and flange for 1300 coupling. No fan. Large sump.
No oil cooler will be used on run as it is short duration.

We should be pleased to have a rough layout of this engine before
proceeding, to check in car layout. Total length of unit to be kept
reasonably short as it is to be installed in central chassis position
and driving to the rear axle with a short propellor shaft.

We will supply final details of engine mountings, and gear change lever.
Clutch operation hydraulic. We could supply details of explosion valves
for inlet manifold. Engine to have magneto. No starter,. Rear
gearbox engine mounting plate as for 1.1/2 Riley would be suitable on
provisional layout, also front mounting similar to old T.A.10H.P. Midget,
at the front, at any suitable centres to suit engine condition. We will
supply exhaust stub pipes. Mechanical fuel pump (suggest Plessey special
for Methanol). A Tecalemit Micro pump could be driven off the rear end of
the supercharger for lubricating the supercharger.

Reduction of weight is important, as tyre size is small.

Engines must be checked to ensure they will not exceed 1500 c.c. after
the attempts.

Graphs of estimated power and performance enclosed.

                                            Yours sincerely,

Copies to :-    Mr. W. V. Appleby.
                Mr. E. Maher (Graphs also)
                Mr. J. W. Thornley
                Mr. H. White.
```

of working with Syd, knew most of what he was talking about, but possibly made a few entirely understandable errors (the spelling of Mr Roundtree on the second page – surely it would have been Rowntree? And talking of a 'mount ring' where it seems likely Syd meant simply 'mounting'?) but this is nit-picking; the gist of what Syd wanted, set out in detail, is clear enough for the recipients to understand, without being embellished with flowery prose: it is an engineer's letter. It is clear, too, who in Syd's mind was to be the most important recipient of a copy of the letter, as he marked Eddie Maher's copy to be sent with graphs.

The date of the letter to James Thompson, and the content within, makes it clear that the basic format of the new record breaker (EX181) was already evolving in Syd's mind – in other words the engine would be centrally mounted and in many aspects would be significantly different to EX179, even though both cars would benefit from the latest iteration of the twin-cam B-Series powertrain, using Shorrock superchargers to help generate impressive power outputs well beyond the typical figures for an everyday 1.5-litre four-cylinder in the mid-fifties. The subsequent letter from George Eyston of June 7th 1956 also shows other factors in play – such as the debate as to whether or not EX181 would need a tail-fin (in the end, there was one for 1957 but not for 1959; some of Syd's contemporaries said that the Chief Engineer did not think it necessary in 1957 but that he included it to keep Eyston happy).

In a short report summing up the record-breaking efforts in the in-house Nuffield publication 'Teamwork' of October 1956, it was pointed out that the engines were special; they were described as being '... *basically the B-Series, which are already powering many B.M.C. cars. A twin overhead-camshaft head was designed and built at*

The supercharged twin-cam engine. (Author Archive)

CHAPTER SEVEN: FINAL FURLONGS

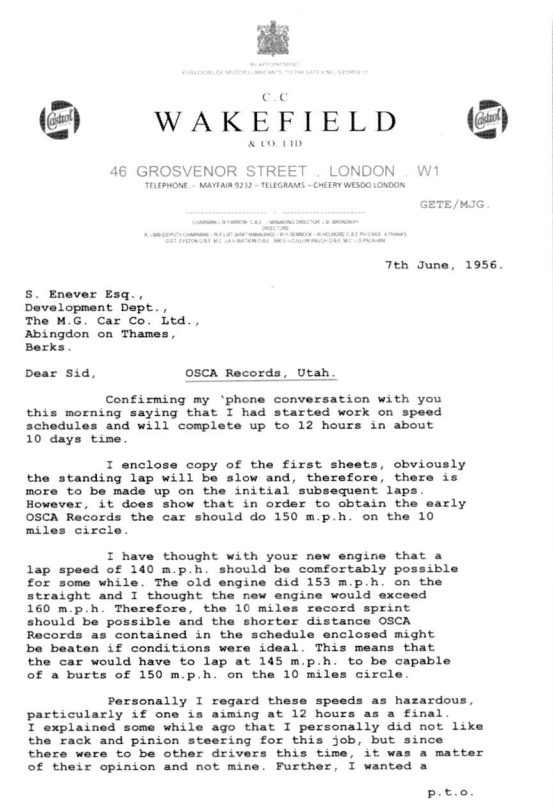

Engines Branch. Mr R. Maher [stet], Chief Experimental Engineer at Engines Branch, and C. J. Law, Chargehand of the Experimental Department, prepared these engines which were shipped to the USA with the car.' There were three engines sent on the trip; two of them tuned to give 100bhp and the third (used in the International Ten Miles Flying Start) developed 120bhp.

The article went on to credit Syd: *'modifications made to EX179 to accommodate the new engine were designed by Mr. Sydney Enever, Chief Engineer of the M.G. Car Company, and these included transferring the driving position from the left to the right'.* The change from left to right hand drive was not to suit the drivers or national pride, but instead to suit the different engine exhaust stacks. The team at Utah, apart from Captain Eyston and the drivers, included Alec Hounslow ('Foreman of the B.M.C. Competitions Department'), Chris Law and Henry Stone, (by this time, Hounslow's Charge-Hand)..

The record tally in August 1956 with EX179 with the new twin cam engine was an impressive sixteen new International and 38 American ones, with the driving duties shared by Ken Miles and Johnny Lockett.

August 15th 1956	EX179 record breaker, now fitted with a prototype 1.5 litre twin overhead cam BMC B-series engine, and re-configured to right hand drive (because of the engine exhaust stack arrangements) secures eight International Class 'F' records at the Bonneville Salt Flats, Utah, USA: 500km, 142.97mph; three hours, 143.09mph; 500 miles, 141.17mph; 1,000 km, 141.66mph; six hours, 142.28mph; 1,000 miles, 141.46mph; 2,000 km, 141.86mph; twelve hours, 141.71mph. Drivers are Ken Miles and Johnny Lockett. Colour scheme is 'traditional' metallic 'MG EX Green' over a bronze lower section.
August 17th 1956	EX179 record breaker secures seven more records at the Bonneville Salt Flats: 50 km, 148.39mph; 50 miles, 150.89mph; 100 km, 151.75mph; 100 miles, 153.12mph; 200 km, 153.66mph; one hour, 153.98mph; 200 miles, 154.30mph.
August 19th 1956	EX179 record breaker secures its final record for 1956 at the Bonneville Salt Flats, with the ten miles at 170.15mph.

With EX179 at Abingdon are, left to right, Tom Haig, Bunny Hillier, Jim Cox, Cliff Bray, Henry Stone (looking towards Syd), Alec Hounslow and Syd. (Enever Archive)

EX179 on the Bonneville Salt Flats with David Ash outside the cockpit; both alongside a long black oil line 'course marker' marked on the salt lake surface – something that would surely outrage modern environmentalists. (Enever Archive)

Syd Enever already knew that in order to raise the targets even higher, EX179 was not sufficient, even though that car was still new, and hence the work on the new car in the background, first thoughts of which, according to Peter Neal, were already germinating in Syd's mind as early as 1954 – which probably explains why the record breaker has an even earlier number than that of the 1955 Le Mans race cars. It was obvious that the older car (i.e. EX179) still had great potential, but there was limited scope to overstretch its abilities, and with George Eyston lending his weight – personality, connections and sponsorship – MG was able to get the necessary funding for a brand new, more revolutionary record breaker capable of reaching into the region of 250mph or more. John Thornley would later claim that some of the budget which supported EX181 was obtained with the aid of some subtle sleight of hand with the publicity budgets at his disposal.

In planning the new record breaker, Syd turned again to Terry Mitchell and the two discussed their options; the world of aerodynamics and wider experience of streamlined record chasers showed that the ideal shapes were slim, tapered projectiles akin to modern wing sections, but with the shaping effectively carried around both the horizontal and vertical planes – the latter inevitable meaning that the rear track would end up somewhat narrower than the front.

Aerodynamic profiles were obtained, using sections developed from work by a Russian scientist, mathematician and engineer, Nikolay Yegorovich Zhukovsky, which were known as 'Joukowski profiles'; a good example of Syd spending time in the Oxford Reference Library to teach himself what he needed to know. Syd played with some experimental models with the assistance of Harry Herring, followed by wind tunnel testing by George Beech in the laboratories at 'Sir W. G. Armstrong Whitworth Aircraft Limited' at Bagington (Coventry). Eventually what Syd considered the ideal shape – a balance of profiles and practicalities was tested in model form at the Bagington windtunnels, before the shape was scaled up, in timehonoured wooden 'egg-crate' style, and then the aluminium body panels were formed and fitted by Midland Sheet Metal.

The chassis itself, largely designed by Mitchell, featured a De Dion rear suspension, a TC gearbox and structural members made by J Thompson Pressings, the company responsible for the main pressings for the MGA chassis. As Mitchell explained: *'there were two main members to the chassis, which were made by Thompson, using three-inch diameter 14-gauge tube. They said "we'll do it for free if you can get us free publicity". They phoned one day, saying that they couldn't make the members to the tolerance that we wanted. Syd said to me "you'd better go up there and see" so I went up there, and I found they'd made up 120 sets, which were all stacked up against the wall! They'd made them all up on crude trestles. I said, "how can you do it without a surface table?" They couldn't match our tolerances, which we wanted within a few thousands of an inch. So, I picked the best I could find, brought it back and put it on our surface table, where we managed to heat and bend it to the correct shape'.*

The body of EX181 was created, using the time-honoured timber 'crate' with cross sectional pieces at ten-inch intervals, and the panel work was undertaken, as noted, by Midland Sheet metal. *'They were strict union at Nuneaton'* Terry Mitchell told the author; *'I went up there once – it was a very muddy road leading up to their shop. They were doing Morris Traveller roofs, with the double curves slapped by hand on wooden formers'.* From the Abingdon end it was mostly Henry Stone and Jim Cox.

EX181	Record Car (Special) [*the famous Record Breaker driven by Phil Hill and Stirling Moss, and known to the media as the 'Roaring Raindrop'. Most of the 276 drawings date from 1957 to 1960, but there are later entries from No. EX181/273 onwards; EX181/273 dated August 10th 1966 is for 'radiator front duct' whilst EX181/274, dated July 3rd 1978 is for 'front decal showing GB & USA flags and MG emblem' – drawn in retrospect no doubt to allow restoration. Drawings EX181/275 & 276, dated October 25th 1979 and October 30th 1978 respectively, detail the tail contours*]

Once EX181 was a rolling vehicle, it was taken to RAF Brize Norton, near Witney, for a test session with Tommy Haig driving and Syd accompanied by Terry Mitchell and Geoffrey Iley. As Henry Stone later recalled: *'Tom Haig, who was our tester, drove it at about 120 plus, so that we could assess the stability of the car's nose down attack angle. We wanted to ensure that if it hit a bump, it would not take off'.* On one occasion at Brize Norton, the base commander was on hand, and when John Thornley enquired how much longer the runway would be available, he was astounded to learn that there were at least two quite large military aircraft in a holding pattern waiting until the MG men had 'done their stuff'.

From early on with EX181, there was a link to one of Britain's favourite up-and-coming race drivers, Stirling Moss, although from the outset it was obvious that this would involve a new level of negotiation and diplomacy, aligning Moss's existing calendar of commitments and also ensuring there were no conflicts with, for example, his existing advertising and product endorsements. This was an area where John Thornley excelled; he tended to leave Syd out of the finer points of these issues, but kept his old friend copied in. An example is shown here in the form a letter from Thornley to Ken Gregory, Stirling Moss's agent and image protector, on the topic of which spark plugs would be used in EX181; the letter is typical of Thornley's style, honed before the War during his time in MG's Service Department.

Just a day after his letter to Moss's agent, Thornley was in contact with George Eyston (again, the copy comes from Syd Enever's papers); in it the subject of Stirling Moss comes up again – and alongside skilfully deflecting the idea (which Eyston had clearly postulated) of the 'great man' taking a turn in the new car, Thornley broached the idea of introducing Phil Hill to the record-breaking troupe. He also makes it clear that he had not invited Ken Miles (who was one of the drivers at Le Mans in 1955, and of EX179 in 1956): *'You will notice from the foregoing that I have left Miles out of my calculation. This is deliberate. Miles has gone over to the Von Neumann/ Porsche camp, and only drove last year because I had promised him a drive before he defected'.*

Thornley also floated, as a post-script to his letter

```
COPY:     MR. ENEVER

          KAG/JN.                      JWT/GEVC
                                       28th January 1957.

K.A. Gregory, Esq.,
Stirling Moss Ltd.,
20 William IV Street,
London, W.C.2.

Dear Ken

     Thanks for your letter. I have also heard
From George Eyston, and it seems that he is reasonably
happy on the subject of timing, fuel and oil.

     It is a simple matter for us to ensure that
Ferodo friction materials are used in this car, and
this we will do. On the other hand, I hesitate at
the moment to be too dogmatic on the subject of sparking
plugs. If in the ultimate it proves that there is
nothing to choose between Champion and Lodge, then
Stirling's tie-up with the latter will tip the scales
in their favour, but I can imagine that we will be sub-
jected to pressure from the Champion camp. However,
we are starting off with Lodge and will see how things
work out. The most important thing is, of course, to
get a plug which works, and there are not going to be
so many spare engines about for this motor-car that we
shall be able to afford to ruin any in the course of
experiment, so I would prefer to leave this one in the
air for the time being.

     In a few weeks time when plans have been developed
a little further, it would perhaps be a good idea to
have a meeting between you, me, G.E.T.E, Enever, and
others interested - perhaps even Stirling !

                              Yours sincerely,

                              (Sgd.)    JOHN.
```

```
COPY:     MR. ENEVER
                                        JWT/GEVC
                                   29th January 1957.
Capt. G.E.T. Eyston
46 Grosvenor Street
London, W.1.

Dear George
        Thanks for your letter.

        First drivers :    We must not get any mis-
conceptions about the testing of the quick car. Engine
life at the power it will be giving will be distinctly
limited, and test running must therefore be cut to an
absolute minimum. If we had a second string driver to
do preliminary testing it would still have to go out
again prior to the record runs in Stirling's hands for
his own shake-down purposes. It seems to me only log-
ical therefore that the test runs on the vehicle and
Stirling's shake-down should be combined in one oper-
ation.

        Grand Prix drivers are these days accust-
tomed to speeds of 170/80 m.p.h., and there are not
many even of these that I would trust with an enter-
prise of this kind. Of them you could count those
who have exceeded 200 m.p.h. on the fingers of one
hand, and so the choice of a second string is very
very limited.

        While on this subject I might as well make
myself quite clear on another aspect of it :

        You could get into the quick car. It has
been designed to take a 6 ft. diver. I admire the
pluck and enthusiasm which prompts you to suggest it.
Furthermore, I know you would bring back the informa-
tion better than anyone I can think of, but I am not
going to be responsible for pushing you off into the
unknown. So there! See?

        All that being said and done, I agree that
we still need to cover ourselves against the event of
Stirling not being able to turn up at all. I am
Therefore going to suggest Phil Hill, and will be in-
terested to have your reactions. I think he is the
                                               /best
```

```
                                        JWT/GEVC
                                   29th January 1957.
                         -2-
Capt. G.E.T. Eyston, (Contd.)

best driver in America, and is accustomed to Grand Prix
speeds. One can therefor say as much about him as
one can about most others, and from a publicity point
of view on a local boy makes good basis there is much
to commend him.

        He can have a spell on the Class G. car,
Either with or in place of Stirling, and I think we
should invite Dave Ash from Inskips. You can have the
4th spell if you like. I am not going to be adamant
about this one !

        You will notice from the foregoing that I
have left Miles out of my calculation. This is de-
liberate. Miles has gone over to the Von Neumann/
Porsche camp, and only drove last year because I had
promised him a drive before he defected.

        This only leaves the question of what we
are to do with the Salt from the 10th to the 13th, but
I expect we will able to contrive that everybody is
usefully employed.

        I agree the two operations should be kept
Separate, and indeed for this enterprise I think we
Should call EX.179 a stream-lined Morris Minor 1,000.
This won't fool the cognoscenti, but it is not the con-
verted we are primarily preaching to.

        The fuel/oil situation seems to be satis-
Factory, and on this I await your further news. Ken
Gregory tells me that Moss is tied also to Ferodo and
Lodge. We are therefore specifying Ferodo, which
clears that one, but I am hedging at the moment on the
question of plugs. We have first and last to have a
plug which does the job, and we can't afford to blow
many engines to bits testing doubtful starters.

        We intend to paint the quick car a
metallic blue which we have used on the 1/8th scale model.
                                               /For
```

```
                                        JWT/GEVC
                                   29th January 1957.
                         -3-
Capt. G.E.T. Eyston, (Contd.)

For the Minor I am suggesting that we paint it white
with a whacking great black flash down the side.
The flash will prevent one losing sight of the thing
against the Salt, but my only doubt is whether the
white would fox the timing eyes. As it is a ques-
tion of breaking a beam I think it would work alright.

        That's all for now. I, too, am thinking
aloud.

                              Yours sincerely,

                              (Sgd.)     JOHN.

P.S. On the subject of publicity, whilst adhering
     generally to the principle that we shall have
     no publicity until after the event, it has
     occurred to me that we might do a preliminary
     story in March or early April, with picture
     of the models of the cars, and saying in broad
     terms what we intend to do. There is a very
     good story here, and it would be a pity to miss
     it. With a preliminary story so far in ad-
     vance of the real event no harm can be done,
     particularly having in mind the notoriously
     short public memory.
```

to Eyston, the idea of staging some event in the spring of 1957 to excite interest in the forthcoming project, arguing '*whilst adhering generally to the principle that we shall have no publicity until after the event, it has occurred to me that we might do a preliminary story in March or early April, with picture of the models of the cars, and saying in broad terms what we intend to do. There is a very good story here, and it would be a pity to miss it*'.

In a retrospective biographical note of July 23rd 1964 which Syd prepared – in readiness for a visit along with EX181 to Phoenix Park in Dublin (which was, as ever, typed up for him by the redoubtable Isla Watts) he wrote that the car, '*of almost ideal tear-drop shape, was the first rear-engined MG record-breaker to be built since the Company entered the field of records in 1930, and it was constructed in late 1956 and early 1957, being "tailored" to fit Stirling Moss. Its many unusual features include a cooling flap connected to the braking system, which opens automatically to direct air onto the single brake – there is only one – when the brake pedal is depressed.*'

Clearly following John Thornley's suggestion in his January 1957 letter, press visits were carefully choreographed; the car was panelled and largely built,

CHAPTER SEVEN: FINAL FURLONGS

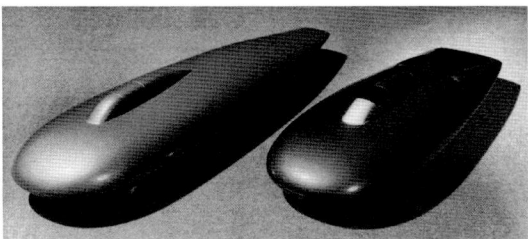

Two of MG model maker and carpenter Harry Herring's models which look close to the end result. (Enever Archive)

Syd and Alec Hounslow (with mirror sunglasses) are nearest the camera and Dave Ash is in the cockpit. EX179, now in two-tone bronze and white, had metamorphosed into a 'BMC Experimental' record breaker, with the A-Series engine, and power unit yet to be seen in a sports car, as the new Austin-Healey Sprite was not destined to appear until the following spring. (David Ash)

but yet to be painted (in two-tone metallic blue, light above dark – see Thornley's latter) and finalised, when Stirling Moss made an appearance at Abingdon for the Newsreel cameras, with John Thornley, Syd Enever and Alec Hounslow amongst those seemingly dancing in attendance, the MG men making theatre for the film-makers by pointing and prodding various parts of the car while Moss, smart in shirt and tie, squeezed his diminutive frame into the compact cockpit with his feet and pedals right at the nose of the car.

Motorsport magazine reported in its May 1957 of a discrete visit to Abingdon, where John Thornley and Geoffrey Iley were the hosts. The writer – almost inevitably Bill Boddy – was able to look into the design nerve-centre: *'a small drawing office, with four boards, serves the experimental department. One board was devoted to a "hush-hush" project, in the form of a new MG record-breaker, not unlike a scaled-down Railton-Mobil-Special, with central engine and very pronounced crab-track. This MG, smaller than Gardner's well-known EX135 record-car, will attempt International Class F records in August, Stirling Moss being flown out to Utah in an endeavour to drive it at four-miles-a-minute over the short fixed-speed distances. Incidentally, an old craftsman at Abingdon makes the necessary scale models for these and similar projects'*.

Two months later, the same publication expanded in slightly greater detail; the magazine reported that the new record breaker was *'... still to some extent "hush-hush" ... but we are able to reveal... [it is the] brainchild of Syd Enever ... the streamlining reduces wind-drag by 37 percent over that of Gardner's EX135, so that 240hp should produce 240mph. Indeed, half-throttle may suffice to lift the records to Abingdon's self-imposed target of four-miles-a-minute.'*

Not everything went smoothly, however; July's Motorsport noted that *'late in May, tests of this engine were held up because the supercharger seized-up, and only about 110bhp had been obtained... '* and *'five weeks before the new record car, EX181, was due to sail it was incomplete and had only a mock-up power unit'.*

These events are confirmed by Jim Cox, for an interview on the MGA Twin Cam Group's fiftieth anniversary book, published in 2008: *'When they ran the first engine the Shorrock blower seized up and was ruined, so they had to have another one built at a cost of £1000. Next time Syd and Alec went up and between them they sorted it out and had a very successful trial'.*

Speaking in 1997, Terry Mitchell explained to the

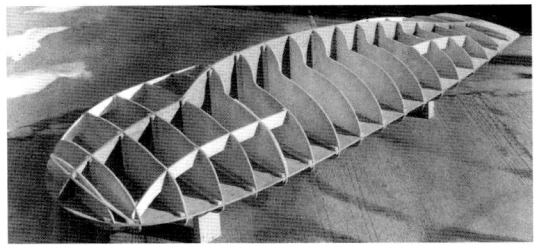

The timber body buck for EX181. (Dick Knudson)

Stirling Moss, Syd and John Thornley confer on the tyre choice for EX181 while the Dunlop representative looks on. (Enever Archive)

Photographed In early August 1957 are, left to right, Jimmy Thompson, Chief Engineer of Morris Motors Engines Branch in Coventry; Jack Goffin and Eddie Maher – who built and tested the engine at Coventry; Alec Hounslow (Foreman of the Development Department, which built the car) sits inside the cockpit; Syd behind; John Thornley leaning in; Geoffrey Iley (Thornley's deputy) behind and last but not least, at right is Terry Mitchell, the clever MG Chassis Engineer who undertook much of the detailed design work at Abingdon on the body and running gear installation. Terry Mitchell once told the author how, when Goff and Maher were having trouble achieving the engine output that was needed, Syd stepped in and with a few changes quickly achieved the desired result... he was truly a wizard with engines... (Author Archive)

author: *'Eddie Maher did the engine to Syd Enever's detailed brief. They had one on the test bed at Morris Motors Engines Branch and they found they could only get 190bhp. They rang up Syd, and he said "have you got this camshaft" and so on, and Eddie said he didn't know. So Syd went up there, they stripped the engine and put all he wanted into it, and it gave 290bhp! The spare engine gave 303bhp...'* It seems that the 'spare' was not used at this stage.

EX181 left the UK on the Queen Mary on July 10th 1957, accompanied by Captain Eyston; this time, Syd was part of the trip (along with Alec Hounslow) as the photos confirm; indeed Syd managed to have quite a good sightseeing holiday once the hard work was over, with a number of photos from his albums testament to the recreation. Meanwhile the objectives included beating those Goldie Gardner Class F records with EX181, soon dubbed the 'Roaring Raindrop' on account of its slippery shape and the noise the twin cam engine, with its vane-type Shorrock supercharger, made when on song. Motorsport confirmed that *'The finish is dark metallic blue below, lighter blue above'* which puts to the lie to popular misconception that EX181 was green in 1957.

Accompanying EX181 on this trip was EX179, but now refinished in a two-tone combination of cream and metallic bronze, the whole ensembled being branded as 'BMC Development Project EX179', using the BMC A-Series engine (contemporary Nuffield PR people asked the press to refrain from calling it a 'Morris Minor record car'; the engine was indeed shared with that car in its latest guise, but the first use of it in a BMC sports car would not be seen for another few months, when the Austin-Healey Sprite was unveiled).

The driving duties of EX179 were shared between American race driver Phil Hill (who had cut his teeth on the TC Midget), his fellow American David Ash and Briton Tommy Wisdom; Ash told the author: *'I shared EX179 with Tommy Wisdom for the twelve-hour run; we split the 12 hours into three, with Tommy doing the middle four-hour stint. I had run J.S. Inskips, the MG importer, and Syd Enever and I had become buddies – he and I went to Las Vegas together. Anyway, Tommy Wisdom was a good driver, but getting on in years, so Syd asked me if I could help out by taking turns with Tommy... two days later, I ran the car with Phil Hill'.*

Between them, the three EX179 pilots went on to secure 56 US and nine international records in six and twelve hour runs, averaging 132mph and 118mph, between August 13th and 17th 1957. EX181 was the 'main event' and was driven for the initial tests by Phil Hill ahead of the arrival of Stirling Moss on August 20th; Moss drove the car on August 23rd to achieve a two-way average of 254.64mph, breaking five Class F records, and delighting everyone at Utah and back home at Abingdon and the boardrooms of Cowley and Longbridge. John Thornley was aware that some commentators wondered at the expense and complications of using Moss, but as he later commented, quite apart from the obvious publicity value, Moss's superb reactions had saved the unique record breaker from imminent calamity on more than one occasion.

EX 181 on the salt flats in August 1957. Left to right we see Phil Hill ('warm up man' in 1957), a representative of Lodge Plugs, Stirling Moss, Alec Hounslow, Syd (in pith helmet) and Ken Gregory (Stirling's manager). Note the tail-fin, included at George Eyston's insistence. (Enever Archive)

CHAPTER SEVEN: FINAL FURLONGS

> **EX181 as Described by *Motorsport***
>
> 'The engine drives via a 1½-litre Riley gearbox and an extremely short propeller-shaft to a de Dion back axle of very pronounced crab-track. Rear suspension is by splayed, trailing very short and stiff ¼-elliptic leaf-springs damped by lever-type hydraulic shock-absorbers. Inboard Dunlop disc brakes are used, and these are the only means of stopping the little projectile, no front brakes being fitted. The final-drive ratio is approximately 2 to 1.
>
> Front suspension is by familiar-looking BMC coil-springs and wishbones, damped by the same type of shock-absorbers as at the back. Steering is by standard Morris rack-and-pinion in a light alloy casing, the geometry being arranged to persuade the car to keep a straight course without much attention from Stirling. Bolt-on disc wheels of standard MG dimensions but stronger material will be used, shod with special smooth-tread tyres made by Dunlop to withstand a wheel-speed of 3,000rpm with a 5 per cent. safety margin.
>
> Moss will recline in a hammock-type bucket seat, a drilled cross-member carrying the steering column, which moves forward to facilitate access and detaches completely for the same reason. The column is nearly upright, 'bus fashion, a large Bluemels wood-rimmed four-cross-spoke steering wheel surmounting it. The gear-change will be left-hand, linked by considerable ingenuity to the Riley gearbox. A fuel tank holding about seven gallons of fuel is set beside the engine on the near side, and there is a small coolant header-tank immediately behind the cockpit bulkhead. The pedals are conventional, mounted on a drilled cross-member right in the nose'.

Record breaking would have to take a back seat in 1958; both EX179 and EX181 made occasional guest appearances, including a demonstration run at Silverstone and a support role to the launch of the new MGA Twin Cam in the summer, but there were other important things happening at Abingdon which demanded Syd's focus; assimilating the Austin-Healey 100/6 production as Riley production was moved elsewhere, readying the aforementioned MGA Twin Cam, and preparing for the arrival of a brand new baby sports car, the story of which is covered later.

The USAAF was on hand to help ferry people and supplies in the forbidding environment at the salt flats. It always helps to know the right people – and quite a few US military officers drove MGs... (Enever Archive)

Syd enjoys whizzing around the site on a miniature motorbike. He seems to have been quite attached to that pith helmet – although the family are not sure what eventually became of it. The Morris station wagon 'service van' behind carried useful spares. (Enever Archive)

Syd is at left, in that pith hat; next is Stirling Moss, Captain Eyston (in straw hat) while Bert Denly stands alongside the open canopy of EX181. (Enever Archive)

In a moment of respite at the Utah salt flats, we see here (left to right) Captain George Eyston, Alec Hounslow (with mirrored sunglasses), Tommy Wisdom and Syd, the latter draining the last dregs of a coca cola. (Enever Archive)

EX181 at the garage at Wendover. (Enever Archive)

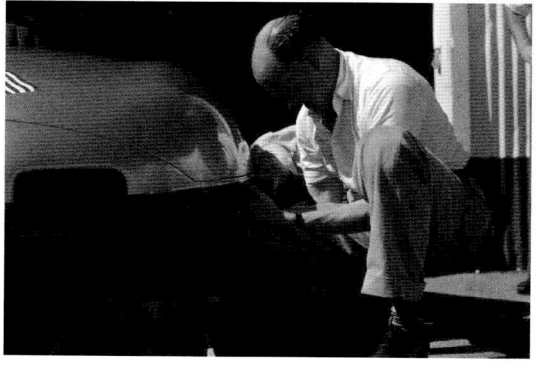

John Law of Morris Engines attends to EX181 at Wendover in August 1957. (Enever Archive)

A striking cloudscape and distant mountains provide a stunning backdrop to EX181 at speed on the salt in August 1957. (Enever Archive)

After the record breaking, there was time to relax – briefly – before coming home to carry on with the day job (the MGA Twin Cam was less than a year from launch – with a production version of the engine in EX181). Here we see Syd and John Law enjoying the swimming pool at their hotel. (Enever Archive)

A stunning contemporary Kodachrome image, showing George Eyston and Syd either side of the tiny 'Roaring Raindrop', resplendent in its 1957 colour scheme of two-tone blue, under the vivid Utah sky, (Enever Archive)

Syd and the Norwegian Children

The 1950s was a period when the dreadful disease of Polio had yet to be largely eradicated by medical advances; many people of all ages could fall victim to this crippling disease, which did not respect any age barriers; for example, as we saw earlier, the highly regarded engine expert Eddie Maher, a great friend of Syd's, fell victim to Poliomyelitis ('Polio'). In 1956, a party of Norwegian journalists happened to be visiting BMC, and when one of them, Fred Kristensen, visited Abingdon to see the MG works, he happened to mention to Syd how he spent a considerable amount of his spare time back home visiting sick children at the Drammen Polio Hospital (nowadays, Drammen Sykehus). Hearing of this, Syd handed him one of the spare Harry Herring EX175 models to take for the children to play with.

Looking Towards the Future

The MGA was a great success, rewarding BMC and MG's faith in the bold leap it had involved, but as we have seen, neither John Thornley or Syd Enever were ones to rest on their laurels. Design ideas were always springing from Syd's creative mind and whilst he was the Chief Engineer, he also oversaw the MG design philosophy because, as nearly always seems to have been the case, neither Cowley nor Longbridge took much of an interest in sports car affairs, especially after the departure of Gerald Palmer. One of the Design Team members was Pete Neal, whose recollections have peppered the text; he frequently found himself being passed magazines or photos of the latest (typically Italian, but also American) automotive creations, and being asked to trace them. As he recalled, one which stood out was a Farina-bodied Alfa Romeo show car, the 'Super Flow' concept of 1956; as Neal wrote in Safety Fast: *"With its recessed headlights, wraparound windscreen and overstated tail fins it may have been the original inspiration for the MGB."*

It is clear that Syd was quite taken by some of the features of this concept, notably the 'pocketed' headlamps (set back into the tops of the wings rather than prominently right at the front), the thrusting nose and the 'tri-tone' colour scheme; the headlamp style also featured on the 1956 Ferrari California and the stunning Ferrari 250GT cabriolet which wowed the crowds at the spring 1957 Geneva Salon. With the Frua MGA described earlier having been seen and assessed, one of the tasks given to Pete Neal was to trace a photo of the full-size car and superimpose

Photographed by Norwegian journalist Fred Kristensen, these are some of the children in a Polio hospital in Dremmen, to which Syd had donated a surplus EX175 model for them to play with. The author reached out to the present-day hospital; they were enchanted by the story, but had no records of what became of the 'toy'. (Author Archive)

The Alfa-Romeo Superflow Concept of 1956; Syd got hold of a photo or a magazine and tasked young draughtsman Peter Neal to make an MG out of it. (Author Archive)

Syd's then favoured rounded nose with quite bulky, bulbous rectangular grille and – yes – those recessed headlamps.

As we shall see, there would be further thoughts and influences towards the eventual successor to the MGA; it could be said that various threads led into the basis of what ensued.

Peter Neal

Someone who knows more about post-war MG history than most is MG Car Club Archivist and former MG Design Office team member Pete Neal. Neal came to Abingdon in October 1954 as a sixteen-year-old apprentice; as he told the author in 2017: *"I had already learned quite a bit about perspective because I wanted to be a technical illustrator when I set out. I was a little bit artistic, I liked drawing and I liked mechanical things; I bought a little book on technical illustrations, and in fact I applied to Morris Motors, to their technical publication department, and they said yes when they saw some of my work, and they said I would have to do a five year apprenticeship and go to college, but they said they didn't have any vacancies at the time – I think this was in the summer – when the schools had broken up – so they said there might be more vacancies in September or the New Year".*

About a month after his interview, Neal received a telegram stating that MG were looking for an apprentice to work in their (new) drawing office; *"my father asked me what I thought – I replied that it wasn't really what I had wanted to do, but it was in the car industry – and so he said I should go for the interview as I had nothing to lose... they gave me a start date, and then they put it back a couple of weeks to some date in the middle of October. I subsequently worked it out that why they put it off was so that it came after the Abingdon Fair which was always a bit disruptive to this [MG works] end of town. So I started in the middle of October [1954]. Roy Brocklehurst had just come back from his time in National Service around the time that I started".*

"Jim O'Neill and Terry Mitchell had already come over [from Cowley] in June-July 1954, so they were still feeling their feet, but already by the time I got there, there was a big layout table where they'd laid out the chassis of what was to be the MGA. I think that Roy Brocklehurst was quite pleased to see me there, because it slightly elevated him so that he was now 'one up' from the boy!" Neal credits Roy Brocklehurst – who had been in a not too dissimilar position when he had started at Abingdon – for taking the new apprentice under his wing. This also meant the occasional especially memorable events that have stuck with him: *"one evening when we were leaving the office at finishing time, [Roy] showed me the MGA prototype, EX175, which was kept under a dust sheet just below the stairs in a corner of 'A' building... I still remember the thrill of seeing for the first time this streamlined two-seater that was so very different from any MG I had ever seen before. The contrast with the TFs that were going down the line at that time was incredible".*

Early experiences included carrying drawings through the works – the drawing office and experimental section were at opposite ends of the factory – and by a process of osmosis as experience grew, altering and cataloguing drawings as part of the day-to-day life of the MG design function. Neal also found himself plotting some of the important graphs which were linked to work under Syd's direction in the engine testing section, including the EX182 Le Mans cars. Sometimes his trips around the factory brought Neal to the Competitions Department, especially when working on performance graphs: *"they also had the test bed in there; I mean, that was the worst thing: I had to go over with a bunch of drawings and a verbal message for Alec, and I would be trying to shout in his ear right next to this engine going at about 5,000 rpm! That was just inside the door as well".*

Although, as we have seen, a design office had been re-established at Abingdon in June 1954, this was effectively housed in a temporary home until re-arrangements of some of the other sections took place the following year. These plans were primarily to accommodate the new Competitions Department, but within the changes it was found possible to create a new drawing office within 'B' Block: *"the project was handled by MG's factory planning engineer (also ex-Cowley), Mike Inston. It just so happened that Mike's office (that he shared with Jim O'Neill) was right next door to Syd Enever's and Syd had managed to persuade him to include a new drawing office in the plans as well".*

Over time the team grew: *"I suppose it was a bit of a cottage industry at first; Syd's department expanded, bit by bit, and he was also able to recruit some of the people who didn't want to go to Longbridge when Morris's design office was shut down and moved up to Longbridge. There were people like Don Butler and Des Jones who came over. Don had also previously worked on loan to Jim, at Bodies Branch, on the MGA, with Eric Carter."* Although a modest 'junior' at first, by the time he had completed his apprenticeship, Pete Neal was a much-valued member of the design team, and remained a key part of it for the rest of his time at Abingdon, although he was away from the spring of 1960 until the summer of 1962 on National Service in the RAF, which meant a small gap when the MGB was being finalised. From time to time he was given photos or drawings of obscure concept cars and asked to draw them up in some MG form – like the 1956 Alfa Romeo 'Superflow' concept car mentioned in the main text.

As Neal noted: *"Despite proposals over the ensuing years to relocate us first to Longbridge and then to a green field engineering centre in the Midlands, this office would remain our 'home', substantially unchanged, until the factory closure at the end of 1980. Reasonably large by Abingdon standards, this new facility would allow space for both chassis and body departments to have two full size layout tables each, plus a number of individual drawing boards at either end".* This all came about during the exciting period after the MGA launch, with all the many projects mentioned in the main text; Peter Neal credits Denis Williams as being another great guide towards his own developing skills, both of them reporting to Jim O'Neill (and in turn to Syd).

After the factory closed, Neal worked for a while as a consultant on SAAB projects until General Motors took that business over in 1990, and later with Tom Walkinshaw at Kidlington (joining Don Butler there), including development of the Aston Martin DB7 sports car – another of those projects to succeed despite a lack of a generous investment budget. *"They eventually had an influx of young graduates, and so they decided to get rid of us old codgers"* he told the author; he retired slightly early at 63. In retirement he has written eloquently of his time at MG and is the MG Car Club's esteemed Archivist.

Abingdon Adopts a Baby – The Austin-Healey Sprite

With senior BMC management having the bit in their teeth for a new small saloon car, it was evident that they were as enthusiastic about the idea of some kind of small sports car to go with it. The MG design team were therefore not going to be left out; as we saw earlier, there were various entries in the EX-Register linked to ideas for small sports cars of one kind or another, but as far as John Thornley and Syd were concerned, few of these had significant appeal; their scoping included ideas such as reskinning a Morris Minor or even creating a cheapened MGA with an 'A' series engine. Geoffrey Iley remembers that the two-fishing line approach was a typical Lord-Harriman ploy; set two entirely separate teams off on broadly the same brief, and then watch to see which one sunk and which one floated.

In the midst of this, therefore, Donald and Geoffrey Healey crafted the basis of what was to become the new Austin-Healey Sprite, using a bespoke monocoque open-topped bodyshell (there was no boot lid, and the front wings were effectively built into the opening bonnet) and in effect hopped-up Austin A35 running gear. Len Lord swiftly adopted this proposal, which he could clearly see as a winner, but the consolation prize would be for MG at Abingdon to build it – the story of which is covered in this chapter. If by now they still had any doubts about the MGA being chassis-less, these must have been abated by the arrival of the new Sprite and soon – according to the grape vine from Syd's friends at Pressed Steel – a new sports car coming from the Rootes Group (who procured most of their bodies from Pressed Steel, then still separate from BMC).

There appears to have been some rival lobbying between Pressed Steel (favoured by MG) and Jensen (favoured by the Healeys, as Jensen already supplied the bodies for the 'Big Healeys') but by the time that the BMC Board decided to shift sports car building out of Longbridge, in favour of Abingdon, the pro-Jensen contingent found their case undermined. As a consequence, the new Sprite – project ADO13 – was built up by Pressed Steel, using a sub-assembly from John Thompson Pressings and after shipment

Production at BMC was seldom simple; these ADO13 Sprites seen at Swindon had started off as base units from John Thompson Pressings; from here they went to Cowley for painting and part trimming, and only after that to Abingdon. Early ones had to be reworked at Abingdon when Syd uncovered a structural weakness. (Author Archive)

from Swindon to Cowley to turn them into painted and partially-trimmed bodyshells, the end product of the foregoing was finally delivered to Abingdon for assembly; production flows were seldom simple in the world of BMC. It was not all plain sailing at Abingdon, however; for one thing the fact that the body did not have an opening bootlid, but had a substantial void accessed from the cockpit, meant that on the line the production worker responsible for gluing in place the lining had to be equipped with a helmet and airline which made him resemble a deep-sea diver.

Of greater difficulty however was the fact that early testing of the first production specimens of the new car swiftly revealed a fundamental structural flaw, which – as explained in the side panel comments by Geoffrey Iley – meant that in severe road use, the body could collapse. The cure was effected by Syd and his team, and had to be implemented quickly by the expedient of bringing partly-completed specimens backwards along the assembly line, stripping the cars out sequentially to allow reinforcements to be added (obviously production changes were effected for the subsequent build). It was a great demonstration of Syd's pragmatic problem-solving skills; identifying and fixing a problem with the minimum of fuss.

Geoffrey Iley on the First Sprites

Geoffrey Iley was at Abingdon, reporting to John Thornley, when the new small sports car to the design of Geoffrey Healey and his colleagues was added to their list of production responsibilities, not long after all Austin-Healey production had been substituted for the previous Riley lines.

'This of course had been a competition between MG and Donald Healey as to who should do the sports car, and John always claimed that Syd Enever's design was actually better, but the reason the Sprite won the day was that some very phoney accountancy had gone on to say that the Sprite was cheaper to make, but that was not actually the case. We built the first thirty, and Syd Enever, who had already said, right at the beginning there would be problems, was proved right.

We had a nightmare getting the bits for it, and when we did get the bits, I had to make trips up to Yorkshire, to Beverley, for the very special rear suspension bits, which were the long-arm shock absorbers and for some quarter-elliptic springs, which came from somewhere else in Yorkshire, which were the necessary bits for the rear suspension, with the quarter-elliptic below and the shock-absorber above; in theory it wasn't a bad idea; the trouble was, they fixed it all on to a piece of tin! Syd said, 'this is going to fail on the pavé' and so they took a couple of cars out on the Belgian Pavé at MIRA, and sure enough, they broke their backs.

At about that time, I was at a Wolseley ex-apprentices' dinner, and one of the chaps there was called Arthur Burton, and he was Works Director at Longbridge; and he got me in a corner, and said "what are you bastards at Abingdon up to?" He said, "you're trying to prove the Sprite's no good: stop mucking us about or we're going to take the production back to Longbridge – and you can tell that to Syd Enever from me!"

But they had to back down; and what happened was that Syd put the cars backwards along the line and took them all to pieces, and then in our own facilities – I'm not sure whether we made them on site ourselves – fitted some channel pieces, which were welded across the floor from the scuttle across the floorpan, and then there was a bigger and heftier bit up the back needed behind the seat squabs, to give reinforcement for the mountings for the quarter-elliptic springs and the shock absorbers.

And so that was the fix done to sort out the very early cars, and then a proper production solution came in some way down the road. Then we had the launch of the Frogeye Sprite, and that was a circus!'

What the BMC 'Buzz Box' ultimately spawned – the ADO 13 Austin-Healey Sprite. Even if it wasn't Syd's own design, Abingdon would get to build this cuckoo in their nest, and his input would prove vital to its success... (Author Archive)

MGA Twin Cam

Arguably one of the more frustrating things that MG lacked was a bespoke engine; such a luxury was unlikely due to the obvious costs and the handicap of production logistics, and being firmly wedded to the requirements for mainstream production was a constraint. However, the benefits included a more liberal spread of the fundamental development and tooling costs, and more manageable unit cost, the wider availability of spares and servicing expertise – so the need to get the balance right was as important as the need to ensure that what was under the bonnet was a worthy power unit for a sports car.

The transition from the old XPEG Nuffield engine to the newer Austin B-Series was one that MG made with good grace; Syd had found during the work to develop the EX182 Le Mans cars how the B-Series could be tuned effectively, and it formed a good basis for the MGA in production. If there were some respectful differences of view between Abingdon (Syd) and Cowley (Gerald Palmer, in the main) on the form of future MG sports cars, where the two parties had common ground was in a plan to develop the B-Series as the basis for a much more powerful, sporting engine.

We saw earlier how development work at Abingdon was under way barely after the paint had dried on the first MGA chassis; Gerald Palmer's ambitious plans for fuel-injection were soon abandoned (there seems little doubt that SU was a factor in that decision; they similarly blocked later ideas for fuel injection) and the engine capacity was increased by 90cc to 1,588cc. At this time, Morris Motors Engines Branch at Courthouse Green was the section responsible for the detailed design of the twin cam engine; as explained earlier, under the lead of James Thompson it was another of Syd's pals, Eddie Maher, who detailed the actual unit. The changes from 1.5 to 1.6 litre capacity came at a relatively late stage in development and necessitated some changes to the block which inevitably introduced subtle changes to the character and performance which had not been tested to the same extent with the new capacity. The story of the short-lived 'Austin' twin cam engine of 1955 was told earlier in this chapter.

The role of the twin cam B-Series unit in record breaking – including how Syd helped stretched it to deliver 300hp – has been partly covered already; it was also destined for the road-going MGA Twin Cam, which as we saw earlier was referred to briefly at Abingdon as the 'MGB'. Detailed develop of the road car was overseen by Syd (the EX Register records it as EX187 – 'Twin overhead-camshaft version of MGA with disc brakes' – entries go from June 2nd 1955 to November 26th 1962) although the day-to-day detailed development was undertaken by Alec Hounslow. That did not stop the pair of them taking a development car on a trip to Switzerland, at which they met up with their good friend and ally Heinz Keller. At one stage, as we have seen, the thought was that the Twin Cam might receive bodywork changes to justify it being called the

Syd Enever (left) and Alec Hounslow stand by the prototype MGA Twin Cam 'ORX 885' and an MG Magnette at the Flüela Pass in the Swiss Alps. As part of their trip, they called on their good friends the Kellers, the Swiss MG agents in Zürich. (Enever Archive)

Syd Enever at a demonstration of the new MGA Twin Cam at Longbridge, with George Holmes of BMC Publicity, who was Exhibitions Manager for Nuffield. (Enever Archive)

At the MGA Twin Cam launch, we see left to right, Ernie Longshaw (MG Transport), Tommy Bownes (Riley Service), MG test driver Tom Haig, Syd and Alec Hounslow. (Enever Archive)

'MGB', but most efforts to restyle the front or rear end of the MGA failed as seen in the photo on Page 154, they lost the purity of Syd's original concept. The MGB name, therefore, was held back for later use. The red scale model was rescued by Peter Neal when the factory was being closed.

The launch of the definitive production MGA Twin Cam in July 1958 was at the 'Fighting Vehicles Research and Development Establishment' (FVRDE) at Chobham, Surrey, a venue used for the first time by BMC for such an occasion (the company would return a year later for the press launch of the ADO15 Mini) and naturally Syd was on hand to explain the inner secrets of the new model to the invited press; obviously much capital was made from the record breaking successes of both EX179 and EX181 with the new engine (and EX181 was destined to continue these a year hence). Finally, it seemed that John Thornley and Syd had achieved what they secretly wanted – a thoroughbred for road and track with state-of-the-art specification, including elegant centre-lock wheels in place of the outmoded wires.

If only subsequent events had been kinder; the saga of the MGA Twin Cam is fairly well-known; there were problems in service (especially when the car was put to arguably the wrongs use, or maintenance regime) but in the end production was limited and finally curtailed; the MGA on which it has been based (see last chapter) outlived the Twin Cam – excess chassis of the Twin Cam type, complete with four-wheel disc brakes – were used up as the 'MGA 1600 Deluxe' (in both Mark I and Mark II forms). Any plans to use the engine in the MGB – the real MGB, that is (ADO23) – were abandoned in favour of other ideas.

Ironically, as is so often the case with such specialised products, the solutions became apparent when it was too late – extensive investigation by Syd and Alec Hounslow eventually determined that there were some initially elusive but ultimately resolvable solutions to problems that had not manifested on the record-breaking cars.

Last Time in Utah: 1959 Record Breaking

The MG record breaking effectively skipped a year from 1957 to 1959; in the meantime, the production version of the twin cam engine had materialised, bringing an additional dimension to the publicity benefits of the runs at Utah. Planning the return naturally proceeded throughout the intervening period in between work on more pressing projects, not least the beginnings of the MGB. There was another angle too; the addition of the Austin Healey Sprite to the BMC sports car portfolio meant that there was an opportunity to publicise the merits of that model too. Syd explored the potential of a streamlined version of the ADO13 bodyshell, under the EX219 project code;

Alongside EX 181 during a press invitation session just before the record cars (EX181 and EX219 behind) at Abingdon are, left to right, Eddie Maher, Chris Shorrock, Jim Thompson (Morris Engines), Syd Enever and Alec Hounslow. (Enever Archive)

Syd is interviewed by a radio journalist at Silverstone. (Enever Archive)

Alec Hounslow (left) and Tommy Wisdom inn the cockpit of the newly-liveried ('Austin-Healey Sprite') EX219 at Abingdon. (Enever Archive)

the EX Register records 19 entries, mostly from mid-April 1959, against this code.

A December 1958 letter shown here from Dunlop to Syd shows how two parallel options were under consideration.

There was a prototype of the ADO13-based car built, and it was photographed at Abingdon with Carroll Shelby surrounded by some of the Development team, but rather as Syd had found four years earlier with the attempt to turn EX175 into a record breaker, the Sprite-based car simply was not good enough. In the end, the simpler albeit slightly cheating solution was to re-livery EX179 (already run in 1957 with the A-Series engine) as an Austin Healey, and to call it EX219 as though it was an all-new car. At least there was no longer any need for soul-searching in terms of thinking of it as a 'Morris Minor' record car.

> **Utah 1959 (from a single page memo by Syd Enever)**
>
> **1. Intention**
> (a). MG to increase the existing Class F (up to 1500cc) record of 246mph beyond the 250mph mark.
> (b). Austin Healey to take Class G (750 to 1100cc) records for distances and times up to 12 hours at speeds of the order of 130mph.
>
> In each case there are subsidiary tasks to be undertaken as opportunity affords:
> (c). MG to take Class E (up to 2,000cc) records at speeds comparable to those in Class F.
> (d). Austin Healey to increase Class G records up to one hour (presently held by Lotus) at speeds of the order of 140mph.
> (e). Austin Healey to increase the Class G records for five miles, ten kilometres, and possible ten miles, which at present stand at approximately 114, 142 and 138mph respectively.
>
> **2. Drivers**
> Stirling Moss and Phill Hill have been engaged as first and reserve drivers for the MG. It is probable that Moss will drive in the Class F condition and Hill in Class G.
> For the Sprite, a three-nation team is being arranged, consisting of Tommy Wisdom, Great Britain; Ed Leavens, Canada; and Carroll Shelby, USA. This latter will be confirmed when it has been shown that we can get the six foot four Texan into the Sprite and get the lid down.
> (the original intention was that this three-nation team for the Sprite should consist of Leavens, Moss and Hill, but the timetable and the intervention of the Monza Grand Prix will almost certainly prevent this).
>
> **3. Time**
> The Salt has been reserved for the whole of the month of September. Dead-line date for the arrival of the vehicles in Wendover is therefore September 1st, and the dead-line date for the completion of the vehicles should be taken as 31st July (this latter will be made more positive when shipping has been arranged).
> Personnel, other than Hill and Moss, will be phased to arrive Wendover between 1st and 6th September, Moss and Hill will fly from Italy after Monza, and planning assumes they will arrive at Wendover September 15th latest.

As the side panel headed 'Utah 1959' shows, Carroll Shelby was still being considered as one of the drivers, but records show that there were doubts that his lanky frame would fit in the diminutive cockpit of EX219. Meanwhile in the EX Register, later entries (dating from June 6th 1959 onwards) relate to the three engines ('Sprint engine', '12-hour engine' and '12-hour spare engine' – respectively EX219/ 16, 17 and 18).

It is not well known that the original plan for an Austin-Healey badged record breaker for 1959 – Project EX219 – was to have used a car based directly on an ADO13 Sprite bodyshell; the prototype is seen here at Abingdon, with guest Carroll Shelby in the cockpit. Also on hand around the car are, left to right, Jim Cox, Frank Daunton, Bunny Hillier, Tony Proudfoot, Harold Wiggins, Alec Hounslow, Peter Neal, John Pike, Pete Owens and Cliff Bray. There was much work done in this by Syd and his team before it was abandoned in favour simply re-using EX179. (Author archive)

The big question for EX181 remained the need – or not – of the tail fin that had been used in 1957, supposedly at George Eyston's insistence; testing ensued at Armstrong Whitworth Aircraft in their wind-tunnels, under the management of Syd's friend George Beech. The conclusion appears to have been that the fin would create drag which would reduce the achievable top speed; it seems that Syd had the ammunition he needed to persuade Eyston that it would limit the potential of EX181 to achieve the top speed he desired.

By the summer, the plans – including the itinerary – were set, as explained in a letter from Syd to David Ash at Inskips; George Eyston would be the elder statesman, John Thornley would be the senior MG representative, and Syd would be accompanied by Alec Hounslow and Jim Cox, the last three flying out of London Airport, via New York, Denver and ultimately Salt Lake City. It seems that the people involved would be Stirling Moss again, following his participation in the 1959 Grand Prix race in Monza, Italy on September 13th (in the event, Moss won Monza in his Cooper-Climax and Hill was second in his Ferrari). Moss was unable to come; Phil Hill worthily gained the honour of the top-slot in EX181.

As for EX219, the so-called 'experimental Austin-Healey Sprite' with 950cc A-Series engine was driven by Tommy Wisdom, Canadian Ed Leavens and American Gus Ehrman. The latter was well known for his role in US sales and marketing as well as racing endeavours, and like David Ash was regarded by John Thornley and Syd as an honorary MG 'family member'; he experienced a fright when out on the ten-mile circle, averaging some 135mph, the engine cover burst open and formed an impromptu and entirely unwanted 'air brake, causing the car to spin well off course. Likewise, Ed Leavens – a well-respected driver who also drove MGAs at Sebring and elsewhere – experienced a crack in the normally rock-hard salt, which again caused the car to veer slightly off course.

The record-breaking contingent at Utah in 1959 around EX219 – effectively the same car as the previous EX179, but now in Austin-Healey livery. (Enever Archive)

John Thornley and George Eyston stage a bit of theatre for the cameras – almost like a case of 'fancy seeing you here!' whilst others looking on in quiet amusement include Gus Ehrman (nearest Eyston) and Syd (in dark shirt and light slacks at the right). (Enever Archive)

Bert Denly, Syd and Henry Stone look over a map of the course. (Enever Archive)

CHAPTER SEVEN: FINAL FURLONGS

Extract From a Subsequent Paper by Syd Enever (Written in 1964):

'*The second outing was again at Utah, in September 1959, when the engine was bored out to 1,506cc to put it into International Class 'E' (2,000cc). On this occasion Moss was again supposed to drive, but the record attempt was delayed repeatedly by bad weather conditions on the Salt Flats, and the car was eventually driven by Phil Hill, the 1962 World Champion racing driver. On this occasion six Class 'E' records were taken at speeds of up to 254.91mph. To date, this has been the last appearance of EX181 in record-breaking.*

The wheel and tyre construction may be described as a technical triumph by the Dunlop Company, who had never before been asked to produce wheels and tyres of such small dimensions which would be capable of standing up to such high speeds. It goes without saying that they did their job magnificently.'

With the immediate record breaking adventure over, Syd pauses on his journey in a big finned Chevrolet in the Rockies, near Steamboat Springs, in September 1959. (Enever Archive)

By the end of 1959, the appeal – as far as the corporate management of BMC were concerned – of record breaking with smaller engines seems to have begun to wane, and behind the scenes, there were already moves that would see some restructuring of the BMC engineering teams. Syd nevertheless held out hope that there might be more derring-do on the salt flats, and with the arrival of the BMC Mini in 1959, he had some ideas of how to exploit its novelty: that story is covered later.

Ted Lund and the Le Mans MGA Twin Cam

We saw earlier how Syd's prize EX186 bespoke Le Mans race car project was stymied by BMC bureaucracy; not to be outdone, he and John Thornley hatched a plan with Ted Lund, stalwart of the MG Car Club and one of the participants in the 1955 EX182 affair (he had co-driven Car No. 64 with Hans Waeffler). Much of the effort involved with the actual car to be raced was down to Abingdon, but provided this could be painted as customer support for a privateer who was flying the MG flag, then corporate eyes appear to have been satisfied. Both Syd and Ted were naturally disappointed that they could not bring EX186 into the glare of daylight, but the opportunity to race again at Le Mans, albeit with a car built up from a motley collection of worthy components was a fair compromise.

Ted Lund was emotionally connected to MG in a number of ways; his father had gone to school with Cecil Kimber at Manchester, and both had been active in the early days of the Manchester Motor Club. He later raced various MG Midgets, sometimes through official or semi-official factory entries, and so when it came to the Le Mans efforts of 1959, 1960 and 1961 (tentative plans to go to Le Mans for a fourth session in 1962 were abandoned, although an entry, by Lund with Mike Reid, was accepted by ACO Le Mans), he was almost an insider in MG terms. The car was SRX210, essentially a new car built from parts of the 1955 Le Mans cars.

Ted Lund had hoped to be able to drive the new MG EX186 -which we saw earlier – at Le Mans; the BMC edict against motor racing prevented that, but instead there was a cunning plan where the UK's North West Centre of the MG Car Club entered a specially adapted MGA Twin Cam; the car participated in 1958. 1959 and 1960. (Author archive)

179

In the June 1959 race an unfortunate collision with an errant Alsatian dog in the 21st hour of the race (on the Mulsanne Straight) led to over-heating and retirement from the race. The following year, the car had been rebuilt with a sleek coupé body, styled by Don Hayter (code EX212), fabricated by Midland Sheet Metal near Nuneaton and the whole ensemble painted the striking Abingdon favourite experimental colour of metallic silver-green, not that far from the shade seen on the 1959 iteration of EX181. This race was better for Lund; the car, with its twin-cam engine bored out to 1,762cc and fitted with twin Weber 40DCOE Carburettors, finished twelfth on distance and won the two-litre class. Back at Abingdon, John Thornley, Syd Enever, Alec Hounslow and their colleagues could hardly have been more delighted.

Ahead of the 1961 race, the nose of the car was re-shaped (Jim Stimson – see later in this chapter – played a part in this); this time there was another 1,762cc engine with twin Weber 45DCOE Carburettors. Unfortunately, the car retired after 15 laps with engine trouble. It was a noble effort, but by now the Abingdon team were thinking of saying au revoir to the MGA as new sports cars were on the way.

MG Midget and MGB

We saw earlier how the plans to replace the MGA soon crystalised into a new model with its own monocoque bodyshell. As with the MGA (DO1062) before, the new model (EX205, then EX214, later ADO23) was very much the product of Syd's fertile mind. Even though it was swiftly decided that the new MG sports car would have no separate chassis, and the (Cowley designed) MG Magnette offered some learning experience, there was no precedent at Abingdon for a fully Abingdon-designed open-topped MG without the obvious structural benefits of a roof. However, the ADO13 Sprite had certainly proved educational, and as soon as it was apparent that there were to be a pair of closely related 'Austin-Healey Sprite Mark II' and 'MG Midget' models (ADO41 and ADO47 respectively) then there was much focus in 'getting it right' and taking the opportunity to almost go back to the MG Midget roots, with a small-engined, low-cost compact sports car.

In the early stages of the process, however, the curious BMC policy of divide-and-conquer, exacerbated by the old Austin versus Nuffield rivalries, came into play in terms of the new body design. The Healeys were given a loose brief from the 'Austin' office at Longbridge for facelift from the front of the Sprite, but originally that was as far as it went. Works started on a new front end, drawn up by the Healey's Body Draughtsman Les Ireland, As Geoff Healey wrote: *'we had been told not to talk to MG about what we were doing, but part way through, Syd Enever rang me and told me that he had something to show me at Morris's Bodies Branch a Coventry, where we had a somewhat guarded conversation about what was going on. It transpired that Syd was producing a new back end with Eric Carter at Coventry. He felt that we ought to get together, as he was worried that his design might not have agreed with our own. Since Syd had been officially informed of our own development work, I was more than happy to reveal to him all that we were fabricating! As a result, we were able to produce a much more uniform design than would have been possible if both sides had continued to work in total isolation'.*

Work thereafter was better aligned, delivering a more homogeneous result, with the body masters being made at Pressed Steel's Swindon works and eventually tailored to meet both Geoff and Syd's requirements; as Geoff Healey states: *'from then on, Syd bore the brunt of the work needed to get the car into production.'* The two new models were launched – separately, a few weeks apart – in the summer of 1961, and whilst the MG Midget got a good reception, there was some muttering in the enthusiast world at the loss of 'character' with the corresponding Mark II Sprite, which had now lost the distinctive protruding headlamps and 'smiling' grille shape. It was perhaps a curious echo of the uproar when the TF had given way to the MGA; after all, traditionalists in the sports car world are seldom the foremost advocates for change.

Denis Williams told the author: *'With the introduction of the 'Bug Eyed' Sprite, the body and trim content became my responsibility and remained so until the face-lifted Sprite and Midgets finally went out of production. The MG Midget Mark I and Sprite Mark II were developed using the original under-frame of the original Sprite as a basis, having a completely new re-styled Front End and Rear*

A beautifully drawn illustration by a Pressed Steel artist of the new ADO47 MG Midget; note the central bonnet plinth which never appeared in production. (Author archive)

End, the scuttle and doors remaining unchanged. The new Rear End full-size layout was drawn by me at Abingdon and the Front End in collaboration with Pressed Steel and Swindon, except for the Radiator Grilles and surround which were designed at MG'. It has sometimes been suggested that Williams took the emerging MGB lines as his basis, but this was not the case; indeed, both the Midget and the MGB lines began with the direction of Syd through Jim O'Neill, and the launch of the so-called 'Spridgets' predated the bigger car by more than a year.

Bigger changes with the Sprite and Midget family saw larger engines (progressively 1,098 and eventually 1,275cc during the 'Enever era'), a change from the original ADO13 type of quarter elliptic rear springs to the more conventional semi-elliptic arrangement, and in the wake of the MGB (described below), a new windscreen, front quarter lights, wind-up door windows and a folding hood. Although the latter was scoped by the Healeys, the serious development work was undertaken by Syd's team at Abingdon, notably Jim O'Neill and Denis Williams, with body detailing achieved in conjunction with Eric Carter at Coventry. By now, the small sports car which had begun as something of cuckoo from MG's perspective had been fully adopted into the Abingdon fold, and the twin-track approach of a slightly more basic Sprite and a moderately more expensive Midget seemed to satisfy the marketing channels of 'Austin' and 'Nuffield'. The EX Register records the first entry under the ADO47 project code as 'ADO47/ 1 – Chassis Number for No. 1 Prototype Car' (dated March 23rd 1960) whilst 'ADO41/ 6', dated March 22nd 1960, was the equivalent Sprite Mark II prototype.

In due course the Midget would prove the stronger seller, and ultimately the survivor, but much of that story belongs at the end of our period of concern.

Syd stands proudly alongside the uniquely finished 100,000th MGA, a Mark II 1600 resplendent in metallic gold paint, matching gold wire wheels, and a white leather interior. By the time it appeared at the April 1962 New York Motor Show, those wheels had been replaced with chrome plated versions. Later sold 'by accident' from a US dealership, the car survived, fell into decay but was later beautifully restored. (Author Archive)

100/6, to become the Austin-Healey 3000, the MGA needed some final ministrations. Syd was rightly proud of the MGA, which achieved 100,000 sales in the spring of 1962; he was photographed proudly alongside a specially-finished MGA 1600 Mark II with a pearlescent gold paint finish (selected by Syd) with cream interior, gold-painted wire wheels and white-wall tyres. The car was shipped off to New York for the April 1962 New York Motor Show and survives in the hands of the Skomp family of Florida. By the time of the MGA's final motorshow appearance in New York, work at Abingdon was nearing completion on the new model – the MGB. By this point, over 70,000 MGAs had been exported to the USA alone.

As soon as it had been clear that the MGA

> 'We aim to give sports car motoring to as many people as possible and to give it to them at the right price. We do not wish to make a small quantity of high priced, specialised cars for the few. At the same time, we set out to provide the fastest possible car combined with the greatest possible degree of safety.'
>
> ... Syd Enever quoted in Press Release for the 100,000th MGA, Nuffield Organisation, March 1962

Last Lap for the MGA – 1600 Mark II

Although by 1960 all serious sports car attention at Abingdon was on the forthcoming Midget and MGB, alongside the latest developments of the Austin-Healey

An MGA with a set of tail-lamps laid out as part of the exercise leading to the definitive MGA 1600 Mark II. (Enever Archive)

When he retired, Syd took with him the experimental MGA Coupé KMO326, finished to Syd's choice of Gold paint (mixed with Mother of Pearl – an early pearlescent paint finish – and possibly the same as the '100,000th' car) with a cream roof. Roger Enever took it on, changed the gold to red, and raced it. The car survives and in recent years has been returned to the gold and cream colour scheme. (Roger Enever)

> ### Chief Body Draughtsman Jim O'Neill on the Beginnings of the MGB
>
> 'The first thing was when Syd said 'look, we want to get a new body made up; all we want is a nice, rounded car'. He loved this rounded business. So, I did a quarter scale drawing of that, and it was all rounded as he wanted, and I took it to George Smith at Cowley for him to make an eighth scale model, which they did. And it looked atrocious, quite honestly; it looked like a pig because the wheelbase was so short and it was a great big fat thing, because of the 'rounded' look. When it came back, I was so disgusted with it that I chopped it up. And I have got an idea I must have destroyed the drawing, because I've never found it, although I suppose it might still be around somewhere. So, what we had to do then was to make it look longer and flatten the sides. When Don Hayter joined us, that was more or less his job to do. He didn't know what the 'rounded pig' was because it didn't exist anymore'.

On the way towards the MGB – note the two-tone paint and bulky radiator grille shape in this model, as well as the recessed headlamp nacelles. (Author photo)

replacement would be of monocoque construction, Syd was determined to avoid the risks of scuttle shake that had afflicted many open cars. Through the usual channels Syd gave Roy Brocklehurst and Don Hayter the task of creating a representative model section for the sills of ADO23, which they took to Pressed Steel for testing for torsional strength. The eventual outcome was a very robust structure which not only ensured the shell was rigid where it needed to be, but also provided a very sound base for the impact legislation that would follow in the future.

One of the best summaries of the development story of the MGB was written, unsurprisingly, by Syd and typed up by Isla Watts; we are fortunate that he attached a copy to a letter he sent in April 1970 to Clive Richardson, then at *High Road* magazine, a short-lived in-house British Leyland publication intended to draw in all the formerly disparate marque magazines under one house monthly. The summary takes the story from the days when the MGA was still in production right through to then recent 'BLMC' facelift of the MGB, but is worth including at this juncture because it provides such a great overview from the creator of the MGB:

The article appeared in the August 1970 issue of *High Road*. Aesthetically, the new MG sports car gained smoother lines – sometimes likened to a 'cigar' – without the characteristic dipped door line and 'hipped' rear wheel arches that the MGA had inherited from the T-Types (and, to some extent, as noted earlier, the Jaguar XK120). Initially there were suggestions of tailfins (all the rage, and Syd was not averse to following some trends) and a boxy shaped radiator grille not unlike a cross between the factory and Frua MGA versions. In due course, the tail fins were judiciously cut down to their familiar form, and the grille shape was lowered and broadened. The inspiration for the latter came direct from Syd, following his visit with Jim O'Neill to the Geneva Salon, where Syd clambered around the new Floride on the Renault stand, to moderate consternation to the officials from the Regie who were on hand.

As Jim O'Neill told the author, subsequently Renault tried to claim that BMC had infringed the design copyright of their Caravelle and Floride models, which necessitated some testimony on paper by Syd and his team, who successfully refuted the claims; it was easy to show that there were various Ferraris with headlamps set back into pockets like those of both the Renault and the MGB, and any debate about the MGB grille was a moot point because the rear-engined French cars had no front grille. It was all soon forgotten, but clearly Syd saw the need to be circumspect in subsequent public discussions. As we saw earlier, Peter Neal had been, from around 1956, tracing photographs of show cars at Syd Enever's request, and alongside the use of those 'pocketed headlamps' on the Alfa Romeo Superflow II show car, and soon there was also the similarly inspirational Ferrari 410 Superfast; Renault really had no case.

Irrespective of the inspiration behind Syd's decision to go for those 'pocketed' headlamps, it was nevertheless a feature he fought to keep despite some push-back from Pressed Steel; Dave Osman, of the latter organisation, liaised mostly with Jim O'Neill or Don Hayter as Syd's intermediaries: *'Don kept coming back and telling me that he couldn't alter that feature. In the main, that sort of issue was dealt with at the prototype stage...'* It was certainly something of a headache in production terms, proving to be quite an unpleasant job for the 'Straighteners' at Swindon – but not enough of a headache to preclude well over a million repeats, counting two front wings per car plus spares.

In an interview with *Motor* magazine in June 1966, just four years on from the MGB's global launch, Syd reiterated his frequent statement that like its predecessor, what became the MGB drew some of its lines from those of the latest record breaker.

'The MGB shape, though you might not realise it, was basically borrowed from the EX181. We streamlined that in conjunction with Armstrong Whitworth and when we started the MGB we took this shell and developed it into a passenger car. All our cars are reasonably streamlined – we can't make them as good as we'd like because they'd look so peculiar. When you've got a nice body and then you have to stick a windscreen and a hood on it, the shape is spoiled. The same with the MGA which started from Goldie

Getting closer to the finished article; this is a Harry Herring model of 'EX214', a precursor to the definitive ADO23 that became the MGB. The grille is still somewhat like that of the MGA, while there is a small 'kick up' behind the door for the modest tailfins. Note the two-tone EX205 Coupe and Frua models in the background. (Author photo)

Gardner's car. I know it's a long, long way from it but the two or three versions we did before the production MGA were more like Goldie Gardner's car than ever'.

If you look at the MGB and the EX181 from certain angles, there is some degree of roundness, it is true, but the resemblance is not immediately obvious. Jim

When Syd Enever (accompanied by his Chief Body Designer Jim O'Neill, who took the photo seen here) saw Renault's new 'Floride' at the 1959 Geneva Salon (the car debuted at Paris the previous autumn), he excitedly alighted on the basis of what would become the famous wide, squat MGB radiator grille. The pencil sketch was added to O'Neill's photo by Syd, using an HB pencil. (Jim O'Neill)

The first 'MGB' prototype with coil-sprung rear live axle. (Enever Archive)

O'Neill, who was principally responsible for developing the shape, with Don Hayter developing the detail, was rather dismissive of the suggestion; O'Neill said to the author *'for people to say that the MGB was derived from the "Raindrop" is nonsense, really. But Syd was certainly always on about wanting it "nice and rounded" – that was one of his favourite terms – and in fact it became quite a joke in the end'*. Then again, as we have seen, there was a sound reason for Syd to champion the cause of internal styling inspiration over any external sources.

At first, there were thoughts of new suspension at the rear, perhaps with coils and even a DeDion set-up, although Syd had his doubts about the latter even if his chassis draughtsman Terry Mitchell (who designed the set-up for EX181) remained keen. Syd said in 1964 that he could see the benefits of independent rear suspension, with caveats *'...it will be more expensive, and the average customer may not notice a big improvement. [You] certainly get better damping features with IRS. I wouldn't have De Dion myself – it's a very stable design and the unsprung weight is not much more than with independent but it's only a halfway house – in total weight it's heavier than IRS and it's still liable to tramp'*. The prototype featured coil springs and a Panhard Rod, and a two-tone paint finish divided by the stainless-steel side strip; the latter remained a feature throughout the life of the MGB and all its variants (even if, from time to time, someone made the case to lose it) but the two-tone paint was a fashion which had arguably had its day, and never appeared on the MGB.

This early prototype for what would become the MGB fascia is interesting by being body coloured – rather than the familiar 'crackle black' of production cars – and many other detail differences. Some of this work was undertaken to Syd's direction by 'the two Abingdon Dons' – Butler and Hayter. (Enever Archive)

Independent and Coil Sprung Suspension Ideas

Writing in *Safety Fast*, Peter Neal spoke of the experimentation with independent rear suspension that began with studies by Harry White, prior to his departure in 1958:

'Before his move to Rootes, Harry had been working with Roy [Brocklehurst] on a form of independent rear suspension, in an attempt to get away from what was considered by this time as the old-fashioned arrangement of 'cart springs' with a solid back axle. This was driven both by a desire to improve the handling and the fact that the market was beginning to dictate that any self-respecting sports car, especially one that had pretensions of being a car that you could take on the racetrack, should have a form of all round independent suspension. Harry had studied closely all the cars on the market that featured either fully or semi-independent rear suspension systems before opting for a relatively straightforward independent set-up with radius arms and coil springs. It is understood that such a system was built into a development MGA but Syd's in-built aversion to IRS as the result of his experience with the pre-war R-type, coupled with Tractor & Transmissions Branch's reluctance to manufacture a special differential unit just for MG, meant that there was no particular enthusiasm for going down this route.'

In the end, all these more adventurous suspension ideas were cast aside; for the MGB, IRS was never really a serious contender in any case, as there was nothing suitable beyond the Austin Gypsy differential, and when Tom Haig reported rear axle steer with the coil sprung live-axle set-up, the design reverted to conventional leaf springs, again bearing the traditional live axle. The changes back to leaf springs meant that Syd – through Jim O'Neill – tasked Don Hayter with re-working the rear body skin lines for Pressed Steel so that they could adopt the rear part of the bodyshell for final tooling.

Three prototypes were recalled in later years by Des Jones, who had come to Abingdon from Cowley in 1960, and was soon working alongside Don Hayter on the MGB. '*In August 1960, two ADO23 prototypes were around. The third was to appear later with a few design alterations. The outside shape remained, as Pressed Steel at Swindon were preparing the skin panel drawings.*' There were several detail changes, which we need not cover here, but the key challenge came when the third prototype was built, and it was Syd who solved the issue: '*there was front end shake*' Jones recalled; '*Syd solved in by fitting a square sectional member across the car and between the 'A' posts, and a substantial reinforcement between the cross-member and the gearbox tunnel, with the steering column attached to a bracket welded to the square-section tube*'.

These changes necessitated a number of last-minute alterations to other components: '*All the instrument mountings and heater controls and switches, and the glove box, had to be re-worked to clear the cross-rail*'. Jones remembers another instance of an Enever solution that was needed: '*Tommy Haig, our Chief Tester, took the prototype out on the pave, and with his thoroughness the aluminium reinforcement in the bonnet front cross member collapsed and made the lock useless. Syd Enever again solved the problem by adding a steel reinforcement which was rivetted to the aluminium cross-member*'.

Des Jones

Desmond Griffith ('Des') Jones (January 22nd 1919 – June 15th 2006) started at Cowley in August 1936 as a clerk on the production line. Whilst there, he took a mechanical engineering course at the Oxford School of Technology, which entailed one full daytime and three nights a week. '*My school reports were sent to S. V. Smith… he offered me a position as junior draughtsman in the Body Drawing Office at Cowley.*' Les Hall was the Chief Body Engineer and Jones had a short stay initially; he joined in January 1939 but was called up on October 16th for war service.

Like many of his ilk, Jones seldom spoke of his remarkable War service, but it included the conflict in North Africa, Sicily and the D-Day landings. As far as his younger colleague Peter Neal was concerned, Des was something of a quiet hero, but his war experiences had affected his hearing and somewhat shaken his personal confidence. As Peter Neal told the author: "*on the D-Day landings, Des was, as he always put it to me, on 'D-Day Plus One'. And that was Des, being very modest, saying that 'I wasn't in the first landings; I went on the second day', but from what I've read about it, the second day was pretty, pretty horrendous – awful. And you know, they were still shipping trips over there for weeks and months after the initial landings, and so the second day was very much like the first day, I think.*"

With the war over, Des Jones was soon back at Cowley; as he told the author, skating over what had gone before: '*after six years and three months, I was back in the drawing office in January 1946*'. There he worked on the Morris Minor ('*I was allowed a free hand to produce the Morris Minor Tourer*' he told the author), the Oxford and related Traveller (again this was largely Jones' work), the MG Z Magnette and Wolseley 4/44. Also at Cowley at this stage was Jim O'Neill: '*Jim gave me the side finishers on the new MG Z Magnette that ran from the door around the front wheel opening to blend in with the front bumper.*'

When the merged BMC started work on the 'Farina line' badge-engineered ranges, Jones worked at Cowley on the ADO10 Austin Westminster and Wolseley 6/99; started at Longbridge, when it was decided to launch the Wolseley first, all the initial work – wooden templates from the Pininfarina prototype and working drawings – were passed from Longbridge to Cowley – at a time when there were still two separate, discreet drawing offices and design centres for 'Austin' and 'Nuffield'. On the ADO16 Morris 1100, Des Jones was responsible for the panel work for the front end.

When the decision came in 1960 to close the Cowley drawing office from July, many staff like Des Jones looked for opportunities to remain near their homes in the Oxford area, and he managed to secure a job at Abingdon in August 1960; '*Syd Enever offered me a job at Abingdon – he said "come over and see Jimmy" – when I visited Abingdon Don Hayter was Chief Draughtsman overseeing the MGB, Denis Williams and Don Butler were Senior*

Body Designers; I was very happy to join them'. He thus arrived in time to contribute significantly to the design of the forthcoming MGB and Midget; some of his recollections of the solutions that Syd developed are related in the main text. Like several of his colleagues, Jones went on to contribute to the Triumph Acclaim project at Cowley., from where he retired in June 1981.

Don Butler

Donald William ('Don') Butler (June 1930 – 14 January 2012) came to Abingdon in 1959 but had worked from Cowley on the MGA bodyshell in 1954, when Jim O'Neill had co-opted his assistance to work alongside Eric Carter in Coventry – primarily on the inner structural body panels. After that work, Syd Enever asked Butler's manager at Cowley, Leslie Hall to release him to work at Abingdon, but initially without success. Butler told the author: '*Leslie said no – he wanted me to work on the Farina ADO9 – including the MG Magnette Mk.III of course – and I also did the windscreen for ADO10. We did the Morris, Riley, MG and Wolseley (which I worked on) versions of ADO9 at Cowley while the Austin A55 Cambridge version was done at Longbridge.*'

Circumstances changed in 1959 as mainstream BMC car design work was withdrawn from Cowley, and Butler was able to move over to Abingdon in the spring of 1959. After initial work on the MG Midget, alongside Denis Williams, Butler also worked on the MGB family, designing the definitive crackle-black facia, and worked on such concepts as ADO34 and ADO21; he later followed Roy Brocklehurst to Longbridge to work on LC10 – eventually the Maestro hatchback, before leaving the 'Austin Rover' business in 1984 to go freelance; he was later involved at Tom Walkinshaw's business at Kidlington alongside Peter Neal on what became the Aston Martin DB7.

Approval of the design of the MGB came very quickly; in time-honoured fashion, it had to be presented to the BMC Board for approval, with George Harriman having the ultimate say; in 1974, Syd recalled Harriman agreed to the MGB quickly: '*that was the one he took to quickest; we sent him the whole complete car, and he put it in the studio, and then more or less the next day he said "yes",* – *he didn't even query the door handle or anything*'.

Speaking to the author some years later, Jim O'Neill, who sometimes accompanied Syd on such trips to Longbridge, spoke well of Harriman (who, in contrast, John Thornley blamed for many of BMC's later problems): '*George Harriman was the main man; he was the bloke that Syd and I used to go and talk to – something that probably wouldn't happen nowadays – I imagine that it is doubtful that you would get to see the Chief Engineer – and yet in those days, we would be talking directly to the chairman of the company. Harriman was very receptive, and I was very sorry about the bad press he got subsequently when he was finally pushed out. I thought that Harriman was a man that you could talk to – he was an engineer himself, and he knew what he was talking about – at least as far as we were concerned*'.

Launch of the MGB

The first public acknowledgement of the new MGB – albeit still a sotto voce announcement aimed at a selected few – came with the first statements in the summer of 1962, coupled with some 'advanced news' leaflets which were discreetly made available for would-be customers and distributors, the earliest known dates for these being June 1962. The advanced information leaflets included black and white imagery of one of the early prototypes, but under the kind of 'gentlemen's' agreement' that governed the press (in particular the motoring press, which relied to some degree on advertising revenue just as much as a relationship based on mutual trust) the

The bootlid of the coil-sprung live-axle MGB opens to reveal the narrow fuel tank and boxing between the inner rear wheel arches. (Enever Archive)

appearance of the new car was kept under wraps.

The Nuffield Organization Press Release of June 25th described the new model as being tasked with 'carrying on a great name', going on to say *'today, the 25th of June, the British Motor Corporation is proud to announce the latest upholder of a fine tradition to come from the Abingdon Sports Car Factory. It is the MGB. Designed as a successor to the MGA, the MGB is in the modern tradition of sports cars. It is sleek and lithe, though a little more blunted than the MGA, and gives the feeling of space, power and that built-in-safety which has always been the hallmark of MGs'.*

Notwithstanding the odd comment about the MGB being 'a little more blunted' than its predecessor, there is little doubt that the announcement was greeted with some excitement (and perhaps, among the new-era traditionalists who had grown to love their MGAs, with trepidation). The autumn of 1962 was peppered with new MG models; the MGB was in showrooms with the Midget Mark II and ADO16 MG 1100 – the latter available in export markets in a neatly-styled two-door coupé version. In addition there was the MG Magnette Mark IV ('ADO38') but like the 1100, this had little relevance to the Abingdon design and production teams – although Syd Enever did drive a 'Farina' Magnette on occasions.

> **Speech by Syd Enever for the Press Launch of the MGB**
>
> *'Our aim is to give Sports car motoring to as many people as possible, and to give it them at the right price. We do not want to make a small quantity of high priced, specialized cars for the few. At the same time, we set out to provide the fastest possible car, combined with the greatest possible degree of safety. The MGB was evolved with these intentions, and in this car, although the ride is much softer, we have good controllability and with no vices under extreme conditions.*
>
> *Similar to the MGA, the MGB is extremely robust; this is a most important feature to the occupants at critical times. As needed in a fast car the braking is powerful and smooth. With regards to performance, we have fitted an 1800 c.c. engine (which gives a torque of 107 ft. lbs.), and we have made use of this to increase the acceleration and general performance, and not to increase the top speed, which is quite sufficient.*
>
> *As regards bodywork, we hope you will approve its clean lines. Although this car is three inches shorter than the MGA, we have arranged for much*

A very early US-specification MGB; as originally conceived, bumper over-riders were going to be optional extras. (Enever Archive)

> more room in the cockpit. The cockpit is amply upholstered in real leather, with comfortable diaphragm seating. The backs of the seats are adjustable for rake to enable the owner to choose his best position for control and comfort. In this car we now have a considerable amount of luggage apace, behind the seats and in the boot. You have easy wind-up windows, also with side ventilators, there is also separate fresh air ventilation at the centre of the cockpit.
>
> As you know, the MGA was a highly successful car, and the MGB should be more so'.

EX233 – The Record Breaker That Never Was...

To build on the success of EX179 and EX181, both John Thornley and Syd Enever wanted to build another new record car from scratch, the objective being to reach for the tantalising goal of 300mph early in the following decade. Drawings were prepared and a beautiful model made by MG's Harry Herring. Syd spoke about the project in 1974: *"It was going to be much smaller than the others; the engine lay over at an angle and the driver more or less sat face down; the whole front of the car was to have been made of Perspex, to allow the driver to see out"*. The car got no further than the model and planning stage; *"but I got certificates to show that it would've done over 300 miles an hour... we'd have got all the parts for it... the only thing was, Dunlop were going to make some very special sports wheels for it, to achieve 300 miles an hour"*.

The new record car would have been remarkably needle-like: *"when you've got the bulkhead, and the wheels, and things like that, you've got a larger and larger area, you see... you're stuck with that as well... so you have to put it awfully close to the road, very square up. And the chap was laying absolutely flat, and it was only about fourteen inches high... the engine was laying flat in the back as well, with the transmission coming forward...it was rear drive... the drive was across this way, a bit like a Mini, only laying flat... there were no components or any sort of business on it ... no carburettors or anything like that; so's to keep the whole thing down to a very small size... oh, it would've gone all right!"*

The author also spoke to body draughtsman Jim Stimson, who became involved in drawing up what Syd wanted: *"I designed various ideas for record-breakers [for Syd] that never proceeded beyond paper studies; but I laid them all out in some detail. One [presumably EX233] was a record breaker based on a Mini under Appendix J rules, and so I decided to use*

In this image, we see Syd, photographed in 1979, when the press came to see him and ask him for his views on the breaking news about the MG factory, with the model of EX233 in the foreground... little did they know, but the table on which the model was sat was also the table on which Syd had laid out his plans for the MGA... (Enever Archive)

CHAPTER SEVEN: FINAL FURLONGS

a Mini Van which had a slightly longer wheelbase. I laid out a complete car which would have had an engine in the back lying over on its side, and driving the back wheels. Appendix J even stipulated things like the window sizes! I laid this out at one eighth size; but it didn't go forward. At the time we were advertising the benefits of front wheel drive, so it didn't fit with BMC's philosophy.".

Isla Watts typed up a typical 'thought sheet' from Syd, dated September 9th 1963, in which he describes an outline brief for this new-generation record breaker, described as a 'Mini Record Car, with transverse engine'; the note describes EX233 as being a 'car of simple construction, very small frontal area, with low weight so small tyres can be used...engine can be built from 'A' or 'B' block, with special casing comprising gearbox, rear axle and combining complete I.R.S. mounting... could make 500/ 750 or 1100 c.c. engines with special cranks and running up to 12,000 rpm.' There is correspondence to and from Syd which shows that he explored the potential of chasing both Class 'G' and 'H' records, in the form of a letter received from the RAC's Competitions Department, which advised him of the various records extant.

In the end, it seems that the BMC Board vetoed funding the project; John Thornley was perhaps no longer able to manipulate funds in the way he had done with EX181 to get that project started, and it would have been highly probable (although Syd's own records do not record this) that Alec Issigonis, BMC Technical Director from November 1961, may have been one of the people who spoke against it; it's use of a transverse Mini engine could have been seen by the proud designer as treading on his toes. Issigonis soon took control of BMC's technical side when he came to power; poor S. V. Smith, who had up to then been his superior as well as technical director above MG, was swept out of the door to his retirement with scarcely any acknowledgement of his own achievements. It was like many such palace revolutions: out with the old, and bow to the new emperor.

John Thornley was fairly sanguine about the abandonment of EX233; *'Anything more extreme than EX181 went into the realms of impracticality... the idea of somebody going for a Sunday afternoon drive lying flat on his face, you know? i.e. fourteen inches off the ground...'* In other words, even if the aesthetic leap from EX181 to MGB seemed tenuous, the idea of EX233 simply had no obvious road-going parallel.

Le Mans and the MGB

With some care – mindful of the ongoing BMC sanction against road –racing – John Thornley, Syd and their colleagues managed to arrange for a 'private' MGB entry at the 1963 Le Mans race, with the driving duties shared between Paddy Hopkirk and Alan Stuart Hutcheson. Syd decided to help make the MGB more aerodynamic, to compensate for its comparatively low power against the leading opposition, and he worked with Jim Stimson to design an alloy nose cone which was fitted first to the 1963 car, entered under the guise

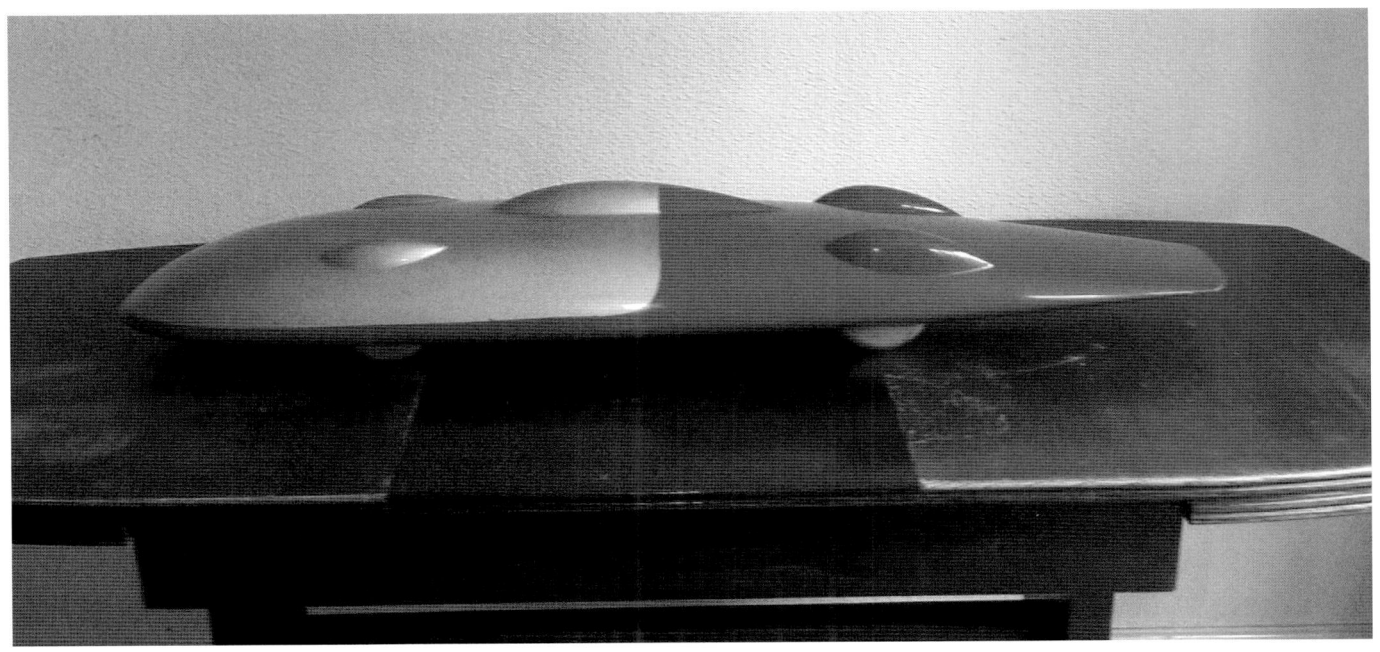

... the photo from thirty years later was taken for the author by Roger Enever, the Harry Herring made scale model of EX233. That dining table is where, Syd recalled, he had laid out his original design for what had become the MGA. (Roger Enever)

SYD ENEVER

BMC was always good at celebratory advertising after its motorsports successes (a more pedestrian advertisement might fill the reserved slot if the racing efforts had gone off the boil). This ad celebrates the success of the MGB at Le Mans 1963 – complete with an aerodynamic nose cone specified by Syd. (Author Archive)

The following year (1964), the trusty MGB won the coveted Motor Trophy for the highest placed British car at Le Mans. The tall, thin figure at the far left is Wilson McComb, later to become the seminal MG historian of his time. Syd shakes hands with John Thornley whilst they admire part of the trophy; behind him we can see Cecil Cousins and at the far right, Reg Jackson, with Les Lambourne, Thornley's deputy at the time, next to him. (Enever Archive)

of 'Ecurie Safety Fast'. The same nose cone, albeit on a different MGB, also appeared at the 1964 and 1965 events, the latter being the final Le Mans outing for the MGB.

Genesis of the MGB GT

From well before the finalisation of the form of the MGB Roadster – or Tourer – there were thoughts at Abingdon about a coupé of some kind – and Syd asked his body design team to draw up a number of options, many with the rounded shapes that he was known to like. The fixed roof version of the MGA had shown one way forward, but there was a desire to create something sleeker with more of a sloping fastback rear end. Some work was done on the Frua MGA which showed the way, and Syd asked Peter Neal in the Design Office to sketch some concepts along similar lines, but to Syd's brief and derived from his own sketches.

Peter Neal told the author how some of the sketches were lacking in terms of proper perspective, and he spoke to Jim O'Neill about 're-interpreting' the basic lines before starting work with the airbrush bought for the purpose; O'Neill said that Neal had better stick to what he had been given to work with. Reminiscing to a colleague at Jensen (Andrew Bee) in around 1971, Syd claimed that he had come up with the basic idea of the MGB GT '*on the back of a fag packet, in a pub*'.

Meanwhile John Thornley too had expressed his desire to see a smart, compact sports car with a fixed roof – he and Syd shared the view that in due course, this was the way that the sports car was likely to evolve, and certainly the hard top was more popular in Europe; it was the North American market which tended to dictate the desire for an open top, and wire wheels. The EX Register lists a project against EX227 as an MG 1,600cc GT coupé 2-seater (there are fifty entries, beginning on January 4th 1962; EX227/2 shows quarter-scale arrangement) but as a standalone coupé it seems unlikely to have gained much traction even if Syd was keen on the idea.

Jim Stimson

Jordan James (Jim) Stimson (March 1926 - May 2nd 2016) worked for many years at Cowley, at one time being a member of the team working on what would become the 1948 Morris Minor; he told the author that he spent twenty years at Cowley in the Body Office there, and amongst other MG-relate projects he drew the factory body arrangement drawings for the 1946 TC Midget. Stimson's

CHAPTER SEVEN: FINAL FURLONGS

> father had worked at Oxford in the beginning: *"my father used to work for Bill Morris in the early days – they were on first name terms. Old Bill Morris used to like to support the 'little man' who helped him. The factory was on the east side of Oxford, and yet the railway was on the west side, and when parts came into Oxford, they naturally went to the railway station first. Bill Morris found a chap at Littlemore named Harding who had a horse and cart and got him to collect the parts and bring them to the factory. After the war, just prior to nationalisation of the transport business, that chap had a very big transport business!"*

In the 1950s, although initially still based at Cowley, Stimson became involved in Abingdon-centred projects; for example, working to Jim O'Neill's brief on the later modifications to the front of the MGA Le Mans MGA Twin Cam for its final 1961 race. After moving across to Abingdon, Stimson became involved in various 'advanced design' projects, mostly – he said – directly for Syd; this included some work on the EX233 record car that Syd wanted to build, and closer to reality, the aerodynamic noses for the 1963-66 Le Mans MGBs: *"the RAC Appendix J rules were crucial – and they meant that we couldn't alter the radiator on the MGB and so the aerodynamic nose on the MGB was a little higher than I'd have liked, but it still gave us 2-3 mph extra – and over 24 hours that could well have saved us one or two pit stops".*

In the midst of that also came the initial work on the MGB Coupé concept which became the MGB GT, once Pininfarina had tackled it (see main text). Further exercises included drawing up prototypes, such as a quarter-scale plan and elevations of the EX234. *"I worked wholly with Syd in the boiler house in those days. At that time, Don Hayter was still in the Production Drawing Office with Jim O'Neill – I was the only draughtsman in the boiler house. I did a number of things apart from body stuff – there was a change on the Sprite/Midget to a crossflow radiator – I did that instead of the chassis people who would normally have done such a thing; in fact, I had one of the chassis men detailing the drawings to my instruction".*

With the MGB in production, attention could more easily turn to the hard top version, and whilst Chief Body Draughtsman Jim O'Neill and his colleague Don Butler deserve the lion's share of the credit for the third-party manufactured removable hardtop, it was to former Cowley draughtsman Jim Stimson that Syd turned for what would eventually become the MGB GT of 1965. The separate project office in which Stimson worked was upstairs within the same block as the MG plant's boiler house; it was a good place to work up top secret projects away from the hustle, bustle and curious eyes in the rest of the plant, away even from the regular Development Department.

Stimson (see panel) was one of several largely unsung heroes who had worked at Cowley on the Morris Minor, in the shadow of Alec Issigonis, and his previous MG involvement, long prior to his arrival at Abingdon in 1960, included the general arrangement drawings for the MG TC Midget. Stimson worked on the aerodynamic nose cone for the MGB for Le Mans, and also on various concepts behind what were sometimes referred to as 'Enever's Toys' – notably the record breakers.

For the coupé version of the MGB, Stimson took the shape of the MGB Roadster and overlaid a fairly conventional roof structure on top, working closely in tandem with Syd and with relatively little direct input from the main design office. Indeed, from the brief 'history of the MGB', by Syd referenced earlier, we can see that he drew some inspiration from the coupé shape of the original MGA replacement concept, EX205.

Before long, it was abundantly clear that trying to stick

The original model that was made up to Syd's specification by Harry Herring, with the draughtsmanship by Jim Stimson. This contemporary black and white photo was taken in the store room at Abingdon which at the time was home to 'Enever's toys'. (Enever Archive)

191

Fortunately the model survives – albeit slightly the worse for wear, having at some time in the distant past had plasticene rather crudely applied to the front end and wheel arches. Author Photo – with thanks to BMM Gaydon

A contemporary Pininfarina Studio sketch, given to the author by Sergio Pininfarina; it does not look all that far removed from the Enever/ Stimson model shown above. (Pininfarina SpA)

with the low roadster windscreen would be completely unsuitable for a car with a fixed roof; not only would headroom have been compromised, but all efforts also to create an attractive style were hamstrung by the beetle-browed style which was an almost inevitable consequence. Furthermore, feedback from the USA showed that drivers of MGBs with the hood erected often found it difficult to see high-mounted signs and traffic signals. For all these reasons, the decision – by Syd Enever and not Pininfarina, despite what has been stated a thousand times – was taken to increase the depth of the windscreen by a couple of inches or more, to give much improved proportions; Stimson recalled drawing up the longer door glasses. Syd was evidently delighted with the outcome and had a model converted at Morris Motors Bodies Branch to show the style he had co-developed with Stimson and took it to show George Harriman at Longbridge.

Evidently Harriman was not entirely convinced by the Enever/ Stimson design and directed that the work be passed over to Pininfarina, then still engaged in consultancy work for BMC (the apogee of which would be seen in early 1968 with their design for a new version of the ADO16 and ADO17). Stimson told the author *'Syd came back to Abingdon, and he was clearly upset at the way they had treated him; but he told me to roll up my drawings and to send them off to Farina along with an open car, which we did – and the Italians built a steel prototype'*.

What came back in a matter of weeks was, without doubt, a masterpiece; Pininfarina had added a sharply-tailored roof structure, with creases in the roof shape that echoed those of the Austin A40 and also a concept from 1962 and added an opening tailgate – creating one of the first 'sports hatchback sports cars' at a time when the term 'hatchback' had yet to be coined. Sergio Pininfarina told the author: *'The hatchback solution was conceived and realised in Pininfarina: it was certainly the preferred option between some others conceived for the car.'*

When the steel prototype came back, everyone agreed that the style was magnificent; indeed, despite having had his nose a little out of joint at Harriman's reaction to his original model, Syd knew that the style was just about perfect, and indeed there were few significant changes made when making what was dubbed the 'MGB GT' production reality. Sergio Pininfarina was happy too: *'In my opinion, our work was one of the most successful we made for BMC: it was received very favourably, approved and converted into production with no difficulty.'* John Thornley was also delighted, proclaiming that the MGB GT constituted a car in which a managing director would be happy to arrive at the office and to park on view in the works car park; he even referred to it famously as a 'poor man's Aston Martin', harking back in part to the Aston Martin DB2/4 which he had originally thought of as inspiration for the MG. In various interviews over the ensuing years he would infer that the clever idea of raising the windscreen height and the roof was all down to Pininfarina; it is true that the Italian designer did increase the height of the screen and made it squarer in the process, but this unfortunately omits the roles of Syd Enever and Jim Stimson.

Timing of the new model was good; the MGB Roadster was in process of changing over to a new five-bearing engine for greater refinement, and there were a number of minor body, trim and hardware changes in the pipeline which could be dovetailed with the launch of the new coupé in the autumn of 1965. A few weeks after the launch, Syd was given a standing ovation at the MG Car Club's Annual Dinner of October 1965, where John Thornley proclaimed his old friend and colleague as a genius.

To ensure that the slightly heavier GT handled as well

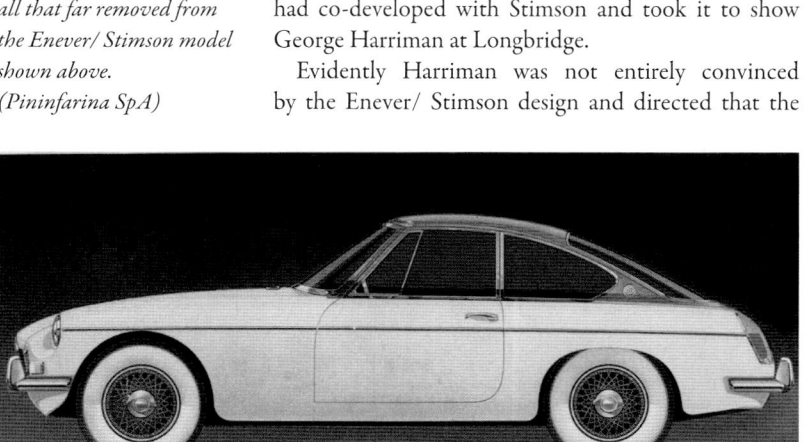

CHAPTER SEVEN: FINAL FURLONGS

A side view in Turin of the original steel Pininfarina prototype for what became, with very few changes, the definitive MGB GT seen below. Sergio Pininfarina said that he felt the MG was perhaps the best resolved BMC design his company had produced. (Pininfarina SpA)

as the open-topped car, Syd worked with Alec Hounslow and the development team to specify different springs and suspension settings (although the basic architecture remained broadly the same) and a new sturdier (and quieter) Salisbury rear axle was specified. According to Syd, when reminiscing in 1974, the rear axle of the MGB (presumably the Salisbury axle on the MGB GT) began with the requirements for a mainstream model: *'they designed a new axle for a future Austin, but as it turned out, they never used it in an Austin..'* he recalled.

Syd Enever on the handling of the MGB GT versus the MGB…

(*Motor* magazine, June 4th 1966)
'Well, of course the weight distribution is different – more tail-heavy – and so we had to start on the springing again. We put stiffer springs on the rear, and this increased the oversteer further and so we were compelled to put an anti-roll bar on the front, we had to take some of the weight transfer from the rear and add it to the front. We even had to stiffen the front springs and so you've got front springs of 100lb rate on the coupe whereas they are only 90 on the MGB. It does give you a slightly harder ride – it must do – but not much as the car's that much heavier. Of course, you can for the roll bar to the open car if you like it stiffer – it's an optional extra on the home market and a standard fitting for certain export markets where the price is higher'.

Syd Enever in *The Oxford Mail*, October 1965

Around the time that the MGB GT was first announced, a journalist from the Oxford Time interviewed Syd for a profile that formed part of a running series in the paper entitled 'Other People's Jobs'. The piece, published on Friday October 22nd 1965, was appropriately sub-titled 'Sports Car Designer':

'Everybody has seen them, those fast low sports cars, that pass in a flash of colour, accompanied by

a low growl from the exhaust. Who is responsible for designing them, for finding a body shape that is both fast and practical? To answer these questions, I went to see Mr. A S. Enever, the head of the design and engineering department at the M.G. Car Company, Abingdon. Mr. Enever joined the M.G. Company in 1928, in the Experimental Department, and went through the various engineering departments, reaching his present position in 1954.

The 1964 edition of "Who's Who in Motor and Commercial Vehicle Industries" lists him as being "designer of the series of M.G. cars that broke many world records in 1938, 1958 and 1959." It was the design of these cars that led to many of the safety factors in new cars today. "We set out to provide the fastest possible car combined with the highest degree of safety." Said Mr. Enever. This is his philosophy of design, the thought that is in his mind when he designs a car. He works in close conjunction with Alec Issigonis, Technical Director of B.M.C., inventor of the Mini series. At Abingdon the whole car is styled, developed, tested, and eventually assembled – none is sent outside for finishing.

It takes nearly three years to design and complete a sports car, from the drawing board to the production line. It begins life as an idea, which is put on to paper, and the proportions are worked out. A small wooden mock-up is then made. This is subjected to wind-tunnel tests, to obtain a workable aerodynamic shape. The room below Mr. Enever's office is stacked full of wooden models of cars that have been produced, and of more adventurous ones that have not got past the model stage.

It was while Mr. Enever and I were walking towards one of the design rooms, and passed an estate car, that Mr. Enever stopped and told me one of the basic principles of design.

"That estate car will go faster than its saloon counterpart," he said. I must have looked surprised, because he then went on to explain how this is so. "With a saloon car, the airflow hits the front windscreen, is compressed and travels over the roof. As it reaches the back window, the pressure on it is released suddenly. This hits the boot and acts as a brake." "With the estate car, this does not happen. The airflow hits the windscreen and is compressed in the same way over the roof. But when it reaches the back, it drops down, as before, but there is nothing for it to drag on."

We then reached the building where all the experimental models are made and worked on. It seemed to me that there was nothing that had not been tried on various sports cars. Among the usual shapes – Austin Healey 3000s, M.G. "B"s Midgets and Sprites – there were some new ones ... but it would be more than my life is worth to describe them. But it is here that they experiment with new engines, gearboxes, and new types of suspension. Tucked in a corner room, covered by a dust sheet, was not the latest model, but the oldest. It was a beautifully renovated 1908 Riley, resplendent in gleaming black paint with distinguished yellow trimming on it. I couldn't help but think of the difference between this and those others outside. And it was there that I left Mr. Enever, surrounded by his work, which is his life'.

Syd stands alongside a new MGB in the factory compound in 1965; note the Bluecol sticker on the windscreen. (Enever Archive)

CHAPTER SEVEN: FINAL FURLONGS

Midget Detours: ADO34 and EX234

As BMC moved into the sixties, it was soon obvious where some of the design principles were headed; the new generation of Austin and Morris models were going to follow the Issigonis philosophy of fluid suspension and transverse engines, primarily front wheel drive. Whilst Issigonis is said to have felt that sports cars needed rear wheel drive, the astonishing success of the Mini Coopers showed how front wheel drive performance cars were not only practicable but race and rally winners.

John Thornley and Syd Enever were happy to explore how the new BMC technology could work in an MG context; the key problem was that Issigonis was very protective of what he saw as his fiefdom, and resisted most attempts to adapt his drivetrain to other uses. Their first effort is recorded in the EX Register as EX220, described as 'New Midget based on Sputnik FWD' and the entries ran from April 4th to May 29th 1959 – in other words, before the launch of the definitive Issigonis 'ADO15' Mini in August. Issigonis presided over the launch of the revolutionary small saloon (the 'Sputnik' nickname came from the tiny 1957 Soviet satellite) and the venue just happened to be the FVRDE in Surrey where the MGA Twin Cam had appeared the year beforehand.

In the meantime, in early 1959, Issigonis seems to have encouraged Jack Daniels to work on a BMC concept for an MG Coupé under the project Code ADO56; it seems that Abingdon had no significant part in this, although having said that, Jim O'Neill once told the author that Issigonis drastically modified one of his proposals for an MG based on the Mini Van platform by cutting the nose short.

The records show that Syd had envisaged both MG and Austin-Healey variants of EX220, and a coupé version (EX220/ 19 was dated May 29th 1959). Before long, EX220 gained more formal BMC authority through a suite of ADO code numbers – 34, ADO35 and ADO36 (MG, Coupé and Austin-Healey and versions of both, respectively). There were in due course two versions of ADO34 – one designed and built at Abingdon under Syd's control, and the other having more overt Longbridge involvement, and a bodyshell designed by Pininfarina to a BMC brief. The basis was the slightly longer platform of the Mini Van – with a wheelbase of 84 rather than 80 inches.

According to Don Butler: '*Syd really started it off, really; he had Jim Oates at Cowley do a scale model, and it evolved from there... we had to keep it quiet from Longbridge at first!*' The Abingdon prototype bore quite a strong resemblance to Syd's MGB – it shared the 'pocketed' headlamps and many general design themes – and Terry Mitchell recalled it as being finished in

A wooden model of the nose of EX220/ ADO34, showing an obvious similarity with the MGB. (Enever Archive)

Here is a finished full sized version of ADO34 in MG badged form. The idea was to use running gear from the contemporary Mini Cooper and/ or MG1100 models, complete with their transversely mounted A-Series engine. (Enever Archive)

Alongside the 'new MG Midget' intended by ADO34, the intention was to similarly replace the Austin-Healey Sprite, in the form of 'ADO35'; as with the contemporary ADO41/ 47 Sprite and Midget pairing, there would have been fairly little beyond trim levels to distinguish the new front wheel drive sports cars, which would have been typically retailed through BMC's separate 'Austin' and 'Nuffield' dealer chains. (Enever Archive)

Simple rear lines on the Abingdon front wheel drive sports car. (Enever Archive)

The Abingdon version of ADO34/ 35 was built as a single running prototype (with alternative radiator grilles for 'badge engineering'); note the retention of sliding side screens. (Enever Archive)

blue. On the other hand, the metallic green Pininfarina 'Longbridge/ Pininfarina' prototype (which survives as part of the British Motor Museum collection at Gaydon) was more blunt-faced, bearing some similarities to the MG version of the ADO16; models showing this style of 'nose' feature in the Enever photo albums. The green car was also a little more sophisticated, with wind-up door glass and hinged front quarterlights.

Denis Williams was one of the MG team that worked on the Abingdon version of ADO34: *'it was based on mini subframes. I did the full-size body layout for this, assisted by Don Butler. This car although basically a two-seater could, by means of a removable tonneau panel, be made into a four-seater, although somewhat cramped in the rear seats. This project came to nothing, being killed off by Alec Issigonis as it did not, in his view, make full use of the advantages of the mini sub frames'.* Don Butler confirmed Williams' story to the author, adding: *'Dickie Wright did the mechanicals... it was quite a nice little car its days – and it even retained side-curtains.'*

ADO34 got as far as being allocated a Pressed Steel Project Code ('257' in late 1966) but it ultimately went no further.

A basic and pleasantly uncomplicated fascia.(Enever Archive)

The piece de resistance of the Abingdon front wheel drive Sprite/Midget was the opening rear tonneau which concealed a lifting back cushion, allowing occasional rear seating. It was a clever idea and it is perhaps a shame that it never saw the light of day. (Enever Archive)

CHAPTER SEVEN: FINAL FURLONGS

> **Three Rival BMC Routes for a Small Sports Car...**
>
> Geoffrey Healey wrote about BMC's thoughts about a way to replace the 'Spridget' in his book 'Healey – The Specials':
>
> *'Any alterations to the fully tooled body produced by Pressed Steel would be expensive, and although Austin had thoughts of a new car they were not sure what it should be. Alec Issigonis, Charles Griffin, Syd Enever and I had a meeting at which a strategy was laid down. Austin would build a prototype using their well proven transverse front-wheel-drive layout, MG would build one with a conventional front-engine, rear-drive configuration, and we would build one with the transverse engine at the rear, with Hydrolastic suspension. Austin thus had to attempt to control the efforts of three prototype units simultaneously, and although three different machines finally evolved, none went further than working prototypes, none of which could be called a sports car'.*
>
> The EX Register also records an MG entry under '*EX228 – transverse rear engine A-Series car*' although frustratingly there are no detailed entries; probably a case of Syd keeping options open...

The next avenue that Syd explored was adapting the Hydrolastic suspension to rear wheel drive; he began with a Midget which was adapted to feature the new system (*EX229 – 'MG Midget with Hydrolastic – rear wheel drive'*; three drawings in the register dated between October 16th and November 21st 1962) and the following spring, another code was taken out and much more work done against it (*EX231 – 'Hydrolastic Suspension on ADO41/ 47'* which comprised 66 drawings from April 1st to December 20th 1963). The development and testing was clearly thought promising, but nobody – least of all Syd – wanted to develop a revolutionary Midget using the monocoque that had started with

Donald Healey's ADO13 Sprite; the consequence was a further project, which involved the commissioning of a new Pininfarina design; this was EX234 ('*Hydrolastic Sports Car Prototype*' – 136 drawings ranging from February 2nd 1964 to September 4th 1968).

EX234 was rather special because it was viewed as a neat way to replace both the Sprite/ Midget pair (the 'Spridget' in popular parlance) and the MGB, including a neat 'GT' coupé version) whilst above it would – in theory – be a joint replacement for the MGC (and its still anticipated Austin-Healey sister model) although no serious work seems to have been undertaken at Abingdon on such a car; instead a large 'BMC Grand Tourer Sports Car' was conceived independently at Longbridge under the ADO30 project code (also known as 'XC 512' and irreverently as 'Fireball XL-5'

The EX234 prototype was a Hydrolastic suspended front engine rear-wheel-drive concept for a sports car that might have replaced both the MG Midget and the MGB, with A-Series and B-Series engines respectively. It was overtaken by other priorities – a lack of funding for a brand new sports car at a time of growing Federal legislation. Work on it had begun after Syd had experimented with an MG Midget converted to Hydrolastic suspension, under Project Code EX229. (Enever Archive)

The style of the Longbridge ADO34 Midget bore less resemblance to the MGB than the Abingdon effort; neither made it to production, however – as much down to BMC internal politics as budgets. (Enever Archive)

Just for scale, here we see Issigonis's ADO17 Austin-Morris 1800 alongside the Longbridge iteration of ADO34. (Enever Archive)

from the name of a contemporary Gerry Anderson TV series). Some work was undertaken on a one-off fitting of a 1,600cc B-Series engine into an ADO41 Sprite (EX221, dated March 23rd 1960) but it is not clear to what extent this was intended as part of the process which led to EX234; indeed the notion of squeezing the B-Series into a 'Spridget' appears several times throughout the EX Register (e.g. EX238, of July 1966), but seldom with any thoughts of suspension changes of such a dramatic nature as EX229-231-234.

> **Summary of Midget Development Projects in the EX Register**
>
> The list below covers the main EX Register entries; it should also be noted that there are many entries in the 'ADO41' and 'ADO47' series (450 and 843 entries respectively) which include such references as chassis numbers, rear suspension work, even some Innocenti-related work and a myriad other developments. The entries drawn out below are concerned with more radical programmes.
>
> **EX220**: New Midget based on the future ADO15 Mini (referred to in the EX Register as 'Sputnik') (April 23rd to June 4th 1959)
>
> **EX221**: An Austin-Healey Sprite with a 1.6-litre B-Series engine (EX221/ 1 is 'chassis number for No. 1 prototype car') (March 23rd 1960)
>
> **EX229**: Midget with Hydrolastic suspension (three layout drawings related to the front end) (October 16th to November 21st 1962)
>
> **EX231**: Hydrolastic Suspension on ADO41/ 47 (April 1st 1963 to December 20th 1963)
>
> **EX234**: Hydrolastic Sports Car (the first drawing, EX234/ 1, is a layout of the actual Pininfarina car, drawn by Jim Simpson) (February 2nd 1964 to September 4th 1968)
>
> **EX238**: MG Midget with 1800 cc engine (two drawings only, referenced 'propellor shaft') (July 10th 1966 and February 20th 1967)
>
> **EX243**: Sprite with heel-board moved rearward (no drawings listed; Terry Mitchell told the author that this was a piece of work responding to criticism of the Spridget's tight cockpit). (December 13th 1968)

A rolling underframe was prepared at Abingdon and shipped to Italy late in 1963, where Pininfarina proceeded to clothe it in a pretty if slightly petite and anodyne roadster body which had echoes of the Alfa Romeo Spider. The single completed EX234 prototype which returned in the New Year of 1964 was well received at both Abingdon and Longbridge; different exterior trim details were fitted with the intention of modelling modest differences between projected 1,275cc A-Series and 1,798cc (or even 1,994cc) B-Series versions, although the prototype featured the former. The design excited Syd and his team and they were optimistic that they would be given the go-ahead to develop it further. Unfortunately the concept arrived at a difficult time for both MG and BMC; the MGB GT and some of the contemporary changes provided something of a boost for the four-year-old MGB range, lessening the urgency of its replacement, but the parent company was entering a difficult patch which would ultimately contribute to the major events of 1968, and meanwhile the early onslaught of US Federal safety and emissions standards was occupying more and more of the design team's time and budget.

Roy Brocklehurst, Mike Holliday and Jim Stimson undertook much of the experimentation with EX234, with Syd overseeing their work. Several former MG design and development staff told the author of Syd's personal interest in the EX234 project; how he experimented with varying flow between front and rear Hydrolastic displacers using simple domestic gas taps plumbed in, and how he specified larger ADO17 displacers in place of the ADO16 originally fitted.

The EX Register shows that after initial work between February 1964 and April of the following year, activity slowed – there was a single entry in November 1966 and then nothing again until January 4th 1968, whereupon there was a flurry of activity until the last entry of September 4th 1968.

A simple entry (EX234/130, dated August 19th 1968) explored the potential of installing the new BMC E-Series engine that was destined to appear in the forthcoming ADO14 Austin Maxi. By then, of course, the British Leyland merger had taken place, and Federal requirements were necessarily the first priority for Syd and his team. As was so often the case, the EX234 project was placed in abeyance and in the event, was never resurrected. Fortunately the prototype was not cut up; it was squirrelled away in the Syd Beer collection and passed through an auction in June 2016, and was put up for auction again in September 2022.

Last Lap at Le Mans

As we saw earlier the MGB appeared at Le Mans on three occasions; in 1963 it was a 'private entry' although factory supported, whilst for the next two years, the subterfuge was avoided and the teams were fully-fledged factory efforts.

However, Syd was not satisfied with just a modified MGB; he made tentative plans in March 1965 for a bespoke GT prototype, based on the 1965 Le Mans regulations, presumably for an entry at the 1966 event.

The logic was understandable; the MGB was, like most other roadgoing sports cars, being left behind by the exotica also racing, and there was an argument that if Ford could turn their focus to cars like the Ford Mark II and GT40, should not BMC follow suit. In the meantime, too, the Healey team had been increasingly ploughing their own furrow with Special Sprite entries at Le Mans and Sebring among others.

Thus in the spring of 1965, a full-sized body MG 'Le Mans' concept under EX-Register code EX237 was modelled in Plaster-of-Paris and photographed for the records; it seems to have used basically either front-engined Midget or MGB proportions, but with a smooth fast-backed shape. The intended powertrain is less certain, but there was talk within the Competitions Department at the same time of a de-stroked 1.6 B-Series with overhead camshaft and fuel injection; as noted in the 'other engines' panel, once Jaguar joined up with BMC, there was the potential to consider a V8 from either Daimler or Coventry Climax. It was all academic, however – 1965 proved to be the last factory MG entry until long after the Abingdon era had ended. The Healeys persisted until 1970, their last cars being highly specialised machines; Andrew Hedges and Roger Enever drove the final Healey SR37 in the 1970 race.

EX237	GT Prototype to 1965 Le Mans regulations [3 drawings, dated 10/3/1965, showing body lines (EX237/1 & 2) and windscreen glass (EX237/3)]	10/03/1965

Hefty Six: The MGC

We saw earlier how Syd wanted to create a new post-war six-cylinder MG, and ideally make a coupé version; his original thoughts of a unique MG was tempered by the realism that from 1957 onwards, any larger-engined MG would have to share some of its architecture with

This was an idea from Syd for a special MG coupé for Le Mans, perhaps in 1966; it never went further than this plaster model. By this time, the Healeys were 'doing their thing' with first special-bodied Sprites and ultimately a bespoke racing car. (Enever Archive)

Syd's aerodynamic nose for the MGB lasted three seasons. Here in the pits for the 1965 Le Mans race, we can see BMC Mechanic Gerald Wiffen in the background. It is possible -but yet to be proven with certainty – that this work came under Project Code EX235. (Author Archive)

a new Austin-Healey. The fact that Syd liked the idea of a smooth six is illustrated by his enthusiasm for the unique C-Series powered MG Z Magnette that we also saw earlier. The problem was however the universal one that MG had so often faced; powertrain specifications were largely determined by volume car requirements, and when it came to larger six-cylinder models, those volume cars were inevitably aimed at a more sophisticated sector where smoothness was the chief requirement, and weight was often a secondary factor.

Much as Syd would have liked a different set of parameters for his ideal sports car, his voice was simply not likely to be given enough weight at BMC Longbridge, where Alec Issigonis presided over just about every aspect of engineering. Efforts were focused on enhancing refinement, which mainly mean adding additional bearings to make the C-Series smoother; experience with the cut and thrust of rallying in the Big Healeys showed that the basic engine was probably tough enough, and maximum power outputs could be prodigious.

Other Engines

Above all other aspects of development, Syd was keen and knowledgeable about engines. He may have lacked some of the mass production and theoretical design expertise of some of his peers, like Bill Appleby, James Thompson and Eddie Maher, but he certainly knew how to get the best from an engine and loved nothing more than experimentation aimed at improving performance. We have seen earlier how these skills served him well right through his career, the apogee arguably being in his record-breaking exploits; by the sixties, although the peak of those exciting adventures had passed, he had not lost his appetite for creativity. The most revolutionary line of thought within BMC came with a programme to develop a new narrow-angle range of V4 and V6 engines which would have shared almost nothing with the existing powertrain ranges; Syd tried a V4 out in an MGA (EX-Register project code EX216, from September to December 1958) and there was talk of both this two-litre (EX214/ 2) for the MGB along with the related three-litre V6 but in the end BMC scrapped the project as too costly.

In the wake of the twin cam engine saga, and despite the work by Syd and Ted Martin described earlier, it was evident that achieving another almost bespoke MG engine was unlikely, but that did not prevent Syd telling his friend Gordon Whitby what he really wanted to do in that area: *'Syd Enever confided in me that he had every intention to design and produce a number of new overhead camshaft engines of different configuration (four-cylinder, six-cylinder with single and multi-overhead camshafts) hopefully with aluminium cylinder heads, that would propel the MGs of the 1960s and beyond and ensure Abingdon's dominance in the world's sports car market and to power future BMC sedans. Unfortunately, the directions given to Syd Enever from the Longbridge Top Brass was to "Build your overhead cam engine so long as you utilize the existing Austin designed "B" or "C" engine blocks"'.*

Also on the subject, Denis Williams – a member of the MG Design Office – told Jon Pressnell: *'Engines were Syd's first love. He knew all the engine people within the group. He designed an engine [for the MGC]. He just came up against brick walls all the time.'* Fellow designer Pete Neal added: *'Syd got on very well with George Harriman. Harriman wanted Syd to go to Longbridge to head engine design. Syd and Harriman were a pair. Both had come up from the shopfloor. Harriman was very friendly with Syd.'* Clearly such a move, had it come to pass, would have involved a schism for Syd from his role at Abingdon.

Meanwhile, Eddie Maher was happy to explore any developments of existing BMC powertrains and his work on the A-series was legendary. He also helped eke more power from the C-Series

The MGC Prototype, 'FRX 692C', wearing a proprietary hardtop and clearly having ensured extensive road testing. This car was later acquired by MG Apprentice Bob Neville and survives today in the hands of MG enthusiast Tim Hodgkinson. (Author Archive)

six-cylinder, and even worked on a larger 3.3-litre version, which would have suited a more powerful Austin-Healey which would presumably have been built at Abingdon. BMC had developed a six-cylinder version of the B-Series four, and although originally conceived in the UK, the resultant engines were only built and used in Australia. A small number of these units were imported to the UK and Syd got hold of one which was tried in an MGB – but without a wider production application beyond sports cars, Longbridge would not countenance its use. The MG records show that a test was undertaken in late 1962 ('Graph 577 – Provisional Power Curve 2.433 litre six-cylinder engine').

The desire for a two-litre engine also prompted Syd to consider a four cylinder derived from the C-Series six, through the expedient of omitting cylinders three and four (EX214/ 4) ; it would have been an interesting if still quite heavy unit, but again no other users were seen. In tandem with this, the EX Register tantalisingly refers to an 'MG Two Litre Engine' (EX214/ 5) – unfortunately another non-starter. An idea in a similar vein was to update the ageing Austin Taxi 'big four' last seen in the first-generation Austin-Healeys, but reducing the stroke to make a 2.2-litre unit; once more, one assumes that Alec Issigonis turned his nose up at a powertrain clearly unsuited to his transverse front-wheel-drive maxim, which also dictated the format of such important new powertrains as the E-series, in both four and six-cylinder guises.

The marriage of BMC and Jaguar which created 'British Motor Holdings' in 1966 brought fresh opportunities, and before long slide rules and tape measures were being directed at powertrains in the Jaguar and Daimler areas, including the Edward Turner designed Daimler V8 (both the 2½ and 4½ litre engines), Coventry Climax and even the classic XK six-cylinder – and gradually usurped such units as the four-litre Rolls Royce six. So long as Syd and his Longbridge cohorts did not tread on the toes of the E-Type, it seemed that there could be many new opportunities.

Competition aspirations also prompted some adventurous thinking, such as fuel injection and overhead camshafts, but despite the Competitions Committee supporting many of these bright ideas, relatively few got very far; one exception was EX239, which relates to 'competition and fuel injection for the ADO47 Midget' and covers 25 entries from November 1967 to April 1968, and likewise a few entries under EX223 'Competition Mini-Minor' around the same time which refer to fuel injection.

In due course, other units such as the ex-Buick Rover V8 and even potentially the Triumph Slant-Four and V8 engines came into play later, but strictly speaking were not considered in Syd Enever's time at Abingdon.

ADO24 – a Rolls Royce Healey

The relationship of Syd and Geoff Healey and the latter's eponymous cars has been touched on already; there would be a strong association between the Enever and Healey families even after the Austin-Healey itself faded away, through Roger Enever racing various Healeys. Before then, however, there were efforts to sustain the traditional Austin-Healey line which were supported by both the Abingdon and Warwick camps, despite the development of the MGC and, at George Harriman's insistence, a putative 'Austin-Healey 3000 Mark IV' cloned from it.

In 'The Story of the Big Healeys' Geoffrey Healey relates how he and his father conceived the idea of a wider body version of the classic 3000 with a Rolls Royce four-litre unit as sued in the Vanden Plas 4-Litre R. It was intended to help sustain the traditional Big Healey market as much as form

One of the ADO24 Rolls-Healey prototypes (ADO24-1002). It was six inches (150mm) wider than a standard BN8 Austin-Healey 3000 Mark III. Syd's work on this project was referenced by Geoff Healey in his own books about the Healey marque. (Enever Archive)

a counter to the BMC 'Fireball' sports concept referred to earlier. Once the concept had been viewed and well-received by BMC top brass in 1966, the project was allocated the code of ADO24 and sensibly, Syd was given overall charge. *'Syd quickly and clearly defined the areas of responsibility'* Geoff Healey recalled; *'we were to arrange the chassis redesign and the collection of material and assembly. Jensen were to be responsible for the body... Syd's careful planning and clear instructions ensured that the project proceeded very smoothly and rapidly.'* Eventually, two cars were completed, one of them with automatic transmission, but in April 1967, BMC cut the budget and programme from six cars to the two now built, and not long afterwards stopped the programme entirely.

Geoffrey Healey subsequently recorded: *'Unbeknown to us and to BMC, Rolls Royce had suspected that BMC wouldn't be taking its full allocation of engines, and had got rid of a lot of tooling, so it wasn't really in a position to start immediate production of the engine – certain critical castings weren't available... also BMC was running out of money. It was in a very bad way. When it found its commitment to the engine disappear, and discovered there would be additional expenditure on tooling needed...'* Add to this the fact that BMC was by now tied up with Jaguar, and the raft of Federal legislation in train, and it is easy to see the new 'super Healey' as being regarded by the top tier of management as superfluous.

The EX-Register has a small section for the ADO24 project; dated February 27th 1967, which refers to the 'Healey-Rolls'. The single page sets out ADO24/1-1000 as being allocated to Jensen, ADO24/1000-2000 to the Healeys and those above 2000 to Abingdon. There are just four entries, ADO24/2001 to 2004 inclusive. The familiar automatic transmission prototype registered as TNX 65G, bore the chassis number ADO24-1002; three surviving prototypes in total are known, the other two both having Jaguar manual gearboxes.

When it was clear that a redesigned C-Series was going to be the way forward, Syd set out to tailor it to his preferences through planning both a shorter stroke and enlarging the bore, the aim being a higher-revving sporty engine with reduced height and a 2.5-litre motor sport-friendly capacity, but Alec Issigonis refused. Dick Wright told the author that he thought this was partly because new transfer machinery, recently arrived from Germany, although equally obviously the corporate requirement for the next generation Austin Westminster and Wolseley 6/110 to have three litres (and not to forget the existence of a four-litre Vanden Plas too) meant that adding a special capacity for MG alone was ruled out. If BMC had been in a stronger position, or projected sales of the new six-cylinder MG and related Austin-Healey had been higher, then perhaps the situation might have been different, but such debate is academic.

Geoffrey Healey, when interviewed by Jon Pressnell, offered some defence of Syd's position with regard to the MGC – a car which Donald Healey famously detested: *'It's my personal view that he never wanted the MGC. He didn't think it right, and he didn't put his heart into it. That reflects a certain caution and wisdom. He foresaw that the car would understeer and would always be a problem.'*

In a similar vein, as we saw in the 'other engines' panel the six-cylinder B-Series engine; designed largely in the UK, but only manufactured and sold in Australia, this unit had no potential future beyond MG; the MGB that Syd fitted with one proved to be fast enough to attract the interest of the constabulary when Roy Brocklehurst took it out on test. As the project moved forward, there were notionally two versions – ADO51 was to be an Austin-Healey (replacing the 'Big Healey') and ADO52 was the new MG six-cylinder sports car. Almost inevitably, under the badge-engineering BMC regime of the early sixties, the two versions were gradually whittled down to the point where there were hardly any differences; the Healey family eventually (at a late stage) declared that they wanted no part of it, and ultimately ADO52 became the MG MGC.

The bulky, heavy cast-iron engine – coupled with the desire to offer a version with the Borg Warner BW35 automatic gearbox – made packaging a challenge for the Abingdon team; it necessitated a complete re-design of the front suspension and engine bay panels. Whilst the new suspension was drawn up by Pat Rees, the body changes were shared by Roy Brocklehurst and, for the only obvious exterior alteration, Des Jones. *'The initial prototype of the modified bonnet was done, but there was an extra bulge required in the bonnet to give extra clearance to the rear carburettor on the left side. The forward-mounted radiator meant that the front-end panels on the body supporting it had to be altered, and in addition the bonnet release lever was reversed. Syd Enever and I went over to Pressed Steel at Cowley, at the request of Reg White, to approve the mock-up of the MGC bonnet before releasing to the die-cutting machine.'*

CHAPTER SEVEN: FINAL FURLONGS

The end result of all this work, the production MGC (in Roadster and GT forms, and with the option of a Borg Warner automatic transmission) was announced for the 1967 Earls Court Motor Show – at time when BMC was in trouble, both financially and in terms of corporate image. The Healey family decided not to support a planned 'Austin-Healey 3000 Mk. IV', despite fairly advanced planning of sales and service literature. A botched launch – not the fault of Syd and his team, it should be stressed – also did the poor MGC no favours, nor its task of effectively replacing the much-loved Austin-Healey 3000 Mk. III. Coupled with this was the extensive (and growing work) needed to meet new Federal emissions and safety legislation, in order to maintain any US sales of the BMC sports car range; by the time that BMC slipped into a union with the Leyland Motor Corporation, the future of the poor MGC began to be increasingly in doubt.

Syd and the MGC

It was during one of his visits to see Syd at Abingdon that David Ash stumbled across a prototype of the MGC; he was not overly enamoured of the large cast-iron six-cylinder that had been stuffed into the reworked MGB engine bay, but when Syd sought his opinion, Ash simply said that it was 'interesting'; he wasn't about to upset his friend and host. Eventually, Syd pressed Ash on his thoughts, and he said how frustrating it was that MG appeared to be poorly served by its BMC masters. Ash later wrote what Syd nodded in reply: *'it won't change – at least, not in my time. There is no money for anything new. We have to simply make do, and hope for the best. There is no other way.'*

Barely two years after its launch, the MGC was discontinued; UK monthly CAR, in its October 1969 issue, referred to a trip to Abingdon: *'When we called to see the latest in MG and Austin-Healey models, everyone was feeling gloomy about the demise of the MGC. Chief Engineer Syd Enever felt, like the rest of his staff, a little hurt and upset that the Press had killed it because, he claimed, most of the people who had bought one liked it immensely. He felt that the Press expected too much from it, hoping for handling like a B but performance like a rally Healey 3000. That wasn't the intention at all, claimed Mr Enever; it was intended as a fast tourer which would cruise along easily and quietly with good but not sports-car handling. He admitted that the engine had a rather strange lack of power when installed in the MGC, which was due to a distribution problem in the carburetion and could have been overcome, given time. The automatic versions suffered chronic starting problems which also mystified them for a long while, but again it was traced to carburetion. A Downton head cures all those problems, but the Press had killed it before they had a chance to implement any major changes.'*

In the aftermath of the arrival of the MGC, there seems little doubt that there was understandable concern at the press reception accorded to Abingdon's crucial new sports car; however there was hope that if the model could be given scope to evolve, then MG's pre-eminent role as British Motor Holding's seminal sports car marque (excepting Jaguar) could be sustained; the MG Midget and MGB remained the top priority, and some of the investment that bore fruit in the MGC (like the all-synchromesh manual gearbox) also benefitted the MGB.

The Lightweight Cars – Midget and MGC GTS

Dick Jacobs, who we saw earlier with the unfortunate incident at the 1955 Le Mans race, had subsequently migrated to running his MG dealership alongside a racing team. A few years with the MGA Twin Cam was

Syd leans into the cockpit to talk to John Wilkinson, seated in the cockpit of the John Milne MG Midget Coupé (138 DJB); the occasion is the September 5th 1965 'ADAC 500 km Rennen auf dem Nürburgring'; the car finished in 26th place. The Mini Cooper alongside (No. 57) was drive by German driver Willy Kauhsen, who did not finish. (Enever Archive)

followed by musing over what might be next; as he set out in his autobiography *An MG experience* (Transport Bookman, 1976) the solution came about almost by chance:

> 'Early in the year, going back now to 1961, the first catalogues of the new MG Midget arrived. Inside I noticed the small side elevation drawing of the car. This did not appear to be to any set scale but was used to show the overall measurements such as height and length. By pure chance I had on my desk a Motor road test of the original Aston Martin DB 4 and I noticed the overall length of a similar drawing for the DB 4 was the same as the MG Midget drawing. I took a tracing of the Aston Martin outline and laid it on the MG Midget and I had the silhouette of an MG Midget coupe. Armed with this pleasing shape, I visited John Thornley at Abingdon, who was enthusiastic and made a lot of encouraging noises. Syd Enever was called in and he too was interested. The drawing office lads had done a rough sketch before I left, and Syd Enever was asked by John Thornley to go ahead'.

> 'As bumpers were not required by racing regulations, Syd designed a new nosepiece with better air-penetration qualities. Wind tunnel tests showed that, at 100 mph, the Midget in this form required 13 bhp less than the production car, although the basic shape from headlamp to tail lamp and from the top of the doors down, was standard. With aluminum bodywork throughout and the removal of all un-necessary weight, the car weighed 11 cwt. As production of these rather special cars involved many departments, it was obvious that 1962 would have to be our first season'.

The 'drawing office lads' referred to by Jacobs were Jim Stimson and Denis Williams, the latter as we have seen the Body Draughtsman with responsibility for the Midget range. There is little doubt that Syd would have liked the Midget GT to be turned into a production car, but there was insufficient business case to support the idea. Fabrication of the racing cars utilised aviation standard rivets and Araldite glue to join aluminium alloy to steel, and Syd took a great deal of personal interest in this; he would have gained some expertise from the work on earlier projects such as EX181.

The MGC GTS is for some MG enthusiasts the apogee of the MGB MGC family; it combines lightweight outer body panels, including flared front and rear wings in aluminium alloy, styled by Eric Carter.. Syd was at the heart of this project, taking a keen interest in the aviation techniques used to glue and rivet the alloy panels on to the base steel monocoque. He was keen to reduce the engine stroke to create a competition-compliant 2.5-litre, as well as a lightweight three litre six – there was even fanciful talk of using the Daimler 2.5-litre V8 (at a time before the BLMC merger made the ex-Buick Rover V8 available). Thornley and Enever dreamed of a low-volume road car – but their ambitions were ultimately thwarted. (Author Archive)

> **The Lightweight Midgets in the EX-Register**
>
> Work on improving the 'Sprite' began almost from the outset – and with even greater fervour by the time that the 1961 MG Midget (ADO47) and Austin-Healey Sprite Mark II (ADO41) arrived. The chassis number for the first MG Midget is recorded as ADO47/ 1, dated March 23rd 1960 and entries continued over the years up to ADO47/ 843 of May 25th 1978. Meanwhile the original Sprite entries ran from ADO13/ 1 of January 20th 1958 to ADO13/ 176 of April 13th 1961, before 'handing over' to ADO41, which had already begun with ADO41/ 1 of November 11th 1959 ('heraldic badge – bonnet panel') and continued until ADO41/ 450 of June 9th 1970.
>
> One of the entries buried in the MG factory records for the Midget Coupé is within the graphs , where Graph 572 of May 4th 1962 is concerned with 'Power – road load – ADO47 GT (Jacobs)'. However we are also fortunate that within the main ADO47 listing, those entries relevant specifically to the coupé have been given a special 'GT' prefix. The first of these is ADO47/ GT/ 46 for 'flexible pipe, filter to cooler' (dated June 15th 1961) and this is followed by interspersed entries within the overall ADO47 listing such as ADO47/ GT/ 54 'Panel – luggage floor – modified for GT – 15.4 gallon tank' (November 24th 1961); there are sixteen bespoke 'Midget GT' entries in total, ending in November 1963.

Don Hayter told the author that from his recollection, it was Jim Stimson who was responsible for the shape of the Jacobs car; as he put it *'Jim [Stimson] drew a streamlined fastback shape based on my Le Mans car [EX212] and Denis Williams' Midget [ADO47]'*. There has been some confusion in the past over which 'Jim' was involved – i.e. Stimson or O'Neill – but the simple answer should be both of them, as the former reported to the latter, who was in overall charge of MG's body design at the time. The lightweight Midget coupés went on to have a whole racing career of their own, but there is insufficient space here to do that story justice; only to record that there was another lightweight Midget that had special relevance to both Syd and Roger Enever.

This was '138DMO' which started life as the prototype MG Midget Mark III, registered by the MG Car Company on October 7th 1963 and bearing the factory-owned registration number 'MG 1' (seen before and subsequently on other MGs). This Midget, the first with wind-up windows and quarterlights, was re-registered '138 DMO' the next year and was allocated to the Development and Experimental Department where it was turned into a factory race car. It was fitted with experimental 1,275cc A-Series Mini Cooper specification engine ('XSP 2195-3') on July 2nd 1964. The bodywork and fixtures were lightened as far as possible, and the little red Midget was given an all-alloy, long-nose resembling the Dick Jacobs coupés. Thereafter it was raced between 1964 and 1967 by Roger Enever – a story told later in this chapter.

The lightweight MGC GTS race car – a project in which Syd took great interest – seemed to offer a great competition future, and as Don Hayter told the author, Syd was very keen to see a lightweight version of the new-generation straight six as the basis of a good motorsports and upmarket sports car engine.

The bodywork relied on alloy panels – developed with the aid of Pressed Steel – which were then Aralditied and riveted to a steel MGC GT monocoque. To do this, Syd built on his earlier experience with the 'Jacobs' Midget. The style of the distinctive 'Sebring' wheel arch flares – which have been replicated by hundreds of enthusiasts ever since – was credited by Don Hayter to Eric Carter; *"Eric created a wooden model – I went up and saw them with Syd, and Eric told us that Abbey panels were in the process of making the first set off those wooden blocks whilst we were at Coventry."*

The first MGC GTS was built up with the new interior body structure and torsion bar suspension, but its racing debut at the Targa Florio in May 1967 was well before the production MGC had been revealed to the public; accordingly, this prototype was fitted with a B-Series engine – the only time that such a combination was used. In the wake of the MGC's show debut in October 1967, it was possible for the MGC GTS to be made public, and its debut was the 1968 Sebring race, and it appeared at other events such as the Targa Florio and Marathon de la Route, the latter even involving the input of Roger Enever, as explained later in this chapter in a section about Syd's son.

The Impact of American Legislation

From the formation of the corporate slogan 'Safety Fast' in 1929, the idea of fast but safe motoring was firmly ingrained in MG road cars. Syd was an exponent of safety in design and engineering terms, even if his occasional predilection for what in some colleagues' eyes seemed to be 'over-engineered' components sometimes added weight to production sports cars. However, to Syd, and indeed the vast majority of his industry contemporaries, the most importance was felt to be in terms of ensuring that his cars were safe in terms of performance, including road-holding, handling and braking. The idea of making a car into some kind of padded survival cell suited for driving by a driver of least competence seemed anathema – and in MG's case, the cars were clearly aimed at an enthusiast market which at least implied some degree of interest in the art of driving on the part of the customer. In common with most of his peers with an interest in US sales, this worldview was somewhat upended in the 1960s, the pressure for change coming largely on two convergent fronts.

First came the matter of air-pollution, a growing concern in urban areas in particular, where the tetraethyl lead added to regular petrol (gasoline) had been found

In 1967, the major concern at Abingdon was being able to keep the MG range on sale in the USA. Here Syd poses alongside a new MGB GT at the factory as part of press coverage of the challenges being faced with growing Federal legislation. (Author Archive)

to have health impacts for the broader community. The bowl-shaped Los Angeles basin was often home to unpleasant smoke-addled fogs – the term 'smog' stemmed naturally from this – and public pressure from the late 1950s onwards led eventually to the nationwide US 'Clean Air Act' of 1963. Early approaches to reducing the toxic elements of vehicle emissions were inevitably somewhat rudimentary; the engine driven air-pumps on many cars were simply designed to recycle unburnt petro-carbons through the engine by the simple expedient of pushing exhaust gases back through the combustion sequence a second time; an obvious consequence of this was a loss of power – obviously more of an issue on smaller-engined cars like the imports from Europe: it was a beginning of an inexorable trend towards ever-better air quality measured at the tail-pipe.

The second front was that of road safety, long an issue of some concern but policed effectively by bodies largely financed by the domestic US automotive industry. Deaths on American roads was a matter of increasing discussion, but many automotive engineers – unsurprisingly supported by the corporate accountants and management focused on the bottom line – remained wedded to the views that it was the roads themselves which needed to be made safer (and many obviously needed this) and focus within the vehicle should be upon the so-called 'nut behind the wheel'. Over the years, as the motor car had evolved, there had been many advances in vehicle safety terms, such as padded interior surfaces, safety belts and dual-circuit braking systems, but the car makers often argued that 'safety didn't sell' and so many potential advances stalled at conception.

In the mid-sixties the cosy industry status quo was rudely shattered by a hitherto-unknown young New York lawyer called Ralph Nader, whose crusading book 'Unsafe at Any Speed' galvanised the American public, caught the attention of politicians, and was largely dismissed as scaremongering by many in the auto-industry. The full thrust of Nader's polemic need not concern us here, other than to note that it spawned an embarrassing episode for General Motors (culminating in a very public apology by the GM Chairman) and helped kick-start some transformational legislation, 'The National Traffic and Motor Vehicle Safety Act', which steam-rollered its way through both US houses in the summer of 1966.

Rather than blithely placing fault with the 'nut-behind-the-wheel', the changes to vehicle construction standards also embraced the themes of survivability – in particular the ability of those inside (and outside) a vehicle to survive the consequences of a vehicle collision – so-called 'secondary safety'. In due course there would be almost an obsession with the idea that the occupant of a vehicle needed to take no personal action to ensure their safety within it – which led to the creation of the air-bag – whereas a sports-car engineer like Syd Enever would wish to focus on making sure that the car could be driven safely and competently, for the benefit of the driver in particular, in the expectation of some personal accountability and a modicum of skill on the part of the person involved – that 'nut-behind-the-wheel' again. Safety systems are now taken for granted, but in the context of the time, many inside the industry viewed some of them as an affront to automotive engineering.

On September 9th 1966, US President Lyndon B Johnson formally signed the new legislation, in the form of two complementary safety bills (the 'motor vehicle safety act' and the 'highway safety act'), during a ceremony in the Rose Garden at the White House. Immediately beforehand, President Johnson noted that over the recent 'Labor Day' weekend, 29 Americans had died in Vietnam. During that same weekend, 614 Americans died on the Nation's highways. In the 20th century, he said, nearly three times as many Americans died in traffic accidents as died 'in all our wars'. Every day, 9,000 were killed or injured; Johnson added:

"It makes auto accidents the biggest cause of death and injury among Americans under 35. And if our accident rate continues, one out of every two Americans can look forward to being injured by a car during his lifetime – one out of every two!"

The legislation empowered the US Federal Government to set and administer new safety standards for motor vehicles and road traffic safety, and this was facilitated by the creation of the National Highway Safety Bureau (later the National Highway Traffic Safety Administration). Emboldened by this presidential mandate, and heightened public and political expectation, the new body wasted little time in drawing up a raft of new standards, and whilst these were subjected to industry consultation, the response times were short and the expected roll-out of compulsory standards hardly less so.

For the big domestic car makers in Detroit, these changes were a corporate headache, but one they could not avoid, and would need to resource; their sheer size and obvious reliance on their home market meant this was a challenge they would have to accommodate on their financial balance sheets, but the consequences for importers like BMC, whose sports cars sales relied upon open access to North America, the implications were arguably more serious because of their relative poverty and the fact that as yet much of this raft of new legislation was largely irrelevant as far as the vast majority of their own domestic vehicle output was concerned. In simple terms, the current ADO15,

ADO16 and ADO17 Austin-Morris saloons did not have to meet the full extent of these new US rules, and yet the MG Midget and MGB clearly had to align with the new legislation in order to remain on sale.

For MG, matters soon came to a head; Syd was photographed and interviewed by the Oxford Mail in January 1967, and some of the challenges were already apparent. The drive for changes had actually started before the new legislation, when the 'General Service Administration' (which was responsible for Federal fleet purchases) had set its own standards (mostly affecting domestic car makers; for obvious reasons, government agencies tended to 'buy American') and then individual States started imposing their own standards – which pre-empted a raft of paperwork for Syd and his colleagues to handle. However, the new legislation was rolled out with great urgency and unsurprisingly many of the new standards were either biased towards larger US cars or were arguably mis-judged.

There were an initial set of 23 standards which were issued in consultation form on November 30th 1966, with a very tight two-month turn-round time, with a deadline for feedback of the end of January; public comments from the US motor industry were at the forefront, with Henry Ford II, Chairman of the Ford Motor Company, complaining that many of the standards were "*unreasonable, arbitrary and technically unfeasible.*" He said, ominously, that they could even lead to plant closures. BMC said the legislation "*... could result in serious disruption of our production, if our cars were unacceptable to them.*" The timetable for the necessary changes to be in place had been set for September 1967, and this meant that Syd and his team were forced to re-design the Midget, MGB, MGB GT and MGC versions to keep them on sale in their primary sales market.

An obvious problem was that the standards were really aimed at the 'standard' American cars – which were very different in size, layout, proportions and structure to the small sports cars from Abingdon. As the Oxford Mail reported: "*An example of this is that seat belt anchorage points have been stipulated at certain angles from the seats. In most American cars the driver and passengers are in a "sit-up-and-beg" position – quite unlike the more stretched out position in an M.G. One result of this is that on the M.G.B. one of the anchorage points required is at a spot above the actual body of the car – in thin air.*" This was not all; Syd told the paper that "*with the original standards, twin reversing lights had to be fitted. B.M.C. designed, tooled and prepared to make these for the M.G. at a cost of several thousand pounds, only to find that in the latest standards only one reversing light is ordered...*" The twin rectangular reversing lights on the MGs first appeared in the spring of 1967, ahead of the MGB Mark II facelift already planned for later in the year. At the time, Syd's team of engineers and technicians was reported by the newspaper as being fifty strong; the BMC submissions to the US agency were reported as filling two suitcases.

Changes clearly had to be made; refusal to meet the requirements was not an option, but delivering them for the MG and surviving Austin-Healey range became almost the sole focus at Abingdon, alongside the concluding development phases of the MGB Mark II and the related MGC, to be launched at the October 1967 Earls Court Motor Show. Around the same time, the final fate of the 'Big Healey' was also sealed, despite efforts at Abingdon and Warwick to save it.

We saw side reflectors, changes to lighting, the infamous padded fascias (the so-called 'Abingdon Pillow') and a peculiarity of several contemporary British sports cars, the triple windscreen wipers for Federal-market open models. Jim O'Neill, working under Syd, told the author how the team had been involved: '*that was one area where Don Butler did a great deal of work. The only way we could get the specified wiped area was to use three wipers – everybody thought it looked stupid, but there was no other way; and if you didn't comply, you couldn't sell any cars*'. The idea also extended to Jaguar E-Types for North America, now under the same 'British Motor Holdings' family.

For a period in the autumn of 1967, there was even a brief hiatus while no cars were built, as the changes were variously still in design, commissioning from suppliers, or subject to alterations to the production facilities. For Syd and his team, the pressure was enormous – almost as heavy as those far-off motorsports days of the thirties. It did mean, however, that work at Abingdon on all-new sports cars had to be largely put off for another day. This did not prevent ideas being pursued elsewhere in the BMC organisation, as new design talent arrived; even so there would be more big challenges to come.

Interviewed for *Autocar* of February 29th 1968, Syd commented that the amount of paperwork associated with the American regulations was frightening; every word had to be read; and with hundreds of people writing the rules, reading them was a full-time job.

> **Roy Haynes – BMC's New Stylist**
>
> In October 1967, just as the MGC was being launched, the British Motor Corporation was embarked on an unprecedented recruitment spree, bringing in new talent to oversee aspects of the business where rivals already had experienced

executives – namely styling and sales & marketing. It was painfully evident that the tried and tested philosophy of relying on chairman's hunch and Chief Engineer's peccadilloes was no longer enough for a business building some of Britain's top selling car lines. On October 19th 1967, during the Earls Court Show, just as press and punters were poring over the new six-cylinder MG (and bemoaning that it was too much like the MGB and not enough like the Austin-Healey 3000 Mk. III), it was announced that BMC – or more properly British Motor Holdings – had recruited Roy Haynes to become its 'Director of Styling'.

Roy Douglas Haynes (March 12th 1924 - March 22nd 2020) was already fairly well known in the industry as a leading Ford UK designer. Educated at Bromley Grammar School, the Bromley College of Art and the Southeast London Technical Institute, Haynes secured an apprenticeship at J. Stone & Company of Deptford before war intervened. After the war, he spent time at De Havilland on airliner interiors (such as the famous Comet), spent a couple of years as an 'advertising creative artist' at Vauxhall Motors and then ran his own industrial design business in London for five years. His big break came when he joined Ford in 1954 in a senior styling capacity. After a three-year stint away from Ford with Lansing-Bagnall, he came back to Ford in 1963, and by 1966 he was the Executive responsible for all car and truck styling for Ford of Britain's design office, with the highly regarded Ford Cortina Mark II (launched the same year) to his credit

With his modern Anglo-American auto industry outlook and mannerisms, and understanding of the way that the big US-owned car manufacturers worked, Haynes could hardly have been more different from the BMC 'old guard' typified by Alec Issigonis and Dick Burzi. There is little doubt that BMC needed a jolt in terms of engineering, design and product planning, and the arrival of Haynes and his contemporary Sales Director Filmer Paradise (a cigar-chomping larger-than-life recruit lately of Ford of Italy) was an eye-opener throughout BMC, and not everyone welcomed these brash incomers.

MG was a little different, for as we saw earlier Haynes had spent time at the Abingdon works during WWII, working alongside the team there on tank design work, and he and Syd Enever had met and collaborated during his fairly brief spell at the factory; possibly others such as Cecil Cousins and Reg Jackson may have remembered him too, although the author knows of no specific recollections in print from any of them. The point was, there was a link, no matter how tenuous, that probably nobody at either Cowley or Longbridge could match. That does not necessarily mean that the Abingdonians would welcome all that Haynes would bring forward – just that they had a connection.

So, when Haynes began work on one of his pet projects to create a related family of mid-sized high-image cars on a common base platform, he turned to Syd for advice. By this time – probably sometime in 1968 – BMC had already merged with Leyland and Haynes' concept would evolve gradually into the ADO28 Morris Marina. When the author interviewed him in 1995, Haynes said *'Syd was a good engineer who understood what I was trying to do; I asked him what he would need me to do to create an MG out of what became the Marina, and he went away, thought about it, and came back to say that he would like a bracket spot-welded on the underframe to accommodate a Panhard Rod for the back axle.'*

Also in the MG world, it was Haynes who initiated a review of the existing MG sports car range which culminated – after he had left the company – in the 1970 Model Year facelifts which brought in such changes as new colours, vinyl upholstery, recessed satin black radiator grilles and Rostyle wheels; the latter were actually discussed in 1968 for both the MGB and MGC, and a memo from that year which recently came to light records that the introduction of painted and chrome plated Rostyles had been deferred to January 1969 (in reality they arrived that autumn, and only for the Midget and MGB – the MGC had been discontinued).

It is not recorded exactly what Syd thought about these styling changes (some of his colleagues were more outspoken; one of them told me of Syd's disdain for vinyl in lieu of leather, and there was the occasion recalled by Jim O'Neill when Haynes came up with his thoughts on the MG badge: *'we got on well with Haynes. Syd and I went over to see him at Cowley lots of times. The classic occasion was when I saw on the wall, at Cowley, a beautiful representation of an MG badge, and I said to Syd "look at that!" – we couldn't believe our eyes – it was an MG badge drawn as a hexagon! We called*

> *Haynes over and said to him "come on – have a close look at this – what about that then?". "It's not bad, is it?" he replied; "but it's a hexagon" I said"; "yeah, that's right" he said. So I said "but it should be an octagon" – and his face fell – and he realised of course that although he'd seen plenty of MG badges before, he'd missed this fundamental point. I don't know who had done it – one of the stylists, I suppose. It quickly came down and that was the source of a few laughs...'*
>
> Mirth notwithstanding, it seems likely that Syd may have realised, pragmatically, that such changes as the facelift ideas from the Austin-Morris studio at least served to keep MG relevant at the start of a new decade, albeit one in which Syd's own role at MG would be short-lived.
>
> Nevertheless, perhaps in part because of their past connections during war time, Syd and Roy Haynes clearly maintained something of an alliance; Haynes told Barney Sharratt in an interview about the Morris Marina in 1995: *"I remember Syd asking me if I realised that they were going to spend £1.9 million re-tooling the Triumph gearbox for it. He showed me the drawings and said: 'they must be out of their minds. Look at the distance between those shafts and the size of the bearings. You can't put the horsepower into that gearbox that can into a B-Series. If we spent £750,000 putting synchromesh on the B-Series first gear, then that 'box would never cause any trouble.' But Harry Webster wouldn't listen. The Marina could have sold a lot better. The front suspension was a mess and we were in trouble with the Triumph gearbox from the word go, with horrendous reports in 'Which' magazine."*
>
> As it happened, Haynes had gone by the time the Marina was launched, and as we shall see, before long his unlikely ally at Abingdon would be gone too.
>
> In the midst of this period, a bridge between

normal MG and Austin-Healey ranges.

Given the project codes of XC512 and later ADO30, this project was largely unloved, even by those tasked with its development, and was certainly despised by the sports car experts at Abingdon and Warwick. It was nicknamed 'Fireball', a play on 'Fireball XL-5', a popular contemporary Gerry Anderson children's TV puppet science fiction show. In the event, 'Fireball' went nowhere, beyond wasting both finance and resources, and was eventually shelved. Roy Haynes seems to have no input so it probably had been largely forgotten even before he arrived in 1967. Few mourned.

> ### Syd's Alternative
>
> During the course of his own research into the somewhat vexed development story behind the 'Fireball' sports coupe, Jon Pressnell uncovered this Memo to Alec Issigonis from Syd Enever, dated April 27th 1964, with a Ford Mustang catalogue attached. Pressnell notes that this shows that *'Syd was on the ball'*:
>
> *'Herewith, for your interest, copy of Ford Mustang literature.*
>
> *Don't you think that the new big sports car should be reconsidered and made so that variations can be offered of full four-seater etc (and suitable engines) similar to this range?*
>
> *We should then have the MG Magnette, Healey range, etc which everyone thinks we should have'.*
>
> Part of the problem of course was that Alec Issigonis, now Technical Director BMC, was unlikely to take such advice from Syd or any other of his peers.

Here We Go Again: The Coming of Leyland Motors

January 1968 saw a major upset when the news broke that the Leyland and BMH businesses were going to merge; the rivalry with Standard-Triumph's sports car family was well established, but it was evident that MG and Triumphs were soon going to become siblings, and as the merger was consolidated, it soon became obvious where the power would lie. To John Thornley and Syd Enever, it looked like 1952 all over again; a takeover by overtly hostile outsiders. The aforementioned Fireball was already dead by now; Sir William Lyons could doubtless have seen it as a pointless rival for his Jaguar E-Type, especially when 'his' powertrains were being contemplated.

the golden era of BMC and what came afterwards, there were some peculiar things which only peripherally involved Syd and his team, but we can be reasonably sure that he probably knew about them, and also would have shared the views of other people who were similarly outside looking in. The key project in this category was a proposal for a larger sports car – initially a rival to the Jaguar E-Type, but refocused when Jaguar joined BMC in the short-lived British Motor Holdings – which was seen by Chairman Sir George Harriman as a flagship project to sit above the

For the time being, Syd – now in his early sixties – continued to be afforded the respect that his position as MG's Chief Engineer commanded, but with the abandonment by the autumn of 1968 of his EX234 Hydrolastic sports car project described earlier (it was never formally cancelled; merely side-lined), the rapidly rising workload consumed all resources in ensuring that the entire export range could remain on sale in North America, in the face of rising safety and emissions legislation.

Meanwhile, new management structures were taking shape within what was now 'British Leyland Motor Corporation' or BLMC for short, and what had briefly been the MG Car Division in the closing months of British Motor Holdings effectively became a subsidiary of 'Austin Morris', whilst Triumph, along with Rover and former MG allies Jaguar, became a part of the 'Specialist Cars Division'. Even though it was pretty obvious to anyone with a pulse that MG remained the corporation's best-selling sports car brand, the marque now had to justify investment needed as part of the cash demanded to nurture the volume car part of the business. For a while, Syd was still a key member of the group of key people making decisions about MG, but his role began to be gradually eroded; engineering was increasingly masterminded by Longbridge and design by first Roy Haynes (initially at Cowley) and then by Harry Webster, and engineering by Charles Griffin.

Although the merger to form the new BLMC was announced to the world in January, this was followed by negotiations and senior structural changes to corporate management; old allegiances became less relevant and new faces appeared at meetings where crucial decisions would be required. In February 1968, we learned that Alec Issigonis had asked to be relieved of executive responsibility for BMC engineering, handing the reins to Charles Griffin, who as an ex-Nuffield man was already well known to the folk at Abingdon; meanwhile Issigonis would assume a role as a Technical Director looking towards future developments. It was undoubtedly a side-shuffle which was insisted upon by Stokes, who knew that some of the blame for BMC's woes could be laid at Issigonis's feet.

By May 1968, the new structures were largely in place and naturally Abingdon's fiefdom had to yield to the new regency. In Syd Enever's files is a copy of a meeting at Longbridge to discuss the future of sports cars within what had hitherto been the orbit of BMC, and was gradually emerging from its chrysalis as 'Austin Morris'. It is notable above all for the fact that instead of being number one or two on the list of those attending, Syd's name was simply one of fourteen people attending, and as for John Thornley, he was merely 'copied in'.

Strictly Confidential

**Notes on Meeting at Longbridge
On 6th June 1968**

Sports Cars

Present: Mr. H. J. L. Suffield – Chairman
Mr. H. R. Barber
Mr. B. H. Bates
Mr. J. F. Bramley
Mr. F. F. R. Clarke
Mr. P. N. Davies
Mr. S. H. Dews
Mr. S. Enever
Mr. C. A. Griffin
Mr. R. Haynes
Mr. G. W. Rose
Mr. B. Stockdale
Mr. H. W. Webster
Mr. D. Withall

The meeting was convened to discuss short- and long-term proposals for sports car models in the Volume Car and Light Commercial Vehicle Division.

ACTION BY

Short Term

1. It was agreed that the Sprite/ Midget (ADO.41/47) and MGB /C (ADO.23/ 52) facelifts as shown were uneconomic and should not be pursued in that form.   H.R.H.
2. For July 1969 it was agreed that the following changes should be investigated, in addition to those necessary to meet legal requirements: –
   (a) Distinctive changes without major sheet metal tooling. Styling to prepare and MGB or C Model with all possible changes for viewing and discussion. Model to be available within one month.   R.H.
   (b) Increase in engine power.   C.A.C.
   (c) 4 ½ J wheels and bigger tyres (Sprite/ Midget only).   S.E.
   (d) 4-speed synchro gearbox (Sprite/ Midget only).   H.G.W.
   (e) Improved hood mechanism.   S.E.
   (f) Stylish hard top option. Product Planning to prepare profitability exercise.   R.H.
      F.F.R.C

Long Term

3. Mr. Barber stated a time base requirement for new bodies of 2 to 2 ¼ year. This sets Spring 1971 as the earliest possible date for the introduction of a new body shell.
4. Sales agreed to conduct a Market Research Study to determine their requirements and forecast volumes for one and/ or two body shells and/or engine options bearing in mind the possibility of coupé versions of the Maxi. Study is to be completed within 3 weeks.   H.J.L.S
5. Engineering agreed to provide outline specifications 4 weeks after Sales requirements are known. C.A.G.
6. It was agreed that the order of priority should be:
   (i) Sprite/ Midget replacement
   (ii) MGB /C Replacement

Distribution:
All present plus:
Mr. W. H. Davis
Mr. J. W. Thornley

Key to personnel listed above:

Mr. H. J. L. Suffield – Chairman Lester Suffield, Sales Director; Suffield had been a deputy managing director of BMC, with particular responsibilities for the group's worldwide sales. He survived into the new Corporation but soon left for another appointment in the arms industry

Mr. H. R. Barber – Harry Barber of Pressed Steel; responsibility for body styling, structure, trim and finish Harry Barber, was the assistant managing director of Pressed Steel Fisher,

Mr. B. H. Bates – Bernard Bates – Sales Director. A long serving BMC employee, Bates had come through the role of 'Home Fleet Sales Supervisor, for BMC'. By the time of this meeting, he was 47 years old and director of home sales.

Mr. J. F. Bramley – Jim Bramley – Sales... Export

Mr. F. F. R. Clarke – Fred Clarke – Austin Morris Planning Director; according to Ian Elliott, Fred Clarke, who had come from Ford, was known (not to his face one assumes) as 'Fitted For Radio' Clarke on account of his initials.

Mr. P. N. Davies – ? Davies – Finance?

Mr. S. H. Dews – Stan Dews – Development/ Proving role; ex Ford. From February 1968 he became Deputy Director of Engineering, reporting to Charles Griffin

Mr. S. Enever – Syd Enever – Chief Engineer, MG

Mr. C. A. Griffin – Charles Griffin – Chief Engineer, Austin Morris; responsible for all aspects of the division's engineering and design direction.

Mr. R. Haynes – Roy Haynes – Chief Stylist

> Mr. G. W. Rose – Geoffrey Rose (ex BMC Board)
> Mr. B. Stockdale – Bert Stockdale – Technical Sales Manager
> Mr. H. W. Webster – Harry Webster – Austin Morris Technical Director
> Mr. D. Withall – Doug Withall – Sales Director
> Mr. W. H. Davis – Bill Davis – Production Director
> Mr. J. W. Thornley – Director, MG

Last Laps With the Healeys – Le Mans 1968

Although BMC – yet to be fully subsumed within BLMC – had already abandoned racing, the Healey family maintained their more independent approach to motorsports, building their own cars, either highly modified production cars or bespoke one-offs. The 1968 Le Mans event (clearly planned as far as entrants were concerned before the spring BLMC merger) included a special Austin Healey Sprite, to be driven by Roger Enever and Alec Poole, and complete with a 1,293 cc A-Series engine. The latter was largely the handiwork of Syd; as Roger confirms, despite some historic rivalry between Healey and MG camps, the relationship between the two groups was always cordial and mutually supportive

'They were all friendly; they all appreciated one another. For the Sprite – the streamliner, my father did the engine – he built the engine for them up at Abingdon, and sent it to Warwick: anything to do with engines, that was his forté! And that car used a pint of oil in 24 hours – I always remember him saying that it went like clockwork – and we were the first British car home! And that meant that we won the Woolf Barnato Trophy through the BRDC. It wasn't super-fast, I suppose, but it was certainly very reliable, and it was the first British car home!'

Roger is of course correct; a cursory study of the 1968 Le Mans results shows that their car, bearing race number 50, finished in fifteenth, third in the Prototype 1.3-litre class and the only cars ahead of them with the same engine class was a brace of Alpines with Renault Gordini power units, and most of the top ten had very specialised multi-cylindered or otherwise exotic engines of between two and 4.9 litres in capacity. Notably the Healey's other self-created car, the Healey SR with its Coventry Climax 1968cc V8, expired after three hours while the little Sprite kept going all through.

Although Syd's role in planning future models had clearly been diminished (and his old ally John Thornley, having had health problems in 1966, chose to retire before him, aged sixty in July 1969 – leaving him without one of his key defenders) the fact remained that the factory was as busy as ever, with the focus now on maintaining sales in the US market. Increasingly it would be Roy Brocklehurst, finally beginning to segue into the leadership he had long been promised by his mentor, who would cross the Atlantic and ensure that the MG range remained saleable in its principal market. Surely Syd himself would never have envisaged the MGB that he created going on to live for a further decade without replacement.

One of the casualties of British Leyland rationalisation was the poor MGC; it was targeted for possible euthanasia in January 1969 and the sentence of death was formalised in May, by which time, ironically, the car itself was somewhat improved. The MGC quietly slipped off the new car prices lists with little publicity from the press office, who were simultaneously putting the Riley marque to rest. The MGC had never really recovered from its rather botched launch and the prejudices of those who liked to latch onto the coattails of the negativity which had come to surround the old BMC; it had been scheduled to receive a package of upgrades not unlike those which would appear in late 1969, including five-spoked chrome-plated Rostyle wheels, but these changes were delayed so far that they never materialised.

Of course there was a lot going on in the Corridors of Power – not just at Longbridge, but also the new Corporate Headquarters in London's Grosvenor Square, and even more inside parallel organisations within the wider Corporation – most obviously the 'Specialist Cars' people, dominated by Jaguar and Triumph and to a lesser extent Rover. Everyone had some self-interest in terms of 'feathering their own nests' and with Triumph having worked hard on the development of some new sports and luxury car offerings – the TR, Stag and a planned 'Lynx' coupé to supplant the TR line (represented since the beginning of 1969 by the TR6) – it was not hard to see how, in a climate of post-merger rationalisation, that the poor MGC – hampered by a fractious birth – was soon lined up for Euthanasia. Syd might have had mixed feelings about the MGC as it appeared in production, but it was his creation and he was hurt when it went.

In the background at MG, Syd Enever's role as master of his own destiny had continued to slip just as the parent organisation – and its associated bureaucracy – enlarged. We saw earlier how Syd's presence at that sports car meeting of June 1968 had been as a contributor to a committee of stakeholders rather than as the person leading the discussion. Indeed, whilst Syd retained his Chief Engineer and Chief Designer title right through this period, in truth he reported to Charles Griffin, who at least was a fellow Nuffield veteran and someone who Syd respected. As British Leyland's structure evolved, it soon became obvious that the new masters were going to favour the old Standard-Triumph teams as part of the new 'Specialist Cars' division, while MG was seen as an offshoot of Austin-Morris, the car-making rump of the old BMC.

Evidence from the meeting books of the various boards within British Leyland show how there were moves to rationalise sports and upmarket car making into a small number of new factories and associated design facilities, but the volume car side would be focused on Longbridge and Cowley. Abingdon, as an avowedly old-fashioned operation with an ageing – albeit still very successful – product range, ensured that MG remained something of an outsider. From the perspective of a new generation of automotive stylists, the MG sports cars were anachronisms to a forward-looking team focused on the latest design trends, and for their engineering and production counterparts, the MG Midget and MGB drivetrains were divorced from most of the Austin-Morris range, even if the Morris Marina would be an exception to the BMC front wheel drive rulebook.

The irony, of course, was that the North American customers still loved their MG sports cars, and exports remained very important as one of the parent company's key revenue sources: there were echoes of those discussions back in the late forties when the top management had bemoaned the fact that Americans wanted 'old fashioned' MG sports cars rather than the company's staider saloons. There is some truth in the thought that some of those old jealousies of the affection in which Abingdon was always held had never really gone away.

Shunted Sideways: New Hierarchies Take Priority

By the summer of 1969, Austin Morris had its own special Product Planning Committee, which generally met at least once a month, and alongside the inevitable focus on development of the likes of the new 'mainstream' offerings (ranging from Mini, ADO16, ADO14 Maxi, the ADO17 and its successor, the beginnings of the ADO28 Marina and ADO67 Allegro, light commercial vehicles and onwards right up to the big ADO61 Austin 3-Litre) and their possible replacements, there was also discussion about the sports cars, even if most of the latter was simply about keeping the existing lines on sale and debating the roles of MG versus Triumph on the broader BLMC canvas. It is notable that the minutes of those meetings, often with twenty or more people present, seldom was there anyone from Abingdon.

In the midst of this period, there were a number of changes made which almost certainly were not popular with Syd; for example, Pressed Steel at Swindon eventually got their way, and the alloy bonnet was replaced with steel. Jim O'Neill told the author that he could see both points of view; Syd was interested in saving weight, but the management at Pressed Steel was interested in production costs and logistics; '*on alloy, you have to use an acid etch primer before you can continue with the painting process, which of course is quite different from steel. So, it meant that there was an added complication with painting. But the main problem that we had, apart from the production ones, was the tendency of the panel to "ding" easily. You could easily push the panel down, and because of the soft alloy, it used to dent*'.

Finally, Ken Osbourne, a director of Pressed Steel at Cowley, put his foot down and was able by dint of his position to over-rule Syd; as Jim O'Neill commented: '*of course that put even more weight on the car – we already had weight problems without that. But that is what they did, and we had no option really*'. David Osman, who had been at Pressed Steel at the time, added: '*I think that the alloy bonnet was in one way a legacy of the old days – the MGA had many alloy panels, and Syd Enever wanted the MGB to have more alloy panels – such as the doors and bootlid. But we submitted a request to replace the alloy bonnet with steel. The process for steel was much simpler...*'

There was a great deal more excitement and optimism at Abingdon when the development team found themselves involved in work on a mid-engined sports car, using a 'mule' based on an MGB GT; the modern up-market sports cars from Lotus, Ferrari, Lamborghini were increasingly built with mid-mounted engines, and Porsche's 911 had an engine and drivetrain at the rear. The story of this project – ADO21 – is covered in the side-panel; even if Syd may have seemed somewhat ambivalent previously concerning this type of mechanical layout, it would hardly the first time that he had changed his mind; after all, as we saw earlier, he was initially reluctant to abandon the idea of a separate chassis for the MGA's replacement.

Mid-Engined Sports Car – ADO21

The abandonment of the EX234 could have marked the end of the Abingdon line, other than the extended lifespans of the MG Midget (in production since 1961) and the MGB (from 1962). However, it was not quite the last gasp in terms of an all-new MG sports car with MG engineers at the fore – that honour goes to a mid-engined concept originally gifted to 'Austin Morris' as a project to replace both the MG Midget and, potentially, the Triumph Spitfire. Although Syd had previously declared he was not a supporter of the idea of a mid-engined MG, John Thornley suggested to journalist Richard Bremner (in an interview published in *Motor* in January 1985) that what became the ADO21 was *'technically the apple of Syd Enever's eye'*.

Photographs here show a scale model called 'Apollo' which was an early effort to secure a style for such a car, possibly with some design input from Jim Oates at Pressed Steel Cowley before styling moved up to Longbridge. In due course, ADO21 involved collaboration between the Longbridge-based Austin Morris design team and the Abingdon engineers – notably Don Hayter (who eventually moved to work on the project for a time at Longbridge, down the corridor from Charles Griffin) and Terry Mitchell, who presided over the chassis side. Mitchell's fondness for De Dion suspension systems (vide the EX186 covered earlier) meant that this was one of two options considered for the mid-engined concept, and a US-specification Mark I MGB GT was hacked about so that a mid-mounted E-series engine could be fitted behind a make-shift bulkhead. The gear-linkage was a challenge, coming out of the back of the Maxi gearbox and having to be turned through 180 degrees and brought forward to the centre of the cockpit; future experience with the cable-operation of the early Maxis suggest that the MG installation might have fallen some way short of the rifle-bolt quality familiar to MGB owners.

The De Dion suspension tube on the MGB GT-based prototype featured a lateral De Dion tube mounted in front of the engine and gearbox package, located with a universal joint mounted on the back of the vestigial cockpit floor tunnel. Struts carried the wheel-hubs with integral coil springs and telescopic dampers. An alternative rear suspension concept considered but not built would have seen semi-elliptic springs and the De Dion tube mounted behind the E-Series package.

Don Hayter recalled that Spen King had been a supporter of the ADO21, just as he had hoped to have seen the larger Rover P9 with its mid-mounted Rover V8 engine as an idea developed from the P6BS concept that survives at Gaydon.

Towards the end of Syd's time at Abingdon, his creative fervour did not dim; this is a model known as 'Apollo' which was part of the exercise to create a mid-engined replacement for the MGB. The fact that Syd retained a whole clutch of photos of this model is testament to his interest in the concept. Thankfully the model survives at Gaydon. (Enever Archive)

However, both concepts ultimately failed for a number of reasons, ironically at least in part due to a fact-finding mission in the USA by Spen King which found that local dealers and distributors liked the idea of a modern style but only if it was married to an easily maintained and relatively inexpensive drivetrain – which for them still meant a conventional in-line front engine and rear wheel drive.

In the meantime, however, as inspiration, Syd managed to 'borrow' the one-off Rover P6BS mid-engined prototype; Tommy Haig and Danny Lloyd from MG were sent to Solihull and brought the P6BS back to Abingdon; former apprentice Bob Neville remembers it being in the shop for a couple of months, with a few surreptitious trips to MIRA to examine how the suspension behaved. When the author spoke to Spen King, who had been part of the P6BS design team, he was surprised to hear that the prototype had had a 'holiday' at Abingdon; MG's Geoff Clarke subsequently commented: *'that was typical Syd Enever – always up to tricks!'*

In addition, the US importer insisted upon the new car, as a supposed MG Midget replacement, costing around $2,000, and despite best intentions the ADO21 resolutely failed to be brought below $2,400. The E-Series engine was also found to be unsuited to forthcoming Federal emissions requirements, and Don Hayter's undoubtedly clever idea to squeeze in the 2.2-litre E6 six-cylinder only made it more expensive still and a putative rival for the Triumph 'Bullet' project which begat the TR7. In the end, ADO21 was killed off in December 1970. It is not certain how much Syd really embraced the project, and his personal involvement is equally unclear; what we can say, however, is that it was the last all-new MG sports car conceived on his watch.

The EX-Register includes a section on ADO21 work; entries ADO21/ 1-499 (dated November 5th 1969) are referenced as being allocated to the 'Project Office'; thereafter, for entries 500-610 inclusive, the Development Shop clearly became involved, with entries from ADO21/ 500 (November 11th 1969) to December 16th 1970. Interesting items include ADO21/ 501 (December 2nd 1969) for 'sketch showing body cut-out for insertion of E-Series engine in MGB GT'; ADO21/ 514 'De Dion Tube – complete'; ADO21/654 'Scheme 3 – De Dion rear axle with coil springs and radius arms'.

The final design concept for ADO21 by Paul Hughes, of the Austin-Morris Design Office at Longbridge; it could have been a winner for MG, but it was not to be. (Paul Hughes)

The period of the work on ADO21 more or less coincided with the cancellation of the MGC (originally slated for some of the facelift changes that appeared eventually at the 1969 Motor Show on the MGB, and in similar form, the Spridgets), the retirement of John Thornley and meanwhile the seemingly relentless onslaught of US safety and emissions legislation: it was a wearisome time for someone like Syd who saw the respect he deserved and the input he could still undoubtedly provide being rapidly eroded. When, eventually, ADO21 was abandoned, and the hierarchy of British Leyland became more and more marginalising, it was sadly nearing the end of a wonderful Enever era.

The meetings of the new Austin-Morris Product Planning Committee continued to debate future sports car ideas and policy, and increasingly the people involved in debating points were those who barely understood, let alone had much interest in or appetite for sports cars. At the same time, the fact that the Triumph team were within the 'specialist' cars group, but poor MG was stuck with Austin and Morris because of its BMC roots, meant that work on 'real' MGs with input from people who appreciated the heritage and context of the sports car, almost fizzled out. There would be one heroic 'last gasp', in the form of the MGB GT V8, but that project arrived after Syd had left, and so is not covered here.

Roger Enever

Although this book is principally about Roger Enever's father, it would be very remiss to leave out the story of the racing career in which a proud father understandably took a great interest. Born in Oxford on June 8th 1944,

Roger's wedding day was a stylish affair; later the couple separated. (Enever Archive)

and living in the family home in Westminster Way, Roger was naturally surrounded by his father's work, growing up knowing many of the same people and their families; the 'Enevers' were good friends with the 'Jacksons' and so on. Many was the time when either his father brought home an interesting experimental car for a blast round the bypass, or there would be Sunday lunch with one of the other families and the conversation would inevitably turn to 'shop talk'.

In those days, too, it was fairly common practice for sons of engineers within BMC to secure an engineering apprenticeship as a sure-fire way to gain wide-ranging experience within the company. Within BMC, those in the know also believed that one of the best places to do this was in 'Morris Commercial Cars' in Birmingham, which had evolved from the earlier Nuffield business of that name. 'MCC' was one part of the corporation where far more of the actual vehicle was made; it was in effect a microcosm of BMC with aspects of just about every side of vehicle design and manufacture, whereas many other parts of the parent business either brought in or supplied significant parts of their production.

Roger secured one of these coveted MCC apprentices, and at the same time so did Alec Poole (born in Dublin on May 21st 1943, and hence a year older than Roger); Alec was the son of William Poole of the well-known Irish 'Nuffield' assembler Booth & Poole. Both Roger and Alec, with cars and motorsport in their genes, soon embarked on racing various BMC cars – typically MGs which had some connection to the Abingdon works in some way. Their early experience included racing an MGB (2GLL) owned by Eddie 'Baggy' Sachs; they soon gained a reputation for 'giant killing' results in UK and European circuit-based distance racing. Roger also raced the MGA Coupé 'KMO326', an ex-development car: *'when I raced it, I just took the radiator grille out and put a blanking piece in there so that there was less air flow. When we sold it, it was to the MG specialists, Toulmin Motors of Brentford, West London; it's a shame, really, but you can't keep all these things!'* he told the author.

The next step was to secure an ex-development MGB, BRX855B, which having endured long-distance engine testing was due to be scrapped; some parental help (from Syd) managed to ensure that Roger and Alec could acquire the car and see its engine rebuilt by MG's Jimmy Cox to Stage 6 tune. The duo took BRX855B to the 1966 Marathon de la Route, playing second fiddle the main factory effort with GRX407D ('Old Faithful'). For much of this gruelling event, the two MGBs were almost unbelievably in first and second place; some bad luck eventually put Roger and Alec out with a broken half shaft just past the pit; as it was, 'Old Faithful' would still go on to score first place. Roger remembers the MGBs with affection: *'BRX855B – that did a lot of racing. When we took that out we won as GT cars at Monza and Spa in 1966 or 1967. And that was beating the Porsche 911s! Bob Neville was along with the team, and we had it all worked out – pit stops and everything – and I think we beat the 911s on the pit stops. André Wicky – we beat him both at Monza, which was a fast track, and then at Spa, which is also a fast track. And then we got to Nürburgring, and I think that the Porsches had got their act together, and that was the end of the MGB, really...'*

In tandem with the MGB efforts, the lightweight MG Midget '138 DMO' referred to earlier in this chapter, but re-painted from red to black, was raced by Roger from 1964 to 1968. In 1967 alone, Roger secured 19 victories, winning the Fred W Dixon Trophy and the Amasco Championship.

More than once, Roger and Alec, either together or individually, proved what could be achieved with the right combinations of driving skill, mechanical fortitude and a smidgen of good fortune, they could achieve seemingly miraculous outcomes; the MGB was not the most powerful, but on many occasions its durability and nicely balanced power-to-weight ratio could deliver great results – not least in the wet, where the MGB did not suffer the problems of the far more powerful competition cars in terms of maintaining grip on wet surfaces. The duo continued their exploits together, and we both back for the 1968 Marathon – this time as part of the factory effort in the new MGC

GTS, a car whose creation, as we have seen, was one of Roger's own father's creations.

Testing took place at Thruxton in July and August (Roger at the latter); for the actual race Clive Baker was accompanied by Roger and Alec in RMO699F, the second of the two factory GTSs; Roger had been involved in the build of the alloy engine in RMO, through time spent at Morris Engines in Coventry. Syd's interest in the MGC GTS extended beyond the special bodywork and other developments at the factory towards the practical problems that had to be fixed on the fly. For an example of the latter, Bill Price the author that: *'Tommy Wellman took out some special wheel-nuts with a steel rung shrunk on the outside to stop it expanding too much and coming loose when they got hot; they had been getting hot and the clamping action on the tapers of the wheels was insufficient; the idea was that these wing-less hexagon nuts – and I'm pretty sure this was a Syd Enever's idea – because of course his son was part of the exercise. Those shrunk-on sleeves did the job!'*

Sadly the engine distorted in the race itself and was forced to retire; it was a great shame according to Roger Enever, but of course to some effect down to the luck of the game; Julien Vernaeve, Tony Fall and Andrew Hedges took the older MGC GTS 'Mabel' to sixth place overall (it could almost have been third), but Alec Poole and Clive Baker had to share Roger's disappointment with 'Romeo'. Not long after the Marathon, changes within MG's parent company, by now British Leyland Motor Corporation, saw Lord Stokes move to close the old BMC Competitions Department. This change did not stem Roger's and Alec's racing exploits; Roger raced as part of the Healey team and also competed in MG Midgets and Minis, and competed at Le Mans no less than four consecutive times within his racing career (his best finish was 15th in 1968, co-driving with Alec Poole in the Healey Sprite with its special Healey coupé bodywork). In 1969 he co-drove a Chevron B8 with Peter Brown, but the car did not finish.

Roger especially has reason to remember his stint in the Healey SR 'XR37', which at one time in the 1970 race was 10th overall and, with just 14 minutes of the race left (23 hours 46 minutes) whilst lying in 14th overall, a ballast resister rivet shook loose and the engine expired. As Roger explained to the author: *'it just stopped on the Mulsanne when I was driving: it was just an electrical contact which worked loose due to the vibration – and that was it; it was something on the ignition side. And I couldn't find it at the time – and they were all waiting back in the pits with champagne! It was a shame, because that would have been a wonderful result'.*

The last British Leyland effort at the Marathon de la Route with Roger's involvement was with the remarkable Roy Pierpoint (May 15th 1929 – January 12th 2023) 4.3-litre Rover P6 V8 in 1970, which at one stage built up a six and half lap lead over the Porsches which ended up winning the event, but had to withdraw after fifteen laps: *'that car was incredible!'* Roger says; *'Oh my God! I just kept it in fourth gear most of the way – I don't recall how many gears we had, but basically I think I went between third and fourth. It streamed past the Porsches; we ought to have won by simply miles, but in the end it was the propshaft which let us down. Because you know they have a split propshaft on the standard car? It was such a long way to the back and we only had a single propshaft – and it went out of balance – we didn't have time to put the split propshaft on...'*

In 1971, Roger continued his exploits in the Huron Auto Racing Developments 'Huron 4A' with, for a while, 'Camel Filters' sponsorship (this was a time before tobacco sponsorship was outlawed) and for his final Le Mans outing, the Huron Lola T212 – again with Camel Filters sponsorship although the car did not finish due to an engine problem. In 1971, Roger decided to retire from active motorsport, the interminable struggle for sponsorship making the life less attractive.

The Complan Mini

The following notes are Syd's own, referring to a turbo-charged conversion of the BLMC Mini.

'You may be interested in the Turbo-charged Mini, which has now successfully run at Phoenix Park and Ingleston with Alec Poole, and at Silverstone with Roger Enever. Fitted in the 'Complan' Mini, and enthusiastically worked on by Alec Poole, it makes a Glaxo Baby bursting with go.'

'The engine is basically the Cooper 'S' 1275 in competition form, with an eight-port head, Lucas Fuel Injection, but the compression is lowered to 8:1 by machining the connecting rods with 1/8-inch shorter centres, and the clutch has a stronger spring to take the increased torque. It is fitted with a 3 LD Turbocharger, restricted to a maximum of 15psi manifold pressure by turning the exhaust turbine housing to suit the engine and the use of a blow-off valve. The accelerator is over-ridden by a control cylinder, which regulates fuel delivery according to the manifold pressure. On test, the engine gave nearly 200bhp, but was derated for reliability to 185bhp as the figures below.'

'The Lucas Fuel Injection system is modified in

that the fuel pump is run at higher pressures and the injectors are set at lower pressures of 30-35 psi.

RPM	BHP	Manifold Pressure (PSI)	Fuel PP BHP
4,000	100	7.0	0.669
5,500	138	10.4	0.665
6,000	160	12.5	0.646
6,500	171	13.0	0.628
7,000	181	14.0	0.606
7,500	185	14.5	0.602
8,000	180	15.0	0.621

Roger Enever recalled that Reg Jackson's son Barrie (who died in 2022) had contributed to the success of this car: '*Barrie reminded me that he made a manifold for a Mini which my father built with a turbocharged engine – and we put it in Alec's 'Complan' Mini...*' Roger says it was another example of his father's almost magical ability extract the maximum output from the smallest of engines: '*he certainly knew how to make an engine work – given what he had. That Mini gave about 192 horsepower from 1,293 cc; it had a turbocharger on it – I think they reduced the compression ratio, or the boost pressure, or something as it used to crack the big end bearings; you had to rebuild it after every other race – it was just too much! I drove it once at Silverstone and when it got up to speed it was phenomenal – we won one race with it*'.

It was not only the Complan Mini that benefited from Enever family wizardry; Roger says '*I campaigned a Mini in the British Saloon Car Championship under JCB colours, and my father did the engine for it: that was a 1,293 cc Lucas fuel-injected unit and he got a lot of horsepower out of that one; he experimented with – I remember – megaphone exhausts and all sorts of things. And I remember that when I was driving it, the Competitions Department were trying to find out what was going on! He was trying different exhausts, and eventually ended up with one coming out of the side. He was so inventive!*' (Roger finished in fifteenth place on the first heat of the 1969 'Evening News Trophy' race at Brands Hatch in this JCB-liveried Mini, but did not finish on aggregate due to an accident).

The special turbocharged A-Series engine in the 'Complan' sponsored Mini.

Chapter Eight: Into the Sunset

Au Revoir Abingdon

The final lap of the Abingdon circuit for Syd came on the last day of April 1971, when he was sixty-five and therefore at the age at which it was usual practice for staff to retire. The Oxford Mail of April 30th 1971 carried a photo of a smiling Syd, standing between a brace of contemporary MGB GTs, with the headline *"Mr Sydney Enever, the man who designed the cars that brought sports car motoring to thousands of enthusiasts at a reasonable price, retires today."*

The smile for the photographer notwithstanding, Syd had previously asked if he could be retained in some sort of consultancy basis, but the rules for retirement at 65 were generally strictly enforced across most companies in those days; even Sir Leonard Lord had retired (as Chairman) at that age, although he stayed on as 'President'. According to Peter Neal, the response came that the Board was simply not prepared to make an exception for Syd, and so his departure was terminal.

> cars have been produced in the last 15 years. His world of motoring started when as a young lad of 14 fresh from the South Oxford School, he was "placed" by the headmaster with Morris Garages in Oxford. Even then his mechanical mind was alive – he built himself a three-wheeled runabout using old angle iron and a motor-cycle engine. When he was twenty, he went to MG in the experimental shop. These were the days when everyone was expected to turn their hand to everything and did. He eventually became the chief of the Experimental Department. he designed the world's fastest 1,100, 1,500 and 2,000cc cars. He was responsible for the construction of the famous EX135 in which Major Goldie Gardner smashed the 200-mph barrier on German autobahns in 1938 and captured more records the following year. And he was also the designer behind the 1,500cc version in which Stirling Moss drove at 254mph in 1957.

> ### Retirement Reported in *The Oxford Mail*, April 30th 1971
>
> **Man Who Designed 254 Mph Car Retires**
> MR SYDNEY ENEVER, the man who designed the cars that brought sports car motoring to thousands of enthusiasts at a reasonable price, retires today. Mr Enever, designer of the MGA and MGB sports cars has been in motor car production and design in Oxford and Abingdon for 51 years. He started as a junior working in the sales department at Morris Garages in Oxford in 1920. He went on to design the world-beating record cars of the 1930s, design tank conversions in the 1939-45 War, to become chief engineer at the MG Car Company, Abingdon, and to draw up the MGA and later the MGB which became the world's top selling sports car. More than half a million of his

Syd's retirement took place from MG on the last day of April, 1971; he is seen here standing at the Abingdon works between two examples of what were probably his favourites of the latter part of his career – the MGB GT.(Enever Archive)

> **Syd's Retirement Reported in *Autocar*, May 20th 1971**
>
> "Quiet Genius of sports car engineering, Syd Enever, has retired" writes Tom Wisdom. He has spent a lifetime designing and engineering MG cars from the day he started "on the floor" at Morris Garages Ltd. Which in 1930, became the MG Car Company. A farewell lunch was given last Thursday by J. Greenborough, managing director of Shell-Mex and BP Ltd., at Shell-Mex House. Syd was supported by many of the colleagues who had worked with him over a very long period, including John Thornley, ex-managing director of MG; Chris Shorrock, who bult the superchargers for many of Enever's race-winning and record-breaking cars; "Jacko" Jackson, for many years in charge of quality control at Abingdon; Alec Hounslow, in charge of research and development; and friends from Shell-Mex and BP who supplied the fuel for Enever's successful record attempts. From America came Captain George Eyston, once holder of the World Land Speed Record and a famous racing driver at Brooklands days and, from the South of France, "Eddie" Hall, winner of many races in a variety of MGs. Tom Wisdom himself co-drove with George Eyston on many of the successful international world record attempts at Montlhéry and on the Salt Flats at Utah, was also at the gathering. Since he started with the late Cecil Kimber at MG Garages, Syd Enever has overseen the production of more than half a million sports cars from the Abingdon factory, and his son carries on the sporting tradition as a most successful newcomer in motor racing."

He was given little choice in the matter, and indeed he was already gone by the time that George Turnbull, who had assumed the title of Director of Austin Morris in June 1968 (soon after the meeting to discuss sports cars described above) turned up at Abingdon to celebrate the production of the 250,000th MGB, a US-specification MGB/ GT, on May 27th 1971. Nobody in senior management at British Leyland felt any need to invite Syd to join the celebration (by coincidence, as this book was being finalised, this car re-emerged from storage in Alabama). As *Autocar* reported in their issue of June 3rd 1971, citing both Syd and Cecil Kimber: '*Syd Enever, whose retirement we announced only a fortnight ago, it would have been a proud day for both of them*'.

On his departure, Syd was seen off by his faithful colleagues at the usual ceremony, with a number of gifts from both the MG works as well as other parts of the business, and as noted in the side panel, he was feted at a luncheon given by Shell-Mex; meanwhile at Abingdon his trusted office ally Isla Watts would stay on for a few years yet, supporting Syd's two successors. Many of those prepared to speak of the events behind this end of the Enever era were less than complimentary of the manner in which it was carried through; Don Butler told the author: '*at the end, Syd was treated very shabbily – he wasn't even allowed to keep his company car. Charles Griffin managed to arrange for an experimental car to be done up for him but there was just no recognition from higher up of what Syd had done for the company*.'

> **Management Changes**
>
> **Plant Management**
> With the retirement in 1969 of John Thornley, after thirty-nine years at MG, the reins were passed over to his deputy, **Leslie 'Les' Lambourne** (March 14th 1931 – October 13th 2010). Lambourne was born in Bicester into a prosperous ironmongery business, but Lambourne senior died when Les was just three years old. An only child, his daughter Karen says that her father was something of an entrepreneur from an early age. After Bicester Grammar School, he gained an

Just days after Syd had been 'sent off' into retirement, Austin-Morris Chairman George Turnbull turned up for photos with the quarter-millionth MGB, a Blaze (orange) MGB GT destined to be given away in the USA as part of a competition. Would it have hurt the British Leyland management to have invited Syd or John Thornley along to help celebrate? The car survives. (Author Archive)

apprenticeship at Pressed Steel Cowley in 1947, attending the Oxford College of Technology, then graduated from the job of process planning engineer to that of assistant to the works manager.

Lambourne came to MG as Supplies Manager in 1959 and rose to become first John Thornley's deputy and then his successor in 1969, at a time when Syd was still Chief Engineer and Designer. He travelled extensively and in April 1972 he supported MG's 25th anniversary of MG sales in the USA by attending the New York Motor Show. He is fondly remembered by one of his US hosts, Bob Burden of the Austin-Morris sales team at Leonia: "*ours was a junior-senior relationship, but he always treated me with respect. He was so unlike most of the Leyland executives I had been in contact with. He was happy, enthusiastic and willing. I thought he was the kind of person Cecil Kimber or John Thornley would have approved of to run MG. I often wondered what happened to him after MG.*"

In an interview in August 1973 with Philip Turner, Midlands Editor of *The Motor* magazine, Lambourne said that his original posting to MG, after three years at Cowley, had come as something of a shock. Before actually taking up his new appointment, he paid a visit to Abingdon and admitted in the article that he had a 'quiet chuckle' when he saw this rural factory with the cars being assembled on wheeled trollies instead of on a proper assembly line. It was such a contrast to anything he had seen before, but in his own words: "*I came to scoff but remained to wonder, and the place has fascinated me ever since.*" By then his job title was '*Director and General Manager, MG and Vanden Plas Assembly*' with plants at Abingdon and Kingsbury.

In late 1973 Les Lambourne finally left Abingdon behind to become '*Director of RALPO (Radiators and Light Pressings Operations)*' headquartered in Oxford with responsibilities across the UK from Llanelli to Birmingham. Lambourne's place was assumed by R. W. 'Bob' Ward, who had previously worked at Longbridge. By the time of Michael Edwards' arrival in 1977, Les Lambourne was one of four key directors, but soon after he left to pursue his career outside BL.

Engineering

Immediately upon Syd's retirement in May 1971, he handed over the reins to **Roy Brocklehurst** (his early story is covered in Chapter Six), whose recent work had chiefly been on keeping the MG range on sale in the USA; however with Abingdon's existence now tied to sustaining the old MG range, only the MGB GT V8 proved to be a distraction from the inevitable suspicion that British Leyland's

Les Lambourne is seen here in the centre of an MG display at the 1972 New York Motor Show (the 'silver jubilee' marked 25 years of post-war MG sales in the USA). Les had been John Thornley's deputy but took over when the latter retired in 1969. (Lambourne Family)

Roy Brocklehurst had been Syd's deputy for a number of years and briefly took over his mentor's mantle in 1971 – but moved onwards and upwards inside British Leyland just two years later, at which point Don Hayter took charge. (Author Archive)

small to medium sports car future would be dominated by a curious alliance of Canley and Longbridge. Brocklehurst's reputation meant that he was soon tempted to become part of the advanced Austin Morris design team, initially at Longbridge and eventually at Gaydon.

In 1973, just two years after Syd's departure, Brocklehurst had left too, and handed the keys in turn to **Don Hayter** (see also Chapter Seven) who had also made a positive impression on Charles Griffin through his work on ADO21, the SSV1 MGB GT 'safety car' and federally-mandated testing and systems for the MG range. The workload remained high, and the input of the MG team was still crucial, but the corporate structure of British Leyland meant that technically, there was no longer such thing as a 'Chief Engineer' of Syd's former stature; as Don Butler explained to the author: *'Body and chassis engineering were now directed from Longbridge, and so MG's Chief Engineers of Body and Chassis Design – respectively Jim O'Neill and Terry Mitchell – actually reported in turn to Tom Penny and Harry Webster at Longbridge.'* Clearly this generated inefficiencies in terms of MG production, and so in practical terms, Don Hayter led the technical side at Abingdon while a series of managers presided over production.

MG After Syd...

The MG factory and its prodigious output clearly went on notwithstanding the retirement of its distinguished Chief Engineer; by the summer of 1971, the first prototype of the MGB GT V8 was under construction, and a year later the first work on the future impact-absorbing bumper systems was under way (and the MGB in particular would benefit enormously from the basic inherent strength of the monocoque, thanks to Syd). Meanwhile, however, the next raft of Federal legislation seemed likely to kill off the open sports car, and this helped underpin the choice of what would become the Triumph TR7 as British Leyland's new corporate mid-sized volume sports car. Remarkably enough the legislation was dialled back, and the MGB and smaller Midget gained a stay of execution, lasting for much of the remainder of the decade. Abingdon survived until financial pressures led to a new management swinging the axe; the Midget went first and the last MGB went down the line in October 1980, around the same time that 'BL Cars' was in the throes of launching the Austin Mini-Metro. Syd joined his old colleague and mentor, John Thornley, for a photo-opportunity on the line.

The tortuous subsequent history of what became of the MG Midget and MGB, as well as the story of the creation of the Triumph TR7, are beyond the scope of this book, because they extend beyond Syd's involvement; in retirement he was always welcome and came back to see the factory on occasions, such as the landmark half-millionth MGB.

Jensen

Upon retirement from MG, Syd was approached by Kjell Qvale to provide consultancy work for Jensen Motors. Until recently, little was known about this period of Syd's working life, but the author is extremely grateful to Vincent van Gerven, the fortunate owner of the sole surviving prototypes of one of the last Jensen sports car projects, the G-Type, which not only survives (albeit after much necessary engineering work to turn it into a road-going vehicle) but was accompanied by extensive paperwork, which includes reports and letters both written by and addressed to Syd. Combined with the memories of Roger Enever and other records, such as the archives at Warwickshire County Records Office, it is possible to piece together this chapter.

The archives at Warwick include a neat, well-composed two-page critique of the first Jensen-Healey prototype after he drove it on a 230-mile road test on September 7th 1971. *'Generally the car is pleasant, easy and relaxing to drive, and you become more at home with it as you go along. Seating comfortable and firm, the car rides soft and flat and yet is quite firm enough to give it precise handling'*. He then went on to list a raft of insightful, constructive suggestions that were clearly born of his decades of experience.

His work there also included help in adapting the famous Jensen Interceptor to a convertible version; *'it was a bloody awful job to do because it was a power-operated drop-head'* he recalled shortly afterwards; he even recruited the assistance of his former Morris Motors Bodies chum Eric Carter to help draw everything up; indeed Vincent van Gerven's papers include a copy of a letter from Carter to Syd dated November 17th 1971 written just after the former had had a successful job interview with Jensen's Chief Engineer Kevin Beattie; Beattie's letter included the following:

CHAPTER EIGHT: INTO THE SUNSET

"*Dear Mr. Carter,*
This letter is to confirm the agreement which we reached during our meeting yesterday at this office, when we discussed your appointment to work for this company on a 'contract basis' with respect to a new convertible Interceptor model. Briefly we agreed that you would work under the control of Mr. S. Enever on this project, and that you would work for those hours per week which were necessary it ensure the earliest possible construction of a prototype car, and following this, and depending on the acceptability of the prototype, the eventual production engineering requirement..."

In his letter to his old friend, Carter wrote:

"*Dear Syd,*
I have today replied to a letter from Mr. Kevin Beattie, confirming details of our meeting last Monday and he suggested I report to you on Monday 29th November at 9.30 am and work under your control. I mentioned it was pointed out last Monday that this model could present many difficulties, but I accepted the challenge, also I appreciate the Company could discontinue the project should detailed investigation prove disappointing. I hope during the next few days to find time to give some thoughts to the project, but information I have is very limited, just the 1/10 scale outline and no styling lines. However, when I start I hope there is a little information available to enable me to get "stuck in" and get something moving..."

In the papers that Syd left behind for his family was a copy of the publication Car Styling that featured this 1972 Pininfarina Alfa Romeo 'Alfetta 1800 Cabrio' in which Syd had bookmarked this photo. Around that time he had begun consultancy work at Jensen Motor Company, encouraged by his old friend Kjell Qvale. (Author Archive)

A scale model of the proposed Jensen 'F-Type' – one of a handful of projects at Jensen with which Syd became involved. (Author Archive)

In addition, Syd had considerable input to the prototype work on new Jensen models – the F-Type (an Interceptor replacement) and the G-Type (the van Gerwen car, complete with gull-wing doors(; Roger Enever remembers his father travelling to Turin to see various coachbuilders as part of the project, and the late William Towns, who is credited with the eventual design of the G-Type, told Jonathan Empson (for an article in the May 1993 issue of *Thoroughbred & Classic Cars* magazine) of a visit by Syd to his design studios to discuss structural design requirements. The files show how Syd visited and corresponded with Giancomo Bianco of a business called Indestor, based in Turin, which had agreed to build the prototype G-Type bodies including ones for crash test purposes.

Another aspect of the work on the G-Type was trying to find a suitable proprietary powertrain; at one stage a special version of the Simca-Chrysler 180 engine and transmission was considered, and there is copious evidence of Syd's work on this in the van Gerwen papers.

For example, a letter from Syd to Madame Guillaume of Chrysler France of April 1972, which makes reference to Joe Farnham, who much later would go on to work for Austin Rover:

"*Dear Madame Guillaume,*
As discussed with Mr. J. Farnham some time ago, we are now pursuing a cost and technical investigation into the possibilities of a four valve cylinder head on the basic 2 litre 180 engine.
At the moment we have discussed this with Mr. Neale Johnson of B.R.M. and also Mr. D. Downs, Managing Director of Ricardo Engineering.
Mr. Johnson (of Mr. Windsor Smythe, Chief Engineer) of B.R.M., wishes to have drawings of the latest 2 litre block and head for initial consideration, and we should be grateful if you could let them have these direct, perhaps with some arrangement drawing. Ricardo's do not require any drawings for their cost and timing programme proposals. This is, at present, only a

cost investigation exercise, when and if we wished to proceed, Mr. K.Beattie would then discuss these proposals with you.

Mr. Beattie says he is also interested in the three valve cylinder head, and he would be pleased to see some arrangement drawings and any technical details of cubic capacity, BHP compression ratio, fuel consumption, number of carburettors etc., also any effect you consider it may have on emissions HC, CO and NoX.

Would you please send these to Jensen Motors for the attention of Mr. A. S. Enever.

Yours sincerely, A. S. Enever. JENSEN MOTORS LIMITED"

Geoffrey Healey alludes to Syd's work on the G-Type in his book 'The Story of the Big Healeys', stating that *'the "G" or Gull Wing was the have been a small four-seat saloon of advanced appearance. Syd Enever worked on this project for some time after he retired from MG but it never reached the stage of running.'* This rings true; the sole surviving G-Type bodyshell was turned into a running vehicle by an enthusiastic Dutch Jensen fan who commissioned Lynx Engineering to motorise and trim it in the 1990s.

In the end the Jensen work faltered and Syd finally called it a day when one of Jensen's increasingly frequent problems – in this case redundancy for a large part of the workforce in October 1974, made it untenable for the management to justify keeping a consultant on the payroll. Syd finally retired for good, although for a man with few hobbies, this was a difficult transition. In 1975, he was invited back to Abingdon along with his old sparring partner Cecil Cousins to witness a demonstration of the new vehicle crash-testing facility, built on a shoestring budget by Don Hayter and his colleagues; the MGB GT V8 that was propelled into a concrete block at 30mph performed superbly under test, the strength of the sills a testament to the foresight of the man who had made MG his life.

The present-day owner of the gull-winged Jensen 'G' Type inherited a significant volume of paperwork with the car, including project notebooks, letters, memos and plans with Syd's handiwork very evident. (Vincent van Gerven)

Roger Enever on His Father's Later Works

Syd was often lauded at race meetings when people realised who he was: *'he was always positive – keen to help. He would always try to find a way, as it were – and people used to go to him if they could... whenever I went to race meetings, you know, people would always praise him – I was only quite young but I got this idea from seeing this of someone who was very much appreciated. I think he was very helpful to people and if he could help, he would – that was just his way...'*

'A lot of people used to come to him for advice, because I suppose he was quite generous with his advice, you know: he was a fountain of knowledge! I remember, even, Joe and Sir Anthony Bamford coming along and having a meeting with him to talk about a record breaker because of his knowledge about record breaking. He even gave a lecture at Oxford University's engineering department on the demise of Donald Campbell's Bluebird, setting out why in his view the accident happened. He believed that once it started going out of line, the gyroscopic action operated in the wrong direction and contributed to it going out of line; I think that in aircraft design they have to design to compensate for this. But I do remember sitting at the back of the lecture hall; that was at the engineering department in Oxford University – at Keble College'.

Requests for help also came from unexpected directions: *'Colin Crabbe came to him, when he bought the famous pre-war Mercedes-Benz W125 racing car, and he didn't have a carburettor! He learned that my father had the only large SU carburettor in existence, that had been made for the Roaring Raindrop. He must have had a spare one – because if you look at photographs of the engine, you can see it. And the engine was running on some kind of exotic fuel with methanol; anyway, I remember that Colin Crabbe came along and nabbed it for his car! So that Mercedes runs an SU!*

Even so, the day-to-day challenges from MG were much missed by Syd; Roger explains: *'the Jensen thing helped for a while. But after that he didn't do much: of course, people would come to see him, from time to time, at the house. But he wasn't so happy, I think, in retirement. His hobby really was 'MGs' really, and if you take that away... he didn't have fishing or anything...'*

Oxford Mail, October 12th 1979 – Syd's Reaction to News of the End of Car Production at Abingdon

Oxford Mail October 12th 1979

Roaring Raindrop Man: 'Great shock'

Sydney Enever can hardly bring himself to talk about the fate of the MG company he helped to build.

"It came as a great shock to me. It is hard to say anything because it is such a big thing," he said.

He left nine years ago. Now 73, he lives in retirement at Westminster Way, Oxford.

He started in Morris Garages sales office in 1920 as a 12s 6d a week assistant. But the mechanics improvising streak which once led him to make a home-made bomb which blew up in his face soon turned to better ends.

He became famed as a speedy and ingenious car mechanic.

Cecil Kimber took him to Abingdon as an experimental mechanic. He went on to become chief designer and produced the Roaring Raindrop.

His revolutionary MGA was first sketched on his dining room table at home. "I had been mixed up in the speed record breakers and it was dreamed up from that. It was put on one side for a couple of years, then they realised they had to make some changes and told me to get on with it," he said.

In his later years, Syd enjoyed family life, being a grandfather and all the pleasures that status enjoyed, and occasionally he entertained visits from old friends, but his time was not filled with hobbies because, to be frank, he had none beyond the natural love of his family; whereas someone like Terry Mitchell, who was

In Syd's time, crash testing by MG generally involved sending cars to the independent facilities at MIRA; in 1975, the resourceful MG team created their own facility at Abingdon, using a concrete block and a Jaguar engine-powered steel hawser. As part of the 1975 'Golden Jubilee' celebrations, British Leyland invited journalists to see a test performed on an ex-development MGB GT V8, telling their audience that this facility, which had cost a grand total of £17,000, saved some £1,000 for every test that could now be conducted in-house. Among the guests, appropriately enough, were Syd Enever and Cecil Cousins. The photo shows the test car having just been propelled at the concrete block at 30mph; note how the structure is largely intact, a consequence to a significant extent of Syd's insistence on designing strength into the MGB sills from the outset. Although the MGB GT V8 project only gained momentum shortly after Syd retired, by 1975 he was invited back – although British Leyland may not have stressed the significance of Syd's role, in conjunction with that of Roy Brocklehurst, Jim O'Neill, Terry Mitchell and Don Hayter, in helping ensure the car was so strong and safe... (Author Archive)

On the day that the 500,000th MGB went down the line at Abingdon in January 1980, local BL Plant Director Alan Edis invited Syd along to join in the celebrations. It was a nice gesture, against the backdrop of the threat of the end of car production, if not necessarily at that stage full plant closure. The car itself, a black US specification Roadster, is now owned by MOSS California, a major British sports car parts specialist. (Author Archive)

Syd pictured in October 1979 around the time that he was interviewed by the local paper for his views on BL's announcement that car making at Abingdon was to cease. (Author Archive)

very much of a similar engineering ilk, enjoyed model railway engineering (and true engineering at that; Mitchell had a magnificent garden railway with home-designed and built locomotives and rolling stock) and messing about with his home-built specials, Syd's life had been MG and so with no really hobbies, he sometimes seemed bereft.

Syd was invited to see the half millionth MGB come off the line in 1980 and later that year, to join John Thornley and a handful of other old colleagues on the occasion of the last car leaving the Abingdon line on October 23rd. By then he was clearly getting fairly frail and complained of occasional forgetfulness. When he eventually suffered the early onset of dementia, it was, as always the case with that invidious disease, a cruel affliction, as it slowly robbed him of his memory and his faculties. The author corresponded with Syd in this period, but the disease was already upon him, and a clear source of frustration.

'*He had problems with his memory in later days*' Roger Enever confirms; '*he could remember everything from the early days, but not what was happening currently. He eventually lost his licence; his last car was BMC 1800 and he was caught speeding up the Southern Bypass, I think; I never really knew all the details – I never asked – but anyway, he stopped driving after that. Maybe he had a 'last hurrah' – 100 miles an hour up the Southern Bypass, perhaps?*'

Syd's last curtain call came on February 9th 1993, his beloved Ivy having gone before him the previous September. His passing was hardly covered in the press other than through a worthy obituary from one of his protégés, Don Hayter, in *Safety Fast!*; there was no public oration in his memory, unlike that for the likes of Alec Issigonis, who as we saw earlier, Thornley felt was hardly more worthy of his 'genius' accolade than Syd. It is the author's hope, therefore, that this book has gone some small way to redress the balance: it has been a way to say "thank you" to one of the people who actually brought into existence the very MG cars that so many of us now cherish.

Appendix

The Ex-Register During Syd Enever's Career

EX Numbers	Model(s) [Author comments in square brackets]	Date
EX101	Midget front wings and lamp supports [12 drawings for 'M' type Midget]	06/11/1929
EX102	Brake cross-shaft bearings and cables, Mark I [nine drawings dated 14-29/11/1929 for the MG 18/80]	14/11/1929
EX103	Brake cross-shaft bearing modification [seven drawings, undated, for the 18/80]	-
EX104	Mark 3 type experimental front and rear wing fittings [4 drawings for the Mk.III 18/100]	-
EX105	Mark 3 petrol tank and fittings [25 drawings, for the 18/100]	-
EX106	Mark 3 exhaust system [seven drawings, for the 18/100]	-
EX107	Mark 3 headlamp assembly [seven drawings, for the 18/100]	-
EX108	Mark 3 miscellaneous [23 drawings, for the 18/100]	-
EX109	Brooklands type MG Midget: exhaust and induction [six drawings for the Brooklands Double Twelve Midget]	-
EX110	Midget (Brooklands type) wings [one drawing]	-
EX111	Mark 3 controls [15 drawings for Mk.III 18/100]	-
EX112	Mark 3 instrument panel on chassis [2 drawings for 18/100]	-
EX113	Mark 1 and 2 miscellaneous [15 drawings for the 18/80 Mk. I & II]	-
EX114	Midget (Brooklands type) petrol tanks [two drawings for Brooklands Double Twelve Midget]	-
EX115	Frame and suspension, Midget 1931 [21 drawings for 1931 Midget, which saw the changeover from the Morris Minor 'M' type chassis to a purpose-designed MG one]	-
EX116	Shock absorbers [six drawings for 1931 Midget]	-
EX117	Mark 2 close up of wings [two drawings of 18/80 Mk. II]	-
EX118	Mark 3 oil tank [two drawings of 18/100 Mk.III]	-
EX119	Mark 1 servo brakes (DeWandre servo) [two drawings detailing the chassis-mounted brake servo on the 18/80 Mk. I]	-
EX120	Midget 750 c.c. [no less than 372 drawings listed for this car, which was Eyston's Montlhéry Midget, which gained several international class records in 1930/1931. It was the first car, for example, to extract a speed of over 100 m.p.h. from under 750 c.c. EX120 does not survive; following a record-breaking run-in September 1931, it caught fire and the remains were cut up at Abingdon soon afterwards]	-
EX121	Midget miscellaneous (two-seater, 1931) [two drawings for 1931 Midget]	-
EX122	Mark 2 fan [nine drawings for the 18/80 Mk. II]	-
EX123	Midget anti-squeak [three drawings for MG 'M' type]	11/09/1930
EX124	Midget blower equipment [seven drawings for Midget supercharger]	-
EX125	750 c.c. blower equipment [139 drawings]	-
EX126	Midget change-speed (sliding type) [Midget gear selector]	-
EX127	Single seat racing car [93 drawings for Eyston's second record breaking car – the 'Magic Midget' which achieved 120 m.p.h. from less than 750 c.c. Bobby Kohlrausch (see also EX154) later achieved over 140 m.p.h. EX127 was eventually reworked into EX154]	-
EX128	'E' type [22 drawings; this appears to have been an abortive project. The 'D' type became the new Midget, and the 'F' type emerged as the Magna.]	-
EX129	'F' type chassis with three-foot, ten-inch track [16 drawings, possibly for the 'F' type Magna, although that car had a track of three-foot six inch]	-

EX Numbers	Model(s) [Author comments in square brackets]	Date
EX130	AB type engines [33 drawings. EX130/32 and 33 are for 'J' type engine camshaft details.]	-
EX131	Experimental 'K' type engine items [11 drawings for K type engine]	-
EX132	Experimental K3 type [six drawings related to the famous K3 Magnette]	-
EX133	Girling brakes [three drawings]	-
EX134	Crankshaft thrust bearings (ball type) [five drawings]	-
EX135	Single seat, 1,100 c.c. [233 drawings; this became the famous record breaker EX135, after a few incarnations; in original form, effectively a single seater MG K3 Magnette – number K3023]	-
EX136	Crankshaft steady – roller bearing type [seven drawings]	-
EX137	Cadmium-plated big-end [one drawing]	-
EX138	J2 brake cross-shaft with single point adjustment [one drawing]	-
EX139	Reverse stop assembly [four drawings]	-
EX140	Reverse stop assembly [two drawings]	-
EX141	Laycock propeller shaft [two drawings]	-
EX142	Experimental brake gear [51 drawings, including proposed brake gear for K3 Magnette, designed by Cecil Cousins]	-
EX143	Special parts for Mille Miglia K3 cars (1934) [11 drawings]	-
EX144	'N' saloon [two drawings, which only depict the bonnet]	-
EX145	Petrol and oil sealing devices on K3 Marshall blowers [19 drawings; sealing problems with Marshall superchargers]	-
EX146	(No title – only 'superseded by EX147') [118 drawings giving all chassis, suspension, engine mounting details for the 'R' Type single seater]	-
EX147	'R' type [106 drawings for the famous independent suspension 'R' type single-seater of 1935]	-
EX148	'P' type sundries [13 drawings, including details of Le Mans fittings]	-
EX149	Not taken [in other words, not used! The following is purely conjecture on the author's part, but it is quite possible that EX149 was to have been the so-called 'S' Type single seat racing car which Cecil Kimber hoped to produce]	-
EX150	3½ litre independent car [1,106 drawings including what is referred to as 'banana type rear suspension'. This car was nicknamed the 'Queen Mary'. Abandoned, along with EX147, with the sale by William Morris of the MG Car Company Ltd to Morris Motors Ltd.]	-
EX151	10/4 engine (TA etcetera) [41 drawings detailing the engine for the 'TA' Midget]	-
EX152	R.A. experimental chassis (anti-roll experiments) [CANCELLED]	-
EX153	Experimental work on the Two-litre [72 drawings for the SA]	-
EX154	Special car for R. Kohlrausch esq.; specification as follows: Chassis No. EX154; Engine No. 2443A; P-type chassis frame; P-type front axle; P-type rear axle; Q-type brake drums; J4 torque-reaction cables; Straight-cut gears to back axle; rear axle nose-piece through-bolted with tubular distance pieces; J4 body, petrol tank and spare wheel carrier; J2 cycle type wings and P-type wing stays; three inch diameter prop-shaft balanced to 8,000 r.p.m. (200 series joints, four and a half inch O/D flanges, five sixteenth inch bolts on a three and $^{61}/_{64}$ inch P.C.D., thirty six and $^{1}/_{16}$ inch long); Q-type engine with pre-selector box and Zoller supercharger mounted between front dumb irons; P-type steering cam gears; special road wheels and tyres supplied by Mr. Kohlrausch. [72 drawings for the special Bobby Kohlrausch car, built using some parts from EX127. EX154 was later destroyed in Germany.]	-
EX155	'T'-series Midget; allocated for experimental chassis and cars. [Chassis No. EX155/1, engine no. 6594/1 – dated 22/2/1938. The following MG Midget TA series cars were converted to competition models and fitted with 1½ litre engines:	-

APPENDIX

EX Numbers	Model(s) [Author comments in square brackets]	Date
EX155	Chassis No. Engine No. To EX155 chassis and new engine no.	-
	TA.2017MPJG.2285EX155/2TPBG.1383	
	TA.2018MPJG.2286EX155/3TPBG.1373	
	TA.2019MPJG.2291EX155/4TPBG.1397	
	TA.2020MPJG.2295EX155/5TPBG.1384	
	TA.2092MPJG.2368EX155/6TPBG.968	
	There are 20 drawings also listed, covering such items as police equipment and supercharger fixings. The chassis numbers may relate to the new 'Cream Cracker' team cars of 1938.]	
EX156	Valve spring experiments [two drawings – CANCELLED]	-
EX157	Not allotted	-
EX158	SA Type Two Litre [85 drawings; including Mille Miglia car]	-
EX159	VA Type 1½ litre [36 drawings; includes cars EX159/1, with engine 6591/1, and EX159/2, with engine TPDG 6720/2, featuring wider rear track and special body]	-
EX160	3½ litre car designed at Cowley [no entries; probably the idea to produce a large Wolseley engined MG saloon, which was quickly abandoned in favour of the WA – EX161]	-
EX161	2.6 litre [WA 2.6 litre saloon. 19 drawings including three related to chassis: EX161/1 with engine QPHG-2523; EX161/2 with engine 6608/1; and EX161/3 with engine QPJG-648 (described as 'working show chassis')]	-
EX162	Two Litre – front independent suspension designed by Mr. Girling of Pratt and Manley [4 drawings; cross refers negatives with EX158 MG SA. Includes modified 'Jackall' arrangements]	-
EX163	10 H.P. XPJG engine; now 10.8 HP XPAG [five drawings of the XPAG engine exhaust valves. Cross refers to EX155 TA Midget; this is probably the TB Midget]	-
EX164	10 H.P. Midget (DO 811) independent front suspension [one drawing. Note the reference to a Cowley 'DO' project code]	26/10/1939
EX165	10 H.P. Midget (DO 825) [note reference to Cowley 'DO' code number]	27/11/1939
EX166	1¼ litre saloon 1945. [engine number 6946/3; EX/MG/76. Comment in register: 'Guarantee plate issued to Cowley Experimental Department 7/1/1945']	-
EX167	'Bitsy' [Engine No. XPAG 529. 'Bitsy' was a sort of tractor built from bits and pieces – hence its name – during war time]	-
EX168	1¼ litre saloon 1945 (DO 914) [engine number 11527/1. Morris Motors Experimental Number EX/MG/125]	-
EX169	1¼ litre saloon 1945 (DO 914) [engine 11527/2; EX/MG/126]	-
EX170	1¼ litre saloon 1945 (DO 914) [engine 11527/3; EX/MG/127]	-
EX171	TD Midget converted to road racing specification (Dick Jacobs) [44 drawings]	25/09/1950
EX171A	MG 1 11.9 HP engine no. EX171/1. 69.5mm bore, 102 mm stroke; 1,548 c.c. [this is the re-registered chassis number of 'Old No. 1', allocated an 'EX' Number retrospectively in 1956]	1956
EX172	TD Midget for Le Mans with streamlined body. Chassis Number TD/C.5336 [16 drawings; this is the famous 'UMG 400', with the Syd Enever designed body which ultimately inspired the MGA. The body was very similar to the MGA, and the styling was adopted for a road going prototype – EX175 (see below)]	05/01/1951
EX173	TD engines for Record Car – Job No. ZM.13366; Cowley DO1008 [36 drawings]	10/01/1951
EX174	DO1009 2-litre converted Wolseley 6/80 engine for Record Car [62 drawings]	01/02/1951

229

EX Numbers	Model(s) [Author comments in square brackets]	Date
EX175	1,500 c.c. streamlined Midget two-seater [44 drawings; drawing EX175/1 is car outline; this is the second stage in the evolutionary process which led to the MGA. EX175/1 – registered 'HMO 6' – was the car shown to Leonard Lord but rejected by him in favour of the Healey 100]	-
EX176	72mm bore by 90mm stroke four-cylinder 1,466 c.c. TD engine for USA – Job No. ZM.15838 [44 drawings; this is presumably the origins of the later TF 1,500 engine. Curiously, drawings EX176/42,43 & 44 refer to 1,588 c.c. MGA engine for Sebring 1961 and cross-refer to EX178, although it is likely that this is a simple case of mis-booking]	-
EX177	TF Midget [27 drawings, not all dated in register; EX177/15 is dated as 7/5/1953]	May-53
EX178	Austin 1,500 engine tuning [68 drawings. This was clearly involvement of MG with the Austin-designed 'B' series, which appeared in the ZA Magnette and later in the MGA. Not all drawings dated – but drawing EX178/63 is dated 21/3/1957, and drawings EX178/67 & 68 refer to 1,622 c.c. version of engine, and are dated 2/3/1961]	1953-1961
EX179	Record Car for 1954 (Job No. ZM.18757) [115 drawings of this famous Record Breaker. Only drawings EX179/70 onwards are dated; 13/4/1956 for EX179/70 up to 9/1/1959 for EX179/115]	1953-1959
EX180	Morris Minor tuning [11 drawings, related to valve springs, rear springs, shock absorbers, 40 DCOE (Weber) carburettor manifold etc.; dated 11/3/1958 to 29/6/1960]	1958-1960
EX181	Record Car (Special) [the famous Record Breaker driven by Phil Hill and Stirling Moss, and known to the media as the 'Roaring Raindrop'. Most of the 276 drawings date from 1957 to 1960, but there are later entries from No. EX181/273 onwards; EX181/273 dated 10/8/1966 is for 'radiator front duct' whilst EX181/274, dated 3/7/1978 is for 'front decal showing GB & USA flags and MG emblem' – drawn in retrospect no doubt to allow restoration. Drawings EX181/275 & 276, dated 25/10/1978 and 30/10/1978 respectively, detail the tail contours]	1957-1978
EX182	Special parts for Series MGA. [note stops in MGA!] for Le Mans 1955 [68 drawings detailing parts such as oil cooler, tanks & mountings, brakes etc. Nos. EX182/38, 39, 40 and 41 are listed as 'chassis numbers for Le Mans cars nos. 1, 2, 3 & 4 respectively, although it is not clear from this which car is which. Last two drawings are dated – 15/3/1960]	-
EX183	Experimental 1956 Le Mans car (tubular chassis) [27 drawings]	-
EX184	Special parts for Weslake T.S.P. cylinder head [six drawings]	-
EX185	Special parts for competition Pathfinder [15 drawings detailing road springs, engine mountings etc.]	-
EX186	Twin overhead-camshaft 'Le Mans' type 1956 with MGA type chassis [202 drawings detailing 4½ J x 15 alloy disc wheels, suspension, chassis reinforcements etc.. Last entry dated 3/9/1959]	?-1959
EX187	Twin overhead-camshaft version of MGA with disc brakes [318 drawings; 2/6/1955 to 26/11/1962]	1955-1962
EX188	New Midget with [Austin] A30 ['A'-series] engine – MGD [no previous mention of MGB or MGC in register! No drawings or anything else listed, but this may have been related to Cowley's DO1035]	n/a
EX189	4-seater version of MGA – MGE [another 'kite flyer', like EX188; nothing listed in register]	n/a
EX190	Competition Magnette [three drawings; modifications to petrol tank to increase capacity from 9¼ gallons to 14 gallons. Drawings 16/5/1955 to 21/6/1955]	May-June 1955
EX191	Development work on production MGA [450 drawings; dated from 19/5/1955 up to 7/2/1961. Also referred to as ADO31]	1955-1961
EX192	Development work for rallies on Austin cars [20 drawings of such things as: EX192/1 engine number for Le Mans type engine in Austin Cambridge – dated 28/6/1955; EX192/2 rear spring for Austin A90 – dated 15/7/1955; EX192/19 ten-gallon petrol tank for Austin A35 – dated 13/6/1957. The Austin A90 was one of the early choices for rallying by the BMC Competitions Department, managed at Abingdon from January 1955 by Marcus Chambers]	1955-1957
EX193	Magnette (for Bermuda only) [16 drawings detailing different number plate finishers and assemblies, front wing flash and rear bumper blade (split in two – left and right hand), jacking fixings on rear bumper etc.]	September-October 1955

APPENDIX

EX Numbers	Model(s) [Author comments in square brackets]	Date
EX194	MGA Police Modifications ['C' type engine dynamo and larger batteries. 17 drawings]	-
EX195	MGA 'cheap version' [72 drawings, dated from 11/11/1955 to 31/8/1959, detailing ideas for a lower cost MGA with Austin A30 steering box, 13 inch or 14-inch wheels, single $1\frac{3}{4}$ inch SU carburettor, Morris Minor propshaft etc.]	1955-1959
EX196	MGA Hardtop [1 drawing]	07/02/1956
EX197	Fixed-Head Coupé MGA [no entries in register at all]	n/a
EX198	[Riley] Pathfinder (Mark II) Push-Rod 'C' type engine [29 drawings, dated from May 1956 to 31/7/1956, and detailing the changes from the Riley engined Pathfinder into the Riley Two-Point-Six]	May-July 1956
EX199	Competition Magnette [four drawings; 13/1/1956 for ventilated brake drum to 10/1/1958 for sump shield]	1956-1958
EX200	Magnette facelift [no entries. Judging by date, this could be Varitone or even first thoughts about a successor to the Z-Magnette. With no entries to go on, this is pure conjecture. Note also D.O 1071 and D.O. 1091]	n/a
EX201	[Riley] Pathfinder with semi-elliptic rear suspension [39 drawings, dated 5/3/1956 to 4/12/1957]	1956-1957
EX202	Magnette with 'C' series engine [five drawings, of May 1956, covering respectively: rear axle scheme, rear shock absorber, scheme showing 'C' type rear axle, radiator casing grille and radiator block]	8 & 9/5/1956
EX203	Magnette with extra-long column [four drawings]	-
EX204	[Riley] Pathfinder series RMJ 6/90 modified [63 drawings, including chassis number of prototype car – EX204/56]	-
EX205	MG Two-Seater (ADO23) eleven drawings [all described as having been 'transferred into ADO23 book'; from June 1957 to February 1958. Includes drawing of Frua bodied MGA]	1957-1958
EX206	Three Litre Riley [no entries; Don Hayter recalls that this was another 'kite flyer']	n/a
EX207	Twin Cam [Riley] Pathfinder (DO1067) [cross refer Appendix I. Note that there is reference to 'Chassis No. EX207/1 – Export Car'. Presumably drawings were done by Cowley and all booked to DO1067? The engine was designed by Gerald Palmer as a twin-cam conversion of the 'C' series six. Work began in November 1955 but was abandoned in March 1956]	1955-1956
EX208	1½ litre Riley [four drawings, all related to the 'Riley One-Point-Five'. EX208/1 is listed as 'chassis number for runabout car' (dated 12/11/1957); EX208/4 is a 4J x 13-inch wheel arrangement, dated 19/11/1959. This car was also DO1100]	1957-1959
EX209	Long term development power units [No entries. This may have conceivably have been intended to have included Abingdon's own thoughts about a two-litre four cylinder 'cut down' from the six-cylinder 'C' series unit]	n/a
EX210	2.6 litre MG (4-seater sports) [six drawings detailing, respectively; EX210/1 ¼ scale body general arrangement – dated 28/8/1957; EX210/2 described as for previous but annotated 'H. Harris' and dated 28/2/1958; EX210/3 ¼ scale 'schematic layout' dated 28/5/1958; EX210/4 sketch showing installation of pedals – dated 28/5/1958; EX210/5 isometric sketch of front end and EX210/6 ¼ scale frame (the last two both dated 28/5/1958). This is clearly a precursor of the 'MGC', complete with 'C' series engine]	1957-1958
EX211	Anti run-on and fuel economy device [four drawings. An anti run-on device was an attempt to cure the common problem with 'running on' of hot engines after the ignition had been switched off]	08/02/1957
EX212	Fixed head coupé MGA Twin Cam [no entries in register, but this is the Don Hayter schemed coupé built on the basis of Ted Lund's MGA twin cam roadster SRX 210 – chassis no. YD3-627S – for Ted to race at Le Mans]	-

EX Numbers	Model(s) [Author comments in square brackets]	Date
EX213	Competition [Austin] Healey BN6 [75 drawings, ranging from EX213/1 25-gallon fuel tank – dated 20/5/1958 to EX213/75 shock absorber link bolt – dated 1/7/1964. The Austin Healey 100/6 (later the 3000 Mk. I, II & III) was built at Abingdon from 1957]	1958-1964
EX214	Replacement for MGA – body facelift, wings etc. [12 drawings detailing the first thoughts for what became the ADO23 MGB (see also Appendix III). Drawing EX214/1 is for ¼ scale body lines, dated 9/6/1958; EX214/12 is for ¼ scale body lines with wide radiator grille – i.e. the prototype MGB with coil sprung rear suspension – dated 1/5/1959]	1958-1959
EX215	Competition equipment for 1.5 litre Rileys [two drawings, both detailing flexible oil cooler pipes]	03/06/1958
EX216	V4 power unit in MGA [13 drawings detailing modifications to front cross member and other installation requirements. The V4 engine was one of a proposed new family of Longbridge-designed BMC units which was eventually abandoned because of cost and balancing problems. Its demise was not a disappointment to Abingdon. Drawings dated 16/9/1958 to 3/12/1958]	late 1958
EX217	'B' type box on 'C' type engine [one drawing only, for adaptor plates]	-
EX218	[Austin Healey] BN6 Development (including BN7, BN8) [50 drawings, dated from 22/7/1958 up to 2/9/1960]	1958-1960
EX219	[Austin] Healey Sprite 24-hour record car [there is often confusion over the history of this car. Originally, EX219 comprised a special streamlined version of the Austin Healey Sprite body, with faired in nose and 'bubble' canopy. However, wind tunnel tests showed that this body was not aerodynamically effective, so instead EX179 was revised and presented as an Austin Healey. 19 drawings from April 1959 to 16/7/1959]	1959
EX220	New Midget based on Sputnik F.W.D. (Superseded ADO34 [see Appendix III]) [21 drawings, dated from 23/4/1959 to 4/6/1959. Clearly there was some thought about a number of possible variations on a theme – as both MG and Austin Healey variants are included, as is a coupé proposal (EX220/19, dated 29/5/1959). 'Sputnik' was the code name given to the ADO15 Mini prior to its launch.	1959
EX221	[Austin Healey] Sprite with 1,600 'B' series engine [EX221/1 is described as 'Chassis Number for No. 1 Prototype Car']	23/03/1960
EX222	ADO10 [Austin A99 & Wolseley 6/99] and ADO53 [Austin A110 & Wolseley 6/110] Competition [2 drawings related to rear spring modifications; dated 23/8/1960 for the ADO10 version (EX222/1) and 28/6/1962 for the other]	1960-1962
EX223	Competition Mini Minor [162 drawings, all related to the Mini Cooper and Cooper 'S'. Dates from 13/10/1962 to 19/2/1973]	1962-1973
EX224	Mini Minor ADO15 – conversion to Austin Healey sports model [no entries in register]	-
EX225	Mini Minor ADO15 – conversion to MG sports model [no entries]	-
EX226	Modifications to the ADO9 Magnette MK. III [two drawings; EX226/1 steering wheel – dated 4/4/1961; EX226/2 engine – dated 10/4/1961. These drawings may be part of the exercise to improve the appalling handling and performance of the ADO9 range, which culminated in the ADO38 replacement (including the Magnette Mk. IV) of 1961. It is also worth noting that John Thornley sought styling improvements to ADO9 and/or ADO38 – to no avail.]	Apr-61
EX227	1,600 GT coupé two-seater [50 drawings, dated from 4/1/1962. EX227/2 shows ¼ scale arrangement, dated 4/1/1962; drawings undated after EX227/34. EX227 is generally considered as the MGB GT project code, although as can be seen Abingdon originally envisaged it as a 1,600 c.c. coupé – presumably because it was originally envisaged that the MGB would receive the 1,622 c.c. engine, and only received the 1,798 c.c. engine at a fairly late stage prior to launch]	1962
EX228	Transverse rear-engined 'A' series car [this sounds rather like a project by the Healeys known by them as 'WAEC' – or 'wheel at each corner'.	-

EX Numbers	Model(s) [Author comments in square brackets]	Date
EX229	Midget with Hydrolastic – rear wheel drive [three drawings described as EX229/1 steering geometry – dated 16/10/1962; EX229/2 chassis frame front end – dated 21/11/1962; and EX229/3 front sub-frame, dated 21/11/1962]	late 1962
EX230	ADO15 [Mini] with integrated sub-frames [one drawing detailing underframe scheme, dated 29/3/1963]	29/03/1963
EX231	Hydrolastic suspension on ADO41/47 [Austin Healey Sprite Mk. II & MG Midget Mk. I] [66 drawings, all during 1963 (first 1/4/1963; last dated 20/12/1963) concerning the conversion of the 'Spridget' to Hydrolastic suspension.]	1963
EX232	1,800 c.c. engine development [16 drawings, ranging from EX232/1 set of triple valve springs – dated 25/4/1963 – to EX232/16 scheme for swirl chamber induction heater – dated 17/10/1967]	1963-1967
EX233	Record car with transverse engine [no entries in Register – but a project overseen by Syd Enever personally]	09/09/1963
EX234	Hydrolastic Sports Car Prototype [136 drawings for this pretty, Pininfarina styled sports car. Prototype survived as part of Syd Beer's collection, having been bought in the 1970's after many years of 'mothballed' storage; sold through auction]	from 11/2/1964
EX235	Competition MGB [12 drawings from 29/7/1964]	1964
EX236	Comps [i.e. Competition Department] ADO17 [35 drawings dating from 26/11/1964; ADO17 is Austin Morris 1800 'landcrab']	1964
EX237	GT Prototype to 1965 Le Mans regulations [three drawings, dated 10/3/1965, showing body lines (EX237/1 & 2) and windscreen glass (EX237/3)]	10/03/1965
EX238	Midget with 1,800 c.c. engine [two drawings, dated 10/7/1966 & 20/2/1967, both of propshaft]	1966-1967
EX239	Competition and fuel injection Midget ADO41/47 [25 drawings, ranging in date from 8/11/1967 to 9/4/1968]	1967-1968
EX240	Mini 850 c.c. [Red saloon with engine no. 8WR/U/H/4214 built by MG Show Shop in December 1967. After 'Comps' had finished with it, John Thornley bought EX240 for his daughter. Sadly, in his words, '*she impaled it on a Southern Electricity Board Land Rover. She survived, but EX240 did not*']	04/01/1968
EX241	Competition ADO52 [MGC] [4 drawings, dated 8/2/1968 to 30/7/1968, covering inlet manifolds and triple SU HS6 carburettors. EX241 is the famous MGC GTS]	1968
EX242	MG GT version of ADO28 [see Appendix III]; for all part numbers see sheets in Project Office Book – Don Hayter 13/11/1968 [15 drawings detailing Abingdon's proposals for a coupé based upon the forthcoming Morris Marina, on a 102' wheelbase. Drawings dated from 8/2/1968 to 30/7/1968 and detail, among other things, the 'E4', 'E6' and Rover V8 engines. This project may be related to ADO68]	1968
EX243	[Austin Healey] Sprite with heel-board moved rearward	13/12/1968
EX244	Triumph 2.5 P.I. for competition [the first and only Triumph mentioned in the EX-Register! 'Comps' were preparing the fuel-injected Triumph 2.5 P.I. for rallies. Ten drawings, dated 29/7/1969 to 16/2/1970]	1969-1970
EX245	Competition Maxi [ADO14] [four drawings dated from 1/1/1970 to 27/1/71]	1970-1971
EX246	ADO28 [Marina] Special Tuning. For all part numbers see sheets in Project Office Book – M. Holliday 22/2/1971	22/02/1971
EX247	Mini with 12 inch wheels and larger brakes [19 drawings, dated 9/3/1971 to 3/5/1971. Interestingly, 12 inch wheels would be gradually adopted on all production Minis, starting with the Mini 1275GT later in the decade]	1971

Index

100,000th MG MGA – 152, 181, 182
1923 (first known use of MG octagon) – 36
1924 (date claimed retrospectively as first use of MG octagon) - 36
1928 (date of registration of MG Car Company Limited) – 36
1940 MG model range – 103
250,000th MGB – 220
500,000th MGB – 222, 225, 226

A

A.W. Hawksley Ltd of Gloucester - 106
AAA - American Automobile Association – 128
Abbey Panels - 205
Abbot Road (Abingdon-on-Thames) - 35
Abingdon Council Girls' School - 114
Abingdon Factory – see MG Factory
Abingdon Fair - 172
Abingdon Fair, The – 14
Abingdon Grammar School – 156
Abingdon Museum – 108
Abingdon Pillow (facia) - 207
Abingdon School - 130
Abingdon-on-Thames – 10, 14, 19, 60, 65, 68, 77, 114, 219
AC Cars Limited – 33, 38
ACO Le Mans – 179
ADAC ('Allgemeiner Deutscher Automobil-Club') – 99
ADAC 500 km Rennen auf dem Nürburgring' - 203
Adam, Douglas ('Doug') – 137
Adderley Park – 123
ADO10 Austin A99 Westminster & Wolseley 6/99 – 185, 186
ADO13 Austin-Healey Sprite – 174, 180, 197
ADO14 Austin Maxi – 199, 211, 213, 214
ADO14 Maxi Coupé idea - 211
ADO15 Austin Se7en/ Morris Mini Minor – 155, 176, 195, 206
ADO16 Austin, MG, Morris, Riley, VDP, Wolseley 1100 range – 185, 187, 192, 196, 198, 207, 213
ADO17 Austin, Morris & Wolseley '1800' – 192, 198, 207, 213
ADO21 Mid-engined sports car concept – 186, 213, 214-215, 222
ADO23 MGB – 176, 180, 182, 183, 185, 211
ADO24 Austin-Healey 4-Litre ('Healey Rolls') – 201, 202
ADO28 Morris Marina – 208, 213
ADO30 BMC Grand Tourer sports car concept (XC512 'Fireball') – 197, 202, 209
ADO34 Mini based sports car concept – 156, 186, 195, 196, 197, 198
ADO35 – 195, 196
ADO36 – 195
ADO38 – BMC Farina facelifted range – 187
ADO38G – see MG Magnette Mark IV
ADO41 Austin-Healey Sprite Mark II, III, IV et seq – 180, 181, 195, 198, 204, 211
ADO47 MG Midget Mark I, II, III et seq – 180, 181, 195, 198, 204, 205, 211
ADO51 – Austin-Healey equivalent of MGC – 197, 200, 202
ADO52 MGC – 202, 211
ADO56 MG Coupé concept of 1959 – 195
ADO61 Austin Three-Litre - 213
ADO67 Austin Allegro – 213
ADO9 – 'Farina' 1.5-litre saloons – 159, 186
Africa – 24
Air Pollution (and cars) – 205, 206
Alabama - 220
Albemarle aircraft (Armstrong-Whitworth) – 106
Albert Place (Oxford) – 25, 107
Alexander Engineering - 144
Alfa Romeo 'Alfetta' 1800 Cabrio - 223
Alfa Romeo Giulietta - 159
Alfa-Romeo Superflow Concept (1956) – 171, 173, 183
Alfred Lane (Oxford) – 37, 47
Allison, Mike (author) – 8, 14, 15, 35, 40, 41, 43, 46, 71, 73, 75, 81, 82, 97, 111, 133, 134
Alnwick (Northumberland) - 147
Alpine (Renault Gordini) - 212
Alpine Rally, the - 150

Alvis - 142
Amasco Championship - 216
American Express - 127, 128
Americans (USA) – 110
An MG Experience (book) - 204
Anderson, Gerry (TV Producer) – 198, 209
Anderson, Mr. (Morris Garages staff) – 28
Andrews, Bill – 149
Any Questions (BBC TV) – 32
Apollo sports car concept - 214
Appleby, William Victor ('Bill') (1903-1984) – 147, 162, 200
Arab Motor Company – 88
Araldite epoxy adhesive – 204, 205
Archer, Alan – 79
Ards (race circuit) - 66
Armstead, Edwin Clipsham – 28, 29
Armstrong-Siddeley – 147
Armstrong-Whitworth – 91, 106, 136, 147, 164, 178, 183
Arnold, Matthew (Thyrsis: 'that sweet city with her dreaming spires') – 22, 25
Ash, David – 16, 164, 166, 167, 168, 178, 203
Asnière, Eugéne Affovard – 50
Associated Octel – 43
Aston Martin DB2/4 - 192
Aston, Hilary – 42, 43
Aston-Martin – 77, 79, 156
Aston-Martin DB4 – 204
Aston-Martin DB7 – 173, 186
Athens (Greece) – 57
Austin A110 Westminster - 202
Austin A30 – 155
Austin A30 & AS3 engine – 139
Austin A35 – 173
Austin A40 ('Farina' – ADO8) - 192
Austin A40 (1948) – 43, 147
Austin A55 Cambridge (ADO9A) - 186
Austin A90 Westminster – 158
Austin A99 Westminster – 185
Austin Atlantic – 138, 143
Austin Engines Dept., The – 14, 147, 149, 150
Austin Gypsy – 185
Austin Maestro (LC10) - 186
Austin Maxi – see ADO14
Austin Metropolitan – 139
Austin Mini-Metro - 222
Austin Morris Design Studio – 209, 215
Austin Morris Division – 210, 213, 214, 215, 220, 221, 222
Austin Motor Company Ltd. – 43, 57, 59, 60, 73, 118, 119, 120, 121, 122, 132, 134-135 (BMC merger), 138, 157, 180, 181, 185, 195, 197
Austin Rover business – 186, 223
Austin Rover newsletter – 143
Austin Seven - 57, 59, 67, 154
Austin Seven Gordon England Special - 85
Austin Taxi - 201
Austin Twin Cam Engine (1955) – 149-150, 175
Austin, Herbert (Sir) – 134
Austin, Lord Herbert – 57
Austin-Healey – 14, 16, 138, 151, 154, 155, 157, 160, 174, 177, 195, 200, 201, 203, 207, 209
Austin-Healey 'Streamliner' (1954) – 141, 212
Austin-Healey 100/4 – 135, 136, 138, 139, 141, 149
Austin-Healey 100/6 ('Big Healey') – 16, 154, 155, 158, 159, 169, 173, 181
Austin-Healey 3000 Mark I – III – 157, 181, 193, 201, 203, 208
Austin-Healey 3000 Mk. IV - 203
Austin-Healey Special Sprite – 199, 212
Austin-Healey Sprite ('ADO13') – 17, 139, 154, 160, 167, 168, 176, 177, 178, 181
Austin-Healey Sprite Mark II et seq ('ADO41') – 143, 181, 193, 198, 204
Australia – 12, 93, 116, 173, 181, 201
Autocar Magazine (also The Autocar) – 17, 60, 81, 89, 95, 99, 127, 207, 220
Automobile Quarterly - 137

Automobile Quarterly – 17
Automotive Products Ltd. - 42
Auto-Union record cars – 89, 93, 96, 101
Avenall, 'Reg' – 127, 131
AVRO Lancaster (bomber aircraft) – 155, 156
Avus Circuit – 73

B

Babs – Leyland Eight racing car – 88
Baghdad – 57
Bagington (Coventry) - 164
Bailey, Bill (Morris Garages staff) – 29, 34
Baines, Alec & Kenneth – 111, 113
Bainton Road (Oxford; MG factory) – 38, 46, 47, 48, 108
Baker, Clive - 217
Baldt, Artur – 73, 74, 77, 101
Bamford, Sir Joseph – 224
Bampton (village formerly in Berkshire, now Oxfordshire) – 57
Banbury (Oxfordshire) – 38, 124
Barber, Harold (H.R.) (Pressed Steel) – 210, 211
BARC (Brooklands Auto Racing Club) - 87
Barnes, Frank Stanley – 65, 66
Barnet (town) – 41
Baron, Barclay (Author of The Doctor) – 21, 22
Bartlett, J. H. - 67
Barton, Frank George (1869-1957) – 29
Basingstoke – 56
Bates, Bernard (B.H.) – 210, 211
Beans cars – 38
Beattie, Kevin – 222, 224
Bee, Andrew – 190
Beech, George – 164, 178
Beer, Syd - 199
Belfast (city) – 66, 71, 150
Belgian Pavé - 174
Belgium – 90, 95, 105, 127, 134
Bellevue Garage – see Evans
Belsize cars – 30
Benn, Richard ('Dick') – 113, 121, 126, 127, 128, 134
Benson, Mr. – 20
Bentley cars – 39, 49, 68, 71, 74, 80, 93
Berengaria, RMS (Ocean Liner, 1912-1938) – 20
Berkeley, California – 87, 88
Berlin (City) – 93, 101
Berlin Motor Show (March 1938) – 80, 89
Bermondsey (London) – 23
Bertelli, Augustus Cesare – 76, 77
Bertram, K. - 109
Bertram, O. H. J. – 64, 67
Beverley (Yorkshire) – 174
Bicester (Oxfordshire) – 220
Bicester Grammar School – 220
Bicknell, Alan – 95, 96, 99
Big Healeys – see under Austin-Healey
Binsey (Oxford) – 70
Birkin, Sir Henry Ralph Stanley ('Tim') – 74, 75
Birmingham (City) – 28, 76, 107, 131, 134, 147, 216
Bitsy (wartime MG tractor) – 105, 107
Bitterfeld (near Dessau) – 96
Black, Norman – 51, 64, 65, 66, 67
Blackburn Aviation - 147
Blackburne engine – 80
BLMC Mini – see BMC Mini
Bluebird record breaker – 59, 60, 68, 224
Bluecol (antifreeze) – 194
Bluemels steering wheel – 169
BMC (British Motor Corporation, The) – 9, 13, 16, 17, 45, 54, 59, 95, 132, 134-135, 139, 142, 146, 153, 157, 161, 171, 173, 174, 176, 179, 187, 192, 195, 197, 199, 202, 204, 206, 207, 212, 213, 215, 216
BMC 1800 (ADO17) -226
BMC A-Series Engine – 147, 154, 167, 168, 173, 181, 195, 198, 200, 205, 212, 217

INDEX

BMC Australia 'Blue Streak Six' – 201, 202
BMC Board, The (combined) – 11, 132, 136, 161, 168, 173, 179, 186
BMC B-Series Engine – 12, 14, 43, 124, 129, 131, 138, 146, 147, 151, 161, 162, 163, 175, 198, 209
BMC Competitions Dept. (Abingdon) – 172, 179, 199, 216, 217, 218
BMC C-Series 2.5-litre concept - 202
BMC C-Series based four-cylinder - 201
BMC C-Series Engine – 147, 156, 158, 159, 200, 202, 203
BMC Development Project EX179 – see EX179
BMC E6 – six-cylinder engine - 215
BMC Engines - 147
BMC E-Series engine – 201, 214, 215
BMC Experimental Record Breaker (EX179) – see EX179
BMC Mini (see also Morris Mini-Minor) – 44, 179, 188, 194, 217
BMC Mini Van – 189, 195
BMC Mini-Cooper (and 'S') – 195, 203, 205, 217, 218
BMC Publicity Dept. - 175
BMC road testing in Europe - 151
BMC Tractor & Transmissions Branch - 184
BMC V4 and V6 engine concepts – 160, 200
BMW MINI – 27
BOAC (airline) – 127
Boars Hill (Oxford) – 25
Boddy, William ('Bill') – 61, 92, 167
Boden, Oliver – 33, 108
Boeing 377 Stratocruiser - 127
Bofors gun & 'Quad' - 106
Bonneville Salt Flats, The – 16, 128, 133, 134, 163, 164
Booth & Poole - 216
Borg-Warner BW35 Automatic Gearbox – 202, 203
Bourdon, Beatrice Hestel – 19
Bownes, 'Tommy' - 175
Boyle, Robert – 83
BP (British Petroleum) – 29, 220
Bradbury, Mr. (Morris Garages staff) - 29
Bradford (Yorkshire) - 124
Bradstock, George – 64, 66, 147
Bramley, James (J. F. – 'Jim') – 210, 211
Brands Hatch race circuit - 218
Bray, Cliff – 160, 164, 177
BRDC (British Racing Drivers' Club) – 67, 212
Breeden, Charles ('Carl') – 28
Bremner, Richard - 214
Brentford (London) - 216
Brescia (Italy) – 111, 112
Brescia-Bergamo Road (Italy) – 111
Brighton & Hove Motor Club – 113
Brighton (Sussex) – 19, 20, 121
Bristol Aeroplane Company - 43
British Leyland Mirror magazine - 116
British Leyland Motor Corporation ('BLMC') – 13, 17, 45, 133, 182, 199, 210, 212, 213, 215, 217, 219, 220
British Motor Corporation – see BMC
British Motor Holdings – 201, 203, 207, 208, 209
British Motor Museum, The (Gaydon) – 36, 56, 91, 134, 136, 192, 196, 214
British Saloon Car Championship - 218
Brittains Ltd. – 126, 127
Brize Norton (Oxfordshire) – 165
BRM - 223
Broad Street (Oxford) – 28
Brocklehurst, Roy – 13, 16, 114, 116, 132-133, 135, 143, 172, 182, 184, 186, 198, 202, 212, 221-222
Brooklands (race circuit) – 59, 60, 61, 62, 64, 65, 67, 68, 69, 73, 76, 82, 85, 87, 88, 117, 220
Brooklands 'Double-Twelve' Race – 15, 34, 40, 49, 50, 51, 52, 56, 59, 60, 61, 62, 64, 65, 68, 70, 84, 85
Brooklands BRDC 500 Race (1931) – 67, 70, 79, 129
Brown, E. G. & Company Ltd. ('Brown Brothers') – 87, 89
Brown, Peter - 217
Browne, John – 46
Browning, Peter – 14
Brussels - 90
BSA motorcycles – 38, 39
B-Series engine – see under BMC B-Series
Budapest - 89
Bugatti cars – 30, 32, 92, 128
Buick cars - 82
Bull, John – 46, 109, 129
Bulldozer conversions to tanks – 104-105, 107, 219
Bullingdon Road (Oxford) – 19

Bullnose Morris – 27, 28, 29, 42
Bullock, George (Morris Garages staff) – 27, 29
Burden, Robert W. ('Bob') - 221
Bürgermeister of Dessau - 101
Burma - 85
Burton, Arthur, 174
Burzi, Ricardo ('Dick') – 208
Busby, Mr. – 20
Butler, Donald William ('Don') (1930-2012) – 137, 172, 184, 185, 186, 191, 195, 196, 207, 220, 222
Buzz Box (small sports car idea) – 154, 155, 174

C

C.C. Wakefield – see under Wakefield and Castrol
Cadman, Chris – 60
Caldecott Road (Abingdon-on-Thames) – 38
California – 88
Calling All Arms (book) – 105
Callingham, Leslie – 68
Cam Gears Ltd. – 43
Cambrai – 39
Cambridge (city) – 28, 55, 155
Cambridge University – 55, 57, 58, 59
Camel Filters (cigarette sponsors) – 217
Campbell, Donald - 224
Campbell, Sir Malcolm – 57, 58, 59, 60, 68, 76, 85, 88, 91
Canada – 144, 177
Canley (Triumph, Coventry) - 222
Cannell, Mr. – 68
Cannes (France) – 112
CAR magazine - 203
Carbodies Ltd. – 36, 37, 156
Carfax Assembly Rooms (Oxford) – 37
Carter, Eric – 17, 136, 136, 143, 144, 145, 151, 152, 172, 180, 181, 186, 204, 205, 222, 223
Castle Mill Stream (Oxford) – 21
Castrol Oil – 59, 140, 163
Caudron Bi-Plane – 88
Cemetery Road (Abingdon-on-Thames) – 55
Centaur Tank - 105
Centric Superchargers – 94, 97, 111
Champion (spark plugs) – 165
Charing Cross Hospital, The – 23
Charles Raworth & Sons (coachbuilders) – 36
Charles, Hubert (H.N.) – 14, 15, 34, 35, 40, 41-43, 44, 45, 49, 50, 51, 55, 56, 57, 58, 65, 68, 71, 75, 77, 81, 82, 83, 84, 104, 147
Charles, Mrs Constance - 41
Charles, Mrs May (née Dardon) – 42
Charles, Thomas – 41
Chelsea (London) – 76
Cheltenham (City in Gloucestershire) – 43
Cheshire (county) – 88
Chetwynd, Hon. Mrs – 64
Chevrolet Impala – 179
Chevron B8 – 217
China – 57
Chivers Drapers (Abingdon) - 114
Chobham (Surrey) – 105, 176
Chrysler France - 223
Churchills Nightclub (London) – 13
Citroën cars - 63
Clarendon Hotel, Garage & Yard (Oxford) – 26, 27, 29, 34, 37, 39, 44, 45, 47
Clark, Geoff - 215
Clarke, Bill – 149
Clarke, F. F. R. ('Fred') – 210, 211
Clifford, Hon. 'Freddie' – 79, 121
Clifton Hampden (village in Oxfordshire, between Abingdon and Oxford) – 67, 68
Clonfin Ambush, the – 92
Clover, J. H. P. – 64, 67
Coatelen, Louis – 39
Cobb, John – 58, 88, 91
Cockburn, 'Jock' – 27
Colden Common (Syd Enever's place of birth) – 19, 20
Collector's Car magazine – 17
Collinson, Andrew – 148
Collis 'Topper' – 48
Cologne (City) – see Köln
Colombes (Paris) – 50

Colombo (Sri Lanka) – 85
Complan Mini, the – 217-21
Connolly, Harold – 37
Cook, Arthur Leslie – 20, 24, 37, 39
Cook, Jean (née Kimber) – 33
Cooper, George – 83
Cooper, Miss (Morris Garages staff) – 29
Cooper-Climax – 178
Cornmarket (Oxford) – 25, 26, 27, 29, 44
Cotswolds, The – 16
Cotton, Billy – 70, 161
Courthouse Green (Coventry) – 122, 147, 162, 175
Cousins family, The – 34
Cousins, Henry Edward Cecil (1902-1976) – 9, 16, 24, 29, 33, 34-35, 36, 37, 38, 40, 42, 46, 48, 49, 55, 57, 58, 59, 60, 62, 63, 64, 65, 66, 67, 71, 83, 103, 104, 106, 108, 109, 110, 118, 119, 121, 122, 123, 129, 139, 140, 190, 208, 224
Cousins, Henry Snr, & Fanny – 34
Cousins, Mabel Maude (née Nutt) – 34, 35
Coventry (City) – 77, 110, 119, 120, 122, 123, 142, 147, 153, 156, 164, 168, 181, 186
Coventry Climax engines – 199, 212
Coventry Evening Telegraph - 148
Coventry Technical College – 148
Cowley (Morris Motors) – 12, 14, 15, 29, 31, 32, 35, 41, 44, 45, 46, 84, 103, 104, 108, 124, 127, 132, 153, 160, 168, 182, 185, 186, 191, 195, 208, 213
Cowley (Pressed Steel Ltd.) – 136, 143, 144, 202, 210
Cowley Parish Church, The – 19
Cowley Road (Oxford) – 19, 20
Cox, G. K. – 62, 64, 66, 67
Cox, H. – 109
Cox, Sydney John ('Jim' or 'Jimmy') – 8, 12, 13, 14, 59, 120, 127, 129-130, 146, 150, 164, 165, 167, 177, 178, 216
Cox's of Watford - 159
Crabbe, Colin – 224, 225
Crabtree, S. A. ('Stan') – 66, 67, 68
Cranham Street (Oxford) – 20
Cream Cracker MG trials cars – 53
Crease, William ('Copper') – 27, 29, 31, 46, 48
Cripps, Sir Stafford – 108
Critchall, Mr. – 27
Crook, Jack (aka 'Johnny') – 14, 57, 59, 64, 66, 72, 76, 82, 121, 125, 127, 128-129, 131
Crossley, 'Freddie' - 148
Croydon – 117
Crusader Tank - 104
C-Series engine – see under BMC C-Series
C-Series Engine, The – 13
Cullimore, Mr. (Morris Garages staff) – 29

D

Daimler cars – 27, 30, 78
Daimler V8 engine – 199, 201, 204
Dale, Michael – 18
Daniels, Jack ('William John Daniels') – 34, 35, 42, 44-45, 46, 47, 55, 65, 68, 75, 77, 80, 83, 110, 195
Daniels, Mrs Edith (mother of Jack Daniels) – 44
Daniels, Mrs Mabel (wife of Jack Daniels) – 45
Daniels, Roger - 45
Daniels, Stewart – 42, 78
Daniels, William John Snr. (father of Jack Daniels) – 44
Darwin (Lancashire) – 93
Daunton, Frank – 177
Davies, P.N. – 210, 211
Davis, Sarah (née Muddock; mother of Mrs. Ivy Enever) – 22, 25
Davis, William (W.H. - 'Bill') – 211, 212
Daytona Beach – 59, 85, 86
D-Day - 105
D-Day Landings - 185
De Dion cars – 31
De Dion suspension – 160, 161, 169, 184, 214
De Havilland Aviation – 208
Delage cars – 93
Delaunay-Belleville cars – 30
Denly, Albert ('Bert') – 69, 73, 169, 178
Denver (Colorado) – 178
Deptford (London) – 208
Der Adler (magazine) – 100
Deroy (one-off car by Gerald Palmer) – 84
Design Office at Abingdon – 11, 15
Dessau (Germany) – 89, 95, 96, 97, 98, 99, 100, 101, 102, 111

235

Dessauer Rennstrecke (road) – 96, 100
Detroit (Michigan) - 206
Dewar Trophy, The – 9
Dews, Stanley (S. H.) – 210, 211
Dick Jacobs – 11
Didcot (near Abingdon) - 132
Dienemann, Herr – 97
Digne (France) – 112
Dinky Toys – 58
Directorate of Tank Design (Chobham) – 105
DO1008 (Morris Motors design code for EX173) – 133
DO1009 (Morris Motors design code for EX174) – 133
DO1010 (Morris Motors design code for MG Z Magnette) – 143
DO1035 (Morris Motors design code for 'New MG Midget' concept) – 155
DO1062 (Morris Motors design code for MG MGA) – 136, 137, 141, 142, 144, 180
DO1067 (Riley Pathfinder Twin-Cam concept – EX207) - 158
DO934 (Wolseley 6/80) – 133
DO965 (Morris Motors design code for an MG Coupé) – 116
DO967 (Morris Motors design code for MG Y-Type) – 111
DO968 (Morris Motors design code for MG TD) – 111
DO999 (Riley Pathfinder) - 156
Dobson, Arthur – 70
Dodson C. J. P. (Charles) – 66
Doherty Motor Components (see also Morris Radiators) – 107
Dollar-Sterling exchange rate – 124
Don, Kaye - 68, 82
Dono, George E. – 120, 121, 131, 135, 153
Dorset Regiment, The - 58
Douglas motorcycles – 29, 31
Dover (UK Town and Port) – 89, 90, 111, 117, 146
Downs, D. – 223
Downton Engineering - 203
Drammen Polio Hospital - 171
Draper, Horace (Morris Garages staff) – 29
Driskell, John Anthony – 51
Dubai - 116
Dublin – 64, 148, 166, 216
Dublin Grand Prix (1931) – 64, 65
Duckham Oil Company – 111, 127, 128, 140
Duckham, Jack – 111, 127, 128
Duffield, Mr. (of wartime 'MG Joint Committee') – 108
Dugdale, John – 95, 99
Dulwich (London) – 33
Dundrod race circuit – 147, 149, 150
Dunkirk – 90
Dunlop 'Mac' – 113
Dunlop Ltd. - 9, 88, 97, 160, 167, 169, 177, 179, 188
Dunstable (Bedfordshire) – 125
Duralumin (alloy) – 81

E

E. G. Brown & Co. Ltd of Tottenham ('Brown Brothers') – 87, 89
E.G. Wrigley – 33
Eagle-Clarke, Elspeth – 104
Earl of March, The – see under March
Earls Court – see under Motor Show
East Germany ('GDR' - under post-war division) – 101, 111
East St. Helens Street (Abingdon-on-Thames) – 103, 107, 111
Eastbourne (town in East Sussex) – 86, 104, 134
Ecurie Safety Fast - 190
Edis, Alan – 18, 225
Edmund Road (Oxford; MG factory) – 40, 44, 45, 46, 47, 50, 52
Edwardes, Sir Michael - 221
Egypt – 57
Ehrman, Gus - 178

Eire (Ireland) – 148
Éireann Cup (1931) – 65
Eldridge, Ernest – 57
Enever, Ethel – 6
Enever, Eugenie – 20
Enever, Florence ('Flo') – 6, 21, 104
Enever, Francis Albert Sydney Taylor (née Taylor) – 19
Enever, Frederick Francis – 19
Enever, Ivy Mildred (née Davis) – 12, 22, 24, 25, 107
Enever, Jane – 12, 25
Enever, Lena – 6
Enever, Leonora Grace – 22
Enever, Lorna – 20
Enever, Maud Matilda (née Harper) – 19, 22
Enever, Michael – 25
Enever, Roger – 6, 7, 8, 12, 15, 16, 18, 25, 70, 144, 153, 160, 161, 182, 189, 199, 205, 212, 215-216, 217, 218, 222, 224, 226
Enever, Susan – 12, 15, 25
Enever's Toys – concept models – 191, 194
Enfield motorcycles – 29
Enfield-Allday cars – 76
Engines Branch – see Morris Motors Engines Branch
Ennever, Barry (researcher of 'Ennever' and 'Enever' family history) – 20
ENV gearboxes – 64, 76
Essex (County) – 91
Essex cars – 27, 29
Esso Research Ltd. – 130
Eustace, Albert – 48
Evans family, the – 60
Evans, Sir Arthur – 25
Evening News Trophy - 218
Eves, Edward ('Ted') – 17, 89
Ewing, Norman – 8
EX Register, The – 55-56, 126, 161, 173, 197 (see also Appendix, pp 228-233 inclusive, and individual index entries below)
EX101 – 55
EX107 – 56
EX109 – 56
EX110 – 56
EX114 – 56
EX115 – 55, 56
EX120 Record Breaker – 34, 42, 56, 57, 58, 59, 61, 62, 63, 68, 69, 70
EX127 – 56, 58, 68, 73-74, 75, 77
EX135 Record Breaker – 15, 58, 74, 80, 81, 82, 84, 87, 88, 92, 95, 96, 99, 100, 102 (1939 records), 111 (1946), 117 (1947), 119, 120 (1950), 128 (1951), 130, 133 (1952), 140, 167, 219
EX147 (MG R-Type) – 75, 79
EX148 – 79
EX149 – 79
EX150 ('Queen Mary' large MG saloon) – 79, 80
EX151 – 80
EX152 ('RA Experimental Chassis') – 79
EX154 – 73, 75
EX159 (MG VA) – 83
EX167 (see also 'Bitsy') – 107
EX172 (UMG400 - TD Special for Le Mans) – 130, 131, 132, 146
EX173 ('TD engines for Record Car') – 126, 133
EX174 ('Two-litre converted Wolseley 6/80 engine for Record car') – 126, 133
EX175 (HMO6 – precursor of MGA) – 130, 133, 135, 137, 139, 140, 141, 144, 146, 161, 171, 175, 177
EX177 (MG TF) – 135, 139

EX179 Record Breaker – 15, 130, 140, 142, 143, 145, 148, 150, 160, 161, 162, 163, 164, 165, 166, 167, 168, 169, 176, 177, 188
EX181 ('Roaring Raindrop' record breaker) – 11, 15, 65, 95, 130, 148, 150, 160, 161, 162, 164, 165, 166, 167, 168, 169, 170, 176, 178, 180, 183, 184, 188, 189, 204
EX182 (Le Mans 1995 et seq.) – 14, 130, 136, 144, 146, 147, 160, 172, 175, 179
EX183 'Experimental 1956 Le Mans Car (Tubular Chassis)' - 160

EX186 ('Twin Overhead Camshaft "Le Mans" Type 1956 – MGA Type Chassis') – 143, 156, 160, 161, 179, 214
EX187 – ('Twin overhead-camshaft version of MGA with disc brakes') – 175
EX188 ('New MG Midget' concept) – 155
EX195 Cheaper MGA proposal – 151, 156, 173
EX202 Six-cylinder MG Z-Magnette – 156, 158, 159
EX205 MGA replacement – 180, 183, 191
EX206 Riley Three-Litre concept – 158, 159
EX207 Riley Pathfinder Twin-Cam concept – 158, 159
EX210 MG 2.6-litre 4-seater concept – 158, 159
EX212 MGA Le Mans Coupé for Lund – 180, 205
EX214 MGB (see also ADO23) – 180, 183, 200
EX216 MGA with V4 engine – 200
EX219 Record Breaker ('experimental Austin-Healey Sprite') – 95, 176, 177, 178
EX220 Mini-based sports car concept (New Midget based on Sputnik FWD) – 195, 198
EX221 Austin-Healey Sprite with a 1.6-litre B-Series engine – 197, 198
EX227 MG 1,600cc GT Coupé concept – 190
EX228 'transverse rear engine A-Series car' – 197
EX229 'MG Midget with Hydrolastic – rear wheel drive' – 197, 198
EX231 'Hydrolastic Suspension on ADO41/47' – 197, 198
EX233 Record Breaker concept ('Mini Record Car, with transverse engine') – 188, 189, 191
EX234 – ('Hydrolastic Sports Car Prototype') MG Midget/ MGB replacement prototype – 191, 195, 197, 198, 199, 210, 214
EX234 GT Coupé – 197
EX235 – MGB Le Mans developments - 199
EX237 'GT Prototype to 1965 Le Mans regulations' - 199
EX238 MG Midget with 1,800cc engine – 198
EX239 'competition and fuel injection for the ADO47 Midget' - 201
EX243 Austin- Healey Sprite with heel-board moved rearward - 198
Exeter College (Oxford University) – 23, 48
Eyston, Capt. George Edward Thomas, MC OBE – 12, 15, 56, 57-58, 60, 63, 67, 69, 70, 73, 75, 76, 84, 91, 134, 140, 141, 142, 145, 162, 163, 165, 166, 168, 169, 170, 178, 220
Eyston, Edward Robert Joseph – 57
Eyston, Mrs Olga Mabel (née Eyre) – 58

F

Fairfax, Ernest (pseudonym of Miles Thomas) – 105
Fall, 'Tony' – 217
Farina – see under Pininfarina
Farnham, Joseph ('Joe') – 223
Federal (USA) Road Safety & Emissions legislation – 12, 198, 202, 205, 206, 207, 212, 215, 222
Fell, L. – 64
Fellowship of the Motor Industry – 17
Feltham (Middlesex) – 77, 156
Fennemore, J – 109
Ferguson Formula (Four-wheel-drive) - 95
Ferguson, Harry – 95
Ferguson, Victor – 60
Ferodo (brakes) – 165, 166
Ferrari 250GT Cabriolet (1957) - 171
Ferrari 410 Superfast - 183
Ferrari California (1956) – 171
Ferrari cars – 155, 178, 183, 213
Festival of Britain (1951) – 127
FIAT cars in general - 30
Fiennes, C. W. – 64, 66, 67
Filippini, Corrado – 112
Findlater (member of Morris Garages staff) – 28
Fireball sports car – see ADO30
First World War, The – 20, 21, 22, 28, 33, 34, 58, 75, 76, 85, 88, 91, 102
Flockhart, Ron – 150
Florida - 181
Flüela Pass – 175

Flynn, Errol - 131
Foleshill (Coventry) – 122, 123, 124
Folkestone (Kent) – 117, 125
Ford 109E – 144
Ford Cortina Mark II - 208
Ford GT40 & Mark II - 199
Ford Model 'T' – 30
Ford Motor Company, The (and cars in general) – 16, 30, 95, 140, 156, 207, 208
Ford Mustang (1965) - 209
Ford of Italy - 208
Ford, Henry II - 207
Formula Junior – 144
Foster, D. G. – 51
France – 90, 112, 116, 151
Frankfurt Motor Show (1955) – 147
Frankfurt, Germany – 11, 54, 74, 85, 86, 87, 89, 90, 93, 94, 95, 111
Frankfurt-to-Darmstadt Autobahn – 85, 111
Fred W Dixon Trophy - 216
Freeman, N. W. H. ('Bill') – 88
French Customs ('Douanes Francaises') – 90
Frilford Golf Club (near Abingdon) – 77
Frost, Derek – 149
Frua of Turin (MGA re-bodied) – 155, 157, 171, 183, 190
Fuel Injection- 175
FVRDE ('Fighting Vehicles Research and Development Establishment') – 176, 195

G

Gambrell, H.T. – 109, 116
Gardiner, Jack (MG personnel manager) – 46, 48, 116
Gardner Record Car (see also EX135) – 17, 84, 86, 87, 88, 94, 103, 110, 111, 125, 126, 133, 134, 140, 167, 183, 219
Gardner, Freddie (Morris Garages staff) – 29
Gardner, Lieutenant-Colonel Alfred Thomas Goldie, OBE MC ('Goldie') – 11, 12, 15, 17, 40, 58, 59, 62, 64, 65, 66, 67, 70, 71, 79, 83, 84, 85-86, 87, 89, 91, 92, 93, 94, 95, 96, 97, 99, 100, 101, 102, 104, 110, 111, 112, 113, 117, 118, 120, 121, 125, 126, 127, 128, 130, 133, 134, 140, 161, 167, 168, 183, 219
Gardner, Mary Eleanor King (née Boalt) – 86
Gardner, Rosalind – 86, 104, 119
Gardner, Una (née Eagle-Clarke) – 86, 104, 119, 134
Gaydon – see British Motor Museum
Gaydon (Technical Centre) – 133, 222
General Motors – 16, 78, 144, 173, 206
General Service Administration (USA) - 207
Geneva Salon (Motor Show) – 12, 117, 171, 183
German Democratic Republic – see East Germany
Germany (and Germans) – 73, 74, 75, 85, 86, 87, 89, 95, 99, 101, 103, 105, 112, 147, 202, 203, 219
Gibson, George – 45, 56
Gibson, R. – 64
Gillow, Victor – 148
Glasso Paint – 13
Gloster Aircraft Company – 106
Gloucester (City) – 106
Gloucester (Massachusetts) – 20
Gloucester Green (Oxford) – 21
Gloucester Trial – 60
Goffin, Jack – 149, 168
Golden Arrow record breaker – 68
Goldener Beutel ('Golden Bag') – Hotel in Germany - 96
Goldie (book by John Mayhead) – 86
Grasse (France) – 112
Great War – see First World War
Great Western Railway (GWR) – 77
Greece - 116
Green, Malcolm – 52
Greenborough, L. - 220
Gregory, Kenneth A. (1926-2013) – 165, 168
Grenoble (France) – 112
Griffin, Charles – 17, 197, 210, 211, 213, 214, 220, 222
Grimes, Jack - 83
Grisewood, Freddie – 32
Grosvenor Square (London) - 212

INDEX

Guillaume, Madame – 223
Gunderson, Joe & Cathy - 161
GWK Cars - 39
GWR (Great Western Railway) - 143
Győr (Hungary) – 73, 89

H
Haddock, C – 109
Haig, 'Tommy' – 12, 70, 164, 165, 175, 185, 215
Hailwood, S. W. B. (Stanley) – 66, 67, 72
Hall Scott Motor Company – 88
Hall, Edward Ramsden ('Eddie': 1900-1982) – 66, 67, 71, 72, 128, 129, 220
Hall, Leslie ('Les') (Chief Body Engineer, Morris Motors, Cowley) – 155, 185, 186
Hallow (Worcestershire) – 26
Hambro Ltd. – 127
Hamilton, George – 48
Hamilton, H. C. ('Hammy') – 64, 66
Hampshire – 19
Hanks, Reginald Francis ('Reggie') – 108, 117, 119, 121, 123, 124, 131, 135, 138, 139
Harding, J. (J. Harding & Son, later Harding & Moore, of Oxford) - 191
Harper, Maud Matilda – see Enever, Maud
Harriman, Sir George – 54, 135, 155, 173, 186, 192, 200, 209
Harris, H. - 158
Harrison, Donald – 121, 122, 123, 132
Harrow-on-the-Hill - 157
Harry Ferguson Research Ltd. – 95
Harwell Laboratories - 132
Hastings, Harold – 9
Hatchback (on MGB GT) – 192
Hawker Hurricane (fighter plane) – 43
Hay, Captain Max – 56, 57
Haynes, Roy Douglas (1924-2020) – 105, 207-209, 210, 211
Hayter, Don (1926-2020) – 12, 13, 16, 114, 116, 155, 156, 157, 180, 182, 183, 184, 185, 191, 205, 214, 215, 221, 224, 226
Headington (Oxford) - 26
Healey business and family – 153, 154, 180, 181, 201, 202, 207
Healey Hundred – see Austin-Healey 100/4
Healey Race Team – 199, 212, 217
Healey Rolls – see ADO24
Healey Sprite Coupé – 217
Healey SR37 – 199, 212
Healey XR37 - 215
Healey, Donald Mitchell (1898-1988) – 138, 139, 149, 154, 157, 173, 174, 197, 202
Healey, Geoffrey – 15, 16, 138, 141, 153, 157, 158, 173, 174, 180, 197, 201, 202, 224
Healeys – the Specials, book - 17, 197
Heaton Norris (town in Lancashire) – 33
Hebeler, R. – 64
Hedges, Andrew – 199, 217
Heenan & Froude machine – 14
Hellfire Caves (West Wycombe) – 158, 159
Hemmings, Fred – 48
Hendon (Middlesex) – 88
Hendy, G. – 64
Herring, 'Harry' – 155, 160, 167, 171, 183, 188, 189, 191
Hertfordshire – 41
Hertzog von Anhalt - 101
Herzogliches Hoftheater - 100
Higgin, D. ('Dan') – 64, 65, 67
High Road magazine - 182
High Street (Oxford) – 32
Highgate School – 41
Highway Safety Act (USA, 1966) - 206
Hill, Phil – 11, 165, 166, 168, 177, 178, 179
Hillier, 'Bunny' – 160, 164, 177
Hillman Imp – 142, 143
Hispano-Suiza cars – 30, 39
Hitler, Adolf – 18, 27, 80, 89
Hitler's Black Book ('Sonderfahndungsliste G.B.') – 18
HMO6 – see EX175

Hobbs, W. - 121, 123
Hodkinson, Tim - 200
Holbrook, S. V. – 64
Holliday, Michael - 198
Holmes, George – 175
Home Guard, The - 104
Honda Motor Co. – 143
Hong Kong – 129
Hopkirk, Paddy – 189
Horch factory – 101
Hornblower, Sidney - 113
Horndon, Essex – 23
Horsfall, Ewart (1892-1974) – 32
Horton, R. T. ('Ronnie') – 62, 64, 65, 66, 67, 71, 79, 84, 85
Hotchkiss engine – 32
Hotel Vittoria (Milan, Italy) - 112
Hounslow, Alec Leslie – 6, 7, 12, 16, 35, 48, 61, 64, 65, 67, 69, 70, 72, 110, 127, 130, 131, 141, 142, 145, 146, 148, 150, 151, 164, 167, 168, 170, 172, 175, 176, 177, 178, 180, 193, 220
Hounslow, Mrs Margaret - 70
Howard Street (Oxford) – 20
Howe, Lord – 112
Howitt, Captain Cyril – 21, 22
Howlett, John – 106
Hubbards of Basingstoke – 56
Hudson cars – 27, 29
Hughes, Paul - 215
Humber Car Company, The – 17, 29, 30, 137
Humbug ('Magic Magnette' - EX135 race and record breaker) – 58, 80
Humphries, Cliff – 13
Hungary – 73, 89
Hupmobile cars – 30
Huron Auto Racing Developments 'Huron 4A' - 217
Huron Lola T212 – 217
Hutcheson, Alan Stuart – 189
Hydrolastic Suspension - 197

I
ICI (Imperial Chemical Industries) – 13
Iffley (Oxford) – 65
Iley, Geoffrey – 35, 96, 97, 132, 151, 158, 165, 167, 168, 173, 174
Independent Suspension – 184, 185
India – 57
Indian motorcycles – 29
Inskip J.S. (New York MG) – 16, 166, 168, 178
Institute of Automobile Engineers, The – 10
Inston, Mike - 172
IRA (Irish Republican Army) – 92
Ireland, 'Les' - 180
Irish Grand Prix (RIAC Irish Grand Prix - see also under Dublin, Saorstát and Éireann Cups) – 68, 70, 84, 148
Iserante, Herr (Junkers) – 99, 101
Isle of Man – 82
Issigonis, Sir Alec – 9, 17, 35, 45, 83, 132, 139, 141, 155, 189, 191, 194, 195, 201, 202, 208, 209, 210, 226
Italy – 89, 111, 112, 177, 178, 197, 200, 208

J
J Stone & Co. Ltd. – 208
J. S. Inskip – see Inskip
J. Thompson Pressings – see under Thompson
Jabekke Highway (Belgium) – 112, 113, 117, 126, 134
Jackson, Barrie - 218
Jackson, Hester - 85
Jackson, R. R. ('Robin') – 62, 64, 65, 66, 67, 82, 86, 87
Jackson, Reg ('Jacko') – 6, 7, 10, 12, 14, 15, 16, 39-41, 42, 46, 50, 57, 58, 59, 61, 63, 64, 68, 69, 70, 71, 72, 73, 74, 75, 80, 81, 82, 84, 85, 86, 90, 91, 92, 93, 94, 95, 96, 97, 98, 101, 102, 103, 109, 111, 112, 113, 116, 117, 118, 119, 120, 121, 122, 125, 127, 128, 131, 134, 140, 141, 142, 148, 190, 208, 216, 218, 220
Jacobs Midgets – 143, 203, 204, 205
Jacobs, ('Dick') – 124, 146, 148, 203, 205
Jaguar Cars, Inc. (USA) – 18
Jaguar E-Type – 12, 201, 207, 209

Jaguar in general – 199, 201, 202, 203, 209, 210, 212
Jaguar Mark II – 158
Jaguar XK Engine – 118, 125, 159, 201
Jaguar XK120 – 93, 130, 139, 151, 182
Jam Mound, The (Oxford) – 25
Jameson, A. M. C. – 64
Japan - 143
Jaray patents – 87
Jarvis and Sons, Wimbledon – 57, 70
JCB (J. C. Bamford) - 218
Jeffress, J. R. – 67
Jenkins, David Abbott ('Ab') – 127, 128, 129
Jenkins, Marvin – 127
Jennings, Tony – 149
Jensen F-Type - 223
Jensen G-Type – 222, 224
Jensen Interceptor – 17, 222, 223
Jensen Motors – 173, 190, 202, 222, 223, 224, 225
Jensen-Healey - 222
John Thompson Pressings Ltd. – 153, 173
Johnson, (US) President Lyndon B. – 206
Johnson, 'Bubbly' – 32
Johnson, Neale – 223
Jones, Desmond Griffith ('Des') (1919-2006) – 172, 185-186, 202
Joseph Lucas Limited – 28
Joukowski profiles - 164
Jowett cars – 84, 124
Junkers aircraft factory (Dessau) – 96, 99, 101
Junkers JU88 ('Schnellbomber') – 99, 100
Junkers, Hugo – 96

K
K3023 – MG Magnette - 87
Kauhsen, Willy - 203
Keble College (Oxford University) - 224
Kecskemét (Hungary) - 89
Keen, Alfred E. – 121, 123
Kehoe, W. – 65
Keller AG (Swiss MG agents) – 117, 151, 175
Keller, Heinz - 175
Kelly's Directory, The – 22
Kemp, A. ('Alfie') – 68
Kennington, Oxford – 6, 40, 41
Kenpas Highway (road in Coventry) – 147
Kesterton, Leslie Gilbert ('Kes') – 12, 82, 90, 91-93, 94, 95, 100, 101, 110, 112, 113, 121
Kevill-Davis & March Ltd. (see also under March) – 63, 64
Kidlington (Oxford) – 155, 173, 186
Kimber, Betty – 33
Kimber, Cecil ('Kim') (1888-1945) – 9, 11, 28, 29, 32-33, 34, 35, 36, 37, 38, 40, 41, 42, 44, 45, 49, 50, 51, 53, 54, 55, 58, 59, 62, 63, 68, 71, 72, 73, 75, 81, 82, 83, 84, 85, 87, 89, 91, 92, 101, 103, 104, 106, 111, 118, 131, 140, 147, 179, 220, 221, 225
Kimber, Evelyn Irene ('Renee') Phillips (née Hunt) – 33, 37, 42
Kimber, Jean – see Cook
Kimber, Muriel Lillies (Gillie) (née Dewar) – 33
Kimpsey ('Wally') – 130
Kindell, J. ('Freddie') – 59, 64
King, Charles Spencer ('Spen') (1925-2010) – 214, 215
King, Frank – 48
King, George – 48
King's Cross rail station – 33
King's Head (PH in Harrow) - 157
King's Norton – 77
Kingston-Pagpuize - 159
Kinsey, 'Wally' – 131
Knight Sleeve Valve – 38
Knudson, Dick – 78, 87, 140, 142, 167
Koblenz (Germany) – 95
Kohlrausch, Robert ('Bobby' 1904-1953) – 58, 73, 74, 75, 77, 101, 111, 112
Köln (Cologne) – 85, 91
Kristensen, Fred - 171

L
Labor Day weekend (1966) - 206
Lagonda cars – 95, 96, 99
Lamborghini cars - 213
Lambourne, (Mrs) Pan 'Pam' – 13
Lambourne, Karen - 220
Lambourne, Leslie ('Les') (1931-2010) – 13, 190, 220-221
Lancashire – 33, 57, 93
Lancaster (bomber aircraft) – see AVRO
Lancaster (City in Lancashire) – 71
Lancia Lambda – 39
Lands End Trial, The – 36
Langsteiner, Otto – 93
Lansing-Bagnall – 208
Las Vegas - 168
Law, C. J. - 183
Law, Don – 149
Law, John (Engines Branch) – 170
Lawrence, Ernest – 22
Lay, 'Johnny' – 134
Lay, P. – 109
Laystall Engineering – 125
Lazenby, George - 116
LC10 (Austin Maestro) -186
Le Mans 24-Hours Race, The – 11, 14, 50, 51, 58, 76, 130, 131, 146, 148, 149, 160, 164, 172, 179, 180, 189, 190, 191, 199, 203, 205, 212, 217
Leavens, 'Ed' – 177, 178
Leeds (city) - 147
Leica camera – 99
Lempens, Thijs – 31
Levegh, Pierre - 146
Levis (motorcycles) – 29
Lewis, Jack – 83, 129
Leyland Eight car – 88
Leyland Motors (and Corporation) – 88, 203, 209
Light Car Club, The – 70
Lightweight Midget & MGC – 203, 204, 205, 216
Lincolnshire – 39
Little Clarendon Street (Oxford) – 28
Little, 'Jock' – 65, 66, 67
Littlemore (Oxfordshire) – 19, 191
Liverpool – 65
Llanelli (Wales) – 122, 221
Lloyd, 'Danny' – 215
Lockett, 'Johnny' – 163
Lodge (spark plugs) – 165, 166, 168
London Airport – 178
London in general – 39, 56, 59, 87, 91, 105, 114, 157, 212, 216
London, City of - 23
London, East End of – 23
Long Wittenham – 19
Longbridge – 54, 133, 138, 143, 147, 149, 154, 157, 160, 161, 168, 172, 173, 174, 175, 180, 185, 186, 192, 195, 196, 197, 198, 200, 201, 208, 210, 213, 214, 215, 222
Longbridge Body Experimental Shop – 137
Longshaw, 'Ernie' – 175
Longwall Street and garage premises (Oxford) – 27, 29, 31, 37, 47
Lord Nuffield – see under Nuffield
Lord Stokes – see under Stokes
Lord, Leonard P. (later Sir Leonard Lord; Lord Lambury) – 33, 43, 54, 81, 118, 119, 120, 121, 132, 135, 136, 138, 139, 141, 144, 149, 154, 155, 173, 219
Los Angeles – 140, 206
Lotus Elan – 161
Lotus sports car in general - 213
Lowe, Derek – 149
Lowndes, Jack – 34, 37, 46, 48, 109
Lowry, Russell – 121
Lucas – see also Joseph Lucas Ltd.
Lucas fuel injection – 217, 218
Lucas, Oliver – 28
Luftwaffe - 100
Lund, Edward Walter Kingstone 'Ted' (1913-1978) – 11, 124, 160, 161, 179
Lurani, Giovanni Lurani Cernuschi, VIII Count of

Calvenzano ('Johnny' Lurani) – 74, 99, 101, 111, 112, 113, 117, 126
Luther Street (Oxford) – 20
Lyle, T.B. – 116
Lynx Engineering - 224
Lyons, (Sir) William – 117, 209
Lytham St. Annes – 95

M

Mackenzie, Sir Compton (1883-1972) – 32
Macon – 112
Magdalen College (Oxford University) – 32
Magic Magnette, the (see also EX135 & Humbug) – 80, 90
Magic Midget, the (see also EX127) – 56, 68, 73, 75, 77
Magic MPH (book by Capt. Goldie Gardner) – 11, 62, 87, 90, 100, 101, 111, 113, 120
Maher, Edward Joseph ('Eddie') (1910-1976) – 15, 146, 147, 148-149, 150, 162, 163, 168, 171, 175, 176, 200
Maida Vale (London) – 91, 92
Maidenhead (Berkshire) – 39, 143, 156
Maintaining the Breed (book by John Thornley) – 73, 77, 86, 98, 100, 125, 133
Mainz (Germany) – 91
Mainzer Aktien-bier – 91
Malaya - 129
Malta – 116
Manchester (City) – 179
Manchester Evening News - 123
Manchester Motor Club, the – 179
Manchester School of Technology – 93
Manchester, Victoria University of – 88
Manley & Charles (consultancy) – 43
Mannin Beg race (Isle of Man) – 82
Marathon de la Route race – 205, 216
Marcel Wave (hairstyle) – 22
March, Frederick, 9th Duke of Richmond, Lennox and Aubigny (Earl of March) – 25, 62, 63, 64, 65, 66, 67, 68
Marcham Road (between Abingdon and Marcham) – 72, 159
Marchant, L. - 109
Marney 'Nobby' – 63, 74
Marshalls Flying School - 155
Martin engines - 144
Martin, Charles ('Charlie') – 47, 109
Martin, Keith – 42
Martin, Ted – 144, 150, 200
Martyr's Memorial, The (Oxford) - 32
Maserati cars – 75, 155
Mason, George – 139
Massachusetts - 97
Matchless (motorcycles) – 29
Mathews, Wilfrid – 36
Matthews, Keith – 139
Mayhead, John – 86
Maynard, R - 109
Mays, Raymond - 32
McComb, Wilson (author) – 13, 36, 50, 67, 75, 83, 104, 130, 146, 190
McDonald ('Dunlop Mac') – 88
McEoin, Sean (IRA) – 92
McLellan, John (author) – 34, 35, 122
McMullan, C. J. – 65
Mercedes-Benz cars – 32, 74, 89, 96, 146
Mercedes-Benz W125 – 224, 225
Merton College (Oxford University) – 27
MG – Syd Enever's 3.3-litre engine concept – 201, 205
MG & Riley – combined grouping – 54, 116, 120, 122, 123, 124, 125, 126, 136, 143, 156
MG 1¼-Litre Saloon (prototype of later Y-Type) – 108
MG 1100 (ADO16G) – 187, 195, 196
MG 14/40 'Mark IV' – 44, 46, 49
MG 18/100 'Mark III' 'Tigresse' – 49, 51, 53, 55, 80
MG 18/80 Mark I ('MG Six') – 34, 40, 49, 51, 52, 55
MG 18/80 Mark II – 49, 50, 51, 52, 53, 55

MG Car Club, The – 15, 42, 55, 59, 104, 148, 160, 173, 179, 192
MG Car Company Ltd. – 10, 17, 29, 31, 32, 33, 36, 43, 49, 52, 53, 71, 73, 80, 81, 87, 118, 122, 124, 140, 194, 205, 219
MG Car Division (1967) - 210
MG C-Type Midget Mark II (1930s) – 14, 40, 41, 42, 46, 56, 59, 60, 61, 62, 63, 64, 66, 67, 70, 71, 85
MG Development Department (Abingdon) – 47, 70, 105, 129, 130, 160, 168, 177, 180, 191, 197, 202, 205
MG Drawing Office at Abingdon (from 1954) – 141, 143, 144, 153, 167, 172, 173, 181, 185, 190, 191, 204, 222
MG Drawing Office at Cowley – 84, 108, 110, 124, 131, 139, 140, 143, 172, 180
MG D-Type Midget – 50, 69, 70, 71
MG EX Numbers – see under 'EX'
MG Experimental Department/ Shop, The – 34, 46, 49, 68, 71, 76, 83, 87, 89, 107, 108, 110, 128, 205, 219
MG Factory, The (Marcham Road, Abingdon) – 6, 12, 14, 16, 18, 29, 32, 34, 35, 38, 40, 42, 43, 45, 46, 47, 51, 52, 54, 55, 57, 60, 63, 69, 81, 82, 83, 84, 87, 103, 104, 105, 106, 107, 108, 110, 111, 116, 119, 121, 122, 123, 126, 131, 132, 139, 140, 142, 144, 151, 152, 153, 157, 160, 167, 172, 173, 178, 187, 194, 198, 203, 207, 208, 212, 213, 215, 222, 224, 225
MG F-Type Magna – 70, 71
MG J1 Midget – 71
MG J2 Midget – 42, 71, 75
MG J3 Midget – 71
MG J4 Midget – 71, 73, 75
MG J-Type Midgets – 71, 75
MG K3 Magnette (and engine) – 42, 50, 58, 71, 72, 74, 76, 79, 120, 125, 130
MG KN Magnette – 35
MG K-Type Magnettes – 71
MG Magazine – 16, 65, 76
MG Magna – Palmer Midget (1954) – 131, 135, 142
MG Magna (in general) – 50, 51, 55, 70
MG Magnette (in general) – 51, 55, 84, 85, 87, 209
MG Magnette Mark III (ADO9G) – 186
MG Magnette Mark IV (ADO38G) - 187

MG MGA ('MG Series MGA') – 11, 12, 14, 16, 18, 40, 45, 130, 132, 137, 139, 141, 143, 144, 145, 146, 147, 149, 151, 152, 153, 155, 156, 157, 160, 164, 171, 172, 173, 175, 176, 178, 180, 183, 186, 187, 188, 213, 219, 225
MG MGA 1600 (1,588cc) – 152
MG MGA 1600 Deluxe – 176
MG MGA 1600 Mark II (1,622cc) – 152, 181
MG MGA Cabriolet – 151
MG MGA Coupé – 137, 143, 145, 151, 152, 155, 179, 182, 190, 191, 216
MG MGA facelift & replacement ideas – 151, 154, 214
MG MGA Hardtop – 151
MG MGA Twin Cam (and engine) – 11, 18, 131, 142, 144, 148, 149, 151, 152, 155, 159, 162, 168, 169, 170, 174, 175, 176, 179, 180, 191, 195, 200, 203
MG MGB – 10, 11, 13, 14, 16, 137, 143, 145, 146, 157, 171, 173, 176, 181, 182, 183, 184, 185, 186, 187, 188, 189, 190, 194, 197, 199, 202, 207, 208, 211, 213, 215, 219
MG MGB GT – 190, 191, 192, 193, 198, 202, 205, 207, 213, 214, 219, 220
MG MGB GT V8 – 70, 143, 215, 221, 222, 224
MG MGB Mark II - 207
MG MGC (and GT) – 143, 197, 199, 203, 205, 207, 208, 211, 212, 213
MG MGC GTS – 13, 137, 203, 204, 205, 216, 217
MG Midget (ADO47 -1962 onwards) – 12, 47, 137, 180-181, 186, 187, 191, 199, 203, 204, 205, 207, 208, 213, 214, 216, 217, 222
MG Midget '8/45' Double-Twelve Replicas - 52
MG Midgets in general – 84, 108, 117, 142, 147, 155, 204
MG Minor (concept) – 119, 124
MG Monoposto Magnette (never built) – 76, 79
MG Monoposto Midget (MG R-Type) – 76

MG M-Type Coupé - 53
MG M-Type Midget – 40, 48, 49, 50, 51, 52, 55, 56, 57, 64, 70, 154
MG Octagon, use of – 36, 52, 84
MG Old Number One – 32, 34, 35-36, 47, 75
MG P-Type Midget – 73, 75, 78
MG Q-Type Midget – 42, 73, 75, 76, 77
MG RA & RB Types (speculative names) – 79
MG Radiator Grille, the – 46, 52
MG R-Type Midget – 15, 42, 47, 73, 75, 76, 77, 78, 79, 80, 81, 83, 184
MG SA – 43
MG Six – 49, 52, 70
MG sports cars in general – 125, 203, 213
MG S-Type Magnette (speculative name) – 76, 79
MG Super Sports Morris – 36
MG TA Midget – 43, 45, 80, 83
MG TB Midget – 107, 110, 118
MG TC Midget – 11, 35, 108, 110, 118, 119, 120, 124, 129, 130, 190, 191
MG TC Tuning Manual, The – 14
MG TD Midget – 11, 12, 18, 35, 95, 108, 117, 120, 124, 125, 126, 128, 130, 131, 132, 136, 138, 139, 143
MG TF 1500 - 140
MG TF Midget – 45, 95, 135, 138, 139, 140, 145, 172, 180
MG Trials Cars – 53
MG T-Series Midgets in general – 80, 83, 110, 146, 182
MG UA Midget (MGA) – 139
MG VA 1½ Litre – 43, 83, 84
MG version of Morris Minor – 110
MG WA (2.6-litre) – 83, 104, 111
MG Y Type – 35, 95, 108, 110, 117, 119, 120, 121, 124, 126
MG YT (Tourer) – 120, 132
MG Z Magnette – 12, 124, 131, 137, 139, 155, 158, 175, 180, 185
MG Z Magnette Six-Cylinder – 156, 158, 200
MGA Twin Cam Group – 150, 167
MGB – name for MGA Twin Cam – 151, 175, 176
Midgeley, E.L. – 113
Midland Sheet Metal Ltd. – 140, 145, 160, 164, 165, 180
Milan, Italy – 112
Miles, Ken – 140, 163, 165, 166
Mille Miglia (road race) – 51, 58, 72, 74, 75, 93
Miller race car – 57
Milne, John - 203
Mini – see BMC Mini
Ministry of Supply (wartime) – 105
MIRA (Motor Industry Research Association) – 149, 174, 215
Mister MG (book by Peter Thornley) – 7, 10
Mitchell, Terence Henry ('Terry') (1921-2003) – 8, 15, 16, 139, 140, 142-143, 144, 155, 160, 161, 164, 165, 167, 168, 172, 184, 195, 214, 222, 225, 226
Mitchell, Theresa – 16
Modern Wonder magazine (September 1938) – 89
Monarch Airways – 127, 128
Monte Carlo (Monaco) – 111, 112
Monte Carlo Rally – 50, 93
Montgomery, F.M. – 64
Montgomery, Field-Marshall ('Monty') – 105
Montlhéry (France) – 34, 41, 57, 58, 59, 60, 63, 69, 73, 93, 151
Montlhéry Midgets (see also MG C-Type) – 62, 64
Monza race circuit (Italy) – 177, 178, 216
More Healeys (book) – 16, 157
Morlands Brewery (Abingdon-on-Thames) – 45
Mormon Meteor – see Ab Jenkins
Morris 10/4 engine – 80
Morris 1100 (ADO16) – 185
Morris 1800 (ADO17) – 198
Morris 2½ Litre six-cylinder engine - 34
Morris cars in general – 30, 110, 118, 119, 120
Morris Commercial Cars Ltd. – 18, 54, 80, 90, 106, 122, 123, 216
Morris Cowley ('Bullnose Morris') – 29, 31, 32, 39
Morris Cowley 'Chummy' – 36, 37

Morris Garages 'Supersports' – 32
Morris Garages Specials 'MG' sports cars – 29, 32, 33, 34, 47, 52
Morris Garages, The – 6, 7, 22, 26, 27, 28, 29, 30, 31, 33, 34, 36, 38, 39, 44, 46, 47, 70, 136, 219, 220, 225
Morris Industries Ltd. - 80
Morris Isis (1955) – 158
Morris Marina (ADO28) – 208, 209, 213
Morris Midget - 49
Morris Mini Minor (see also ADO15 and Mini) – 9
Morris Minor (1928 et seq.) – 40, 49, 50, 52, 55, 75
Morris Minor (from 1948) – 9, 44, 45, 78, 110, 119, 124, 142, 156, 168, 185, 190, 191
Morris Minor 1000 – 155, 166, 173, 177
Morris Minor Tourer (convertible) - 185
Morris Minor Traveller – 145, 185
Morris Mosquito (prototype for post-war Minor) – 78, 118
Morris Motors Ltd. (Cowley, including 'Cars Branch' and Drawing Offices) – 12, 29, 32, 33, 41, 42, 43, 44, 45, 46, 73, 80, 81, 82, 83, 84, 108, 117, 121, 122, 124, 132, 142, 143, 146, 154, 156, 172, 173, 182, 185, 190
Morris Motors Ltd. Board – 108, 117, 121, 123, 126, 127, 130, 132, 135, 139, 144, 152
Morris Motors Ltd. Bodies Branch (Quinton Road, Coventry) – 17, 110, 116, 120, 123, 124, 130, 136, 137, 144, 152, 172, 180, 192, 222
Morris Motors Ltd. Engines Branch – 13, 15, 123, 124, 146, 147, 149, 150, 161, 168, 170, 217
Morris Motors Ltd. Machining Branch – 123
Morris Motors Ltd. Radiators Branch – 35, 107, 122, 156
Morris Owner magazine – 36
Morris Oxford ('MO'; 1948 onwards) – 156, 185
Morris Oxford Taxicabs – 122, 145
Morris Radiators – see Morris Motors Radiators Branch
Morris Ten (1938) – 43
Morris, George – 109
Morris, George – 37, 46, 47, 48
Morris, Sir William Richard, Baronet – 73
Morris, William Richard (see also Sir William Morris and Lord Nuffield) – 26, 27, 28, 32, 33, 42, 56, 73, 107, 191
Morris-Cowley Sports ('Old Number One') – 36
Moscow – 106
MOSS California - 225
Moss, 'Pat' – 147
Moss, Sir Stirling – 147, 165, 166, 167, 168, 169, 177, 178, 179, 213
Motor magazine (also *The Motor*) – 9, 49, 54, 60, 90, 120, 183, 193, 203, 214, 221
Motor Show (1928) – 40, 49
Motor Show (1935) – 80, 81
Motor Show (1951, Earls Court) – 138
Motor Show (1953, Earls Court) – 139
Motor Show (1967, Earls Court) – 203, 207, 208
Motor Sport magazine – 49, 51-53, 54, 57, 61, 66, 67, 92, 167, 168, 169
Motor Trend magazine - 128
Motor Trophy - 190
Motor Vehicle Safety Act (USA, 1966) – 206
Motoring (Nuffield magazine) – 121
Mott, Sue – 35
Moufflet, Claude – 25
Moufflet, Nicholas – 25
Moufflet, Tamsin Genillier – 25
Muddock, Sarah – see Davis, Sarah
Muddock, Will – 22
Mullens, H. C. R. – 121, 123
Mulliners (coachbuilders) – 81
Mulsanne Straight (Le Mans) – 180, 217

N

Nader, Ralph - 206
Napier-Railton car – 88
Nash, R. G. J. – 66
Nash, Sam (MG factory road tester) – 47
Nash-Kelvinator – 139
National Benzole (petrol) – 29

INDEX

National Highway Safety Bureau (USA) - 206
National Highway Traffic Safety Administration (USA) – 206
National Traffic and Motor Vehicle Safety Act (USA, 1966) - 206
Nazi Party – 96, 99
Neal, Peter – 8, 15, 137, 142, 143, 150, 159, 164, 171, 172-173, 176, 177, 183, 184, 185, 186, 190, 200, 219
Neptune amphibious tank – 129
Neville, Robert ('Bob') – 200, 215, 216
New College (Oxford University) - 27
New Marston (Oxford) – 44
New Road (Oxford) – 29
New South Wales (Australia) - 93
New York – 16, 20, 76, 88, 125, 126, 134, 178, 181, 206
New York Motor Show – 125, 181, 221
Newbold, Harry – 27
Newcastle (city) – 147
Newhaven (Sussex) - 93
Newport, Mr. (Morris Garages staff) – 29
Nibbio record car – 101
North & Co. Ltd. – 22
North Africa - 185
North America (and market) – 110, 132, 138, 154, 161, 190, 206, 210, 213
Northampton - 37, 39
Norton – 43
Norway – 171
NSKK ('National Socialist Motor Corps') – 96, 98
Nuffield – philanthropy – 26
Nuffield engine range - 161
Nuffield Exports Limited – 116, 127
Nuffield Factories Reorganisation Scheme (1948) – 122
Nuffield Mechanizations (Cowley) – 108
Nuffield Metal Products – 120, 122, 131, 135, 153
Nuffield News Exchange magazine – 112, 113, 116, 118, 134
Nuffield Organisation, The – 13, 17, 18, 28, 33, 35, 45, 55, 103, 105, 106, 110, 113, 117, 118, 119, 120, 121, 122, 123, 124, 134, 140, 142, 168, 180, 181, 185, 187, 195, 210, 213, 216
Nuffield Pressings - 121
Nuffield Teamwork magazine – 18, 47, 128, 129, 162
Nuffield Tractors – 122
Nuffield, Lady – 33
Nuffield, Lord (see also Morris, William) – 32, 33, 35, 36, 50, 54, 55, 56, 80, 81, 82, 84, 85, 86, 87, 89, 91, 95, 97, 101, 107, 108, 111, 119, 120, 125, 127, 131, 134, 148
Nuneaton (Warwickshire) – 140, 145, 160, 165, 180
Nürburgring – 203, 216
Nuvolari, Tazio – 70, 72
Nye, Doug – 17, 136, 144, 145

O

O'Neill, James Edward ('Jim') (1922-2015) – 8, 12, 15, 16, 35, 110, 111, 117, 131, 135, 139, 142-144, 151, 155, 156, 160, 172, 173, 181, 182, 183, 184, 185, 190, 191, 195, 205, 207, 208, 213, 222
Oak, A. Victor ('Vic') – 83, 84, 108, 110, 121, 123, 124, 131, 141
Oates, 'Jim' – 195, 214
Octagon – see MG Octagon
Old Faithful (MGB, GRX407D) – 216
Old Number One – see MG Old Number One
Old Speckled Hen (car) – 45
Olley, Maurice – 78
ONS ('Oberste Nationale Sportbehörde' – German motorsports body) – 92, 96, 98, 101
Opel cars – 31
Operation Overlord (1944) - 105
Operation Plunder - 105
Organ, H. V. – 116
Osberton Radiators (see also Morris Motors Radiators) – 35, 107
Osberton Road (Oxford) - 107
Osbourne, Kenneth - 213
Osman, David - 183
Osman, David - 213
Ostend (Belgium) - 112

Our Lady's School, Abingdon - 15
Owen Organisation, The – 95
Owens, Peter - 177
Oxford (City of) – 10, 17, 22, 23, 25, 26, 37, 38, 40, 43, 44, 45, 49, 65, 134, 146, 153, 158, 185, 191, 215, 219
Oxford Automobile & Cycle Agency – 29
Oxford Castle – 21, 22
Oxford Central School - 44
Oxford College of Technology – 133, 155, 221
Oxford Crown Court – 27
Oxford Mail, The – 193-194, 207, 219, 225
Oxford Rail Station, The – 29, 35
Oxford Reference Library, The – 10, 164
Oxford Replanned (book) – 23
Oxford Technical School – 25, 185
Oxford Theatre, The – 20
Oxford Times, The - 36
Oxford Tram Lines – 45
Oxford, University of – 23, 156, 224

P

Pall Mall (London) – 56, 57
Palmer, Gerald – 12, 45, 83, 84, 120, 121, 124, 125, 131, 135, 137, 138, 139, 142, 143, 146, 147, 149, 150, 153, 155, 156, 158, 175
Palmes, J. A. ('Jimmy') – 55, 56, 57, 59, 67
Panhard Rod (suspension) - 184
Paradise Square (Oxford) – 20, 21, 22, 23, 25
Paradise, Filmer Melvin - 208
Paris (City of) – 25, 50
Paris Salon (motorshow) 1927 – 50, 183
Parker, Harold (H. D.) – 62, 64, 65, 67
Parry-Thomas, J. G. – 69, 88
Paterson, Oscar - 71
Pavlova Leather Company, The (MG Works) – 45, 47, 52, 106
Peco-Shorrock Developments Ltd. - 95
Pembroke College (Oxford University) - 156
Pendine (beach in South Wales) – 60, 69
Penny, 'Tom' - 222
Perch, The (PH in Oxford) – 6, 70
Perranporth (Cornwall) - 138
Perrett, John B. - 88
Phillips, George E. – 11, 109, 124, 130, 131, 132, 135
Phillips, Gordon – 59
Phillips, W. D. – 67
Phoenix Park (Dublin) – 64, 148, 166, 217
Pierpoint, Roy – 217
Pike, John – 177
Pininfarina (also 'Farina') – 171, 185, 191, 192, 193, 195, 196, 198
Pininfarina, Sergio – 9, 192, 193
Poliomyelitis ('Polio') – 148, 171
Pomeroy, Laurence - 92
Poole, Alec – 18, 212, 216, 216, 217, 218
Poole, William – 216
Porsche 911 – 213, 216
Porsche in general – 149, 165, 166, 217
Powerplus Superchargers – 56, 58
Pratts (petrol) – 29
Pressed Steel Ltd. (see also under 'Cowley' and 'Swindon') – 136, 143, 145, 156, 173, 180, 181, 182, 183, 185, 196, 197, 202, 205, 213, 214, 221
Pressnell, Jon – 8, 15, 17, 158, 200, 202
Preston (Lancashire) – 93, 94
Price, William ('Bill') – 217
Prickett, Jim – 48
Propert, George ('Pop') – 9, 33, 35, 37-38, 44, 46, 48, 53, 62, 103, 104, 105, 106, 108, 118, 119, 121, 122, 124
Propert, Mrs Lily Victoria (née Sephton) – 38
Proudfoot, Tony – 177
Purves, Syd – 37, 38, 48

Q

Queen Elizabeth, RMS (liner) – 127, 134
Queen Mary, RMS (liner) – 88, 168
Queen Street (Oxford) – 22, 26, 27, 29
Quinton Road (Coventry) – 136
Qvale, Kjell – 161, 222, 223

R

RAC (Royal Automobile Club) – 56, 66, 69, 82, 112, 189, 191
RAF (Royal Air Force) – 70, 91, 94, 99, 143, 155, 173
RAF Brize Norton – 165
Railton, Margaret (née Hensman) – 88
Railton, Reid Anthony – 62, 63, 80, 87, 88, 89, 167
Railton, Sarah – 88
Railton, Timothy – 88
Railway Locomotive book anecdote – 10
Rally (French sports car make) – 50, 52
RALPO (Radiators and Light Pressings Operations - 221
Ramsay, Tom - 110
Randall, Cecil J. – 64
Record Breakers & Record Breaking in general – 6, 9, 10, 12, 16, 17, 34, 40, 57, 58, 96, 125, 130, 136, 140, 154, 162, 176, 177, 179, 219
Red Line (petrol) – 29
Rednal, Birmingham - 147
Reece, J. G. – 66
Rees, Pat - 202
Reid, 'Tubby' – 120
Reid, Michael ('Mike') – 179
Rembrandt Hotel (London) - 101
Renault Caravelle & Floride - 183
Renwick and Bertelli (R&B) cars - 77
Renwick, Anne Barbara – 77, 79
Renwick, Mrs Joan Lesley (née Bayly) – 76, 79
Renwick, William Somerville ('Bill') – 8, 75, 76-79, 80, 83
Resuggan, David (Morris Garages staff) – 29, 30
Retirement (April 1971) - 219
Rex motorcycles – 85
RFC (Royal Flying Corps) – 41, 76, 91, 94
Rhine (river) - 95, 105
Ricardo Engineering – 223
Richardson, Clive - 182
Richardson, T ('Tom') – 121, 122
Riggott, A. – 109
Riley – 38, 54, 119, 120, 121, 122, 123, 124, 129, 137, 138, 145, 148, 151, 159, 169, 174, 194, 212
Riley & MG – see MG & Riley
Riley 4/68 – 186
Riley Nine – 50
Riley One-Point-Five – 159
Riley Pathfinder – 35, 131, 135, 143, 155, 159
Riley Pathfinder Twin-Cam concept (EX207) – 158, 159
Riley Two-Point-Six – 158, 159
Riley, Victor – 119
Rising Sun (Public House) – 20
RNAS (Royal Naval Air Service) – 41
Road & Track magazine - 161
Road Safety (vehicles) – 206
Roaring Raindrop (see also EX181) – 7, 15, 165, 170, 184, 224, 225
Robinson, Dave – 68
Robson, A. A. Graham (author) – 124
Rockie Mountains - 179
Rolls-Royce – 43, 148, 202
Rolls-Royce 4-litre engine – 201, 202
Rolls-Royce Merlin engine – 105, 129, 148
Rootes Group – 142, 143, 157, 173, 184
Roscrea (Tipperary, Ireland) – 148
Rose, Geoffrey (G. W.) – 210, 212
Rosemeyer, Bernd – 89
Rostyle wheels – 208, 212
Rotol Airscrews Limited - 43
Rover (ex-Buick) V8 engine – 204
Rover 200 (SD3) – 143, 156
Rover 800 (R17) - 156
Rover Car Company – 106, 210, 212
Rover P6 V8 - 217
Rover P6BS mid-engined concept – 214, 215
Rover P9 mid-engined concept – 214
Rowntree, Beveridge - 162
Royal Aero Club, the – 88
Royal Aeronautical Society - 148
Royal Automobile Club – see RAC

Royal Enfield (motorcycles) – 29
Royal Irish Constabulary (RIC) - 92
Royal Navy - 107
Rubin, Bernard (1896-1936) – 75
Rudge-Whitworth Biennial Cup – 130
Rugby School – 88
Rush, Harry (Riley) – 124
Ruskin College (Oxford University) – 25
Rutter-Harbott, Reuben – 111, 113
Ryder, Harold Alfred (1888-1950) – 35, 107, 108, 110, 119, 131, 132

S

SAAB – 173
Sachs, Eddie 'Baggy' – 216
Safety Fast slogan – 12, 82, 205
Safety Fast! (BMC and, later, MGCC Magazine) – 12, 54, 171, 184, 226
Salisbury Axle - 193
Salt Lake City (Utah) – 128, 178
Salt Lake Flats, Utah (see also Bonneville) – 11, 14, 126, 127, 140, 145, 158, 166, 167, 169, 176, 177, 179, 220
Samuelson, Sir Francis (F. H. B.) – 50, 64
San Francisco – 57, 161
Saorstát Cup – 65, 70, 148
Saunders, Stan – 37, 47, 48
Savoy (London Hotel) – 73
Schäfer, Herr (timekeeper, 1938) – 96
Schloss Stolzenfels (Koblenz, Germany) – 95
Scotland - 79
Scott, Andrew – 77, 79
Scott, Peter – 77
Scott, Walter – 22
Seagrave, Sir Henry – 68
Seaman, Dick – 93
Sebring 12-Hour Race, The – 16, 178, 199, 205
Second World War – 22, 24, 33, 35, 54, 70, 94, 96, 100, 101, 103-109 (Chapter Five), 114, 118, 143, 148, 155, 165, 208
Selby, T.V.G. – 64
Selway, Eric – 83
Seymour, David – 17
Seymour, Peter (Morris historian) – 28, 81
Sharp, Thomas - 23
Sharratt, Barney – 209
Sheffield-Simplex – 33
Shelby American – 140
Shelby, Carroll - 177
Sheldon, Archie (Morris Garages staff) – 29
Shell (and Shell-Mex) Petroleum – 29, 56, 57, 68, 220
Shelsley Walsh (hillclimb in Worcestershire) – 60, 70
Sherman Tank – 104
Shorrock Superchargers – 95, 162, 167, 168
Shorrock, Christopher – 91, 93-95, 96, 97, 101, 111, 112, 113, 119, 121, 125, 126, 127, 176, 220
Shorrock, Doris (née Eaves) – 94, 113
Shorrock, Ernest – 94
Shorrock, Noel – 93, 95
Shotover Hill (Oxford) – 24
Sicily – 185
Silver Bullet record car – 68
Silverstone Race Circuit, The – 7, 10, 169, 176, 217, 218
Simons, Jean – 111, 112
Simpson, June (daughter of Alec Hounslow) – 70
Singer cars – 29, 30, 33, 78
Sisteron (France) – 112
Skinner, T. C. (of SU) – 93
Skomp family, the - 181
Smart, Bob – 149
Smith, Frank (Morris Garages staff) – 29
Smith, George - 182
Smith, H. A. – 66
Smith, Keith – 34, 44, 45
Smith, Sydney Victor (1896-1968) – 35, 108, 117, 119, 121, 123, 131-132, 138, 142, 144, 151, 153, 154, 155, 159, 185, 189
Smythe, Windsor - 223
Solihull (Warwickshire) – 93, 215

239

South Oxford School, The – 20, 26, 219
Soviet Russia – 106
Spa race circuit – 216
Spain – 116
Spalding (town in Lincolnshire) – 39
Sparkfield (Birmingham) – 76
Specialist Cars Division (of BLMC) – 210, 212, 213
Speed of The Wind record breaker – 58, 74
Speedweek (Germany) – 89, 90
Spelsbury – 24
Spoelstra, Cathelijne – 60, 65, 67, 71
Sports Car magazine – 16
Spridgets (Sprites & Midgets) – 197, 198, 215
Spring Gardens (Abingdon-on-Thames) – 129
Springfield, Massachusetts – 97
Sputnik (Russian satellite) - 195
Squire Cars of Remenham - 70
Squire, Adrian – 42, 70
SRX210 (Le Mans MGA) – 179
SS Cars (William Lyons – later basis of Jaguar) – 84
SSV1 – MGB GT Safety Car - 222
St. Aldates (Oxford) – 20, 27
St. Barnabas School (Oxford) – 20
St. Ebbe's (district of Oxford) – 21, 22, 23
St. Ebbe's Church (Oxford) – 20, 21, 25
St. Ebbe's School (Oxford) – 23
St. Edmund's School (Abingdon) – 129
Staffordshire – 95
Standard cars – 29, 30, 78
Standard Triumph – 209, 213
Staniland, Chris – 63, 64
Stansfeld, Janet – 24
Stansfeld, Reverend John – 20, 21, 23, 24
Steamboat Springs (Colorado) – 179
Stein, Jonathan – 137
Stepney, Miss (Morris Garages staff) – 29
Stevens, Dennis – 149
Stevens, Frank (Morris Garages staff) – 32, 34, 47, 75, 109, 116
Stewart & Ardern Ltd. – 28
Stimson, Jordan James ('Jim') (1936-2016) – 110, 180, 188, 189, 190-191, 192, 198, 204, 205
Stisted, H. H. – 51, 60, 64
Stockdale, 'Bert' – 210, 212
Stockport Grammar School – 33
Stokes, Donald Gresham (Sir, later Lord – 1914-2008) – 210, 217
Stone, Henry W. – 13, 14, 70, 72, 110, 127, 130, 131, 140, 142, 150, 164, 165, 178
Stonyhurst College – 57
Stuart, Dr. Duncan – 14
Studebaker cars – 30
SU Carburettor Company – 12, 82, 91, 93, 94, 100, 122, 149, 175, 224, 225
Suez Crisis, the – 144
Suffield, H. J. L. (Lester) – 210, 211
Sunbeam – 29, 39
Sunbeam Alpine – 130
Supermarine Spitfire (fighter plane) – 43, 148
Sutton Courtenay (village near Abingdon) – 65
Swastika – 99
Swindon (Wiltshire) – 143, 174, 180, 181, 185
Swiss Alps, The – 175
Switzerland – 117, 151, 175

T
Talbot cars – 29, 68
Targa Florio road race – 205
Taruffi, Piero – 112, 125, 134
Tatlow, Jack – 54, 124, 125, 126, 136
Tayler, Leonard Cyril ('Frankie') – 14, 64, 65, 66, 67, 82
Taylor, Mike (author) – 15
Teamwork – see Nuffield Teamwork
Teddington (Middlesex) – 43
Temple, John (MG Competions Manager, 1930s) – 68
Tendring (town in Essex) – 91
Tetraethyl Lead (in petrol) – 205
Thames Street (Oxford) – 20
Thames, River – 114
The Insomnia Crew (book by Henry Stone) – 72

The Light Car magazine – 54, 96, 100, 101, 102
The MG Companion book by Kenneth Ullyett – 47
The Motor magazine – see *Motor* magazine
The Perch PH – see Perch
The Story of the Big Healeys, book – 16, 224
The Story of The MG Sports Car (book by Wilson McComb) – 75
The Straits Times (Singapore newspaper) - 56
The Trout PH – see Trout
The Works MGs (book) – 14, 97, 133
Thomas, William Miles Webster (1897-1980) – 33, 36, 53, 54, 81, 105, 106, 108, 119, 120
Thompson, J. – Pressings – 164
Thompson, James Rochester ('Jimmy') (1903-1987) – 146, 147, 150, 161, 162, 168, 175, 176, 200
Thomson & Taylor – 88, 117, 125
Thornley, Joanne – 13
Thornley, John William Yates – 9, 10, 13, 14, 17, 35, 38, 42, 43, 47, 49, 53-54, 74, 77, 84, 92, 98, 100, 101, 103, 111, 119, 120, 121, 122, 124, 125, 126, 127, 130, 132, 133, 135, 136, 137, 138, 139, 140, 141, 142, 145, 146, 149, 151, 152, 153, 154, 155, 157, 158, 160, 161, 162, 165, 166, 167, 168, 173, 176, 178, 179, 180, 186, 188, 190, 192, 204, 209, 210, 212, 214, 215, 221, 222, 226
Thornley, Peter – 7, 10, 54
Thoroughbred & Classic Cars magazine – 15, 53
Three Musketeers MG Trials cars – 53
Thruxton, Race circuit – 217
Thunderbolt record breaker – 58
Thurles Technical School – 148
Tipperary (Ireland) – 148
Tobin, Marguerite – 25
Tobin, Mr. (Morris Garages staff) – 29
Toreador (motorcycles) - 93
Tottenham, North London – 87
Toulmin Motors – 216
Tourist Trophy (TT) race – see Ulster TT
Trinity College, Cambridge University – 57
Triumph Acclaim ('BL Bounty') – 143, 156, 186
Triumph Bullet – 215
Triumph cars in general – 210, 212
Triumph gearbox (for ADO28) – 209
Triumph Lynx (concept) - 212
Triumph Motorcycles – 28, 29, 41
Triumph Spitfire – 214
Triumph Stag – 212
Triumph TR2 – 139
Triumph TR6 – 212, 213
Triumph TR7 – 215, 222
Triumph TR7 Convertible – 156
Trocadero, The – 54, 90, 94, 95
Trojan cars – 45
Trout, The - (PH in Oxford) – 6
TT – see Ulster TT and Dundrod
Tuck, George – 38, 95, 99, 101, 103, 113
Tuck, Mrs Beryl (née Propert) – 38, 113, 118
Turbocharger – 217, 218
Turin (Italy) – 193
Turnbull, George – 220
Turner, Edward – 201
Turner, Philip (*Motor* magazine) – 221
TWA ('Trans World Airlines') – 147

U
Ullyett, Kenneth (author of *The MG Companion* book) – 47, 48, 151
Ulster – 60, 67
Ulster TT ('Tourist Trophy') Races – 11, 65, 67, 68, 70, 71, 72, 85, 86, 87, 128
UNESCO – 95
United States of America (USA) – 118, 124, 137, 138, 139, 141, 143, 151, 155, 163, 166, 168, 177, 181, 192, 198, 203, 205, 206, 207, 215
University Motors – 84, 86, 87, 147
University of London – 41
Unsafe at Any Speed (book) - 206
Upavon – 91

Uppingham – 85
US 'Clean Air Act' (1963) - 206
US Federal Legislation – see Federal
USAAF (USA Air Force) – 169
Utah – see also Salt Flats – 167, 176, 177, 179

V
van Gerven, Vincent – 222, 224
Van Norman Boring Machine – 97-98, 99
Vanden Plas – 71
Varney, Mr. – 28
Vauxhall cars - 208
Vernaeve, Julien – 217
Victoria University – see Manchester
Vietnam War – 206
Villoresi, Luigi – 112
Vines, Victor – 109, 159
Von Eberhorst, Eberan – 93, 101
Von Neumann, John – 165, 166

W
Waeffler, Hans – 179
Wakefield, C. C. (see also Castrol) – 59, 163
Walker, Martin – 117
Walkerley, Rodney Lewis de Burgh – 54, 90, 91
Walkinshaw, Tom – 173, 186
Wallingford – 70
Walters, P. M. – 67
Walton Crescent (Oxford) – 34
Walton Street (Oxford) – 34
War Time Activities of the MG Car Company Limited, Abingdon-on-Thames (book) – 104, 105, 106, 107
Ward End factory (Birmingham) – 122, 123
Ward, R. W. ('Bob') – 221
Warrington Garage (Maida Vale) – 91
Wartime work at MG factory – 38, 47
Warwick (City) – 16, 207, 209, 212, 222
Warwickshire County Records Office - 222
Watford – 159
Watney, R. ('Dick') – 65
Watts – Douglas ('Douggie') – 114, 116
Watts – Michael ('Mick') – 114
Watts, Hilary – 114, 116
Watts, Hilda May Watts (née Williams) – 114
Watts, Isla Evelyn (1916-2001) – 114-116, 161, 166, 182, 189, 220
Watts, John – 116
Watts, John Urry ('Jack') – 114
Webb, C. B. – 127
Weber Carburettors – 149, 180
Webster, Henry George ('Harry') CBE (1917-2007) – 209, 210, 212, 222
Wednesbury (Staffordshire) – 95
Wellman, Mr. ('Tommy') – 149, 150, 217
Wellworthy Ltd. – 106
Wendover (Utah) - 127, 170, 177
Weslake, Harry – 117
West Wycombe (Buckinghamshire) – 158, 159
West, T. G. – 34
Westby, Stan – 80, 156
Westgate Centre (Oxford) – 23
Westminster Way (Oxford) – 135, 153, 216, 225
Wharton, Kenneth – 148
Which? magazine – 209
Whitby, Gordon – 16, 200
White & Poppe engines – 30
White House, the – 206
White, Geoff – 83
White, Harry – 142, 143, 155, 157, 162, 184
White, Reg – 202
Whitehead, Kevin (grandson of George Morris) – 47
Whiteman, Philip – 144
Who's Who in Motor and Commercial Vehicle Industries - 194
Wicky, André – 216
Wiffen, Gerald – 131, 199
Wiggins, Harold – 130, 140, 160
Wilkins, 'Billy' – 110
Wilkinson, John – 203
Willesden (London) - 91

Williams, Denis George (1925-2022) – 8, 155-156, 159, 160, 161, 173, 180, 181, 185, 186, 196, 200, 204, 205
Wills, Margaret – 113
Wilmot Manufacturing Company, The – 28
Wilmot-Breeden – 28
Wimbledon – 55, 57
Winchester – 19, 59
Windsor (Berkshire) - 39
Winterbottom, Eric - 130
Winterhilfswerk des Deutschen Volkes - 95
Wirdnam, H. ('Bert') – 109, 129, 139
Wisdom, Thomas Henry ('Tommy') (1906-1972) – 168, 170, 176, 177, 178, 220
Withall, Douglas – 210, 212
Witney (Oxfordshire) – 156, 165
Wolseley 15/60 - 186
Wolseley 4/44 – 124, 138, 185
Wolseley 6/110 – 202
Wolseley 6/80 – 133
Wolseley 6/90 – 158
Wolseley 6/99 – 185
Wolseley apprentice – 140, 174
Wolseley cars in general – 29, 30, 55, 80, 110, 118, 119, 120, 122, 123, 124, 131, 135
Wolseley engines – 70, 80, 134
Wolseley version of Morris Minor - 110
Wolveridge, W. E. – 56, 57
Woodcock, James R. ('Jim') - 154
Woodhouse, Jack - 85
Woodstock Road (London) – 28
Woodstock Road (Oxford) – 42
Woolf Barnato Trophy - 212
Woollard, Frank – 28, 42, 55
Woolworth's (Oxford) - 27
Worcester (City) – 26
Works MGs – book by Mike Allison – 70
Worsley, Hon. Victoria – 51
Wright, Pat – 48
Wright, Richard Neville 'Dickie' – 142, 155, 157, 160, 196, 202
WRM – see Morris, William
Würlitz (Germany) – 101
WWI - see First World War
WWII – see Second World War
Wycliffe Hall (Oxford University) – 23

X
XC512 – see ADO30
XPAG Engine (1,250 cc) – 15, 95, 107, 120, 126, 128, 130, 134, 138, 140, 142
XPAW Engine (Wolseley 4/44) – 124
XPEG Engine (1,466 cc) – 136, 138, 140, 161, 175

Y
Yarnton (Oxford) - 108
Yorke, Jack – 149
Yorkshire – 104, 174
Young, Vic – 29

Z
Zenith Carburettors - 42
Zhukovsky, Nikolay Yegorovich – 164
Zoller supercharger – 73, 75
Zürich (Switzerland) – 151, 175
Zwickau (Germany) – 101